On Monosemy

To Lou Hammann,
who's made the biggest difference.
From Charles Ruhl '60,
with thanks.

SUNY Series in Linguistics
Mark Aronoff, Editor

ON MONOSEMY

A Study in Linguistic Semantics

Charles Ruhl

State University of New York Press

Published by
State University of New York Press, Albany

For information, address State University of New York
Press, State University Plaza, Albany, N.Y., 12246

Library of Congress Cataloging-in-Publication Data

Ruhl, Charles, 1936–
    On monosemy : a study in linguistic semantics / Charles Ruhl.
        p. 000 cm. — (SUNY series in linguistics)
    Bibliography: p. 000
    Includes index.
    ISBN 0-88706-946-0.   ISBN 0-88706-947-9 (pbk.)
    1. Semantics.   I. Title.   II. Series.
P325.R84   1989
415--dc19   88-17494
                                                                   CIP

10   9   8   7   6   5   4   3   2   1

CONTENTS

PREFACE

In this book I argue for monosemy; I claim that current linguistic theories accept too uncritically the conclusion of dictionaries that words in general have multiple meanings. I argue that words contribute much less to meaning than usually supposed; the apparent lexical meaning of a word includes in large part a contribution of contextual factors, both linguistic and extralinguistic. Factoring out contextual meaning, we find that some words have a single, highly abstract meaning; other words, referring to highly diverse realities, represent the unity of that diversity.

Posner (1980:100) describes two strategies for lexical analysis:

> *Meaning-maximalists* attempt to deduce as much as possible from
> the literal meanings of verbal expressions and tend to assume
> richness and ambiguity in the meanings of words. On the other
> hand, *meaning-minimalists* attribute more importance to the
> pragmatic rules of reinterpretation as opposed to literal meanings
> and tend to accept only minimal meanings and unambiguous
> words.

Posner sees a parallel in Cohen's (1971) contrast of "semanticists" and "conversationalists". It is, broadly, a difference between formalists and functionalists: between those who seek for the explanation of meaning largely or solely in the linguistic system and those who attribute meaning largely or solely to the conditions of language use.

Posner is a minimalist; he goes on to show how variations of meaning associated with *and* can be attributed to contextual factors. He concludes (p. 117):

a. The use of a verbal expression is partially determined by the meaning of this expression.
b. The meaning of a complex verbal expression is determined not only by the meanings of its constituents, but also by their specific use.

Two other minimalists are Garcia (1975) and Andrews (1976), both in the Jakobson tradition carried on by William Diver. Garcia makes two crucial assumptions, as do I: she takes forms (specifically Spanish *se*) to be related in a Saussurean system, deriving their value "negatively" by contrast to the forms most directly related to them; and she calculates, as does Posner, what aspects of meaning are contributed by contextual factors, specifically the pragmatic inferences that arise in (always present) communicational situations. Garcia and Andrews start with the Jakobson-Diver assumption that I will call the MONOSEMIC BIAS: the hypothesis that a form (the Russian suffix-*ka* for Andrews) has a single meaning, and that all the complicating factors that make it appear polysemic have their sources in contextual contributions to meaning.

An extreme example of a maximialist is Empson (1953), exploring ambiguities in literature, and attributing them to words. Obviously, someone with literary perspectives might use this approach very effectively and appropriately, especially so since a richness and diversity of meaning *does seem to focus in particular words*. Further, this effect is not merely literary, but (as dictionaries attest) is ubiquitous to all language use. To use one of my examples, in *The thief took the jewels,* the verb *take* seems to mean 'steal', and would be presented and taken so by the interlocuters. It is a part of users' knowledge that *take* has this effect, and any theory of word meaning must account for it. Yet, is the effect that of *take* alone, or rather *take*-in-this-context?

Bierwisch (1981:341) observes:

. . . the notion of word meaning is much more complicated than it might appear even at second and third glance. More specifically, I will claim that (at least) two aspects of meaning are to be distinguished that are organized according to independent, though interacting principles: *Semantic structure,* determined by the rules of language and thus pertaining to the realm of tacit linguistic knowledge; *Conceptual structure,* based on rules in terms of which mental representations of the world are built up.

Of course, those who accept this in principle may not agree in specifics. Significantly, however, this principle *must be demonstrated in the details,* especially so since it goes against our immediate perceptions and our pretheoretical heritage. There is no available shortcut, no plausible ready idealization; but if we take the Monosemic Bias as a principle, we at least make it equally difficult for a linguist to make either a monosemic or polysemic/homonymic/idiomatic claim. Most of the inertial forces now favor multiple meaning.

Posner and Bierwisch assume a difference between inherent lexical meaning, which is semantic, and additional instrumental meaning, which is pragmatic or conceptual. Many current researchers deny this distinction; Ray Jackendoff in *Semantics and Cognition* (1983) and George Lakoff in *Women, Fire and Dangerous Things* (1987) are two significant examples. Yet the disagreement may be more apparent than real. The semantic/pragmatic distinction, as currently envisioned, has its roots in maximalist conceptions, which attribute too much meaning to words. Thus, it is not surprising for linguists to find that *supposed* word meaning differs little, if at all, from obviously non-lexical meaning; this merely indicates earlier misjudgments.

Strictly speaking, it is misleading to describe Posner, Garcia and Andrews as minimalists. A fully minimalist position would claim that words have no inherent meaning at all, deriving all their apparent contribution from functional context. These three linguists assume, as do I, that words have some inherent meaning. The analytic task of semantics-pragmatics is finding what the balance is. It may seem to many readers that I am taking a severe minimalist position, just barely short of zero.

A linguist like Garcia takes a strongly functionalist stance; it would appear that this is the obvious, even inevitable, orientation for someone who searches for meaning extralinguistically. Thus, I need to define my "theoretical space": I am a formalist, with formalist goals. However, I share many of the global criticisms that Garcia and Givón (1979) direct against the Transformational tradition, with its almost exclusive avoidance or deferral of so-called "performance" factors. Yet while they view this tradition as almost fully misguided, I see it rather as overextended: in its "classical" period (based on Chomsky's *Aspects of the Theory of Syntax* (1965)), it viewed too much of the language in highly autonomous terms. To substantiate my monosemic claims, I must advocate a high degree of functional determination of linguistic meaning; but in principle I agree with Chomsky's theoretical goals, differing only (though extensively) in specific analyses.

This is thus a study in linguistic pragmatics. But I only briefly discuss here topics that are usually considered pragmatic. I am working closer to lexical bone, claiming that meaning almost universally ceded to be semantic should be considered pragmatic. My claims of lexical monosemy imply that lexical meaning must be highly abstract (though still specific to a particular language), and thus highly formal, some of it highly remote from all ambient contingencies. I hope to show functionalists that the most functional linguistic ability is based on a high degree of formal autonomy.

Remarkably, formalist and functionalist alike tend to reach the conclusions about polysemy and homonymy that I here criticize. These conclusions are unavoidable in traditional maximalist thinking, since words must carry so much semantic weight; yet they are also in Lakoff (1987), who adopts a strong functional view and belabors traditional thinking on almost every other point. His following comments on multiple meaning could be taken from any traditional work (p. 416):

> It is common for a single word to have more than one meaning. In some cases the meanings are unrelated, like the two meanings of *bank*—the place where you put your money and the land along the edge of a river. In such cases, there is not one word, but two. They are called instances of homonymy, where two words with two totally different meanings happen to be pronounced the same way. In other cases, the senses are related, often in such a close and systematic way that we don't notice at first that more than one sense exists at all. Take the word *window*, for example. It can refer either to an opening in a wall or to the glass-filled frame in the opening. Or take the word *open*. We open doors and open presents, and though the actions described by the words are very different, we would normally have to think twice to notice the difference. Or the word *run*. It is very different for Harry to run into the woods and for the road to run into the woods. Again, there is a single verb with two senses so intimately related that we have to think twice to notice the difference. Such cases are called instances of polysemy. They are cases where there is one lexical item with a family of related senses.

This certainly sounds familiar, and thus even reasonable. However, what warrants the claim that *window, open,* and *run* have more than one sense? Admittedly, the phrases *open the door* and *open the present* evoke quite different images, but why is the difference attributed to *open,* which doesn't differ, and not also *the?* Why isn't the difference located solely where there is difference: in the door-presents distinction and in the knowledge that people have about these two activities?

Because the maximalist tendencies of traditional thinking put the semantic-pragmatic distinction in the wrong place, both Jackendoff and Lakoff, formalist and functionalist, must deny the distinction, describing their inquiries as "conceptual" or "cognitive" and encompassing wider ranges of human ability. Since I claim that much of what has been considered semantic is really pragmatic, I in effect agree with them; when I use the term "pragmatic" in this book, I intend it to apply to the full range of possible human concepts and cognitions. Jackendoff's and Lakoff's point is especially well taken heuristically; even if linguistic meaning is a special case, addressing that possibility in isolation too narrowly focuses our inquiries. The strategy of idealization adopted in Transformational Grammar, which was well motivated at the time of *Aspects,* has become severely limiting, even for formalists.

Nevertheless, I believe that the *Aspects*-idealization was linked to a legitimate empirical goal: finding the innate universals underlying human linguistic competence. I assume that language is to some degree autonomous, though not fully so, but rather in gradient holistic degree. Accordingly, I assume that there is something autonomously "semantic" that describes a word's potential of meaning in a human language. For some words, the semantic-pragmatic distinction can be clearly drawn, and for other words it cannot. I try to explain how and why. I also claim that some aspects of meaning can be both semantic and pragmatic. To some extent, I am proposing a new definition for "semantic", and for "polysemy" as well (and for that matter, "synchrony" and "diachrony" also). I hope to show that some of our problems with semantic and pragmatic have been confusions about levels of abstraction.

To be precise: I am arguing that many words have only a single, highly abstract meaning. This is the inherent meaning, a word's semantics. I am thus neither saying nor denying that a word has a prototype, as proposed by Rosch (1977b) and others. This is an intriguing area of research, but I think my project is different in significant ways. As researchers explicitly state, or sometimes implicitly evidence, semantics deals with closed, finite systems; prototypes are much more complicated. I assume that they are phenomena of a less abstract nature, including perceptual, acquisitional, and instrumental modulations: that is, details of pragmatic diversity.

In my opinion, this makes them even more valuable than if they were purely semantic. Particularly, they show why words (and sentences) seem to have meanings in "isolation"; such prototypic meanings actually reveal the implicit modulations we make under conditions of minimal explicit context: they reveal our biases, stereotypes, preferences, purposes, tyrannies, hidden agendas. In contrast, the meanings I "approximate to" for some words (I usually won't be able to paraphrase them) may seem both mysterious and useless.

Not all words are monosemic, but I argue that this should be our standard expectation (especially when appearances seem otherwise). Typically monosemic words have the quality of being (to use Bierwisch's term) INDETERMINATE. (I say UNSPECIFIED, but his may be the better word.) He comments (1981: 347ff.) (my numbering):

> What I am after is indeterminateness. It does not turn on syntactic or semantic ambiguity [like *What did you expect to melt?* and *port,* respectively], nor on vagueness on a continuous domain [like *many, young* and *dark* in *Many young people have dark hair*]. It rather relates to discrete conceptual distinctions which do not correspond to different semantic structures.
>
> Consider the following examples:
>
> [1] a. On Friday morning, Bill came out of the university and took a cab.
>
> b. For two years, Bill has been teaching at the University of Appletown.

    c. The university by now covers the whole area around the
house you lived in.
    d. The university is a typically European institution that
developed during the Middle Ages.

Here *university* denotes conceptually different entities—a building
in (a), an institution in (b), a campus in (c), and something like an
educational principle in (d)—which are related in systematic ways
and cannot be considered as instantiating a semantic ambiguity in
the sense of say *bank* or *port*.

    The same is true in a slightly different respect for the verb
find in the following examples:

[2] **a.** Max found an elegant proof for the theorem.
    b. John finally found the book he has looked for in various
book stores.
    c. John found the book in the mess on his desk.

The type of activity involved in constructing a proof, searching for
a book, and retrieving a particular copy leads to accordingly
different types of finding, though there is no lexical ambiguity
involved.

    The conclusion to be drawn from these and many other
examples is this: The semantic structure *sem* of a word determines
a conceptual unit denoted by the word relative to a given context.
To put it the other way round: *sem* determines a family of related
conceptual units the differentiation of which depends on the context
within which the word in interpreted.

Bierwisch calls [1] an example of Conceptual Shift, and [2] Conceptual
Differentiation. The important point is that *diversity is provided by context.*
What often happens in polysemic analyses is that contextual contributions to
meaning are duplicated into the word; the original monosemic sense vanishes.
Further, without the monosemic sense, we are often unable to see the contextual
examples that we have overlooked (and we always overlook); in many
instances, this changes a word with potentially infinite contextual meanings into
a polysemic word with only few "distinct" meanings.

    I can illustrate some of my argument by returning to Lakoff (1987). As a
formalist, I need to grant functionalists many points, especially when they
expose maximalist thinking so well. But traditional thinking is more pervasive
than we think: Lakoff accepts another traditional assumption, though in a
different guise. One of his important points is that we as humans use our bodies
as a point of reference and extended imagery; he demonstrates this, to my
satisfaction, with many data (among others) relating to anger: *Don't bite my
head off!*, *Why did you jump down my throat?* (p. 394). Yet, even granting this
is a highly prolific part of language, too little noted in the past, it can be
overextended as an explanation. Lakoff gives an example from Johnson (1987)
and then a following comment:

Consider just a small fraction of the operational feats you perform constantly in your daily activities—consider, for example, only a few of the many *in-out* orientations that might occur in the first few minutes of an ordinary day. You wake *out* of a deep sleep and peer *out* from beneath the covers *into* your room. You gradually emerge *out* of your stupor, pull yourself *out* from under the covers, climb *into* your robe, stretch *out* your limbs, and walk *in* a daze *out* of your bedroom and *into* the bathroom. You look *in* the mirror and see your face staring *out* at you. You reach *into* the medicine cabinet, take *out* the toothpaste, put the toothbrush *into* your mouth, brush your teeth, and rinse *out* your mouth. At breakfast you perform a host of further *in-out* moves—pouring *out* the coffee, setting *out* the dishes, putting the toast *in* the toaster, spreading *out* the jam on the toast, and on and on. (Johnson, p. 30–31)

Johnson is not merely playing on the words *in* and *out*. There is a reason that those words are natural and appropriate, namely, the fact that we conceptualize an enormous number of activities in CONTAINER terms. Lindner (1981) describes in detail what is involved in this for 600 verbs containing the particle *out,* not just physical uses like *stretch out* and *spread out,* but in metaphorical uses like *figure out, work out,* etc. As Lindner observes, there are a great many metaphors based on the CONTAINER schema and they extend our body-based understanding of things in terms of CONTAINER schemas to a large range of abstract concepts. For example, emerging *out* of a stupor is a metaphorical, not a literal emergence from a container. (Lakoff, p. 272)

Lakoff here echoes traditional views in the assumption that *in* and *out* have literal meanings that are physical/directional, and metaphorical meanings that are abstract. He makes the same assumption in a later lengthy analysis of *over,* based on Brugman (1981). Both that traditional view and Lakoff's body-as-a-container schema reveal a human preference for the concrete when analyzing language, but this preference can have various explanations. I attribute it to stereotyping, the conscious mind's limited awareness. (Anyone doubting the pervasiveness of stereotyping should look up the noun *bank* in *Webster's Third New International* and see if it is as simple, or 'river edge' so special a sense, as our ritualistic discussions of homonymy suggest.) Instead, I claim that *in, out, over,* and all prepositions have highly abstract meanings, of which the concrete are simply a pragmatically modulated subspecies.

Lakoff's proposal is somewhat like the theory of localism (Anderson (1971)), which derives abstract meanings from prior concrete, localized senses. Both proposals are apparently quite widely supported by details. Yet their plausibility can be explained by a hypothesis that claims precisely the reverse: if *in* and *out* (and even *contain* and *container*) are highly abstract categories, they could thereby provide the cognitive means for making, and making believable (at various times), the traditional view, localism, and Lakoff's container schema.

Stated thus, my suggestion seems arbitrary and vague; it is the purpose of this book to make it seem less so. I might note that my claim does not diminish in any way the impressive work done by Lindner, Brugman, and Lakoff; the extended studies at the end of Lakoff's book are relentless both in their detailed differentiations and in their unifying proposals.

However, as impressive as those analyses are, they must be tested by an even wider range of data. As only one complication, the concrete-abstract variation is trickier than polysemic theories allow. To address just the quote above, *stretch out* and *spread out* can be abstract also, and *figure out* and *work out* can be somewhat concrete: *He figured/worked out the details on the tablecloth.* Additional data must also be actual data, not only intuitional invented isolated sentences. As I hope to show by example, large bodies of actual data can challenge assumptions that restricted, intuitional data have left untouched.

Lakoff's key point is that we think through multiple, often contradictory, cognitive models, and not only through the "objectivist", single-truth, faithful-to-reality traditional model. I agree. Further, he argues, a word is accordingly polysemic (and not homonymic) when its meanings in various models can be seen as related, notably by prototypic, radial organization: one or more central meanings, related to one or more partly motivated peripheral meanings. Here I differ: on what grounds are the word meanings considered different in the first place? Why can't we say that the differing models produce varying effects on a single, general meaning?

The resourcefulness of words like *in* and *out* can be best explained by highly abstract meanings; these require the ambient modulating schemas that Lakoff illustrates. It is too limiting to suppose with such words that we are merely metaphorizing our own bodies (although we do this in many ways). We will find that our linguistic capacities are far more complex; I hope to show that the most functional part of our linguistic resourcefulness is a highly abstract, formal and autonomous collection of categories that seem overwhelmingly baffling and unreal to our conscious understanding.

ACKNOWLEDGMENTS

This book has been fifteen years in the making, and portions have appeared earlier in the LACUS Forum series, published by Hornbeam Press, Columbia SC; the titles below should make obvious what is borrowed (Fourth LACUS discusses Bolinger's "Meaning and memory."). I thank the editors and publisher for permission to reprint.

Primary verbs, The First LACUS Forum 1974
Pragmatic metonymy, The Second LACUS Forum 1975
Idioms and data, The Third LACUS Forum 1976
Two forms of reductionism, The Fourth LACUS Forum 1977
Alleged idioms with *hit*, The Fifth LACUS Forum 1978
The noun *ice*, The Seventh LACUS Forum 1980
The verb *kick*, The Eighth LACUS Forum 1981
Figurative *kick*, The Ninth LACUS Forum 1982
The verb *slap*, The Tenth LACUS Forum 1983
Primary verbs revisited, The Eleventh LACUS Forum 1984
"Particles," The Twelfth LACUS Forum 1985

I must also thank the many linguists at the LACUS (Linguistic Association of Canada and the United States) meetings, who gave support unqualified by the fact that I identified myself as a transformationalist, a breed rare at those annual meetings: Adam Makkai, Valerie Becker Makkai, Saul Levin, Allen Gleason,

Ulf Bäcklund, Roger Wescott, Peter Reich, Ernst Pulgram, Victor Yngve, Toby Griffin, James Copeland, Sidney Lamb, Michel Paradis, Konrad Koerner, Peter Maher, Kenneth Pike, Earl Herrick, Robert DiPietro, William Sullivan, Janet Collins, Peter Fries, David Lockwood, Allen Walker Read, Carleton Hodge, Michael Cummings, John Morreall, Alan Melby, Yakov Malkiel, Hans-Heinrich Lieb, Richard Gunter, and Robert A. Hall, Jr..

I also need to thank the following regional colleagues in the Southeastern Conference on Linguistics (SECOL): Karl Nicholas, Ronald Butters, Walter Cook, Michael Montgomery, Reza Ordoubadian, Jeutonne Brewer, Greta Little, Peter Menzel, Boyd Davis, Chauncey Chu, Salikoko Mufwanee, Marvin Ching, William Smith, Katherine Leffel, Gary Miller, Guy Bailey, and Dee Ann Holisky.

I give special thanks to the following at the University of North Carolina-Chapel Hill, past and present: Connie Eble, Lloyd Anderson, James Gaskin, Carroll Hollis, Robert Howren, Michael Dressman, Lester Woody, David Edsall, and Robert Rodman.

I also give special thanks to my colleagues at Old Dominion University: Janet Bing, Carole Hines, John Broderick, David Shores, William Riley, Heinz Meier, Judy Andre, and Larry Hatab. Ken Daley drew the figure on p. 178.

They and the following have given me advice, insights, reservations, cautions, cease and desist orders, and especially data: Arnold Zwicky, Charles Fillmore, Robert Kirsner, James McCawley, William Cantrall, Terry Langendoen, John Ross, Earl Stevick, Daniel Laferriere, and Catherine Chvany.

Belatedly, I thank two people who died before I could adequately acknowledge their generous interest and support: Helmut Esau and James Gough.

This book interweaves with two other books to come, on the verbs *break* and *take*. I would like to thank Old Dominion University for a summer grant and the American Council of Learned Societies for a year's fellowship, both of which make possible all three books.

All of these, and others who are victims of my forgetfulness, should claim credit for what is good here and attribute the rest to me.

Finally, I thank Dwight Bolinger, who taught me the important thing: a linguist should attend first to the language and to the various many who use it variously. As will become apparent, I both rely on and quarrel with him in this book, so it is only fitting and necessary that I dedicate it to him.

Norfolk VA, March 1988

Chapter *1*

MONOSEMY

Anyone using a dictionary is accustomed to finding that most words have multiple meanings. This is especially true for the most common words of English: verbs like *come, go, bring* and *take,* or prepositions like *of, to, from, on, in* and *at.* Multiple meaning is so pervasive in dictionaries that it has the force of evident fact; its ubiquity leads us to assume, usually without taking thought, that multiple meaning is in the nature of things, an established reality that we need not and cannot question.

This book takes issue with the ubiquitous fact. I hope to show that many common words of English, such as those noted above, each have only one single general meaning. I argue that many examples of multiple meaning are the result of dubious assumptions about language: assumptions perhaps necessary for the practical work of making dictionaries, but damaging when carried over almost intact into linguistic theories on semantics.

A case in point: one particular shortcoming of dictionaries in a habit of overspecifying, of attributing to words meaning that in part is supplied by the context. I can illustrate this briefly with some data that I will discuss more extensively later. Consider the expression *take off.* Dictionaries treat some combinations of these words as single units, unrelated to the verb *take* and the preposition *off.* One attributed meaning is 'become airborne' (or 'take flight'), sometimes with the additional 'from land or water'. This meaning is inferred from sentences [1] and [2] and perhaps [3]; but what about the others?

[1] Planes were landing and taking off like clockwork. (Malcom X)
[2] They heard the grouse take off without ever being quite able to locate its position. (Robert Murphy)
[3] They [small frogs] move only when actually dispossessed, taking off in a long leap that is almost a flight. (Marjorie Kinnan Rawlings)
[4] Of course, ability plays a part in whether or not a real tackle-buster will be landed, but if one [fish] does latch on, take off for the horizon, and pop the line, the small loss is well worth the excitement. (Joseph D. Bates, Jr.)
[5] However, he was unable to hold them [horses] and they took off. (Walter R. Fletcher)
[6] He gave the cab driver the address of the hotel, and the taxi took off with a lurch. (Bernard Malamud)
[7] . . . Jones took off at a gallop down the right sideline. (AP)
[8] We put on our skating shoes, knotted the laces of our regular shoes together and hung them around our necks, got out on the frozen lake, held the sails in front of us, and took off. (Bruce Catton)
[9] When they [surfers] got out to where the waves were breaking, they swung their boards around and straddled them, waiting for the right moment to take off. (William Murray)

In each of these sentences, *take off* seems to mean that something is in motion; but in [4–9] the motion is horizontal, not vertical as flight in part requires. Does this mean that [1–9] illustrate several different meanings of *take off*? Given that the same words describe all these motions, on what basis can we assume that the horizontal-vertical distinction makes a difference in this expression? These data show that the meaning 'become airborne' is a mistake. *Take off*-motions are neutral between horizontal and vertical directions; giving a separate meaning for flight needlessly divides a unified sense. It is comparable to giving *dog* a separate meaning when it applies to collies. This book will be filled with many demonstrations of this type; later I will show that attributing 'motion' to the expression *take off* is yet another overspecification, comparable to a mistake that gives *dog* a particular meaning for all dogs that have shaggy hair.

However, my chief concern is not with dictionaries, but with linguistics; this book is intended as a contribution to theoretical semantics. Yet dictionaries are crucially important because they are part of our pretheoretical heritage; linguists, like everyone else, have been conditioned by the model of dictionaries to expect words, as a matter of course, to have multiple meanings. We require semantic theories to be much more rigorous and precise than dictionaries; but if dictionaries lead us to expect widespread multiple meaning, our theories are severely compromised right from the start. We then begin with dubious axioms and spread their distorted implications throughout our theories. Keeping in mind that dictionaries have severe limitations (recognized most clearly by lexicographers themselves), linguists must question not only the specific analyses of dictionaries but their design and purposes as well. My goal here is to test multiple meaning: to argue that its seeming abundance does not represent a fact about human language, but is rather a consequence of mistaken premises.

1.1 MONOSEMIC BIAS

My original inspiration for this book was a remark by Uriel Weinreich regarding *take* (1963: 180):

> When we contemplate the varieties of "meanings" which a word
> like *take* has in English (*take offense, take charge, take medicine,
> take notice, take effect*, etc.), we come to the conclusion that this
> is a case not of abnormally overdeveloped polysemy of a word, but
> rather of its semantic near-emptiness.

These comments suggest that *take* has only one highly general meaning. Can such a possibility be taken seriously? Dictionaries provide *take* with many separate definitions, which become little less than chaotic in *Webster's Third New International Dictionary* (1976) [W3]. What theoretical assumptions support the dictionary treatments? Conversely, what theoretical assumptions would support a semantic theory that posits only one meaning for *take*?

We can begin answering these questions with Ullmann's three types of multiple meaning (1957: 114):

1. Several aspects of one sense: SHIFTS IN APPLICATION: e.g.,
   healthy climate, healthy complexion
2. Several senses of one word: POLYSEMY: e.g., *human head, head
   of department, bridgehead*
3. Several words: HOMONYMY: e.g., *sea, to see, a see*

The distinction between polysemy and homonymy is a commonplace of semantic research, although scholars sometimes loosely use either term as a cover label. In addition, judging an expression idiomatic implies multiple meanings for its constituent words. I will use MULTIPLICITY as a cover term for all of these. Of particular interest in Ullmann's types is Shift. He refers to the "elasticity" of words, their ability to make small adjustments in different contexts without the need for distinct meanings. He gives as an example the noun *wall*:

> A simple word like *wall* will have different aspects according to its
> material (stone, brick, concrete, timber), its functional role (wall of
> a house, a fortress), and also according to the background and
> interests of its users (bricklayer, architect, art historian, etc.). All
> these shades of application are felt as contiguous facets of a
> coherent whole. . . .

These remarks imply that perception of different meanings does not necessarily imply that an involved word should be given multiple meanings; there are many shades of red, but we do not parallel them all with separate senses of *red*. In general, human beings can in some perspective count as "the same thing" what in a more discriminating perspective appears as "different things". That is, we have multiple means of interpreting: each particular use of language can be judged in some highly differentiating perspective to be unlike any other use of language. But multiple perspectives are not solely provided by words; a difference of perceived meaning does not automatically require different lexical meaning. A linguistic theory must have ways of determining when multiplicity is inherent in a word, and when it is supplied by other words or even extralinguistically.

A theory requires an associated methodology that specifies a preferred way of making and testing hypotheses. Ullmann gives a pertinent suggestion when he emphasizes that his three types are not fully distinct, but form a continuum; when a word's status is hard to determine, he advises the following (p. 115):

> . . . it may be wise to lay down a golden rule to give the benefit of the doubt, in borderline cases, to the closer of the two alternative connections: to shifts in application against polysemy, and to polysemy against homonymy. Naturally, each case will have to be examined on its own merits, and often there may be no hard-and-fast solution at all.

I infer from this the following methodological implication:

[A] MONOSEMIC BIAS

First Hypothesis: A word has a single meaning.
Second Hypothesis: If a word has more than one meaning, its meanings are related by general rules.

In other words, a researcher's initial efforts are directed toward determining a unitary meaning for a lexical item, trying to attribute apparent variations in meaning to other factors. If such efforts fail, then the researcher tries to discover a means of relating the distinct meanings. If these efforts fail, then there are several words. This approach initially assumes that lexical form and meaning are fully congruent, and that claims of polysemy, homonymy, and idiomaticity must be substantiated by detailed study, not merely asserted as intuitive insights. This Monosemic Bias implies a priority of research: a full detailed exploration of a word's variant range before considering its possible paraphrase relationships with other lexical items. For example, it claims (as does Kirsner (1972)) that Postal in his treatment of the verb *remind* (1970) should have first considered a possible unity for all posited meanings for *remind* before attempting to link one of those meanings to other expressions such as *strike as similar*.

Objections to such an approach come readily to mind, even too readily. An approach that initially considers form and meaning to be highly congruent may seem hopelessly naive, especially with the massive evidence of dictionaries to the contrary. But an initial presumption of monosemy does not question the existence of multiplicity; rather, it implies that current analyses find too much multiplicity too easily, and so provides a means for testing each particular claim. Thus, while I will grant that the noun *orange* is polysemic and the noun *bank* is homonymic, I will show that the verbs *bear* and *hit* are monosemic. Also, while I agree that *white elephant* is an idiom, I will show that *take off, hit the beach,* and *break the ice* are not. Even the favorite exemplar, *kick the bucket,* is not an idiom; it relates to other expressions.

Actually, the full-range implausibility of the Monosemic Bias is perhaps its best recommendation. Methodologies can easily become self-confirming, finding only supporting evidence. What begin as hypotheses, to be confirmed as factual, often turn into axioms, yet still treated as fact; language enables us to use the same means either to describe or to dictate. The hypotheses I propose have the virtue of being in direct contrast with some of our most pervasive assurances, and they thus serve as necessary counterbalancing cautions, a check on what we too easily take for granted. Without such an explicit check, current methodologies and assurances are even more naive.[1]

1.2 MODULARITY

Because dictionaries try to be as informative as possible, they typically assume that the message of a particular sentence is completely supplied by words. Thus, each word in a sentence must carry as much information as possible, as illustrated above by *take off*. However, if in those sentences *plane, grouse, frog, taxi, surfer,* or other words show (directly or indirectly) what kind of motion is involved, *take off* does not have to show it again. In fact, if other information is minimal, as in *It took off,* the expression *take off* by itself cannot provide the details. This is precisely the attribute of any general term: *dog* by itself cannot indicate the size or breed of a dog, but it can be interpreted more specifically when the context occasions it: *the dog tried to pick a fight with a cat twice its size.* Our ability to imagine several possibilities for *It took off* (horizontal or vertical motion, and others) does not require us to give *take off* several distinct meanings, just as our ability to conceive of several types of dogs does not require us to give *dog* several distinct meanings. Without the horizontal-vertical distinction, we can still posit a general meaning for *take off,* just as we can with *dog*. Admittedly, genuine examples of multiple meaning, such as the homonymy of *light* in *She wore a light dress* ('not dark' or 'not heavy'), may seem to have the same attribute I have just noted for general terms; I must give additional reasons why *take off* is not multiple like *light*. My purpose here is to note the possibility, until now neglected, that *take off* is a combination of *take* and *off* and that each of these words and their combination have only a single meaning.

My argument assumes that meaning is MODULAR. The notion of modularity now has a prominent place in linguistics and related fields, and we can illustrate it by a specific application to lexical meaning: what dictionaries offer as definitions and linguists as solely lexical senses are actually complexes of a word's inherent content and contextual inference. What appears to be a number of separate senses, possibly highly different and unrelatable, can better be analyzed as a single general lexical meaning that can be variously "modulated" by a range of specific interpretations.

One consequence of this claim is that I will be confronting throughout this book the notion of COMPOSITIONALITY: that the meaning of a sentence is the sum of its lexical parts, as structured by the syntax. Consider, as preview, these data:

[10] The thief took the jewels.
[11] The thief took his own jewels.
[12] The jeweler took his jewels.
[13] The jeweler took his hat.
[14] John took his hat.
[15] The king took the jewels.

A sentence such as [10] is usually cited in dictionaries under *take* with the sense 'steal'; anyone using [10] would almost always mean that a theft had taken place. A compositional analysis thus seems to require such a meaning, and *take* is the logical place to assign it.

However, stealing is only a particular kind of taking (and *steal* a HYPONYM of *take*). Sentence [11] lessens the likelihood of 'steal'; if the jewels belong to the thief, then it can hardly be stealing. We are alerted to the fact that a person called a thief is not thieving all the time, and thus perhaps is not doing so in the situation described by [10]. Nevertheless, we may suspect a theft also in [11], and even (since we're now aware of the possibility) in [12]. But this is more unlikely, and in [13] and [14] thieving would not occur to us at all without additional contextual information.

What I am claiming is that *take* has the same general meaning in all these sentences, and that we readily and even exclusively reach the conclusion of 'steal' in [10] because of at least four pragmatic inferences:

   (a) that the thief is so described at least in part because of what he
       is doing in this sentence;
   (b) that the jewels do not belong to the thief;
   (c) that jewels are something very likely to be stolen;
   (d) that the thief is acting in the stealthy way that we know thieves
       act.

Given the lexical-syntactic contribution of [10], we infer the most appropriate (likely, typical, plausible, contextually relevant) situation. Of course, additional context can change our judgments. These inferences come from our knowledge of the world, which also suggests:

   (e) that the thief was physically present to steal the jewels in [10].

This inference is less appropriate in [15], because kings can send others to perform the deed. We thus interpret *take* in [10] more specifically as *steal,* just as we can interpret in a context *animal* as 'dog' or *that man* as 'my neighbor Mr. Smith'. We exercise a general inference that I will call PRAGMATIC SPECIALIZATION: we think of a particular kind of taking appropriate to the conditions that are (apparently) described.

Another type of pragmatic inference is illustrated by W3. It defines *break* in the phrase *break an artery* as 'to rupture the surface of and permit flowing out of effusing'. This definition confuses the sense of *break* with the reality to which the whole phrase refers. It is likely that a speaker would say *He broke an artery* and assume that a hearer would know that blood flowed; it is also likely that a speaker saying *He broke an artery and the artery started bleeding* might insult a hearer, by implying that the hearer needed to be told a basic fact about life. Yet, these likelihoods do not require the elaborate W3 definition; *break* here means what it means elsewhere. The full meaning is partly achieved through PRAGMATIC METONYMY, a general inference that supplies appropriate contiguous circumstances: here, a result.

This W3 definition is an especially glaring example of confusion between lexical and inferential contributions, but there are examples in this book that are much more subtle. These two examples demonstrate one of my themes: that our notions of word meaning have been formed by an implicit idealization in which language stands independent of extralinguistic contexts. This idealization thus creates a theoretical entity that seems deceptively "context free"; as a result, factors supposedly outside the isolated domain can be incorrectly included in the idealization. This result is what Bolinger (1971) has aptly called SEMANTIC OVERLOADING.

My point of view parallels modular conceptions in the tradition of Transformational Grammar [TG], particularly current Government-Binding [GB] theory. The transformational rules of Classical Transformational Grammar [CTG]—i.e., those modelled on *Aspects of the Theory of Syntax* (Chomsky (1965)) [*Aspects*]—were, like dictionary definitions, highly specific and detailed; but there were general properties of the transformations that were missed and implicitly denied by the formulations. Now, in GB, there is one general transformation ("Move Alpha"), that is less informative; the details of CTG transformations are distributed among various other modules of the grammar.

The parallel is also practical: the word meanings I will propose or point toward in this book are often highly abstract and remote from practical usefulness, just as the GB model now is remote for those who once thought that transformational insights could be applied to tasks like teaching. Dictionaries are limited by practicalities, sensitive to the demands of (relatively) easy understanding. So were CTG transformations; though their formalism discouraged many mathophobes, they provided insights that could have been captured with little practical loss in prose.

CTG transformations often missed generalizations, especially the most elusive and important: those that provide insight not merely into one specific language, but into language capacity in general. I am assuming, like GB theorists, that a basic task for linguistic theory is to discover what is universal, and possible innate, in human language capacity.

Though I will repeatedly be critical of compositionality, it should become apparent that I have no quarrel with the notion as such, but rather with faulty assumptions concerning what is being composed. In parallel, transformational-ists who now reject CTG rules are not rejecting the notion of 'rule' or even what such rules specifically claimed, but rather those particular formulations: that is, those particular distributions and combinations of theoretical detail, and the theoretical reasons that guided them. What is at issue is the following:

(a) the proper distribution of meaning between lexical items and
    other factors that contribute to sentential and discourse
    meaning, and
(b) the assumptions about universal linguistic capacity that justify
    such distributions.

Thus, I assume that lexical items as structured by the syntax do contribute compositionally to the meaning of a sentence; but this sum can then be altered in a number of different ways, two of which are Pragmatic Specialization and Pragmatic Metonymy.

While this position is not new or unique with me, my claims will probably be more extreme than those of any other scholar in the degree to which I "empty" words of their supposed meaning and assign it to other factors. In effect, I adopt Joos's (1972) "Semantic Axiom Number One": that a word should always be assumed to contribute as little meaning as possible to its context. Joos was thinking first in practical terms, specifically of *hapax legomena,* trying to guard against unwarranted intrusions of extra meaning into a translated text. But like him, I think his axiom has wider application, if supplemented by other theoretical assumptions, and one purpose of this book is to justify his insight.

1.3 SYSTEMATICITY

Modularity is a kind of systematicity; the observations made thus far apply directly to the Saussurean insight that linguistic order is systematic. The notion of 'system' in linguistics corresponds to the broader notion of 'ecology', the twentieth century's major interdisciplinary discovery. There are two kinds of systems that need to be distinguished, "weak" and "strong". A weak system exhibits MODULARITY: that is, all elements of the system exist within certain contexts, in relation with other elements. A strong system in addition exhibits MUTUALITY: elements are not merely related, but mutually defining. The status of each element determines and is determined by other elements; any change in one element means a change in the nature of others. The Saussurean system is a strong system: elements are "negative," their status being simply the non-choice of other options. As I will argue, a language necessarily has both kinds of systematicity, for principled universal reasons. More precisely, these are endpoints of a CONTINUUM OF SYSTEMATICITY: from completely closed classes exhibiting full mutuality with each other, which grade to more open classes exhibiting only modularity.

As is well known, systematicity has implications for translation. Translation from one language into another is at best approximate. A translation may inescapably fail to transfer correctly the division between what is said and not said, or between what is assumed and asserted: that is, it may run afoul of different semantic-pragmatic divisions in the two languages. But also, solely within semantics, systematic status (especially mutuality) may be different; even interchangeable one-word "equivalences" may be part of non-parallel systems.[2]

The same point applies to intralanguage definitions, which also are translations. This point is often overlooked, because translation is usually viewed solely in syntagmatic terms: the criterion is accuracy, which is appropriateness in a particular context. But systematicity more crucially concerns the paradigmatic dimension, whose criterion is comprehensiveness, in all contexts. Translation is possible because it is relatively "easy" to find linguistic means to solve the problem of a single context; semantic theory, however, must meet the systematic challenge of also faithfully capturing a word's full range.

A mistaken attribution of multiplicity is likeliest with the most general words in a language, which by virtue of their generality do not have synonyms that come close to having identical syntagmatic and paradigmatic requirements. To define such words by other words, recourse must be made to hyponyms which, by virtue of being multiple, give the impression of a polysemic word. This problem is particularly severe with verbs like *be, do, have, come, go, take, give,* and *break,* and with prepositions and conjunctions. As an additional complication, many hyponyms can be specifications of two antonymous words (such as *lime* for both *yellow* and *green*), and thus introduce extraneous ("emergent") factors; and, as we have seen with *break an artery,* pragmatic meaning may also be included.

Each definition may introduce only a small distortion, but the need for many such definitions creates many distortions. The resulting "meanings" seem clearly distinct and even unrelated, creating the impression of a polysemic or homonymic word.

Consider a TG analysis, now dated (McCawley (1971)), which concerns the following data:

[16] John is believed to *have* arrived at 2:00 *yesterday.*

[17] John arriv*ed* at 2:00 *yesterday.*

[18] John is believed to *have* drunk a gallon of beer *by now.*

[19] John *has drunk* a gallon of beer *by now*.
[20] John is believed to *have* already met Sue *when he married Cynthia*.
[21] John *had* already *met* Sue *when he married Cynthia*.

The odd-numbered sentences present a three-way time distinction, indicated by the different time expressions and the variation of past [17], present perfect [19], and past perfect [21]. The three-way distinction of time expressions is captured also in the infinitive phrases of the even-numbered sentences; but the other three-way distinction is paralleled only by *have*. The question: what is the status of *have*, given that it seems to be synonymous to three different expressions?

In the CTG framework, and even more so in the General Semantics [GS] model that followed, the answer had to be that *to have* was ambiguous. The parallels were captured by the transformation Subject Raising; since transformations were required to be meaning-preserving, the three-way distinction of [22–24] was assumed to be preserved in the single [25]:

[22] It is likely that John has gone.
[23] It is likely that John had gone.
[24] It is likely that John went.
[25] John is likely to have gone.

This is a clear example of syntax dominating paradigm, for the systems being equated are not parallel: in comparable contexts, there is a four-way paradigm in main clauses (two tenses and two perfects) and only a two-way paradigm in infinitives (infinitive or perfect infinitive). Sentence [25] was judged ambiguous not because it filled different roles in its own paradigm, but because it corresponded to separate roles in another paradigm. In effect, this analysis implies that distinctions made anywhere in the language must be assumed to exist throughout the language. Making [25] monosemic would have required (in that model) relinquishing either Subject Raising or the requirement that transformations preserve meaning. The same eclipsing of paradigm for syntax can be seen in a number of proposed transformations of the CTG period; in retrospect, we can see that Saussure's insight was forgotten, misunderstood, or tacitly rejected. (More recent analyses do not consider *that*-clauses and infinitives equivalent; Subject Raising applies only to the latter, and the two paradigms need not be equated.)

A second example shows definitional shortcomings on the phrasal level. The phrase *break the ice* is said to have both a literal and a figurative meaning. The latter is listed by dictionaries as a set phrase; in his *Idiom Structures in English*, Makkai (1972: 311) calls it an idiom. This requires that *break* be multiple in meaning (or, alternatively, sometimes have no separate meaning). The following examples illustrate the figurative use; it occurs as both active and passive:

[26] Some people use an unusual thing, such as an unusual piece of jewelry, to break the ice. (DAI)

[27] And he led the conversation around to the lovely palm trees which nodded outside the window: a conversational turn which broke the ice and won the admiration of the other visitors. (Lawrence Durrell)

[28] I gave her tea, with milk and sugar and tried to think of something to say. Lovell broke the ice by asking me if I didn't think her hair was beautiful. (John Cheever)

[29] The awkward silence of strangers' first encounter prevailed. Then one man mumbled, "Used to watch my grandfather make brooms. Only he used a different kind of contraption." The ice was broken. (Karen Lingo)

[30] The shyness of the young islanders was rapidly giving way to easy comradeship with the visitors. The American boys seemed to know by instinct how best to break the ice. (James Norman Hall)

[31] On the other hand, when the ice was once broken and the barriers down, the President's charm was unusual and almost unfailing. (Gamaliel Bradford)

[32] Held scoreless and hitless until the fifth inning, the Mariners broke the ice on home runs by Willy Horton and Leon Roberts and went on to beat the Rangers. . . . (*Sporting News*)

[33] That breaks the ice. Rich Yonaker gets the first basket of the second half. (Jim Thacker)

To strengthen his claim of idiomaticity, Makkai says that the definite article is mandatory; but it isn't in [34] and [35]. Example [36], although poetic and dated, also provides evidence:

[34] His cheery Creole broke what little ice we encountered, after which conversation flowed like wine.
(Kenneth MacLeish)

[35] When such results occurred, he always made use of them to break any lingering ice, and establish communication.
(Archibald M. Hill)

[36] And your cold people are beyond all price
When once you've broken their confounded ice.
(Lord Byron, OED)

Both W3 and Makkai give the figurative phrase the definition 'to make a beginning'. Sentences [26–28], especially, appear to support this definition, but it is too general: I have just made a beginning with this book, yet it is not appropriate to say I've broken the ice. In addition, it is significant that in [29] the conversation appears to be delayed before starting, and in [33] the team goes several minutes before its first score. *Webster's New World Dictionary, Second College Edition* (1982) [WNW] is more specific: 'to make a start by getting over initial difficulties'. The "difficulties" are what the word *ice* designates; the modifiers *what little* [34] and *lingering* [35] make sense in this light. In dictionaries that note these difficulties, they are specified as formality, reserve, tension, aloofness, shyness, stiffness, awkwardness, hostility and lack of acquaintance. The last two are specified in [37] and [38]:

[37] Diplomatic experts give the President credit for publicly recognizing the strategic importance of Iran and seeking to break the ice of hostility that has surrounded US-Iranian relations. . . . (Charlotte Saikowski)
[38] They nodded to each other by way of breaking the ice of unacquaintance. . . . (Thomas Hardy)

The above examples also illustrate shyness [29] and various inabilities: to talk [28] and [29] and to score [32] and [33].

Funk & Wagnalls New Standard Dictionary of the English Language (1963) [FW] calls these difficulties "restraints." In definitions, dictionaries talk of "getting through", "relaxing", "penetrating" or "overcoming" these difficulties or restraints. As the phrase indicates, a suitable verb is *break*. An analysis that treats the whole phrase as a metaphor or idiom fails to note that *break* is a verb that co-occurs with a wide range of both concrete and abstract objects; examples [39–48] show *break* in contexts very similar to those of figurative *break the ice*:

[39] Now the emotions with Russ began to sort themselves out; he could feel that curious detachment breaking. (Ben Haas)
[40] . . . the stalemate [is] to be broken by the three-man committee. . . . (Jerry Reed)
[41] Briskly, trying to break the inertia, I looked at my watch, and rose, saying, "By Jove! I had no idea it was so late." (C. E. Scoggins)
[42] . . . once the initial aloofness had been broken the use of synthetic indigotin made strides. (E. J. Holmyard)
[43] . . . an indifference seldom broken by the bitterness toward her that Morgan has seen that night. (Tom Wicker)
[44] . . . [she] treated her son with a formal, icy politeness which broke sometimes to reveal a disappointment . . . . (Catherine Gaskin)
[45] When nothing had changed by the evening of the third day, I knew the impasse must be broken. (New Yorker)
[46] The type of synthesis, I predict, will not prove to break the impasse, the communication-barrier. (Donald Mitchell)
[47] The clown succeeded in breaking the shy, inhibited silence of the crowd. (Francis Irby Gwaltney)
[48] I would have liked to break the silence but couldn't think of anything cheerful to say. (James Herriot)

From this evidence we can see the *break* in *break the ice* is the same word that occurs widely in other expressions; only the noun *ice* is figurative. *Break the ice* is thus not an idiom; it refers to the breaking of a difficult situation. If a difficult situation is broken, then a start on something can be made; I suggest that 'make a start' is an inference of Result, another example of Pragmatic

Metonymy. Such a start can in turn lead to an improved relationship with people, or an improved ability in other activities such as games; but these results are also pragmatic inferences. As we will see later in this book, with phrases like *hit the road* and *hit the bottle,* inferential meanings can become more prominent than inherent meaning, and this is one of the circumstances that lead us mistakenly to conclude that phrases like *break the ice* are idiomatic.

I will also show later, with many more examples, that *ice* has a meaning in *break the ice* which it has in other contexts. Thus, for both *break* and *ice,* I appeal to paradigmatic unity to counter what I consider to be incorrect analyses; I present data that demonstrate that linguistic investigation has slighted the paradigmatic dimension and thus failed to allow for full systematicity. But the nature of the data I have invoked now requires a discussion of data in general.

1.4 DATA: USE AND INTUITION

What data are relevant for any semantic study of English? There has been an ongoing debate in linguistics about the relative merits of data from actual use versus data from the intuitions of those who speak the language. American structuralists, dialectologists, and sociolinguists have emphasized the need for actual data, but the Chomsky tradition has favored intuition for its particular theoretical goals, offering these compelling reasons:

    (a) Occurring sentences are only a small subset of what are possible; there are an infinite number of possible sentences.

    (b) The relevant data include structural and relational judgments by speakers (whether, for example, two sentences are paraphrases) that actual use cannot provide. Sentences in themselves, in fact, are secondary phenomena; of primary interest is linguistic knowledge, the system of rules by which any speaker can in principle produce all possible sentences. Compared to the inadequate resources of use, intuition provides direct access to all of a speaker's linguistic knowledge, making available information that can be extracted from actual speech only with the aid of those same intuitions.

    (c) Actual speech is both too complicated and too simple for a particular theoretical issue. With an example specifically tailored to the occasion, guaranteed by intuition, the researcher can have the equivalent of a controlled experiment with only one independent variable. Conversely, sometimes the needed examples are so syntactically complex that they are unlikely to occur; yet such data can be supplied, under systematic control of the variables, by intuition.

    (d) Intuitions can also supply negative evidence, of what cannot possibly occur or can occur under conditions when rules are being broken. Non-use is uninformative.

In these four ways, intuition overcomes the deficiencies of use and provides relevant and reliable evidence. These arguments are convincing to me, and I accept them completely in this study. But unfortunately the opposite question has not been asked: is intuition alone enough? As a survey of works in the transformational tradition quite readily shows, the answer to this unasked question seems to be "yes": almost all data are invented, produced ready-made for the occasion by the researcher. Is intuition without disadvantages? Can either actual data or intuition alone provide what is required?

These are the advantages of use:

(a) Use does not rely as exclusively on the conscious mind as does intuition. Consider a parallel illustration of typical short-sighted prescriptivism: the campaign to get a /t/ pronounced in the word *often*. While proponents were partly successful, they apparently never noticed the word *soften*. For those "in the know," the mistake is obvious: *often* was treated as an isolated element, with the guiding precept that pronunciation should follow spelling. The basic problem of any prescriptivism (when it poses as descriptive) is that of having improverished data. These data in turn strengthen the guiding assumptions. Someone knowing the full range of words where a /t/ is lost, and systematically, is likely to have second thoughts about the precept that spelling should determine pronunciation.

Linguists see the limits of the *often*-prescriptivist because their procedures allow them access to more data. But these procedures, as Chomsky has repeatedly noted, are not ultimate guarantees of success. We cannot know in advance all the correct procedures and assumptions; these must be discovered by wits and genius, by trial and error. Unfortunately, the conscious mind is rather weak in finding the full range of data; procedures and theories based largely on intuition are always struggling with an unnecessarily meager database.

(b) Use is more likely to provide evidence to undermine our hypotheses. Intuitions are not "pure": they can be conditioned by many assumptions, some tacit or highly complex, others as simple as the wish to justify one's theory. They may be subject to various standards of exactitude: when we say two sentences are paraphrases, how exactly are we applying our standards? Are we able to judge our degree of exactness? Even negative evidence may be suspect: there can be many reasons, some highly theory-specific, why some sentences seem ill-formed. Critics of TG reject the more complex TG examples, arguing that they are too complicated for use and thus cannot be considered well-formed, in spite of systematic extrapolations from well-formed simpler sentences. It is noteworthy that the judgments on both sides correlate with larger theoretical assumptions.

Intuition, limited by conscious awareness, does very

poorly when required both to invent and to judge. As
sometimes (but insufficiently) acknowledged, it is a suspicious
practice when researchers create the data that measure the
worth of their theories; this demands a level of self-scrutiny
only rarely achieved. Data of use, if collected sufficiently
(even overabundantly), can guard against undue
self-justification, reveal tacit theoretical biasing, and provide
our intuition with enough material to make more critical
judgments.

(c) Use challenges the mistaken belief that we can "isolate"
linguistic factors. Given the impure status of intuitional data, it
is questionable whether the intuitional strategy of controlling
example sentences for one variable actually allows data to test
the influence of tacit assumptions; rather, this strategy almost
guarantees their permanent lock on our insight. Chomsky
(1955), among others, has disparaged the worth of experiments
on rats that leave the rat with only two choices. Such
experiments may not be as free of extraneous variables as the
experimenters assume, but rather introduce unacknowledged
effects of minimization, thus informing us merely about the
abilities of rats when limited to only two choices. The prospect
of enlightenment with controlled procedures is proportionally
dimmer with human beings.

(d) Although actual data may be too complex and too simple with
respect to intuition, the converse is also true. As I will show,
the simplified sentences of intuition are always judged more
semantically complex than they should be. Also, invented
sentences rarely show the radical unexpected specificity of
detail and context that actual data provide. Invented sentences
tend to be simplistic even when complex: well-behaved (and
overexemplified) nouns and verbs link in stereotypic ways.
This practice serves to reaffirm the belief that the semantics of
some rarified group of sentences can be determined as if those
sentences were "context free". Context, both linguistic and
extralinguistic, is *always tacitly assumed;* but since we are
rarely aware how much is added, we tend confidently to
believe that we have isolated only what we want.

A linguist who struggles with actual sentences is not so easily fooled; the
bewildering range of potentially relevant factors is too apparent, and the
boundaries between semantic and pragmatic (intralinguistic versus extralinguistic) contributions to meaning are not so intuitively clear. Some meanings that
seem inherent in language when viewed through intuitional data appear rather to
be external when viewed through actual data.

Linguists who attempt to factor out pragmatic effects without investigating
such effects in actual detail are at the mercy of pretheoretical habits that try to
assign as much perceived meaning as possible to words. Intuition alone cannot

break the inherited habits. "Conscious control" is only part of research in the human sciences; "indwelling" is also required. Through actual data, we have the resources of both our conscious and unconscious knowledge; we are deterred from oversimplifying our task and making it impossible.[3]

Thus, this book uses many attestations. It is important to be clear about what this means, especially for those trained in TG (as I was) to associate reliance on actual data with the shallow belief that principles and regularities arise automatically from evidence and that all the scientist needs to do is record the obvious conclusions. To the contrary, no amount of "reality" ever leads automatically to explanation; reasons and conclusions require the interpreting human mind. No matter how plentiful the data, they are never enough. In all except logically exhaustible theories, there are always more possible data and thus there is the open potential for correction. A scientist must always go beyond data, relying finally on intuition. A theory, no matter how well-founded, is more faith than fact.

Actual data without intuition hardly qualify as data at all. But intuition without sufficient supporting actual data is barren; both are necessary. The debate on relative merits has been at best short-sightedness, at worst a barrier to genuine semantic research. The greatest need presently in semantic research is for abundant actual data with which our intuitions can do their work well.[4]

1.5   HETEROGENEITY

If a strong system were fully homogeneous, any idealization would be highly distortive. With every element in mutual dependence on all others, a change in one would imply a change in all, and the status of one element could not be ascertained without equal attention to all the others; the system would thus have to be studied completely. But in a weak, modular system, subsystems can relate weakly to each other, with relative autonomy, so that the effects of any change will be localized. Thus, it is possible to posit idealizations that may be relatively accurate—if, that is, our posited modularities correspond to actual ones.

However, a converse issue then becomes important: how much heterogeneity is there? Are we dealing with a relatively few modularities, or almost countless many? The latter possibility is as despairing a prospect for idealizations as a completely homogeneous system, or no system at all.

Human language capacity is part of a larger system of capacities; GB assumes that it has some modular autonomy, although we cannot know in advance which parts are (relatively) autonomous and which are not. Of course, there is no absolute autonomy, for the character of a module is necessarily determined in many ways by larger systems. GB also assumes that even a near-autonomous module of language capacity can itself be internally modular; some of these submodules seem intuitively clear at present, though they may prove not to be so.

The assumption of a specific modularity of Language Capacity may itself be faulty; Chomsky has repeatedly stressed that such a hypothesis is tentative, as is all scientific endeavor (Chomsky (1980, Chapter One)). With similar tentative assurance, I assume in this book that there is something relatively autonomous that can be "language-internal meaning", which I will consider semantic. But I am also constantly preoccupied with pragmatic, language-external meaning, which interacts with semantics to produce the full meaning of human speech: especially so since what I take as semantic will differ drastically from what is normally assumed. An additional complication is that both semantics and pragmatics can be internally highly modular; also, these modularities, and their interactions, may be more continuous than discrete.

The more heterogeneous a system becomes, the more it may appear in some parts not to be systematic at all. Such a system will be rich in individuation; many interacting rules, conditions, and constraints can enable the creation of many small-scale paradigms, with very few members, perhaps only one. In fact, every lexical item is finally in a paradigm exclusively its own. Yet, with any paradigm of a single member, it is questionable whether there is a larger operative order at all; for those linguists not committed to finding systematicity, a singular phrase may appear to be idiomatic, with no systematic explanation. As further complication, a language may have both types of singularity, with no immediately evident means of determining which is which.

No reasonable theory of language can fail to assume a high degree of heterogeneity. This complexity creates the need for idealization, the purpose of which is to homogenize. That is the purpose of the TG idealization [IDEAL], stated at the beginning of *Aspects,* which assumes an ideal speaker-hearer, in a homogeneous speech community, with perfect knowledge of the language, which is learned instantaneously. Formal register is also implied, with "complete" sentences treated as isolated objects of thought, independent of any discourse use. This homogenized language is a model of competence; all the omitted heterogeneity (plus various kinds of "lapses") is to be incorporated in a model of performance.

What is the status of IDEAL? Hostile and even friendly critics over the years have noted the obvious: it is highly unrealistic, and simply false. No community is homogeneous, no language learning is instantaneous, languages have more than a formal register, and expressions have multiple uses. The idealization even borders on the inconceivable: who or what could the "ideal" speaker-hearer with "perfect" knowledge possibly be? Critics charge that IDEAL illegitimately eliminates the contingencies of speakers, hearers, and language use, leaving a "competence" that appears to be highly remote from any scientific accountability.

It might be argued that IDEAL merely serves as a useful artifice, a descriptive expediency; but Chomsky does not see it as such. He claims that it has a reality independent of our theorizing: it corresponds to a mental grammar that is innate and therefore universal and that ultimately can be correlated to physical brain states. IDEAL thus is meant as a substantive empirical claim, testable by research. But, even if justified, the severity of the idealization calls into question most of our testing measures. Actual conscious human knowledge necessarily involves full heterogeneity, not just that of the idealization. Most current tests (and intuition) fail to assure that they test merely what they intend to test.

This has implications both ways: tests do not necessarily invalidate IDEAL; but on the other hand, the difficulty of formulating a test does not strengthen it, but may make it effectively useless, if no means of evaluation can be applied. The most reliable tests have been (excessively?) formal; over thirty years of the TG tradition, there has been constant change and diversification, created by analytical testing that found earlier models inadequate.

These considerations bear on my running appeal to, and quarrel with, the linguist whose ideas have probably had the most immediate influence on this book: Dwight Bolinger. Through the first thirty years of TG, Bolinger has been its most dedicated and detailed critic. He has two basic disagreements: one that I can support (though not for his reasons), one that I cannot. These issues are stated comprehensively in his article, "Meaning and memory" (1976).

CTG was, according to Bolinger, an inappropriately deductive approach to language, committed to finding an underlying formal system that would be highly homogeneous, and thus explicable by rules that swept grandly across a wide range of contexts. To a man who has spent his scholarly life describing many detailed subtleties and idiosyncrasies, this is highly implausible. He sums up his disagreement thus (pp. 11–12):

> Prime attention to the overarching system and more or less
> incidental attention to the local detail follows naturally from the
> assumption that the grammar is homogenous and self-confirming.
> In a formal deductive system everything is explained when
> everything fits. There is no need to worry about missing a detail or
> two because sooner or later any mistake or oversight will show up
> in a grinding of the gears. It even seems rather petty to insist on
> full and precise documentation in each separate province of the
> realm. The power of the system as a whole to reveal a flaw is so
> great that mastering the grand design outweighs any small help that
> can be picked up from one of its mere neighborhoods. But once
> homogeneity is denied, the security is gone. Separate—and, yes,
> ad hoc—explanations for each part become essential. It is no
> longer safe to assume that the system will correct itself.
> Unquestionably it will in many ways; certainly there are local
> regularities as well as universal ones; but the self-corrective
> remedies must be sought AFTER one has canvassed as thoroughly as
> possible in each neighborhood, approaching the indwellers on their
> own terms.

Bolinger follows these remarks with a sustained argument that a language is basically idiomatic, in large part (his words) "jerry built." In this view, systems are possible and sometimes present, but not necessary or crucial. To counter

CTG emphasis on our rule-directed capacity, he champions the mind's storage capacity, which makes possible the memorizing of many unorderly specifics. This is an argument that Bolinger is perhaps best qualified to make, since he has found the discouraging details to undermine many a proposed generalization.

Yet, without denying any of his special details, I think he is wrong in thinking that language is only contingently or occasionally systematic. To repeat: it is possible to have a heterogeneous system that allows a high degree of complexity. Many "idioms" are the result not of irregularity, but of multiple intersecting regularities that allow only one or a few possible realizations. That is, I claim the following:

[B] INDIVIDUATION CONDITION
    Individuation is the result of highly complex systems. The more complex a system, the more diverse its individuals, and the less likelihood that any one individual can directly reveal the system.

Individuation is a central problem in semantic theory, if only because we must deal with individual lexical items. The excessive degree of homogenization in TG becomes critical every time a linguist tries to argue from the patterning of one word to a supposed class that the word represents. This procedure is successful only when we can isolate just those properties common to the words in the posited class. We have no advance assurance that this can be easily done, and a small database merely hides the problem: discussions of Dative Movement, for example, are compromised if each new researcher sticks only to the verb *give* and a few others (and only part of their ranges). A limited database prolongs the life, not only of a mistaken transformation, but also of a mistaken assessment of the homogeneity of a class.

As this book demonstrates, I agree with Bolinger's methodology. Since words (and, even more so, sentences) can be highly individual, my first priority must be the detailed investigation of "local" areas, with large sets of data, rather than the formulating of general rules with limited data.

The challenge for a theory of semantics is to do justice both to the system and to its individuals. IDEAL can overgeneralize and thus undervalue the individuals. An idiomatic view, conversely, can undergeneralize and thus undervalue the system. IDEAL in effect tries to isolate several fundamental generalized modules that are presumed to be the foundation for additional modules that diversify. As the competence-performance distinction implies (or should), progressively more inclusive theories require a parallel series of progressively more concrete idealizations, incorporating some of the variability eliminated in the first.

It is thus essential for linguists who accept IDEAL to flesh out these more inclusive idealizations, as a necessary part of what Chomsky (1980: 25) calls "the social division of linguistic labor." Of course, this wider range can make the task more difficult. As compensation, however, if the idealization chosen is the one necessary to best describe the investigator's problem, the task should be made easier. We cannot know in advance where everything goes; by trying to solve a problem in the wrong idealization, we can create distortions that may introduce distortions into other problems as well.

Distortive consequences can be most costly at the most abstract level, IDEAL, where we cannot see fully which data are part of those modules we intended to eliminate. Inevitably, the more abstract an idealization, the more likely it will try to describe too much, by homogenizing variations and providing solutions for problems that should simply be ignored at that degree of abstraction. It is significant that with each innovation in TG, less is required of the most abstract idealization, with also less multiple meaning.

My claim in this book is that, under the influence of dictionaries, we have misrepresented linguistically conveyed meaning, attributing too much to a minimal range of modules. I am thus committed to a more inclusive idealization. Obviously, IDEAL must at least be modulated specifically to the range of variabilities that we call English. But any attempt to join "IDEAL-English" and "lexical meaning", *as these notions have usually been envisioned,* will lead to excessive homonymy, polysemy, idioms, and "dummy" elements.

In effect, my procedure involves a search for the more concrete idealizations within which the contributions to dictionary-type definitions can be identified and differentiated. IDEAL was fashioned to avoid, at least initially, the necessity of Bolinger's local methodology; but, to distinguish semantic from pragmatic, I must pay him heed.

1.6 MINDS AND REALITIES

Bolinger's reasoning and methodology do not necessarily lead to the view he champions: that most of language is idiomatic, and that the large resources of our memory, supposedly ignored by TG, enable us to store many set phrases that are only minimally integrated into our full linguistic knowledge. Bolinger's view of memory is somewhat skimpy, for he seems to limit it too much to listed storage. Instead, couldn't this storage capacity be organizationally enabled and enhanced by the complex set of rules that Bolinger feels moved to criticize?

Instead of the idealized speaker-hearer, Bolinger assumes, as do many transformational critics, "normal" speakers [NORMAL], the highly diverse actual human beings who use the language. Unlike the perfect speaker-hearer, normal speakers may not have organized their linguistic knowledge to an optimal systematic degree. Bolinger quotes Antilla (1972: 349) with approval:

> Memory or brain storage is on a much more extravagent scale than
> we would like to think; even the most "obvious" cases [of apparent
> generalization] can be stored separately.

We again meet the problem of individuation, this time with the individual speaker. By positing the ideal speaker-hearer, Chomsky attempted to generalize the notion of "mind"; NORMAL linguists assume that individual minds (or their behavioral evidence) are fundamental. R. Hall comments (1978: 34):

> The only linguistic REALITIES, in the sense of directly observable or
> deducible phenomena, are idiolects and the elements into which
> they can be analysed; all other linguistic entities are abstractions,
> arrived at by either naive or scientific analysis.

However, this is too strongly stated: it contravenes the basic assumption of social sciences that humans are social creatures, in large part (and necessarily so) created by their social context. Yet, Hall's remarks are a needed caution against ignoring individuation, of assuming too much social homogeneity. Conversely, IDEAL cautions us not to overvalue the individual speaker. We must search for the general and systematic conditions that enable individual speakers to develop their particular idiolects. Both cautions are necessary.

Optimally, we need the means of showing both all the degrees of uniformity and all the degrees of diversity. We take the usual leap of faith: if we keep in mind the proportional view that some linguistic facts are universal and some are idiolectal (and even nonce), with a continuous cline in between, we can talk about "the mind" while guarding against reducing our theories to the polar extremes of perfection and idiolect.

We can grant that some speakers may learn singularities as isolated entities; but how much should we generalize such isolated learning? There is evidence that humans retain and use knowledge best when it is integrated with other knowledge: specifically, when it is modularly organized. The hierarchical structure of human language shows this clearly. In contrast, we do poorly on isolated bits of information, such as people's names. While this does not make idioms impossible or even unlikely, it suggests a strong tendency for humans to integrate their knowledge, rather than keeping it in isolated storage. If this observation has any validity, it suggests that an idiomatic-view-in-general presents a highly misleading image of the mind's potential and effectiveness.

However, I think we can make more ambitious claims about the human mind, even while constrained to respect both individual variation and the limits of our present knowledge. The major organizing principle of this book is such a claim about the human mind:

[C] VOCABULARY PRINCIPLE
The vocabulary of a language is ordered in accord with the order of the
human mind. Closed minimal classes in a language reflect primary,
unconscious order, remote from reality. Open maximal classes in a
language reflect secondary, conscious order, related to reality. There is a
continuous cline from closed to open, from unconscious to conscious.

My justification for this claim is the full weight of this book. For now, I note it in order to state the major difficulty I have with Bolinger's view: he seems to drastically underestimate unconscious linguistic knowledge. Ironically,

Bolinger shares TG's greatest shortcoming: he trusts too much in his intuition. (His may be the most brilliant and resourceful linguist's intuition we have going, but it's still intuition.)

Of course, we must note here something that Chomsky has, almost in vain, tried to make clear: that we are not used to thinking of non-conscious order as "knowledge", and so we constantly quarrel with every remark about knowledge that seems to depart from immediate conscious understanding. Unconscious knowledge tends to be highly ordered, conscious knowledge much less so. Thus, those who reason too exclusively from awareness can very easily conclude that linguistic knowledge is "jerry built." With the unconscious mind supplying order, consciousness is free (and specifically able) to be (relatively) disorderly (even to "break rules"); it is low-level disorder that makes consciousness possible.

Chomsky (1980: 133) makes a parallel point about pedagogical treatments of language, which (along with dictionaries) have been our means for conscious language learning and reflection. These concentrate largely on (what is seen as) the exceptional, leaving more generalized order to be intuited or simply ignored. The apparent idiomaticity of language thus looms large by default; yet, again, what does this conscious awareness of language tell us about the whole of our linguistic capacity?

I will be arguing for unconscious meanings with radically different categories and processes that are perhaps beyond conscious comprehension. This possibility is precluded in both IDEAL and NORMAL. While IDEAL does not directly deny unconscious order, its effect is to neutralize the interactive complexity of conscious versus unconscious knowledge; and then its exclusive reliance on intuition tends to limit conceivable knowledge to conscious categories. The effect of NORMAL is to eliminate any categories that depart radically from the awareness of the normal speaker. The unhappy coincidence is that both are too preoccupied with consciousness.

We can see this in Bolinger's "Meaning and memory" (1976: 3):

> Suppose we took the phrase *out of patience* and looked for an
> underlying representation. It would have to contain the same *out of*
> that is found in *out of money, out of time, out of ice cream,* out of
> anything that one formerly had a supply of but had no longer. It
> never dawned on me, till the 24th day of January 1973, that the
> *out of* in *out of patience* had any connection with that other *out*
> *of*—penetrating the source of the expression was one of those odd
> strokes of illumination that we get every so often with something
> we have been using all our lives. It is clear that most people do not
> associate the two, because if they did they would not turn *out of*
> *patience* into a command, or use intensifiers with it (*Don't be so*
> *out of patience!, *Don't be so out of money!*) When we say *out of*
> *patience* we are not pulling *out of* and *patience* separately from
> storage and putting them together but retrieving the whole thing at
> once.

The issue is the status of *out of*. Bolinger appeals to several marginal considerations and is too selective in choosing relevant paradigms, thus assuring an idiomatic conclusion. Because we need not be consciously aware to know something, his discovery of January 1973 is minimally relevant, except to his personal linguistic autobiography, or to illustrate the limits of consciousness. Even if a phrase is stored as a unit, it need not be isolated from the rest of the language; it can still be the same *out of*. What has to be shown by idiomaticians, and not merely assumed, is that the "fixedness" of a phrase necessarily changes the semantic status of its words.

This leaves us with one relevant argument: the different contextual effects of *out of patience* and *out of money*. But Bolinger has not made enough paradigmatic checks. There are other data his intuition didn't find: *Don't be so impatient!*, **Don't be so penniless*. These suggest that the difference comes from the more concrete (real-world) difference between patience and money. Their individualities create a difference, but not necessarily one in *out of*. Why are *I've run out of money* and *I've run out of patience* parallel? Why can *I've run out* or *I'm all out* be elliptical for either? (These data suggest that even *out of* is decomposable.)

While we need not take these parallels totally at face value (they may be misleading, and there are other paradigms to check), we can't ignore them. TG is often accused of imposing order by fiat; but here Bolinger seems to be imposing disorder by fiat. To repeat: the problem for all "impositions" is an exaggerated faith in conscious intuition.

Because conscious awareness underestimates the order supplied by the unconscious, it is relatively easy to find rather obvious order that has escaped everyone's notice. Consider the following:

[49] Jack *broke off ties with* Bill.
[50] Jack *broke ties off with* Bill.
[51] Jack *broke off with* Bill.
[52] Jack *broke ties with* Bill.
[53] Jack *broke with* Bill.
[54] Jack *broke it off with* Bill.

Volume One of *The Oxford Dictionary of Current Idiomatic English* [ODIE], "Verbs with Prepositions and Particles," lists forty-nine different expressions with *break,* including (i) four different *break off* phrases, one exemplified by "*Aren't they getting married then?*" "*No, they've broken it off*"; and (ii) a *break with,* exemplified in *John has broken with his family.* In addition, some dictionaries list *break off with* as an idiom, thus isolating three different expressions that in [49–54] seem closely related.

Are these similarities purely accidental? The differences in meaning appear to correlate with the differences in constituent words. A plausible solution would recognize (a) that *off* is optional and (b) that a *with*-phrase can modify an *implicit* nominal. Composing meaning from the constituents seems rather straightforward. Since this pattern has gone unnoticed, should we take it as merely a homonymic coincidence? Perhaps it will prove to be something quite different in the light of further data and assessment, but to judge these expressions as idioms because speakers need not consciously know the full pattern (or because lexicographers and linguists have heretofore pronounced them as idioms) seems to be too great a preference for precedent or current wisdom over data: that is, a preference for overconscious dogmatism.

Much of what I have said thus far requires considerable elaboration; in particular, I need to say more about unconscious and conscious aspects of language. I also need to do some of the "local" investigation that Bolinger's methodology, and mine, requires. Without such specific demonstrations of what I am driving at, my general theoretical musing (even assuming I did it well) would likely be wildly misunderstood. Throughout this book, I will be doing extended studies of particular words: the verbs *bear, hit, kick* and *slap*, the noun *ice,* and the alleged "particles" of English, which I consider (with Emonds (1972)) to be intransitive prepositions. In these studies I assume the monosemic bias and detail its implications. The next chapter is devoted to a word that seems (according to Bolinger) not to have a meaning at all: the verb *bear*.

Chapter *2*

THE VERB *BEAR*

The best way to explore the possibilities of monosemy is to analyze in depth a particular word. This procedure is severely limited: every word is highly individual, so we are not assured of general paradigmatic insights; we cannot have reliable conclusions without knowing in full a word's semantic field. However, by adopting the criterion of Comprehensiveness, we can find sufficient reason to doubt a number of current assurances. Following the Monosemic Bias, I will assume this word has only one meaning, and attempt to determine what would be required for that assumption to be sustained. I will then develop and justify these requirements more thoroughly in subsequent chapters.

2.1 PRELIMINARIES

I choose the verb *bear* because Bolinger (1976) uses it to argue that languages are highly idiomatic; it appears to be the worst possible candidate for semantic unity and the "freedom" of wide syntactic generalization:

> The best example I can think of to illustrate a struggle toward freedom that never quite makes it is the verb *to bear*. It is a veritable jungle of idioms and collocational restrictions with no heart to pump blood through it but with peripheral organs that

manage to keep functioning anyway. Idioms include *bear up, bear down, bear the brunt, bear right, bear left*. Collocations include *bear a resemblance, bear a grudge, bear a child, bear a burden*—we are less likely *to carry a burden* and quite unlikely *to bear a load*. But the puzzling part is the syntactic possibilities of transforming which are simply not carried out. For example it is normal to have *bear* in a relative clause in an expression like *the love that I bear them* (notice this is affirmative). And a declarative or interrogative is all right with a negation or an implied negation: *bear them no love*. But a simple straightforward affirmative is out of the question: **I bear them love*. How do we generate *The love that I bear them* if we cannot say **I bear them love*? The same goes for infinitives and gerunds; we can say *She bore his neglect bravely* and either *She can't bear to be neglected* or *She can't bear being neglected*, but we do not say **She bore to be neglected* nor **She bore being neglected*, though *She endured being neglected* is normal enough. The only way to explain these phenomena is that a child first learns *to carry* and only later *to bear*, but failing actually to HEAR the verb *bear* in contexts where *carry* is normal and from which metaphorical extensions can be made if one wants to, he never fully dissociates *bear* from its collocations, even though all the transformational possibilities are there for him to do it. This argues for the kind of memory storage and retrieval I have postulated. The fact that it has to be invoked for *bear* suggests that it is potentially present throughout the system. (p. 9)

There would certainly be problems for a thesis of monosemy if Bolinger's observations were correct and the only relevant considerations. But his claim of semantic emptiness for *bear* must be tested by the larger database that he himself requires: we must "canvass as thoroughly as possible in each neighborhood."

We begin with the data of dictionaries. Though dictionaries treat *bear* as a highly polysemic word, there is general consensus on certain meanings. These meanings are integrated by the OED into the following scheme of types and subtypes:

> I. to carry; with its transferred and figurative senses
> II. to sustain, support, uphold
>   A. to sustain weight or pressure, to endure
>   B. to support, keep up, maintain
>   C. to hold up, hold, have upon it
> III. to push, thrust, press
>   A. to push, press
>   B. to thrust (through) [obsolete]
>   C. to press oneself; move, tend, lie in a given direction
> IV. to bring forth, produce, give birth to

In attempting to integrate these senses, the OED notes:

> As the senses of *carry a burden,* and *bring forth fruit* or *offspring,*
> are both found in the word and its derivatives in the Aryan
> [Indo-European] languages generally, from the earliest period, it is
> not certain which is the primitive; perhaps branch IV preceded I in
> prehistoric times.

How can these distinctions reflect (either now or in the past) a semantic unity? Consider this possibility: sense (I) could be a generalized form of (IV), and (II) could be a generalization of (I), subsuming motion in a unity of both motion and rest. Yet, even if this were so, we have the problem of relating sense (III) to the others. In its observations about this, the OED describes well the challenge this verb poses:

> This group [III] seems to have arisen in a transference of the sense
> from *carry* to an action producing the same result (i.e., the moving
> forward of a body) by a different application of force, that of
> continuous pressure. This once established, the extension of the
> idea to pressure of many kinds, both horizontal and vertical,
> followed. There thus result senses of *bear* directly contrary to each
> other, as when a post bears the pressure that is brought to bear on
> it, or a man bears up until calamity bears him down.

Taking the notion "action producing the same result" as a clue, let us suppose that (III) is a further (metonymic) generalization (not merely extension) of (II). Then *bear* would no longer relate directly to *carry* but, as the OED suggests, would indicate "pressure which can be applied in any direction". However, are "pressure" and "direction" supplied by *bear*? If we assumed so, *bear* would have to exhibit these senses in every expression; it does not in *He bears a scar on his arm.* So we look elsewhere: in the contrary senses, pressure and direction could come from the words *up* and *down.*

Before proceeding further, we must make explicit several theoretical prerequisites. First, we prefer a "synchronic" solution that can be correlated with the knowledge of current speakers.[1] Thus, we cannot use prior historical status as a crucial part of our evidence. We can make this stipulation without committing ourselves fully to the idealization implied in the synchronic-diachronic split. However, a caution: the possible relevance of a word's historical semantic development is not something we can fully calculate in advance.

Consider some possibilities. In support of Bolinger, it may be that *bear* at one time had a semantic unity, which is now scattered in an unrelated set of expressions. Conversely, an earlier sense of a word need not be its present "basic" sense, and previous secondary extensions of meaning may have been superseded by a full generalization of meaning. Both the OED and Bolinger assume that *bear* has, or ought to have, a sense of 'carry', reflecting its apparent history; yet this (mis)judgment may contribute to the impression of contrary senses that the OED sees or the lack of meaning that Bolinger sees.

Second, anyone arguing for a general meaning must provide evidence of productivity. To support his conclusion, Bolinger implicitly denies productivity and generality, for evidence of these makes a claim of idiomaticity suspect. Bolinger correctly notes that some generalizations may be only artifacts of a theory; we should not underestimate the resources of memory. But it is equally wrong to assume that if an expression can be memorized it will not be generalized with other expressions. If a word has a general meaning, it will pattern over a wide continuous range. The wider such a range, the greater the demand on memory, and the more likely the range is productive. Thus, to support my thesis, I must show that *bear* has a wide range of general, productive uses.

Third, the point at issue is whether a posited semantic distinction is actually appropriate to a word or rather is supplied by other factors. Two factors are relevant: (a) other words in the context (as I suggested in noting *up* and *down*), or (b) pragmatic inferences. My method is simply to question each proposed distinction of sense for *bear,* to see if we can locate the variation elsewhere. Whatever remains after we have factored out variations will be the word's inherent meaning.

A final point: some readers might think that the amount of following data is excessive. Yet, there are two good reasons why even the examples here may not be enough: I must show that there is a general, productive range; and I must provide enough data of use to keep our imperializing conscious intuitions from rushing to premature conclusions. Thus, it is important that each example be taken fully; the effect is a change of one's perspective, through indwelling.

2.2 INTRANSITIVES

The OED's contrary meanings are a good starting point. These are exemplified by the contrast of sentences [1–16] and [17–27]. Type (II) is exemplified by *bear up under* [1–11], *bear up against* [12–15], and *bear up to* [16]:

[1] The boat will bear up under hurricane winds. (DAI)

[2] Pardee said he never doubted Joe Theisman's ability to bear up under pressure and bring his team back. (George McClelland)

[3] . . . we human beings bear up remarkably well under the load of other people's disasters. (John Skow)

[4] I often wonder how he bore up under the strain of me. (James Thurber)

[5] . . . he could bear up under punishments of even greater shame. (Mark Smith)

[6] ". . . don't you think you can bear up under this one small defeat?" (Ken Kesey)

[7] Late last winter, I went back to Nashpee to see how the Indians were bearing up under the disappointment of Judge Skinner's dismissal of their lawsuit. . . . (Paul Brodeur)

[8] . . . glancing sideways to see how Bea was bearing up under these malevolent overlays of superstition. (John Updike)

[9] . . . suddenly she felt unable to bear up much longer under Sid Jaffe's good intentions. (Philip Roth)

[10] He bore up under the osteopathic treatment of desert driving. . . . (Wallace Stegner)

[11] This teleological view of a succession of better and better theories closing in on the ultimate truth cannot bear up under scrutiny. (Robert Rodman)

[12] How do they bear up against distress and shock?" (William Plomer)

[13] He bore up well against all these misfortunes. (OALD)

[14] The house had been "whispering" worse than ever lately, and, even in spite of his luck, Paul could not bear up against it. (D. H. Lawrence)

[15] Short of some catastrophe, literacy and visual bias could bear up for a long time against electricity and "unified field" awareness. (Marshall McLuhan)

[16] Buck did not like it, but he bore up well to the work. (Jack London)

Several initial points can be made. First, making *bear up under* an idiom is undermined by the variant last word: *under, against,* and *to.* The idiom would also have to be rather permeable: note the intervening material in [3], [9], [13], [15], [16].

Second, for *bear* to have a single meaning in all these sentences, it must be *unspecified for concrete and abstract.* Some words in English may be specified for either, and some may cover disconnected ranges in both; the latter possibility would make the word polysemic. For *bear* to be monosemic, it must range continuously from concrete to abstract. The following general pragmatic condition will apply to any verb that is not lexically specified for concrete or abstract:

[A] CONCRETION CONDITION

The degree of concretion will be computed pragmatically, appropriate to the apparent message and references being conveyed.

This formulation (and others to follow) allows incomplete, vague, and multiple computations; all of these are pragmatic, and require no complication of the semantic status of the verb. I assume that the most abstract sense of the verb is its intensional base line, its sense; with increasing concretion comes increasing extensional applicability to reality. That is, here and throughout the book, I take *concrete* and *abstract* to mean, respectively, 'nearer to reality' and 'further from reality', with an assumed continuum between them.

The verbs *be* and *have* obviously require the Concretion Condition: *be a promise/table; have an idea/book).* *Bear* does too; it co-occurs with the same adjuncts for both concrete and abstract, and *under* can take objects *load, weight, pressure, strain* and *stress* in either. Even if these nouns are polysemic with respect to concrete-abstract, there is no gain in reproducing the distinction in the verb (or even *up* and *under*); if we did, we should also make *the* ambiguous between concrete-abstract. Someone claiming that *bear, up* and *under* are polysemic in this way must show that there is some discrepancy of range that a pragmatic rule cannot supply. Similarly, an inference rule will specify sex for *The parent hurt herself* or *The teacher stroked his beard; parent* and *teacher* need not by polysemic according to sex. It is merely necessary for the unspecified sense to allow either variant in any particular context. Both inference rules (specifying concrete or abstract, or male or female) are examples of Pragmatic Specialization.

However, I do not expect the reader to grant this point readily. Ignoring the concrete-abstract distinction is part of the debt I must now incur; the full book must pay the bill.

Type (III) is exemplified by *bear down on* [17–25] and *bear down upon* [26–27], with an extra *bear downwards* in [20]:

[17] You must not bear down so hard on the crayon. (Scholarly Dictionary)

[18] He bears down on it [hoe] with the file. (Wendell Berry)

[19] Then his face got serious again, and he bore down on Henry's shoulder. (Wallace Stegner)

[20] . . . my pen bearing the pen downwards as ineluctably as the state diviner bears down on his twig. (Cyril Connolly)

[21] At the end of the summer, with the accumulation of grievances bearing down hard on him, Scott wrote Hemingway. . . . (Nancy Milford)

[22] . . . the crushing impact of a new way of life that seemed to bear down on him alone. (James Michener)

[23] . . . her seduction must anticipate the despair and madness bearing down on her. (Gilbert Sorrentino)

[24] How often has the reader had the experience of realizing he is pleasantly immersed in some creative activity, totally unaware of time, solely conscious of the job at hand, only to be brought back to "reality" with the rude shock of realizing that other, preset, frequently inconsequential commitments are bearing down on him. (Edward T. Hall)

[25] . . . golf's perfectionist [Ben Hogan] . . . bearing down totally on the next shot. (Denne Freeman)

[26] The weight of family losses bore down upon her. . . . (Elizabeth Hardwick)

[27] He bears down so hard upon his subject matter. . . . (Lawrence Durrell)

Again, there is intervening material between directional word (*down*) and prepositional phrase [17], [21], [25], [27]. *Down* serves as a contrast to *up*, and thus throws doubt on *bear up* or *bear down* being idioms. Examples are both concrete and abstract.

Taking what is common to these two types, we can minimally say that *bear* defines a relationship between a subject nominal [SN] and another nominal

[PN], the object of a preposition. The verb can also occur with specified 'direction', supplied semantically by *up* and *down*.

Up and *down* semantically give "higher position" to one of the nominals: PN in type (II), SN in type (III). We can posit a pragmatic rule for Dominance Control Effect:

[B] DOMINANCE CONDITION

The degree of dominance will be computed pragmatically, appropriate to the apparent message and references being conveyed. Dominance includes the capacity of controlling or effecting something in a particular context.

Again, the computation may be incomplete, vague, or multiple; these possibilities apply to all pragmatic rules, so I will not mention them again. In the data above, we have "worldly" awareness (possible stereotypic or domain-specific) that what is on "top" controls what is on the "bottom". The directional words, together with the prepositions, enable us to semantically and pragmatically define two specific relationships in which the superior-positioned element exerts an effect on the other.

A note is necessary here about my use of *appropriate* in (A) and (B). I use this as an (unavoidably vague) cover term for all the factors that can ground a linguistic expression and help to provide its full interpretation. Grounding can be controlled by what is (presumed) typical, usual, anticipated, or plausible: that is, by the conditions specified by type of speech act, given and new information, cultural situation, and the like.

As we can already see, and increasingly so in further data, *bear* with its accompanying nominals sometimes appears to have a "causative" sense and sometimes does not. For monosemy, this distinction also must be located outside the verb. Causation has usually been interpreted lexically, as a semantic attribute of the verb or of a noun in some syntactic position (usually Subject, but also Object of *by* in passives). Also, the posited causative alternatives are usually few and discrete: the verb is either causative or not; and the noun (as in Case Grammar) represents one of a few roles, Agent, Instrument, or Force.

I claim that this "discrete-few" assumption is wrong for *bear;* there are many gradient possibilities. The nominal that is the subject of *bear* can range over degrees of activity and inactivity, animacy or inanimacy, causation and effect; the verb meaning varies in accord with the implied role of the nominal. If we include "having some effect" as part of the meaning of cause, any nominal can be involved, as the PN is [1–9] above. Although the verb *kill* is semantically causative (every use of the word exhibits it) and *die* is non-causative (no use exhibits it), many verbs are simply unspecified, negotiable, ranging over all the possibilities: causation is computed pragmatically, not semantically. Also, the nominal positions for such unspecified verbs are also unspecified. The following condition applies over the whole sentence, a verb and its nouns (it may be better to include the Dominance Condition as part of this or vice versa):

[C] AGENCY CONDITION

The degree of agency is computed pragmatically, appropriate to the message and references being conveyed. Agency favors active over inactive, animate over inanimate, deliberate over non-deliberate.[2] Subject position typically invites a high agency computation.[3]

Regarding the last point, even though PN is superior in Type (II) with *under*, its oblique syntactic position seems to require nominals with inherent effectiveness, such as *hurricane winds, pressure, stress,* and *strain; scrutiny* [10] seems overbearing, and *good intentions* [9] is ironic. The semantic contributions of other words also weight the pragmatic computation: *hard* [17], [21], [27], instrumental *with* [18], and *well* [3], [11], [15].

Agency is only half the story: we also have the receiver of the effect, commonly called Patient (in Case Grammar, Object if inanimate, Experiencer if animate). There are several problems with this approach: the soldier in *The sergeant marched the soldier* is both Agent and Patient; the boy in *The boy moved* can be both also. These conclusions can be precluded by the needless requirement that a given nominal cannot fill two roles; yet this is what we also have in the sentence *He bore up under the weight,* where *he* is acting by reacting to the weight. I suggest that a posited role stress not passiveness, but (inversely) the degree of response:

[D] REAGENCY CONDITION

The degree of reagency is computed pragmatically, appropriate to the message and references being conveyed. Reagency applies to a nominal that responds to some agency or prior condition. Reagency favors active over inactive, animate over inanimate, deliberate over non-deliberate. Object position typically invites a low agency computation.[4]

(C) and (D) are parallel: the Agent/Instrument variation corresponds to Experiencer/Object. The Reagent also varies in activity and animacy: something active can recoil, something animate can feel pain, something capable of deliberateness can feel resentment. We infer such possibilities in accord with what the full context seems to permit or require. Of course, we may have no Reagency at all, as normally assumed with the Object role. The advantage of my interpretation is that it allows all degrees, including zero. With *break the window, window* is affected, but not *law* in *break the law.* (This is reflected in the possible *the window broke,* but not **the law broke.*)

Thus, *bear* does not mean 'press' or 'endure'; these glosses conflate semantic and pragmatic, the latter providing inferences of light to heavy agency ('press') or light to heavy reagency ('endure'). Factoring out semantic contributions of other lexical items and pragmatic inferences, we have a verb that can describe a single particular relationship by either type (II) or type (III), the circumstance noted in the OED comment: *John bears up under his troubles, His troubles bear down on John.* The sentences do not mean exactly the same (John is more reagentive in the first), but it is the same verbal meaning in both.

For expository purposes, I will use the following informal terminology: the general relationship that remains constant in all examples is the INHERENT MEANING or SENSE or *bear;* it is simply what *bear* means as a word (its semantics). Any additional sense attributable to it in a sentence is an INFERENTIAL MEANING or MODULATION, what *bear* IMPLIES, SUGGESTS, CONVEYS or EVOKES (its pragmatics). The combination of semantics and pragmatics is the INTERPRETATION or MESSAGE, what it means in a context. (I take the Meaning-Message terminology from Givon (1979), Garcia (1975) and Kirsner and Thompson (1976).)

The usual situation in language is that an interpretation of a sentence differs from what is determined by syntax and lexical meaning. A linguistic expression orients a hearer, but it relies on the hearer to interpret the full meaning, beyond what the language supplies. As Lakoff (1977: 239) puts it (while discussing an actual sentence, from Faulkner):

> The meanings of the parts constrain, but do not provide, the interpretation of the whole. The whole makes sense only because some aspect of the reader's experience has been evoked by the meanings of the parts.

Similarly, Garcia (1975: 41):

> The linguistic signs do but point in certain directions and—most important—exclude certain possibilities. What specific message is intended, however, is inferred by the intelligence of the hearer, who combines the meanings offered by the speaker with his knowledge of the context of the utterance, and figures out 'what the speaker must have meant'.

Continuing with further data: in [1–27] directionality is 'vertical'; but *bear, down* and *on/upon* also indicate 'horizontal' relationships:

[28] The charging horses bore down on them. (Henry Roth)
[29] Late that afternoon the second mate, who was on watch, saw such a wave bearing down on us. (H. M. Tomlimson)
[30] A fierce-looking squall just in from the open sea was bearing down on the wharves. (Sterling Hayden)
[31] Bearing down on us at great speed was an enormous cloud, covering half the sky and black as night. (George Gaylord Simpson)
[32] Meanwhile the woman was bearing down upon the empty seat beside Julian. (Flannery O'Connor)
[33] The fleet bore down on the enemy. (W2, *bear down*)

Toward can appear in place of *on/upon*:

[34] The train came out of the red horizon and bore down toward them over the single straight track. (Nadine Gordimer)

Down can indicate both vertical and horizontal movement. I assume (though it is not needed for the present analysis) that vertical-horizontal is neutralized with *down,* the distinction again made pragmatically, perhaps with a bias toward vertical.

Bear down on sentences can include a "source" nominal, which also contributes to the sense of movement:

[35] We would bear down on them suddenly out of the fog. . . . (S. Dillon Ripley)

[36] When I looked, another wave at least as large as the first was bearing down on us from astern. (C. C. Gilmore)

The examples thus far have all included the directional words *up* and *down*. We can also get *in* instead of *down*:

[37] Kurtz bore in on her a little harder. (John Le Carre)

[38] . . . her eyes bore in upon him. (Joanne Greenberg)

[39] . . . inevitably the decision was borne in on her over many months. (Mary M. Luke)

[40] The presence of his mother was borne in upon him as she gave a pained sigh. (Flannery O'Connor)

Bear in against seems possible too; [28–40] also show that the *bear*-relationship need not involve 'immediate contact'.

We can thus provide a SYNTACTIC–SEMANTIC FRAME (Fillmore (1975)) for *bear* (the Conditions above are PRAGMATIC FRAMES):

[X bears DIRECTION]

Since the same prepositions can be used in both directional and non-directional ways, I must, as a consequence of the monosemic bias, assume that Direction and its subspecies of Source, Path and Goal are all pragmatically specified. *Up* and *down* can determine paths. There may be more than one path; *toward* in [34] is more path than goal. (*To* may also be either pragmatically.)

Directional adjuncts are appropriate for a Movement-verb. Since we have both movement and non-movement for *bear,* we will need a pragmatic rule for computing relative movement. The syntactic inclusion of adjuncts which imply movement adds to the likelihood that *bear* should be so specified. Fillmore, as I remember, once noted the necessity of such a rule for the sentence *She wore her new dress to the party*. The alternatives are to give *wear* an additional movement meaning, or to assume a deleted "(and went)".

[E] MOVEMENT CONDITION

The relevance, degree, direction, rate and specific means of movement are computed pragmatically, appropriate to the apparent message and references being conveyed. Movement is both concrete and abstract.

Down can be omitted, leaving only *on/upon/against*:

[41] But that young man, still bearing steadily on the knife. . . . (Joseph Conrad)

[42] . . . follow the pencil line with your razor blade, bearing lightly on it. (*Popular Mechanics*)

[43] . . . the wall bearing on the floor. (W3)

[44] . . . she, watchful, bore rigidly on the seat with her beautiful bare arms. . . . (Joseph Conrad)

[45] The gray sky is curdled, and it bears very close upon the earth. (N. Scott Momaday)

[46] . . . he bore on his offside rein. . . . (George MacDonald Fraser)

[47] One thing kept bearing on her mind, and as she wrote, she pondered on it. . . . (Mary M. Luke)

[48] All the travail of the last days bore upon her anew. (Willie Morris)

[49] Taxation bears heavily on all classes in Britain. (OALD)

[50] The struggle within the Council to remain in the good graces of Elizabeth often bore heavily on political decisions. . . . (Mary M. Luke)

[51] It [arms control], and it alone, bears directly on the prospects for nuclear war and national devastation. (Joseph Kraft).

[52] . . . it is an abstraction not directly bearing on his individual existence or its meaning except peripherally. (Vine Deloria, Jr.)

[53] There is remarkably little hard evidence of the specific kinds of innate influences that bear on the development of perception. (Peter Marler)

[54] . . . the punishment and feelings of guilt did not bear on the underlying need to bully, which therefore remained intact and unchanged. (Edward T. Hall)

[55] . . . the context was entirely political and bore upon the current election for governor. (Gore Vidal)

[56] Many of the important questions which bear upon the nature and extent of one's obligations to obey the law have been dealt with summarily and uncritically. . . . (Richard Wasserstrom)

[57] an arch bearing against piers. (W3)

[58] Mr. Sadat's direct address to the Israelis departed from previous diplomacy in two ways that bear against Washington's influence. (Joseph Kraft)

[59] The discussion bore against the bill. (FW)

Some contexts here could include *down* [41–45]. Sometimes it is absent because it is obvious, as in [43]. Thus:

[F] IMPLICIT LEXICAL CONDITION

If a word is contextually possible in a sentence but not present, its force may be supplied pragmatically, if the apparent references and total message suggest it.

Bear can contextually take a path adjunct; and even when one is not present, it may be inferrable. Thus, not only for explicit *down,* but also for when it is potential, we need a pragmatic rule that specifies direction.

By now, some readers may have the uneasy feeling that pragmatic rules are beginning to proliferate without restraint. A good theorist is likely to wonder where it will end. But linguists who expect to find a limited number of pragmatic rules, or rules typically with only a few options, are mistaking the task; they are trying to make pragmatic rules into semantic rules. Listing pragmatic rules may be an infinite task: all knowledge of the world can be included. In dealing with language, we are used to expecting only a few possibilities; but pragmatic rules can be much more various, since our full knowledge is much more various. This difference between semantic and pragmatic (between what is relatively closed and what is relatively open) is a key part of this book's argument.

A pragmatic rule is justified if it accounts for data, and as fully as possible: for *John bears hard on his pencil when he writes,* we infer the direction 'down'. Where does that inference come from, if not from worldly knowledge? Similarly, by pragmatic reasoning we conclude that the king need not personally do the confiscating (or accepting of the gift, or . . .) in *The king took all our furniture.* Naturally, the most valuable pragmatic rules deal with more general circumstances than these. The charge of proliferation is serious only if generalizations are being missed. The pragmatic rules worth noting are those that have wide applicability, or which specifically serve the purpose of clarifying semantic status, but we must also allow for possibilities that happen only rarely, perhaps only once.

Most of the time, faulty word senses are too specific; but with abstracts they can sometimes be too general: abstract *bear on/upon* [51–56] are usually glossed 'relate to' or 'have relevance for'. Such a gloss seems to deny outright even the possibility of agency. Agency is often present, even if slight: do influences merely "relate" in [53]? As we would expect, with psychologicals [47–50] both agency and reagency are more obvious. Abstract *bear against* is usually glossed 'opposing,' which seems a little strong for [59]; such a gloss also requires that *against* have two meanings, [57] versus [58–59].

We can also have directional *to*-phrases; [62] has the additional adjunct *away*:

[60] He senses that he's bearing to the right. (Wendell Berry)
[61] After a few hundred yards the pass bore to the left and then to the right again. . . . (Norman Mailer)
[62] He bore away to the left. . . . (Jack London)
[63] Some unpublished observations of my own bear to the contrary. (Julian Jaynes)

To-expressions make 'movement' much more obvious than do *up under* and *down on,* but it is quite possible for the same verb to appear in all of these expressions, given the variations of the adjuncts. The examples thus far give us a range of movements from the very slight to the dramatically obvious. We also see how movement can be abstract, as in [63]. I am appealing here, again, to a kind of generalization that is not noted in our usual theories. These data illustrate one of my themes: there are unconscious linguistic generalizations that our usual theories, based on fractured conscious categories, have not sufficiently acknowledged.

The following show other directionals:

[64] The ship bore out to sea. (W2)

[65] Flying Paster carried 127 pounds in that event, conceding huge chunks of weight to his rivals, and he displayed a tendency to bear out, racing wide all the way. . . . (Joe Marcin)

[66] But Crook bore on relentlessly. (Anthony Gilbert)

[67] The cutter was bearing down the channel at twelve knots. (RH)

[68] . . . taking a course which must produce a collision with the French ships, unless the latter bore away. (James A. Michener)

[69] . . . the vessel bore up the river toward the rock. (Willa Cather)

[70] . . . the road kept bearing in a direction Ralph was almost sure was wrong. . . . (James Agee)

[71] In a graceful curve it [river] sweeps out from the town and bears around the base of Colonel Joyner's hill. . . . (Thomas Wolfe)

[72] He bore left at the Mosholu Parkway fork. . . . (A. J. Russell)

[73] Bear left past the cemetery. (W2)

[74] Hull changed course, bearing northwest toward the Bay of Fundy. (John Jakes)

[75] All sails set, she bore off on a course to intercept the stranger. (John Jakes)

[76] "Hull shortened sail just as we bore into the storm." (John Jakes)

[77] A ship bears in with the land. (W2, *bear in with*)

[78] . . . Hurricane David bore toward the population centers of southern Florida. (*Virginian-Pilot*)

[79] The lighthouse bears due north. (RH)

The *with*-phrase in [77] may modify an implicit 'in line'. The final example illustrates "pointing" movement. We can see now that Bolinger was wrong in claiming that *bear up, bear down, bear right,* and *bear left* are idioms. They came more readily to his mind than the other examples here, which were more elusive to consciousness.

To finish this section, we must note several "periphrastic" expressions with *bring* and *get,* whose infinitival complements pattern like those we are discussing. The goal adjuncts are *on/upon/against/at/in*:

[80] The dog had definitely located the plastic buttons on the stranger's garters and was cocking his head one way and another, thinking out ways of bringing his teeth to bear on those delicacies. (Kurt Vonnegut, Jr.)

[81] . . . the woman was bringing pressure to bear on him. (Aldous Huxley)

[82] . . . to bring guns to bear on a target. (W3)

[83] . . . Houston brought brains to bear on winning the Moon. . . . (Peter Tauber)

[84] In doing this, he brings most of his arguments to bear on two points. . . . (Edward P. J. Corbett)

[85] legislation brought to bear directly upon industry. (Harriet Martineau)

[86] I touch upon this to ensure that we are keeping the range of relevant considerations to be brought to bear upon the debate as wide as it must be. (Gareth Evans)

[87] He got up from his chair, and for many minutes roamed the room unable to get his mind to bear on the issue. (John Galsworthy)

[88] . . . being defeated ultimately through the numbers and weapons brought to bear against them. (John R. Milton)

[89] . . . they can bring their numbers to bear at the point where they will tell. . . . (Henry Fairlie)

[90] He preached that the whole man must be brought to bear in the persuasive process. . . . (Edward P. J. Corbett)

Note that the concrete-abstract variation of *bear . . . on* holds here too. The alternate possibilities of *get* [87] for *bring* and of *upon/at/in/against* for *on* show that *bring to bear on* is not an idiom; rather, we might call it a "(pragmatically) favored phrase". Additionally, *come,* the intransitive counterpart of *bring,* also occurs with *bear*:

[91] It is against this background that the claims of deconstruction come to bear on the wider practice of linguistic philosophy. (Christopher Norris)

At this point, we need to assess what has been accomplished. I have factored away variations of meaning that arise when *bear* co-occurs with directional expressions. To do this, I have assumed that certain distinctions such as concrete-abstract, horizontal-vertical, and movement-nonmovement are (for *bear*) determined pragmatically, not semantically. To state it differently, I have assumed that these distinctions are poles of continua, and that pragmatic rules (or strategies) provide (perhaps inadequately) the appropriate specifics, given all other information. In addition, I have assumed certain implied effects of being "on top", such as control, dominance, and effect, claiming also that these are realized differently in concrete and abstract contexts. I should also note that we need a pragmatic scale of intensity, to account for varying degrees of influence, speed, and the like. Are all these assumptions merely arm-waving? Or do they have promise of leading anywhere?

We can assess the merits of the present analysis with the usual analyses. We here avoid multiple meaning by accounting for various aspects of sentence sense with pragmatic ("worldly") knowledge that can be integrated modularly with semantic knowledge. To the extent that these pragmatic rules make sense independently of our present need for them (and I am presuming so), they avoid all the lexical complications attendant on usual dictionary or linguistic analyses. That is, by drawing the semantic-pragmatic border so that semantics accounts for less, we can generalize what, with the usual border, seems to be (in Bolinger's view) idiomatic complexity.

It might be objected that my approach, though somewhat plausible, has no utilitarian value: for example, it could not be used in artificial intelligence. To the contrary, I think it is the usual multiple-meaning approach, when fully implemented (beyond W3), that will not be useful, because it is so committed to the many idiosyncratic complications of the idiomatic approach. There are sufficient individuations in a language to challenge the storage capacity of both computers and humans. It seems pointless and strange to ignore the possibility of generalizing what we can.

Further, all of the pragmatic assumptions I have appealed to are necessary for a computer. If the computer knows that *bear* can be both concrete and abstract, or that *down* can be both vertical and horizontal, it must, to choose appropriately in a particular context, have pragmatic skills similar to those that humans use to disambiguate. Making *bear* semantically ambiguous accomplishes no more than making *dog* ambiguous between *bulldog, terrier,* etc. If *bear* is unspecified for concrete and abstract (semantically, it is not limited to either), then, by general rule, these are two possible interpretations. Pragmatic inferences can imply ambiguity without a semantic ambiguity, as in *they bore down on the wharf,* both horizontal and vertical.

Given the advantages of desemanticizing some aspects of meaning, we might have no great objection to doing so if the ubiquitous model of dictionaries didn't continue to reassure us that usual methods are somehow justified, and that this new approach cannot account for all the "jerry built" particulars.

2.3 TRANSITIVES

We have thus far considered only intransitive patterns. The *bring*-periphrastics are a means of supplying, in effect, a direct object; but we also have transitives with *bear*. We begin once more with *on/upon/against* goal-expressions; the last again contributes a sense of opposition:

[92] . . . a treat bearing little impact on anyone. (Alan Milberg)

[93] "Told me what?" the sheriff said, in a cold, level voice, bearing upon the other a gaze cold and level. (William Faulkner)

[94] "Corporal, you may think that he wants to bear arms against the foe. . . ." (John Steinbeck)

[95] . . . one of the people who bore true witness against him . . . (Peter Tauber)

[96] "Yet you found my hatred vulgar, and further bear against me the grudge men always bear against women they have conquered." (John Updike)

[97] The Senator is bearing all his resources against the controversial legislation. (RH)

These transitives add a third nominal, the direct object (DN), to the relationship. Transitives also have Path adjuncts; first, *up*:

[98] The old bridge can hardly bear up its own weight anymore. (DAI)

[99] a support that bears up the weight. (W3)

[100] She felt as if the blue waves were bearing her up and sweeping her onward. (Ellen Glasgow)

[101] . . . I place my feet where nothing shows, sure my angel will bear me up. (H. M. Tomlinson)

[102] This was the pride that bore up Spitz. . . . (Jack London)

[103] The feet looked too fragile to bear up such a concentrated degree of being. (Muriel Spark)

[104] "Chance drowns the worthy with the unworthy, bears up the unfit with the fit. . . ." (John Barth)

Again, we have movement [100] versus nonmovement [98] and concrete [98–101] versus abstract [102–104]

We also have the variation described by the CTG rule Particle Shift: *up* occurs before the DN in [98] and [99] and after the DN in [100]. I will later argue that particles are simply intransitive prepositions (Jackendoff (1973)) and that the pattern of [100] is basic (Emonds (1972)), with [98] and [99] resulting from the shift of a heavy noun phrase (Heavy NP Shift) to after the preposition (Yngve (1960)). I here ignore this variation.

Similarly, *down*:

[105] Strange, wild creatures, they hung on him and rushed at him to bear him down. (D. H. Lawrence)

[106] . . . in a crisis he was apt to become reckless and to bear down his natural timidity with a mild bravado. (George Santayana)

Prepositional phrases with *to* can also be directional:

[107] Buck, Lester, and Bobo whirled, grabbed Big Boy about the neck, arms and legs, bearing him to the ground. (Richard Wright)

[108] . . . he jumped up and a leaping brown tide bore him to the door. (James Herriot)

[109] . . . bearing the officer to his quarters. (W3)

[110] The little tin tram bore us with the clicking of its wheels to the sandbeaches of Sidi Bisler. . . . (Lawrence Durrell)

[111] . . . a tide of emigration has borne Scots men and women of the best type to Canada. . . . (Isobel Wyle Hutchinson)

The following are passive, vertical and horizontal:

[112] . . . he was borne to earth and his arms were pinioned. (James A. Michener)

[113] . . . fragile [archeological] finds are borne to the barge by hand. (*National Geographic*)

Additional directionals:

[114] . . . the wind came, bearing the boat away from land, away from the world, out onto the open sea. (Ursula K. LeGuin)

[115] Then at last the great car bore him smoothly away to the Residence on the banks of the Nile. (Lawrence Durrell)

[116] . . . Big Boy, all passion spent, drifts off to slumber on the bed of a truck that bears him away to the North. (Blyden Jackson)

[117] . . . she folded the dress and prepared to bear it out of the room. (Kristin Hunter)

[118] . . . the current bore the broken bridge out of sight around the bend. . . . (Annie Dillard)

[119] "The brown current ran swiftly out of the heart of darkness, bearing us down towards the sea with twice the speed of our upward progress." (Joseph Conrad)

[120] . . . at least one black and mountainous wave, washed to this gulf as from the uttermost boundaries of the earth, bore him up and up through a sky snowy with the falling bodies of gulls. . . . (William Styron)

[121] Then well-wishers bore him away. (Gore Vidal)

[122] He bears away from the table a full belly. (Wendell Berry)

[123] The torrent bears along silt and gravel. (FW)

[124] Once she bore me back against the wall. . . . (James Herriot)

[125] . . . he had borne him over the boundary from death into life. (Ursula K. LeGuin)

[126] . . . she whooped but seemed not fearful as he bore her off. (John Barth)

[127] The pilings produced strange currents which bore him this way and that. . . . (C. C. Gilmore)

[128] . . . [he] swung her across his shoulders. He bore her into the center of their home. (Richard Meyers)

[129] ". . . the dance is barely over before Hughmore bears the dazzling creature off into the tender night." (Vance Bourjaily)

[130] There had been a quick storm while he had his nap, and the windows bore in light cool air. (Reynolds Price)

[131] It was fun to watch them [shorebirds] on the run, their slender legs

going a-twinkle, bearing their small bodies swiftly over the level plane of the beach. (Dudley Cammett Lunt)

[132] . . . the wagon, heaving and rocking like a rudderless ship amid a sea of frozen glass, bore me southward again into the dead of winter. (William Styron)

[133] They bore him home. (RH)

[134] . . . [she] accepted the trout as a present from both of us, put it on a platter, and, bearing it aloft, preceded us into the living room. . . . (Paul Brodeur)

[135] Together, they [policemen] pulled the door open, yanked the Dodds out, and bore them safely through the rising waves to the beach. (Franklin W. Dixon)

[136] He had a destination or his body did. It bore him straight forward; he didn't think *to where*? (Reynolds Price)

[137] . . . a warmly sour and corrupt odor that bore him swiftly into some mysterious, nameless, and for the moment irretrievable portion of his own past. . . . (William Styron)

Additional passives:

[138] . . . boats against the current, borne back ceaselessly into the past. (F. Scott Fitzgerald)

[139] . . . as if in this mindless repose he were being borne yearningly, at last, through the floodgates of his destiny. (William Styron)

[140] The crowd was borne back by the police. (RH)

[141] The whole loftiness of the place, booming hollow to the great voice of the wind, swayed at the top like a tree, would go over bodily, as if borne down this way and that by the tremendous blasts. (Joseph Conrad)

[142] He tried to think nothing at all, to let himself be borne forward. . . . (Ursula K. LeGuin)

[143] Like distant music these words he had written years before were borne towards him from the past. (James Joyce)

I would now like to claim that the intransitives studied earlier have, not the frame noted before,

[X bears DIRECTION],

but actually

[X bears (Xself) DIRECTION],

where an implied DN is not expressed because it is identical to the SN: *the man bore (himself) down on the table, the man bore (himself) up under the weight.* I am not arguing that Xself is "really" there; I am merely noting that it is implied, in the same way that in *John went to the store,* both *went* and *to the store* relate to *John*. (Though it may seem so, I am claiming no new syntactic analysis, but merely drawing an inference from present ones; *to the store* is as much a "predicate modifier" of the subject as *happy* is in *John is happy*.) Adjuncts here modify *the man*, but in the transitives they modify the DN: *They bore the man down to the floor, they bore the man up to the clouds.*

Reflexives can be explicit:

[144] Claudio is first introduced, bearing himself with dignity under his sudden arrest. (R. W. Chambers)

[145] In the boy's eyes at least it was Sam Feathers, the negro, who bore himself not only toward his cousin McCaslin and Major de Spain but toward all white men, with gravity and dignity. . . . (William Faulkner)

[146] It is a small, elderly, once gay, now sober, and very pretty trunk, the lid shallowly domed, somewhat tall and narrow, and thus bearing itself in a kind of serene innocence as certain frame houses and archaic automobiles do. (James Agee)

Sentence [144] exemplifies the *under*-pattern we began with. The explicit reflexive pronoun with human beings brings (re)agent notions like "dignity" and "gravity" into greater prominence.

2.4 REFLEXED TRANSITIVES

We now consider a transitive frame that can be characterized as

[X bears Y prep-Xpart],

where Xpart is "part" of X. The preposition varies: *on, upon, in, across, around, before, between, under, within, over, about* and *beneath*. The prepositional phrase is like a reflexive, and for this reason I will (for convenience only) call it the REFLEXED PATTERN. Some examples, first with *on*:

[147] . . . an enigmatic Irish immigrant who bears on his cheek a large curving scar. . . . (Mary Louise Pratt)

[148] This most dangerous of spiders usually bears a red hourglass marking on its underside. (*National Geographic*)

[149] It is not even clear how the brontosaurs could bear their many tons' weight of body on straight legs. (Immanuel Velikovsky)

[150] This Porto church bears New Testament scenes on glazed tiles. . . . (*National Geographic*)

[151] The village spokesman, who bore huge scars on his abdomen. . . . (Edgar Monsanto Queeny)

[152] On their backs they bore baskets of manioc. . . . (Anne Eisner Putnam)

[153] . . . bearing chalk powder on the tails of my worn tweed jacket. . . . (Philip Roth)

[154] Bearing most of his Lamont's weight on his forearms, he dragged the author into the suite's gas-lit parlor. (John Jakes)

[155] . . . September is a quick, hectic month, bearing on the air seeds for burial. . . . (William Styron)

[156] . . . the stream became lighter and clearer, and bore fragmentary, rapidly moving images on its surface. (Ellen Glasgow)

What is borne varies along the alienable-inalienable and motion-stasis continua; specifics are supplied pragmatically. More examples of Heavy NP Shift are [147] and [155]; the *on*-phrase is fronted in [152].

Some examples with other prepositions:

[157] Soon the hens bore the blank look of despair upon their faces. (Walter Wanergin, Jr.)

[158] . . . the carpet was not dense and darkly red, but was thin, and it bore upon its lugubrious puce background a vapid pattern of flaxen parallelograms. (Jean Stafford)

[159] . . . a proud creature bearing in his veins the tide of all life and in his genes the scars of the ages. . . . (Robert Ardrey)

[160] When a woman bears in her uterus an embryo conceived in another woman's womb, who is the mother? (Alvin Toffler)

[161] He bore in his hand a placard. . . . (Frank Norris)

[162] Bear in mind that your supplies are limited. (W3)

[163] . . . bearing malice in his heart. (W3)

[164] To the South, in Greece, a bog has been discovered that bears in its sediments pollen grains dropped by the winds over the last half-million years. (Wallace S. Broecker)

[165] There is no magic medicine, either, for curing the unprecedented disease it bears in its rushing wake: future shock. (Alvin Toffler)

[166] He was still bearing the pull of the fish across his shoulders. (Ernest Hemingway)

[167] John Ehrlichman bore the weight of the Ellsberg break-in as an albatross around his stout neck. (H. R. Haldeman)

[168] Wild buffalo bore between their horns little round marks like shrunken halos. . . . (John Updike)

[169] . . . she bore under her arm a portfolio. (W. Somerset Maugham)

[170] He bore the cool breath of Kennerly's cud all over his face. . . . (Reynolds Price)

[171] The head [of the hawk], slightly flat, like an eagle's, bore a thin line of green above the beak and a circle of green around each yellow, half-open eye. (Rachel Peden)

[172] Forrest saw all that, bore it through his own eyes helpless to refuse. (Reynolds Price)

Dictionaries usually cite *bear in mind* [162] as an idiom, but here we can see that it fits the general pattern. Of course, we can ask whose mind, but this is a problem of the phrases *in mind* and *to mind* (*keep in mind/put in mind/have in mind/bring to mind/come to mind/call to mind;* note also *bear in memory/have in hand/be in touch,* and others).

Sometimes the reflexed PN is identical with SN; it may or may not be a reflexive:

[173] Her belly bore silver stretch marks on it from carrying twins. (John Updike)
[174] Beer men with big bellies who bore them before them like orbs before kings. . . . (Hunter Kay)
[175] I shall ever bear about me a memory. . . . (Edgar Allen Poe)
[176] The wind bore coldness with it. . . . (Stephen Crane)
[177] The earliest texts bear within themselves proofs. . . . (E. A. Wallis Budge)
[178] . . . the girl steps down one step at a time, bearing the heavy weight of her curving belly against herself as she grips the edge of the doorway . . . . (Natalie L. M. Petesch)

The following reflexed examples are passives. The SN, identical to or inferrable from the PN, is omitted; I have supplied (schematic) active correlates:

[179] . . . I can hear the faint echo of a rifle shot borne on the rising wind. (Hugh Nissenson)
(wind bears echo on itself)
[180] A thunderous detonation sounded once more from the sea, borne on a hot blast of air. . . . (William Styron)
(air bears [sound of] detonation on itself)
[181] Borne on the wind, the cloudburst drummed hollowly on the flat wet hills. . . . (John Steinbeck)
(wind bears the cloudburst on itself)
[182] . . . inactive personnel still borne on the rolls. (W3)
(rolls still bear personnel on themselves)
[183] They hardly seem to tread the earth, but are borne in some more congenial element. (William Hazlitt)
(element bears them in itself)

If the general pattern we have posited is correct, we ought to have additional directions here, and we do:

[184] . . . they bore a wreath of white flowers above them on a pole. (Brian Adliss)
[185] . . . the believer bears about in his body the death of Christ . . . . (Giovanni Miegge, tr. Bishop Stephen Neill)
[186] As evening came on serried lines of clouds rose from the west, borne

on great winds from the sea. (Ursula K. LeGuin)
(great winds bear clouds on themselves from the sea)

[187] He went on playing, borne along on an unthinking devotion to
consecutiveness. . . . (John Cheever)
(devotion bears him along on itself)

[188] . . . he felt himself being borne bouyantly along upon the flood.
(William Styron)
(flood bears him along upon itself)

[189] Then came the coffin of Captain Burrows borne aloft on the shoulders
of his crew. (Dudley Cammett Lunt)
(crew bears coffin aloft on their shoulders)

[190] Cass heard the sound of a saxophone, borne away instantly on a gust of
wind. (William Styron)
(gust of wind bears bears sound away on itself)

[191] . . . Mason found himself borne away from this beautiful seclusion on
the winds of violence. (William Styron)
(winds bear Mason away from seclusion on themselves)

The following are especially noteworthy:

[192] Then a wave comes up from the right like a cavalry charge, bearing
landward on the rubber raft Lathrope Macy with Emerson Crane's
second wife. . . . (John Cheever)

[193] . . . bearing up a fainting Peggy on your left arm. . . . (John Barth)

The syntax of [192] is potentially misleading: the DN is shifted later in the
sentence by Heavy NP Shift, and the *on*-phrase is not the reflexed possibility
(the wave bearing them on itself). In [193], we could wordily specify *bear
Peggy on your left arm up under (the weight of) Peggy,* combining two patterns
we have discussed. In a sense, the reflexed phrases have a slight "instrumental"
or "enabling" function, as also (more obviously) in *I broke the bottle on my
knee/the table,* except that for *bear* the instrumentality is limited to using one's
self.

This might throw some light on the preposition *with,* which is
polysemically described as having both instrumental and "accompaniment"
senses. *With* also occurs in reflexed phrases:

[194] Symphony Hall in Boston was packed when he stepped to the podium,
bearing with him a packet of notes three inches thick. (Edward Weeks)

[195] The sudden draft through the cellar bore with it the familar dank.
(Henry Roth)

[196] In all this, Associative Man bears with him a secret knowledge. . . .
(Alvin Toffler)

[197] It [wave] caught us in a steel grip and bore us with it over the shoals.
(C. C. Gilmore)

[198] The brook sang in the distance and bore me with it into sleep. (Elizabeth Ogilvie)

[199] . . . Polynesian legendary figures whose names had once been borne with Tiki over the seas from Peru. (Thor Heyerdahl, tr. F. H. Lyon) (Tiki bore names over the seas from Peru with Tiki-self)

The following has a double (or complex) reflexed adjunct:

[200] . . . a traveller strives to bear away with him in memory the view of a country to which he may never return. (Marcel Proust, tr. C. K. Scott Moncrieff)

To summarize thus far: we assume a syntactic frame for *bear* that includes an optional direct object and adjuncts appropriate for a movement verb (allowing the possibility that some movement might be slight); we also assume another adjunct that has self-instrumental characteristics. With this frame

[X bears (Y) DIRECTION prep-Xpart],

we can account for all the patterns.

However, this frame allows too much. The prep-X does not occur with intransitives, and the *under*-phrases discussed at the outset do not generalize: I have no data (nor can I reliably intuit them) for *X bear under Y* (*up* missing) or *X bear Y up under Z* (transitive with *under*). Thus, this frame cannot be viewed as a generative rule in the sense of CTG; it merely shows how all the patterns discussed thus far relate to each other.

2.5 CONCRETE-ABSTRACT

I have argued that *bear* is unspecified for concrete or abstract, and my previous discussion has assumed that same status for *on* also. In fact, as I hope to show with the full weight of this book, all the prepositions and many common verbs are likewise unspecified. But such a claim raises a number of difficulties. First, how can we characterize, or recognize, a meaning that is unspecified in this way? Second, how can we recognize that certain pragmatic concrete specifications are related semantically to abstract meanings?

The general response to these questions is familiar to all linguists. Simply, we have no answers in advance. In fact, we have no assurance that the basis for these questions—here, the assumption of monosemy—is itself justified. We seek answers of three different kinds: (a) whether our initial hypothesis is correct, (b) how its implied claims can be implemented, and (c) how we can judge a particular solution successful. This is the norm for scientific investigation, which (d) proceeds from the expectation of order (although none may eventuate where we look for it), (e) derives theoretical and methodological implications (although they may be poorly understood, clumsily applied, or related to nonexistent phenomena), and (f) tries to explain some data (although the whole enterprise, including the status of "data" as data, may be completely misguided or misleadingly "correct"). Such is the status of any intellectual enterprise which is not guaranteed a priori.

Regarding concrete-abstract, we can particularize the problem with the following abstract examples of *bear out*:

[201] The facts bear me out. (RH)
[202] John will bear me out. (OALD)
[203] The foregoing examples bear out his principle. (J. Peter Maher)
[204] Experiments of this kind will be laborious but they seem more likely to bear out the notion that abstraction is an exalted process. . . . (Roger Brown)
[205] And it's not the kind of ballet that can bear out evidence of a "collaboration" between Nureyev and Balanchine. . . . (Whitney Balliett)
[206] Four separate surveys bear out arguments that consumption of alcohol among young people is increasing. (Kevin P. Phillips)
[207] The train was but a mere episode of the open street, and I could not feel it bore out the promise of my railway vouchers. (H. M. Tomlinson)
[208] I chose the moment of the ninth wave, which bore out its tradition of being the largest. (Dudley Cammett Lunt)
[209] But he, chilled a little by her answer, perhaps also, to bear out that pretense that he had been sincere in adopting the stratagem . . . . (Marcel Proust, tr. C. K. Scott Moncrieff)

Me in [201] and [202] is a metonym for 'my opinion/judgment'. The following are passives:

[210] I think she gets a certain pleasure from seeing her philosophy so exquisitely borne out by event. (George P. Elliott)
[211] The skepticism of Budge's on Petrie's conclusion has been fully borne out by subsequent developments in the field of Egyptian chronology. (Donovan A. Courville)
[212] The feasibility in theory of such a procedure is not borne out in practice. (William O. Hendricks)

Syntactically, these fit the frame; but their meanings seem remote from any corresponding concretes with these prepositions. A set of circumstances is said to "bear out" a human judgment or conclusion; *out* implies "decision" or "discovery". I propose that *out* has a general meaning of which the directional meaning is one pragmatically specifiable possibility; another specificity is a (sufficient) "end" of a process, as also in *run out, give out*. In the above examples, some "goal" has been reached; the SN of *bear* is depicted as abstractly "moving" from whatever is represented by the SN to a "point" where a conclusion can be reached. (I said "sufficient" because we can get *bear further out*. Like *to, out* can indicate both path and goal.)

But why *bear* and *out*? If we need an "abstract sense of movement" (if such is a legitimate notion), why use *bear* here, rather than *run, go, move*, which are more obviously motional? Further, *off, down,* and *up* (and perhaps other prepositions) have "goal" meanings too, so why is *out* the choice? These questions are telling; and I have no answers.

One problem with my proposed analysis of meaning is that it is too easy. That is, I have no system to impose constraints. Given enough imagination, I can come up with some way of making the words of a mysterious expression seem motivated. The problem of abstract uses of prepositions and verbs like *bear* is similar to that of mythology. Myths also seem baffling; it is possible to "make sense" of them in numerous, various, and inconsistent ways. In spite of all the work done on myths over the past century and more, there are many scholars who believe, with some good reason, that we may be totally off the track.

But the conclusion to be drawn is not that myths are meaningless or that some linguistic domain lacks a system. The difficulty in finding an answer does not mean the enterprise is bogus. We can at least sketch the solution of abstract *bear out*, which is implicit in the "why not something else?" question: we need a full-scale investigation of all the prepositions and verbs. Unfortunately, that is beyond the bounds of this book. One of the difficulties of arguing for monosemy is that a word cannot be treated in isolation; more than in usual theories, my conclusions require conclusions on related words.

Bolinger's conclusion is simple: no system. This is by far the easiest conclusion; it requires no research at all, just an intuitive judgment. It is also too confident: note Bolinger's words (p. 61): "the only way to explain these phenomena. . . ." Why is an idiomatic view the only way, especially when the view of this book (which is implicit in Bolinger's own professed methodology) has rarely been seriously tried? The idiomatic view that denies a system, and the imperialistic view that imposes a concrete-abstract distinction by fiat, are symptoms of a science that has not yet begun. To judge that something is idiomatic is (or should be) to conclude, after all other attempts have failed, that an expression has no (or little) connection with other words and expressions. An idiomatic stance in general is a strange position to take, especially in advance.

We have similar problems with abstract *to*:

[213] "Those who saw this person tell me that he bore some *likeness* to yourself." (Ursula K. LeGuinn)

[214] He bore not the slightest *resemblance* to the boy general I had known at Valley Forge. (Gore Vidal)

[215] What they discussed, however, bore no *relation* to the blackmail crisis of the previous day. . . . (Theodore H. White)

[216] . . . an elusive ballet of wildly symbolic actions tied to ritual magic

and religious doctrines, with motivations which bear no *parallel* to normal ones. (Giorgio de Santillana and Herta von Dechend)

[217] This canonization of this tentative re-interpretation as unquestionable fact bears *analogies* to the 19th century fabrication of Egyptian chronology. (William Mullen)

[218] There can be no nearer *approximation* than that which a masquerade bears to real life. (Alfred North Whitehead)

[219] Let us instead look more closely at the *relationship* that the new culture bears to the old. (Philip Slater)

[220] At first, my remarks bore a deceptive *pertinence* to the topics under discussion. . . . (John Updike)

[221] . . . the *obligations* we bear to our descendants. (Jacques-Yves Cousteau)

[222] She bears *respect* to clothes in the same degree as she bears it to the people from whose backs they come. . . . (Eudora Welty)

The italicized nouns represent relationships specified in the *to*-phrase; I assume that 'prep-self' is implied, and that these relationships can be borne just like scars, designs, and other concretes we saw earlier. Since *to* is an appropriate preposition after a word like *relationship,* we could interpret the *to*-phrases as part of the noun phrase and thus avoid a direct link to *bear.* But even if a separate phrase, this *bear . . . to* can be the abstract correlate of a concrete one.

In my data, I have some examples with *with* that parallel this last set of data; some people find this *with* strange:

[223] . . . small groups that never achieved much diversity and bear only distant *relationships with* any modern animal. (Stephen Jay Gould)

[224] . . . some technique, which would enable the subject genuinely to bear *comparison with* such patronized, supposedly inferior disciplines . . . . (G. J. Warnock)

[225] The descriptions of the flood bear close *similarities with* the flood stories of other nations. (Vine Deloria, Jr.)

Whether grammatical or not, these do not threaten a monosemic hypothesis any more than the *to*-examples do; however, their force may differ from *to*-examples, as I will explain shortly.

With an expression like *bear relationship to* we have another problem of paradigm, one the reverse of *bear out.* Here we can substitute *have* or even *show,* but the difference in meaning is minimal. The use of *bear* appears to be purely arbitrary. In addition, *bear relationship to* resembles *relate to* (more so than the *bear on* examples we saw earlier). Just as with *take* in *take a walk* (compared simply to the verb *walk*), *do* in *do work* (compared to *work*) or *give* in *give help* (compared to *help*), *bear* seems to function only to convert a verb into a noun. In such contexts, *bear, take,* etc. are often considered "filler" words with a solely "grammatical" status. In abstract contexts, prepositions have the same characteristics.

We have the following usual chain of reasoning. These filler words sometimes substitute for each other and relate to other expressions that lack them, in circumstances with no perceivable difference of meaning. Thus, they are meaningless. Yet, on the other hand, they are not freely interchangeable. Since they have no meanings, this limitation must be purely arbitrary. Since it is arbitrary, with no basis in meaning, these phrases must be idioms. Since there are so many such phrases, a language must be highly idiomatic. Those who champion the idiomatic view can thus point to the multiplicity of idioms as a massive refutation of the order presupposed by TG.

Instead, I suggest, the problem is that we have never clearly understood what we mean by "abstract." We think of it as the opposite of "concrete," but in fact it is also the superordinate. We conceive of abstract meanings as metaphoric appendages to concrete meanings; but when meanings generalize, the exact opposite occurs: concrete meanings become pragmatic specifications of the abstract meaning, which is *the* meaning of the word. Such a meaning may seem nearly empty (as Weinreich noted about *take*) when it has few pragmatic modulations. Pragmatic information includes the additional concretions that apply an abstract sentence to a particular use. The problem of near-but-not-free interchangeability is simply one indication of the highly abstract status of words, which is the major difficulty in assessing them.

General abstract meanings elude consciousness; the interpretations of the conscious mind by necessity are oriented toward reality, and thus are not purely semantic, but compounds of both semantic and pragmatic. The general abstract meaning is unconscious, providing the foundation for more specific conscious distinctions.

If so, how then do we proceed with semantic analysis? Answer: in the incomplete, more-problems-arising-with-every-step way in which we are proceeding now. In other words: as usual, but without some unearned assurances.

2.6   ELLIPSIS

A major difficulty with intuitional data is that by design it is comparatively simple in structure; it can be too elliptical, obscuring relationships and thus inviting faulty analysis. The point has been demonstrated quite often in TG; for example, the shorter versions of the following sentences are deceptively parallel (I use parentheses as usual for optional elements, and brackets for material that is understood, but never lexically provided):

> John is easy (for someone) to please [John].
> John is eager [for John] to please (someone).

The difficulty with such elliptical constructions is two-fold. First, syntactic constituency may be obscured: the phrase *broken broken cookie jar* alerts us to the fact that in *broken cookie jar, broken* can modify either *cookie* or *jar*. Second, and more important here, a syntactic possibility may affect interpretation, even if is not realized. Fraser (1971) has studied related constructions such as the following:

> They loaded hay on the truck.
> They loaded the truck with hay.

These seem to be synonymous, but the second implies that the truck was loaded "full". Fraser shows that this implication parallels a syntactic possibility; the additional modifiers in the following cannot be reversed in the two sentences:

> They loaded hay (bale by bale) on the truck.
> They loaded the truck (full) with hay.

Fraser goes further, noting:

> They loaded a bale of hay on the truck.
> *They loaded the truck with a bale of hay.

Since one bale can hardly fill a truck, the second possibility seems bizarre; that is, we interpret the second of each pair as if 'full' is supplied, even if not lexically there.

We thus have another pretext for multiple meaning. How can we account for the additional sense, and the starred possibility, except by giving *load* two meanings, one of which includes 'fill' and one which does not? (Two more meanings must then account for the exclusive occurrence of *bale by bale*.)

I have already applied Fraser's insight earlier when I suggested that 'down' and 'on self' were implied in certain expressions even if the words weren't actually present. The data we confront now present the earlier patterns in more abbreviated form; but since we have started with more complex expressions, we can see how the abbreviated forms mean what they do. Note first that the *bring to bear* expression (and *come to bear*) need not have a PN; 'on something' is supplied inferentially:

[226] The guns were brought to bear. (FW)
[227] He demanded his mind be sharp. He brought every nerve to bear, and he was ready. (Donald Radcliffe)
[228] As three decades rolled past, a number of coinciding factors came to bear. (Jim Pettigrew, Jr.)

Consider minimal transitives, with a DN and no adjuncts:

[229] He said his forehead bears a bruise from the blow. . . . (Bill Burke)
[230] . . . her wrists bore the imprint of her hair. (Diane Oliver)
[231] The shawls bore fringes in accordance with God's Torah. . . . (James A. Michener)
[232] The mountainous bluffs do bear a kind of clay. . . . (P. H. Newby)

[233] Diamond's ability to bear a sharp, honed edge makes it ideal for delicate cataract surgery. (*National Geographic*)

[234] The ground was too hard, I supposed, to bear tracks well. . . . (Mary Stewart)

[235] . . . [a letter] bearing the postmark of a little Nebraska village. (Willa Cather)

[236] . . . visitor might drink from bottles which at least bore European labels. . . . (H. M. Tomlinson)

[237] . . . a marble shelf bears an assortment of bottles of tonic and lotion. . . . (Wendell Berry)

[238] He bore a faint, unpleasant smell of mud. (Jean Stafford)

[239] A boy stood at the curb near the iron stanchion that bore that bus-stop sign. (Aldous Huxley)

[240] The counter bears a frayed ink-marked green blotter, a crusted inkstand and pen, a small nickel-plated bell. (Wendell Barry)

[241] His cap bore a faint stain of sweat. (Theodore H. White)

[242] It [courtyard] bore the action and odor of use, thought vacant of rider at the moment. (Zane Grey)

[243] Each newly minted coin bore a portrait of Elizabeth. (Mary M. Luke)

[244] Here, it was not even a question that his veins bore royal blood. (James Baldwin)

[245] . . . there is now a constant supply of moisture, bearing its own destructive purities, that can seep into nearby temples. . . . (Anastasia Toufexis)

[246] All faces bore a look of peaceful, holy happiness. (Mark Twain)

[247] The words still bore the aura of an incredible miracle. . . . (Mary M. Luke)

[248] The schoolroom, the laboratory, and everything produced by science bear the stamp of culture. (Edward T. Hall)

[249] It [grace] happens to an individual who bears a unique biography and destiny. . . . (Sam Keen)

[250] She had always borne an excellent character. (George Orwell)

[251] If the suddenly amplified Valentino idyll did indeed bear the taint of a public relations operation. . . . (Paul Sann)

[252] They cannot possess temporal properties or bear temporal relations. (James W. Fernandez)

[253] . . . a word bearing many meanings. . . . (W3)

[254] . . . the Links' concept of race unity bore a distinctive transcendent character. (Nell Irvin Painter)

[255] The papers still bear reports of ambushes and grenadings. . . . (Don Moser)

[256] . . . [McLuhan thinks] we are entering an era which bears the promise of paradise in the form of an undissociated electronic culture. (Neil Compton)

These assume the reflexed adjunct. As usual, a concrete situation seems to impart a more specific meaning to the verb, while the abstract seems to be empty.

In addition to the reflexed adjunct, 'movement' can be pragmatically inferred, from an implicit directional:

[257] . . . each boat bore a dazzling light to summon the fish. . . . (William Styron)

[258] . . . I didn't see him come back through the flickering shadows, bearing four large bowls of chocolate ice cream. (Matthew W. McGregor)

[259] A shrieking car came pushing through the mob bearing two officers . . . . (George G. Simpson)

[260] The black Cadillac limousine bearing diplomatic plates rolled to a stop in front of the administration building. . . . (Harold Robbins)

[261] "Across the tranquil, smiling, midsummer countryside of Europe swept vast armies, bearing more deadly weapons than man has ever known." (Stringfellow Barr)

[262] The tender returned to England bearing letters. (Chauncey C. Loomis)

[263] The stirrings of the air bore the smells of foliage and of hay curing and of the opened ground. (Wendell Berry)

[264] Then the [jet] stream looped and howled back to the south at half again its usual speed, bearing the icy Arctic air that numbed the East. (Thomas Y. Canby)

In the following, *weight* provides the DN with the force of an effect (see [154] for the fuller form):

[265] The pillars bear a heavy weight. (FW)

[266] The ice is too thin to bear your weight. (OALD)

[267] The prop should give the visual impression that it will adequately bear the weight it's subjected to. (*Southern Living*)

[268] . . . in the dream there was no stitch in his side from running too far while bearing too much weight. (Norman Mailer)

[269] . . . as Foreign Minister, [he] had to bear the weight of foreign disapproval. (Edward Crankshaw)

[270] Though he'd borne the weight of her love all his life. . . . (Reynolds Price)

[271] These are no help because the ordinary concepts expressed by these words won't bear the weight of a general semantical theory. . . . (Charles E. Caton)

Movement is implied in [268]. These data show that *weight* is also unspecified for concrete-abstract. 'Weight' can be supplied inferentially, giving the following intransitives:

[272] The timber will not bear. (W2)

[273] They had smashed the ice at intervals, so that it would not bear. (Mary Stewart)

The *weight* examples relate directly to the following; contrary to Bolinger's claim that *bear the brunt* is an idiom, *burden, brunt, load, impact* and *strain* fit the general pattern:

[274] He [Jackie Robinson] bore the burden of a pioneer and the weight made him more strong. (Roger Kahn)

[275] There are, also, rules governing, among other things, the burden of proof, who shall bear it and what it shall be. (Herbert Morris)

[276] The researchers reasoned that upper extremities may bear the brunt of a fall from the outstretched arms of the skier. (AP)

[277] . . . they attempted to make older workers bear the brunt of the economic recession. (Norma Levy)

[278] He could conceive of men going very insignificantly about the world bearing a load of courage unseen. . . . (Stephen Crane)

[279] Examining these radical reanalyses can tell us about the load the transformations can bear. . . . (David Lightfoot)

[280] . . . he would have to bear the impact of the German right wing . . . . (Barbara Tuchman)

[281] The silken texture of the marriage tie bears a daily strain of wrong and insult to which no other human relation can be subjected without lesion. . . . (William Dean Howells)

[282] . . . their sweating, straining backs bore every ounce of their supplies. . . . (Howard La Fay)

Since these data suggest the apparently separate meanings of 'tolerate', 'suffer' and 'endure', I should repeat some earlier comments. I have argued that the SN does not inherently convey notions of causation, agency or effect; these come from the total situation. Entities, perhaps especially the SN, will be interpreted as causing and affecting, and deliberately so, to the extent that they have the capacity and the situation suggests it. Further, this variation of cause is not limited to the SN; the DN can exert it too, as the immediately preceding sentences demonstrate. So can a PN: *He bears up under a weight.*

The same conditions hold for entities affected, again with either SN, DN or PN. Entities will be interpreted as being affected, and reacting emotionally and mentally, to the extent that they have the capacity and the total situation suggests it. Further, an entity (and particularly a human) can be interpreted as both causing and being affected simultaneously: again, *He bears up under the weight.* Of course, the possible complexities and variations are greatest when humans are involved; causation includes 'willing' and affect includes 'responsible for' as pragmatic contributions.

This interpretation does not deny the possibility that some other lexical items might be semantically limited for cause or effect. But when a word exhibits all degrees of these (including lack), then it is unspecified. Semantic distinctions that create plus-minus polysemy are pointless; an interpreter, human or computer, would have to use pragmatic skills to determine the full meaning anyway. The use of binary distinctions also hides the fact that degrees of both cause and effect can be numerous.

The following involve humans, persons or organizations:

[283] He rode on another minute, bearing her look. . . . (Reynolds Price)
[284] Forrest went and sat and bore her direct gaze. . . . (Reynolds Price)
[285] Nobody had ever borne heavier handicaps. (Kurt Vonnegut, Jr.)
[286] Losing a regular flow of shillings to a dog must have been a heavy cross for those unfortunate men to bear. (James Herriot)
[287] . . . he must bear pain, bad luck, and defeat without whimpering or making excuses. (Robert Lipstyle)
[288] He was a good man who bore the asperities of my afflicted mother with dignity and restraint. (Loren Eiseley)
[289] They noticed, too, that he bore his death with pride. . . . (Gabriel Garcia Marquez, tr. Gregory Rabassa)
[290] . . . Southerners have borne too many failures to entertain such illusions. (Matthew Hodgart)
[291] Mr. Burns bore their presence as he did that of all the strangers. (Dan Wakefield)
[292] Deborah came on after, bearing the chains of the relationship. (Hannah Green)
[293] Liberals differ from revolutionaries primarily in their willingness to bear the indefinite continuance of unjust suffering. (Glenn Tinder)
[294] . . . he assured Clarkson the legislature would bear the expense of any necessary action. . . . (J. H. Powell)
[295] Measured against the economic interests of those who bear its costs in environmental deterioration—society as a whole—technology is by no means as successful. (Barry Commoner)
[296] He had to bear the guilty aftermath of his rages all by himself. (Lois Phillips Hudson)

'Tolerate' or 'endure' become dominant with a context expressing ability (*can, able*) especially (as W3 notes) when negated. (*These past few days* in [297] is a metonym.)

[297] . . . the activity of the hunt had made her able to bear these past few days. (Ayn Rand)
[298] When his family learned that he had leprosy, the social stigima was more than they could bear. (William S. Ellis)
[299] "I can't bear disgrace, sir." (Arthur Conan Doyle)
[300] But he could not bear the dark, deep nakedness of her eyes. . . . (D. H. Lawrence)

[301] Many of those who could not bear CP discipline thought to find more sympathy among the Trotskyists. (D. Z. Mairowtiz)

[302] . . . she could hardly bear it any longer. (Katherine Anne Porter)

[303] He himself could never bear an extreme tension. (D. H. Lawrence)

[304] "No longer can I bear my portion of sin." (James A. Michener)

"Tolerate" is also implied in complex DN's, with *that*-clauses, gerundives and infinitives. Ability and negation are prominent:

[305] He could not bear it that he had been touched by the blind man. . . . (D. H. Lawrence)

[306] ". . . she can't bear the idea of facing her father again." (Stuart Kaminsky)

[307] Since running can be addictive, most runners can't bear the thought of being sidelined. (David Bachman)

[308] "I couldn't bear it just sitting around and waiting for you." (Florence Engell Randell)

[309] Nor could she bear the little babies and the old people deliberately left behind to die. . . . (Jean Rikhoff)

[310] . . . Anderson couldn't bear having children sit in his lap. . . . (Harvey Arden)

[311] "I couldn't bear for you to touch him," she said. (Pearl Buck)

[312] He could not bear his shamed flesh to be put again between the hands of authority. (D. H. Lawrence)

[313] I couldn't bear to watch. (James Herriot)

The following sentences need special comment:

[314] The bearded one replied, "Because we bear testimony that God is one." (James A. Michener)

[315] How pervasive was this loss in Britain I have no idea, though a single incident bore witness. (Edward Weeks)

[316] . . . participants in the restoration effort are hopeful that these little salmon will bear a particularly strong inclination to return to their natal river. . . . (Stephen Fay)

[317] Usually, a statement about luck in baseball bears vapidity. (Hy Zimmerman)

Bear witness is treated as a separate phrase in some dictionaries, but it relates directly to *bear testimony;* in the light of previous examples, it loses its apparent idiosyncrasy. The general pattern of *bear* makes the latter two examples understandable too; a view of *bear* as merely a focus of idioms and collocations would not anticipate these possibilities.

Ellipsis naturally deemphasizes what it missing. But it can do likewise for what remains, especially if those words (like *bear* and prepositions) are, as I am claiming, very general and thus relatively uninformative. In his *Degree Words*

(1972), Bolinger notes repeatedly (pp. 45, 94, 208, 218, 233, 237) that simple positive declarative sentences without modification, containing "minimal content" words, often have limitations that do not appear in related forms: note *He talks much, He doesn't talk much; *He walked far, He didn't walk far. Bolinger observes that these limitations arise when a low content word is required to take emphasis: words like much and far are too weak (too lacking in information) to be the locus of prominence. When a sentence form implies their prominence, the sentence seems to conflict with itself. (I see this as a rhetorical deficiency, not a grammatical one, more a problem for writing than speaking, so Bolinger's asterisks are too extreme.) However, modifiers (including negatives, conditionals, modals, and the like) usually take prominence, and thus eliminate the inappropriateness.

Consider other examples without a DN. We can have simple bear up, and DN 'self' and 'under Z' understood. This ellipsis deemphasizes bear up and so is used to direct attention to the manner, which is expressed in an adverbial:

[318] . . . Von Sydow bears up fearlessly and with something like grace. (Jay Cocks)

[319] "Well," he says, "how the old folks bearing up?" (Wendell Berry)

[320] It is inspiring to see them bearing up so well. (RH)

The emphasized modifier need not be present; the effect of elliptical deemphasis is to direct attention to attendant circumstances. Consider the following bear down examples. All of these have implied DN 'self'; [321] has an implied 'on Z', with Z adversely affected, and [322] and [323] have implied 'on the task' and 'to an end'. But while [322] has but good to take the emphasis, something like 'unmercifully' must be supplied in [321] and 'hard' in [323]. That is, we pragmatically supply what we know to be attendant circumstances (purposes, manners, participants, efforts, goals) on an obvious typical situation. If the situation were not obvious (out of context, I need to supply the bracketed information in [322]), then an elliptical expression would not be sufficiently informative.

[321] The silence bore down. (Kurt Nelson)

[322] ". . . when they tell you to bear down [while giving birth], you bear down but good." (Laura Z. Hobson)

[323] We can't hope to finish unless everyone bears down. (RH)

The context for bear may minimally be SN, a reflexive DN, and an adverbial. This ellipsis too is used to emphasize a manner; in addition, the reflexive, by reemphasizing the SN, implies 'character' or 'inherent nature':

[324] . . . they bore themselves upright. (N. Scott Momaday)

[325] There was a porter who bore himself as though it were the last day and he knew the worst. . . . (H. M. Tomlinson)

[326] She had on a clean calico, and she bore herself imperturbably. (Mary
E. Wilkins Freeman)
[327] He bore himself well during our interview. (FW)

Since the adverbial supplies the major point of the expression, variation in its
meaning seemingly can drastically change the meaning: *The Random House
Dictionary* [RH] lists *to bear oneself erectly* and *to bear oneself bravely* under
different meanings of *bear*. These two adverbs imply different attendant
circumstances: physical appearance and psychological fortitude, respectively.

Ironically, Bolinger's insight on emphasis and low content words can be
used to explain some of the idiosyncrasies that he mentioned in the quote with
which I began this chapter. To repeat: "we can say *She bore his neglect bravely*
and either *She can't bear to be neglected* or *She can't bear being neglected,* but
we do not day **She bore to be neglected* nor **She bore being neglected,* though
She endured being neglected is normal enough." But his unstarred sentences
have manner adverbials and negation.

In addition, the positives of his negatives are all right, because of the
modal: *She can bear to be neglected* and *She can bear being neglected.* Also,
*She bore being neglected improves with a modifier like *bravely;* conversely,
Bolinger's *She bore his neglect bravely* becomes less satisfactory when *bravely*
is omitted. *Endure* has more semantic content. Thus, Bolinger's idiosyncrasies
do not imply that *bear* has no general meaning; they in fact help to imply the
opposite.

He also claims (to repeat):

> It is normal to have *bear* in a relative clause in an expression like
> *the love that I bear them* (notice that this is affirmative). And a
> declaration or interrogative is all right with a negative or an
> implied negation: *I bear them no love.* But a simple straightforward
> affirmative declarative is out of the question: **I bear them love.*
> How do we generate *The love that I bear them* if we cannot say
> **I bear them love?*

Again, I would not reject *I bear them love. I bring them love* or *I send them
love,* though slightly better, have a similar abrupt quality. *Bring* and *send* may
evoke relevant circumstances better than *bear.* But any additional context
improves it: *I bear them a desperate love* and *I bear them love with total
abandon* or *I bear them a totally abandoned love.* Consider the following:

[328] He sits there, willingly bearing his love for the woman and child. . . .
(Wendell Berry)
[329] As Nolan looked at the girl, the love he bore for her tore him cruelly at
the horror he saw in her eye. (Jackson Cole)
[330] "King David bears deep hatred for my people." (James A. Michener)
[331] Intolerance, of the sort Cass bore toward Catholics in general, and the
Irish in particular, breeds brooding. . . . (William Styron)

[332] . . . that impassioned sense of awe I bear towards a genuinely antique
        inscription. . . . (Stendhal, tr. Richard Coe)
[333] Philip bore a grievance against Townsend. . . . (AP)

These "datives" have explicit prepositions. They also occur without
prepositions; [334] was spoken at the beginning of a meeting by the president of
the organization:

[334] I bear you greetings. . . . (Greta Little)
[335] That would explain the love his wife bore him. (Glenway Wescott)
[336] "I wouldn't want anybody out there in charge of the guard boat who
        bears me a grudge." (Hammond Innes)
[337] In my heart of hearts I bore her no ill will. (William Styron)
[338] . . . there are still those who bear him an abiding mistrust. (James
        Fallows)
[339] "They won't bear you any resentment." (Richard McKenna)

   A more elliptical pattern has an understood indirect object, giving another
minimal transitive:

[340] Bordelles told him to bear a hand. . . . (Richard McKenna)
[341] 'I don't bear any ill will about it, but I'm not having that happen.'
        (Anthony Burgess)
[342] Tom by next morning bore no grudge. . . . (John Barth)

   The *bear relationship to* pattern can lack the *to*-phrase:

[343] Inside, the room bore a great similarity. (Mary M. Luke)
[344] Colchicum are often mistaken for fall-flowering crocus, and the
        blossoms do bear some resemblance. (Linda C. Askey)

   There is one final pattern that fits semantically with 'tolerate' sentences, but
that I cannot account for fully syntactically: *bear with*:

[345] Please bear with me until I finish the story. (RH)
[346] Your little sister is sick. Try to bear with her when she cries. (DAI)
[347] I bear with the sight of them [dead trees] for the sake of the harvest.
        (Marjorie Kinnan Rawlings)

I suspect, but can't demonstrate, that this *with*-phrase is an additional possible
adjunct for *bear,* not strictly paradigmatic with other adjuncts; these may relate
to [223–25].

2.7   METONYMIC INFERENCES

In Chapter 1, I briefly noted two general types of inferences: Pragmatic
Specialization and Pragmatic Metonymy. Of course, linguistic realities will not
obligingly split up neatly into the highly simplified taxonomy of semantic

change from which I borrow these notions; yet to the extent that they are useful at all, I have interpreted most inferential processes so far as specialization. Consider now the following metonymic implications. If X 'supports', 'tolerates' or 'withstands' Y (these senses derived by specialization), then X can (by metonymy) 'invite', 'attract', 'afford', 'permit', 'need', or 'require' Y:

[348] It's a distinction that could bear adoption in the grown-up world of politics. (Jack W. Germond and Jules Witcover)

[349] . . . the lad may bear a little watching himself. (George Gaylord Simpson)

[350] That would bear scrutiny too. (David L. Shores)

[351] The entire episode bears recall now. . . . (William A. Silverman)

[352] It bears repeating that two wrongs don't make a right. (*Virginian-Pilot*)

[353] Each time, too, the winning team has gotten the better of the matchups. Two bear particular attention. (Mike Littwin)

[354] The accident bears two explanations. (*World Book Encyclopedia Dictionary*)

[355] His book bore heavy praise. (W3)

[356] . . . they think there is no theory about them [mental processes] that bears discussing. (Jerry A. Fodor)

[357] To the south, beyond the Grionde, there is forest, nakedness, animals, fever, chaos. It bears no looking into. (John Updike)

[358] Rob saw he was in the presence of a pain which had not yet decided it could bear exploration. (Reynolds Price)

[359] The point at stake bears restating. (Benjamin DeMott)

[360] A morass of complex, highly questionable transactions that could not bear intense scrutiny. (Robert Ludlum)

[361] I have a list of complaints that bear airing. (Melvin Merkin)

[362] . . . a principle which could not bear the light of absolute honesty and intellectual integrity. (Robert Jungk, tr. James Cleugh)

[363] What was being done to him did not bear contemplating. (John Updike)

[364] He felt no different; but then the quality of consciousness perhaps did not bear introspection. (John Updike)

[365] . . . it didn't bear thinking about that he'd have to run the gauntlet again in a few hours. (Frances Clifford)

[366] . . . it is the central doctrine of Yeats's poetry, yet it cannot bear a confrontation with the dynamic world. (Joyce Carol Oates)

Roughly, this rule of Pragmatic Metonymy is this: a speaker can express X's capacity to attract or its need for Y by commenting on X's ability to support or withstand either. Consider further these examples of *bear examination*:

[367] His claim doesn't bear close examination. (RH)

[368] The answer of this witness will bear examination. (W3)

[369] An ethical term may accordingly be adapted to a broad range of uses, sometimes for purposes that will easily bear examination, and sometimes not. (Charles A. Stevenson)

All three sentences imply 'withstand'. The positive [368] can in addition evoke 'invite' or 'need'. Particular context again conditions interpretation: the positive [369] does not evoke 'need' because of *easily*.

Metonymy may also be operative with the OED's type (IV), *bear a child* 'produce', which it assumes was the original meaning. It is important to note here an example such as [370]:

[370] . . . I think of that baby she is bearing and will give birth to. (George P. Elliott)

Bearing that baby implies 'in herself'; this is another implicit example of the reflexed pattern. But this expression can metonymically imply the birth as well, with implied 'out of herself'. Note in what follows how the special circumstances are the determining factor in whether there is any "birth" or "fruit"; we have "carriers," "enablers" and "producers":

[371] . . . a very wonderful tree, which bore a different kind of fruit on each of its branches. (W. H. Brett)

[372] He took a wife, she bore him sons and daughters. . . . (George Moore)

[373] I think that Dorothea would have had more fun as Mrs. John Paul Jones than she did bearing nine children to Patrick Henry. . . . (Samuel Eliot Morison)

[374] To bring his identity to light means to bear a father god out of himself. (Geoffrey H. Hartman)

[375] Others, such as aquarium fish that bear live young, stop growing when they reach an adult size. (Carl L. Hubbs)

[376] The earliest to bear edible fruit are bush beans. (*Southern Living*)

[377] . . . twigs bearing April buds spin down, clipped from branches and bushes. (Edwards Park)

[378] . . . the branches of the trees against the sky were black, skeletal, bearing only tattered remnants of foliage. (Ben Haas)

[379] Tall trunks bore unexpected pale flowers. (William Golding)

[380] a tree bearing late pears; a bush bearing red flowers (W3)

[381] There were varieties of flowers, plants bearing strange seedpods . . . . (Robyn Davidson)

[382] Next year the tree will bear. (RH)

[383] "And I have a raspberries and strawberries that bear almost all the time." (Clifford D. Simak)

[384] oil-bearing shale. (W3)

[385] This soil bears good cotton. (W3)

[386] a bond that bears interest. (W3)

[387] Why not plant live trees instead and let them bear fruits and nuts and firewood which would then give profit to the farmer? (Wilson Clark)

[388] Meanwhile my other investigations were bearing no fruit. . . . (John J. Healy)

[389] But a fortnight passed before these clandestine negotiations bore fruit, and then they bore a fruit less sweet than expected. (Clayton Robert)

[390] The widening fascination with the dream technology of the Senoi tribe will almost certainly bear experimental fruit. (Marilyn Ferguson)

[391] Such prickly challenges to the North to harness public and private capital for economic recovery, unheard before the current Sunbelt-Frostbelt debate, could bear positive results. (Neal Peirce)

We see the familiar variations: both concrete and abstract, implicit and explicit [371] reflexed adjunct, implicit [372] and explicit [373] datives, a source adjunct [374], intransitives with understood DN [382, 383]. Sentences [387] and [389] have *fruit* as a metaphor.

So what does *bear* mean? It should be clear by now that this question cannot be answered in words; there is no single word or phrase that can comprehensively capture exactly what *bear* contributes. I hope, by trying to show the unity of *bear*'s contexts, to have revealed a unified meaning; but such a conclusion is inferential.

On the other hand, is a polysemic solution warranted? Is it possible, with the previous data, to argue that *bear* breaks into a number of discrete semantic parts?

Admittedly, if we must define in words, and there is no other word or phrase with a similar comprehensive range, then we will have to proceed with separate senses, defining with hyponyms or with words not systematically related but having overlapping ranges. This is essentially the method of the OED, and perhaps it is the only option a dictionary has. But we should recognize this method as inadequate and distortive. The challenge is to understand why all the data in this chapter (and of course many more) *seem to be related*, especially so when *bear* appears to be (for Bolinger) a highly idiomatic word. A better conclusion is that, even with this chapter, we still know very little about *bear*. I hope at least to have created doubts about the presumption of polysemy and the adequacy of conscious intuitions and categories.

Chapter 3

OPENNESS

To support the claim that *bear* is monosemic, we must now begin to define the more inclusive idealizations that will enable us to distinguish between what language provides to meaning (semantic, intralinguistic) and what is provided by other means (pragmatic, extralinguistic). If these idealizations are to be more inclusive than IDEAL, we must provide for the capacity of words to invoke pragmatic inferences and to change semantically. By modulating IDEAL, we recognize the historical and experiential openness of language, allowing for various kinds of diversity and mutability.

3.1 SYNCHRONY

For many antitransformationalists, the epitome of TG "absurdity" is Chomsky & Halle's (1968) *The Sound Pattern of English* [SPE], in which (so alleged) the most basic of mistakes is made: confusing synchrony with diachrony. But the "mistake" is not so simply noted; the Saussurean distinction between synchrony and diachrony is also an idealization, and a rather severe one, which in effect denies the relevance of the past to the present. In some respects, the present is a continuation of the past; it is not only possible but even inevitable that a large measure of the past will remain constant in the present, even evidence of diachronic change.

However, some aspects of the past can be eliminated and obscured.

ECLIPSING CHANGE and REANALYSIS can override and reshape just about anything. Bolinger and I both recognize this as a possibility: he claims that change has reduced *bear* to a collection of idioms and collocations, its (possible) earlier unity (almost) completely obscured; I claim that generalization has unified the meaning of earlier (possibly) distinct, metonymically related senses. One hypothetical result of such change (Bolinger's) is that polymorphemes (derivations, compounds, phrases) became arbitrary, with their full meaning unrelated to that of the constituent parts. An alternate result (mine) is that (possible) past multiplicity is obscured by present unity. For both hypotheses, some past order has no "mirror" reflection in present order; even the still separable nominal ending *-m* in *stream* can hardly be considered a reflection. The most telling evidence is that speakers of a language need know very little of linguistic history to be competent; recognizing this, advocates of both IDEAL and NORMAL accept, in principle, the diachronic-synchronic split.

In short, the relationship of past to present is poorly defined, and perhaps undefinable in many significant ways. The relationship cannot be resolved by one stroke of idealization: it has to be worked out detail by detail. Two crucial factors are RATE and VULNERABILITY: changes may be quite rapid and repeated for some more (exposed) concrete or particular aspects of language, and rare for more (protected) abstract or general ones. To take a highly general example: we assume that all languages in the last several thousand years (at least) have had a set of distinctive sounds. This linguistic property is not as easily open to change (or to dialect variation) as are the specific sounds themselves and their specific relationships. Thus, we can assume that some sort of Phonemic Principle is universal (though not eternal). As this example suggests, any change is enabled by some more abstract order that remains constant. This is the type of claim that SPE makes, in assuming that the Middle English system of vowels still holds in some abstract sense; while this may be mistaken (in general or specifics), it is not in principle absurd.

In fact, strict synchronists can unwittingly evoke the past, in an inappropriate mirroring fashion. Some words with concrete senses in Indo-European languages have evolved additional abstract senses, a historical sequence that is often mirrored in the synchronic judgment that concrete senses are "basic-literal" and abstract senses "extended-figurative". To the contrary, I am arguing that such changes can be so extensive that the meaning generalizes, becoming unspecified for concrete and abstract. This clearly happened with *be* and *have*, where past specifics are completely eliminated. For *break, take* and *bear,* this conclusion may seem odd, but only because our usual judgments of these words are based on insufficient data.

If the connection of past and present is a confusion of significance and insignificance, the distinction between synchrony and diachrony can then be both conducive and damaging to particular descriptive goals. While being exclusively synchronic, we can err in two different ways. The synchrony of

IDEAL, while (in effect) allowing the relevance of the past, undervalues the specificities of present speakers, hearers, occasions, etc. Conversely, NORMAL, while allowing such diversity, too confidently makes actual speakers wholly synchronic creatures, thus overvaluing present specificities.

As synchronic idealizations, IDEAL or NORMAL need not (by principle, should not) try to explain (say) the motivations for the three plurals of *octopus: octopodes, octopi,* and *octopuses.* Yet if these forms are analyzed as purely arbitrary, what are we describing, and with how significant a theory? It is best not to prescribe too strictly in advance what and how speakers know, because linguistic experience is related to wider experience and because the past is present in innate and unconscious order. In a more concrete idealization, the effects of unconscious knowledge, ignorance, and (possibly incorrect) conscious knowledge of history must all be acknowledged.

Yet the biggest difficulty of exclusive synchrony is that it ignores the open present. As linguists, we need the past to alert us to changes in progress now. This is a relevant factor if only because each speaker experiences such change while learning, speaking, and hearing different versions of a language. A good vehicle to illustrate the open present is the expression *kick the bucket* 'die', which is frequently cited as *the* typical idiom. We can ask a purely diachronic question: how did such a combination of form and meaning get into the English language? Also, how was (not is) it motivated? (Such a question assumes that at one time form and meaning were related in some way.) Our discussion will spring a synchronic surprise, one we could easily anticipate if our synchrony weren't so rigid.

The word *bucket,* according to scholarly consensus, once designated a kind of wood; it changed meaning by metonymic specialization: Material to Object-made-with-material (which also has occasioned new meanings of *straw, iron,* and *glass*). Buckets need no longer be made of wood (thus, the second sense has generalized) and *bucket* has lost the first sense. *Bucket* at one time could also mean (by another metonymic specialization) 'beam of wood'; a parallel expression, *kick the beam,* also meant 'die'. The best evidence for motivation (not necessarily correct) is that pigs being slaughtered, suspended by their hind legs from a beam of wood, would as an automatic nervous reflex kick the beam when they were killed. Thus, *kick the bucket* 'die' is a phrasal example of metonymy, exemplifying the pattern Cause for Effect.

Where should such information go in a linguistic theory? It appears obvious that none of this is synchronic; further, on seemingly all criteria, *kick the bucket* qualifies as an idiom:

(a) Historically, it has been deprived of every related reality, linguistic and extralinguistic, that could give its words separate senses.

(b) Formally, it appears to be a verb followed by a noun phrase, but, unlike the compositional "literal" counterpart, the object

noun phrase cannot be separated from the verb, as in
passivation (*The bucket was kicked by John*), or topicalization
(*The bucket John kicked*), or the contrast of *John's kicking the*
bucket and *John's kicking of the bucket.*
  (c) Semantically, replacing *kick* or *bucket* with near synonyms like
  hit or *pail* loses 'die' (Makkai (1977:467)); and there is no
  obvious connection of the words to the meaning.

And yet, astonishing as it may seem, this epitome of an idiom does link
semantically to other parts of the language: all of the following expressions also
mean 'die':

[1] "Maybe she's just afraid I'm going to *kick off* before it's time to pay the
    kids' college tuition." (Nancy Mayer)
[2] He *kicked in* after a long and painful illness. (RH)
[3] "Isn't your father going to dump the lot on the Daltons when he *kicks*
    it?" (Tabitha King)
[4] "I wanna make a will before I *kick*." (*Consumer Survivor Kit*)

How do we explain these data? They are not archaisms such as *kick the*
beam; they are spoken and understood now. Their similarity is not likely a
coincidence: it appears that *kick* in the shorter expressions is a CLIPPING from
kick the bucket. Even if this *kick* is unrelated to *kick* 'move the leg', its link to
the expressions in [1–4] should be noted in a complete analysis of English.
Further, the use of *off* and *in* [1 and 2] and *it* [3] can be linked to similar uses
elsewhere in the language.
  So *kick the bucket* is idiomatic only if we ignore the data of [1–4]. Even
with diachronic information eliminated, there is a synchronic relationship to be
accounted for, one which will at least complicate our notion of idiom. When a
phrase becomes an idiom, it is not forever barred from creating new
relationships.
  I am again appealing to productivity, the best claim for a generalization (no
matter how limited); current facts suggest that *kick the bucket* is not so typical an
idiom, if at all.
  In two insightful comments, Bolinger argues that a language is never "fully
set," but is always open to further development. By implication, he defines a
modular view of lexical meaning. In his critique of Katz and Fodor's (1963)
[KF] proposal for transformational semantics, he (1965: 567) notes that their
conception of word meaning has no provision for openness:

[A1] It is characteristic of natural language that no word is ever limited to its
     enumerable senses, but carries within it the qualification of 'something
     else'.

As a consequence, we can have the circumstance that Bolinger notes (1971a:
522) by rhetorical question in his critique of Postal's (1970) analysis of *remind:*

[A2] "What features of meaning are IN a linguistic form and what features are suggested to our minds ABOUT it, by the actual context or by past associations? This is the question of reference vs. inference. . . ."

"Reference" here is a word's inherent meaning, its semantics (though the terminology is confusing, the point still holds); "inference" is what a word suggests, its pragmatics.

Postal finds examples of sentences where *remind* and *strike as similar* seem to contribute the same information. Yet in other examples Bolinger establishes at least two differences: *remind* need not involve a similarity, and *strike as similar* need not involve a memory. The memory of *remind* may sometimes involve a similarity; and the similarity of *strike as similar* may sometimes involve a memory. Alternatively put, reminding may be triggered by a similarity, but need not be; and a similarity may be triggered by a memory, but also need not be. These possible specifics can be provided, in an appropriate context, by two pragmatic specializations, which make *remind* and *strike as similar* synonymous. With these inferences factored out, we need not make *remind* polysemic.

Of course, KF and Postal were both assuming IDEAL; in principle, they should not recognize Bolinger's points. In practice, however, they have no way of knowing what aspects of meaning to recognize or ignore in IDEAL. The idealization requires prior determination of the relative inherent/inferential status of each word, something IDEAL cannot itself provide. Some of the necessary evidence for determination (such as that showing *kick the bucket* to be no longer idiomatic) may be rather slight; so too is the difference between Newtonian and Einsteinian physics. When theories of word meaning are derived from "slightly mistaken" exemplars like *kick the bucket* and *remind,* the inaccuracies can become quickly compounded, especially so if an eventual theory of linguistic use must be adapted to the already finalized dimensions of IDEAL.

By recognizing how a word's meaning can change, we can better assess how a particular word has already changed and still is changing, and thus correct distortions caused by an idealization that assumes lexical meaning to be fully static. The history of *kick the bucket* can provide some clues, for what happened in the past is happening to some degree now. We can note these points:

[B1] The relationship of form to meaning can be INDIRECT. As one example, a motivated new sense of a word can be more general or more specific than a previous sense, or may indicate something similar (metaphor) or contiguous (metonymy), or other relationships.

[B2] Such indirection applies to words, phrases, and even larger units. But indirection alone does not create idioms: as long as speakers were aware that *kick the bucket* pertained to slaughtering pigs, the relationship of form to meaning was explicable and motivated.

[B3] Indirect relationships of form and meaning are particularly fragile when they rest on minimal (and extralinguistic) connections; if knowledge of all connection is lost, an idiom results, unrelated in sense to anything else.

[B4] All elements of a language, including idioms, are subject to alterations that can REMOTIVATE the relationship of form to meaning, making new connections and new productivity. (Thus, also, the once idiom *hot dog* was clipped to *dog,* then elaborated to *corn dog.*)

Eble (1980, 1981) has reminded us in detail that such motivated changes take place rapidly in slang; thus, IDEAL must view slang as irrelevant, or arbitrary and unmotivated. Notably, the changes of slang are fast enough for the average speaker to notice; for speakers to keep current (if only in part), or to realize they aren't current, they must have some (possibly unconscious) knowledge *that* language changes and *how* it changes. The crucial point: *mutability is part of a speaker's necessary (more inclusive) competence.*

Particularly, this larger competence includes knowledge of the potentials of metonymy and metaphor. Such knowledge is necessary not only for producing and interpreting nonce uses of words, but even for understanding "established" uses. Consider a personal anecdote. I remember wondering about *kick the bucket* when I was fourteen and milking cows, especially one cow that several times (before I learned better) kicked over a nearly full bucket of milk. It occurred to me that since the milk was now useless, it was (figuratively) 'dead.' My solution was not historically accurate; but significantly, seeing no direct link of words and meaning, I resorted to a metonymic-metaphoric explanation. That possibility of (re)motivating a form was part of my competence. If such competence is not available to speakers of a language, reanalysis is impossible.

I did not require a new meaning for any of the constituent words; my solution was pragmatic, not semantic. As such, IDEAL need not take notice of my "dead milk" solution, nor of nonce expressions. These reflect modulations exterior to IDEAL. However, this limited scope of IDEAL must then be maintained through less obvious, parallel examples.

Consider *answer the door*. Stockwell, Schachter, and Partee (1973:721) [SSP] note that the meaning of this phrase does not follow from the words. Though they don't judge it an idiom, they claim that *answer* has a different sense. This is a clear example of my major point: too limited an idealization leads to multiple meaning. *Answer* has its usual meaning; *door,* however, enables the hearer to make a metonymic inference: 'someone who is using the door to communicate'. Similarly: *answer the phone/the telegram/the bell/the letter, get the door/the bell, Did you hear the door?* and *Was that the door?* These exemplify the metonymic pattern Instrument for Agent.

As another example, Borkin (1972) has noted that the names of capitals of countries can indicate the government of those countries, as in *Hanoi refuses to negotiate.* Trying to account for this in IDEAL, she could have made *Hanoi* polysemic, but instead opted for a deletion rule that reduces *the government of the country whose capital is Hanoi.* However, though this rule applies to all capitals, it is a highly specific deletion rule, and Borkin shows there is need for many more. Yet, her solution is probably the best one in IDEAL; the awkwardness indicates the idealization's severe limits.

The phenomenon is much more general. All the following place names are associated with a distinctive event or situation:

[5] Indianapolis, Nashville, Hiroshima, Little Big Horn, Yalta, Kent State, Fort Knox, Chappaquiddick, Pearl Harbor, Bethlehem, Watergate, New Hampshire, Selma, Hastings, Wall Street, Madison Avenue, Broadway, Hollywood, Kitty Hawk

Names such as *Munich* and *Versailles* indicate several distinctive events; *Indianapolis* and *New Hampshire* indicate recurrent events and situations. Other examples follow; Arecibo, Puerto Rico, in [8] is the site of a radar and radio telescope.

[6] "She and the boys were with me in Japan. Then *Korea* broke, and I sent them back home." (Ben Haas)
[7] At *Anzio*, I saw a buddy of mine tied to a tree fifty yards from me, screaming for water, his face blistered by the sun. (Ken Kesey)
[8] *Arecibo*, because of its size and the quality of its receivers, can pick up extremely faint sources of radio waves. (James Gorman)

Some names may lose their capacity to evoke a distinctive event (and the newer *Munich* may overshadow the older), but capitals tend to persist over time, creating the impression that the second meaning has been lexicalized. As *St. Petersburg, Berlin* and *Saigon* should indicate, when a name no longer designates a capital, it no longer (except historically) can metonymically evoke the government. The second meaning is totally dependent on the first, and so I judge it to be pragmatic. This is in contrast to real instances of polysemy like *Mississippi* and *Missouri*, where either river or state could change name without requiring a change in the other.

It is the nature of historical change that there be a continuum, as Ullmann (1957) noted, from Shift (pragmatic variation) to Polysemy (semantic variation) to Homonymy (accidental similarity of different words): examples of place names becoming the last are *china, marathon,* and *limerick.* The continuum includes borderline cases, such as university names: *Chicago, North Carolina;* but when Wake Forest University moved from the town of Wake Forest, North Carolina, to Winston-Salem, *Wake Forest* became polysemic. It is part of a speaker's combined linguistic and extralinguistic knowledge to know all these possibilities; obviously, however, they cannot be fully specified in IDEAL.

3.2. DIACHRONY

This continuum also implies a highly variable synchronic status across the vocabulary. Inescapably, words, phrases, even sentences and discourses, are at different stages of development. (This can hold for phrases and sentences that, at a more abstract level, have generalizable syntactic form.) This was Bolinger's double point in [A]; the boundary of semantic and pragmatic cannot be drawn generally in advance, but must be discovered, word by word, phrase by phrase, even sentence and discourse by sentence and discourse. No reasonable theory can evade or postpone this necessity.

Thus, the success and even plausibility of IDEAL requires that we not defer "performance" to some later stage of research. The TG methodology has justifiably provoked reactions from scholars like Bolinger who are more attuned to mutability. Unfortunately, these reactions have often made complementary polar mistakes. Rejecting too much innateness and uniformity, they claim too much change and individuality.

History and experience are crucially important in that they individualize. Different times involve different people and different expressions, even the same expressions being used in different ways. The point of IDEAL is to minimize diversity as much as possible, attributing as much systematicity as possible to our linguistic capability. Yet each single word is an individual, different from other words; each word is also a collection of individuals, since each use is individual. Any theory that must deal with words-as-such runs the risk of inappropriately or excessively systematizing.

If the goal of IDEAL is to isolate what is genetically innate and universal about language, then it will be depicting that which is highly stable and remote from change, to the extent that genetic inheritance (and how it is differently used by different individuals, and used differently by the same person) is unaffected by change. In parallel, if the function of the unconscious mind is to supply a systematic matrix for consciousness, then it too will be relatively unaffected by change. IDEAL is ahistorical to the extent that our innate capacity is such: almost totally so, and relatively so in the language-particular details that belong to it. This idealization depicts Innate Linguistic Competence, the internally closed, tightly organized, and foundational end of a mental continuum that opens by modular diversification (innate to unconscious) into full-blown Linguistic Experience (including other competence and experiences), which is additionally conscious, externally open, individualized, highly particular, both thought and act, and very much in (and actively creating) history.

From this perspective, I can restate my preference for IDEAL over NORMAL: IDEAL, to the extent that it correlates with unconscious knowledge, implicitly defines what must be supplied by other modules. NORMAL, as I assess it in Bolinger, seems to assume a minimized mind, a knowledge almost exclusively jack-of-all-trades and accumulative; this assumption only partially accounts for conscious openness and interprets much of closed unconscious order as idiomatic.

Of course, anyone who rejects the notion of unconscious knowledge (especially as I characterize it) will have to be highly dubious. But one frequent objection to either IDEAL or the unconscious seems unwarranted. Those who champion NORMAL, or some closely related, "realistic" view, often appeal to the notion of PLASTICITY. Unlike other animals, who have built-in limitations, humans have capacities that are largely undefined, and this (so claimed) provides us with the capacities of consciousness and freedom. The notion of determinative innate linguistic ability is thus viewed as an attack on human freedom, an attempt to make us all automatons.

This is a serious charge, particularly so because linguists (like most scientists) tend to ignore the ideological implications of their work; but I think it derives from a misunderstanding of the relationship between order and freedom. A romantic myth of our society is that order and freedom are polar opposites. Given the overwhelming events of the twentieth century, this myth is hard to oppose, especially since freedom seems embattled by many foes. But we must distinguish different kinds of order. I could be suddenly hurled into outer space, and thus "freed" of gravity and other earthly "limitations," but any freedom I have would be rendered useless. To act freely, I need an order; that is the only freedom possible to me. Some order provides for the many (infinite) choices available to consciousness, plus other common human needs.

Similarly, I need the syntactic order of English in order to say the infinite things that I want to say. It would be pointless to insist on a more plastic language that enabled me to combine words in every possible way. The human order also enables me to suspend the order in part to make another free point. The benefits of plasticity are actually systematic consequences of order. The human need is for a foundational order that makes possible the manifold capacities of a language. Innateness and the unconscious underlie the potentially infinite linguistic capacities.

At issue are the means of representing accurately both systematicity and individuality, both timelessness and change, both uniformity and diversity. To dramatize this point, I would like to test my claims with another idealization, supported by the same "realistic" justifications as NORMAL, which I will call HISTORY, presented rather insistently by one of TG's sharpest critics, Peter Maher. Maher is a historical linguist, who finds the diachrony-synchrony split problematic, with all the reservations of relating them which I noted (with his implicit help) above. Like Bolinger, he knows the many idiosyncrasies of a language, and the lost or reinterpreted connections. He states his adversarial position as follows (1977b:2):

> What Chomsky has forgotten is *the* human species-specific trait:
> this is History, alias Culture, or Tradition. Even those who
> disagree with the sentiments of Ortega y Gasset should take it as an
> astringent: "Man has no nature; what he has is history" (cited in
> Dobzhansky 1962:18). Man does indeed have a nature or
> genetically transmitted characteristics: the major one is the faculty
> to acquire culture, to acquire symbols, to profit from the
> experience of forbears without having to recapitulate history (what
> the man in the street calls "learning the hard way"). The forms of

language(s) and culture(s) cannot be read directly as psychological evidence without the hermeneutic prerequisite of putting them into their contexts (social, material, cultural, geographic, stylistic, etc.) Now that means their historical context, both present and past.

Regarding Maher's first point: strictly speaking, Chomsky hasn't "forgotten" history, he has merely "deferred" it; this need not be fatal, especially when there are variationists of many types, including Maher, to assume the necessary divisions of linguistic labor. However, deferring can effectively amount to forgetting and denying; divisions of labor can (and have) become mutually eclipsing rival self-sufficient empires. Though Maher presents his disagreement with TG and IDEAL in rather absolute terms, there is a potential common enterprise.

I will return shortly to Maher's second point, that our nature is to acquire culture. His third point (similar to the one I have been making) is the most telling. Context implies heterogeneity, diversification, individuation: we cannot read the meanings of words as direct evidence of their linguistic status without accounting for the influence of contextual modulations, including time. These modulations may be multiple, variable, and very particular (recall implied 'down' with *bear*); the methods of locating and defining them must be (in large part) hermeneutic. However, in assenting to Maher's point, am I then contradicting myself in also assuming IDEAL?

An answer can be developed from a lengthy quote Maher takes from Homans (1967:92), which illustrates how historical influences make problematic not only the social sciences but even the "vaunted exact sciences":

> I remember well when I first realized this. During World War II I was commanding a mine sweeper equipped to blow up magnetic mines harmlessly by exposing them to a magnetic field created between two long electrodes towed astern. Under these circumstances, it was vital that the magnetic field of the sweeper itself should be on negligible force. Otherwise the mine would explode, shall we say, prematurely. I discovered that the science of electromagnetism could not predict or, *a fortiori*, explain what the field under the ship was going to be. It was not that the scientists did not have full confidence that they knew the laws of electromagnetism but that they found it difficult to draw specific conclusions from these laws under conditions in which the past history of the ship made a difference. For magnetic purposes a ship may be considered a piece of soft iron, and a peculiar property of iron is that various conditions can create in it a magnetic field which it will later retain. A ship's present magnetic field depends on the latitude and longitude of the place where she was built and on her heading on the builder's ways. It depends on where she has sailed and the courses she has steered during her life as a ship. It depends on the amount of pounding she has received from workmen and the sea. The individual mechanisms appear to be well understood. The

difficulty lies in getting the information that will allow their application, and if the information is available, of calculating the resultant of their interactions over time. The scientists could not have solved the problem even if they had wanted to, which they did not, for their practical purposes could be served, not by predicting the magnetic field of the ship, but by simply measuring it and neutralizing it, through the procedure called "degaussing."

I take this to be a parable of our problem in much of social science. Even if we had full confidence in our general propositions, the equivalent of the laws of electromagnetism, we would still have trouble showing how our empirical propositions, the equivalent of the magnetic field of the ship, followed from them.

I find this an apt parable for several reasons, some perhaps unintended, for Maher's immediate comment minimizes its scope:

Natural language texts are, like Homans's mine sweeper, of a dual nature (see Hockett (1958:574). The paradigmatic and syntagmatic patterns are like the soft iron of the ship's hull. (A ship could be built of some other material and still be a ship.) These patterns have their own character, independent of the varying uses to which they are put in the course of time. Surface structures are handed on from one generation to the next, while the underlying values are subject to revolutionary changes. TG theory stands this universal of human semiotics on its head. For a homely example: we use old things for new ends; you can knock someone on the head just as well with a bottle or a baseball bat as with a club designed for the purpose. You can also use those objects to roll out a pie crust or prop open a window. (p. 5)

These comments stress ARBITRARINESS: motivated linkages of form, meaning, and function can be broken and made arbitrary, as in *kick the bucket*. His "homely example" is of generalization, a process that (as he shows) is not limited to language. For all aspects of human culture, such duality makes it difficult and partially impossible to read the present as a mirror of the past, or a mirror to innate psychic ability. Though historical knowledge is not necessary for "practical" living, such living has limited capabilities; the value of historical knowledge is that it can prevent disastrous generalization and idealization. Even if, in idealizing, we want to factor out the influence of the past, or of variation generally, we must use the details of historical research as a necessary guide. Maher's point is well taken, and to the extent that timelessness is invoked or implied by any theory, we must ask to what extent variation has been successfully eliminated.

But is that all there is to the parable? Even duality is not as simple as Maher makes it. Take the homely example: do we keep hitting-over-the-head constant and generalize its means, or do we keep the bottle constant and generalize over its uses? Actually we can say either, both, or neither. For the last option, arguing from a point of view that makes everything strongly systematic, we could claim that both hitting-over-the-head and bottle have changed their relationships with paradigmatic alternatives, and thus neither exemplifies a temporal consistency.

Consider, then, Maher's charge that TG turns things upside down. Specifically: in SPE, the English phoneme once systematically /e/, and in base forms there considered /e/, is now systematically /i/. According to this treatment of English, the former /i/ and current /i/ are not a surface form remaining constant, taking on new values or functions, but rather manifestations of two different entities. Maher may choose the opposite point of view, that of a constant /i/ changing systematic significance; but how can he then account for the changing phonological form of the continuing morpheme *meet*? Of course, we do choose Maher's point of view when we say "forms change meaning" rather than "meanings change form." In both instances, we keep form constant, assuming that more concrete phonology and semantics are what change.

In all these considerations, we are concerned with the appropriate levels of generality and specificity, including the possibility of a highly general, abstract level that is (relatively) remote from the effects of time. It is revealing that Homans's parable is equally problematic for the physical sciences. In his haste to emphasize (rightfully and with good reason) that the physical sciences are also historical, Maher overlooks the fact that useful physical laws have been discovered with the aid of idealizations that ignore both historical change and particular situations. As a result of our particular historical tradition, we have developed a general method of scientific research that has proven successful (by its own standards) and may prove successful in a new area.

As Homans notes, physics is constrained in the highly specific circumstances "in which the past history of the ship made a difference." Yet these circumstances do not prohibit the idealized notions of iron-in-general and magnetic-field-in-general (or of ships made of various materials). By specifying one particular ship, the parable subtly but necessarily (for its point to hold at all) underestimates the full resources of human thought. Like all linguists, Maher does not feel constrained to study only particular speakers and hearers, or particular discourses; if linguists were so constrained, the possibilities of understanding language would be severely curtailed, because these are the particulars that even the physical sciences have trouble in fully explaining.

Yet, to repeat, Maher's point does become applicable at the level of individual words and sentences; with Bolinger, and me, he argues that TG too often generalizes inappropriately from particular words and sentences, taking special individual properties to be representative of a class, and thus illegitimately homogenizes. Green (1974), when investigating in detail all the words that exhibited Dative Movement (or that should, but didn't), found a bewildering complexity that followed no generally applicable rule; this was typical of anyone who tried to state CTG transformations with total explicitness. That is why CTG was abandoned; its supposedly general transformations contained or entailed too many ungeneralizable particulars, and the explicitness of transformational methods made this unmistakably clear.[1]

HISTORY is an idealization, albeit perhaps a not fully acknowledged one, and not only because Maher abstracts away from some particulars, which nevertheless are part of history. Rather, the more crucial idealization is the one implied in his second point, the characterization of human nature: "the faculty to acquire culture, to acquire symbols, to profit from the experience of forbears." While correct, this formulation is too exclusively specific: it allows Maher to ignore the full contribution of the organism. He seems thus to imply that we are merely mutable and experiential creatures.

It also leads him into a strange extrapolation from the mine sweeper to language, which by implicit conflation idealizes away one essential distinction: he equates the iron and its magnetic field. He thus overspecifies the explanatory problem, and so overlooks what might be the parallel, in language, to the physical laws that Homans too briefly mentions. Iron has an innate potential for being magnetized which can be described as an idealization (along with the idealization of magnetic fields) by physical laws, including electromagnetic. Thus, the potential of this ship's iron and the range of its possible magnetic fields can be assessed scientifically with little historical interference. However, the actual sequence and accumulated effect of this particular ship's magnetized iron cannot be. It is this more specific entity that changes, not the iron; if the iron and fields are kept theoretically separate, the capacity of iron for being magnetized need not be equated with the history of the iron, which is impossible to account for.

In analogy, IDEAL is concerned with the magnetizable iron, while HISTORY recognizes no such independent entity, but only the iron-as-magnetized. Thus, it is no mystery why Maher sees historical influence as total, for his initial idealization is more concrete. But, from my perspective, HISTORY homogenizes too much toward particularity; it obscures the possibility of innate and unconscious linguistic ability that may be only remotely connected with reality and history.

To put the issue more broadly: it is possible to take a Darwinian view that all biological processes are mutable and variable, yet still assume that some processes change much more slowly than others, some to the extent that we can assume in an idealization that they are constant over wide ranges of space and time: that they are innate and universal (though not "necessary" or "eternal").

Of course, if Maher is saying that IDEAL is more difficult to define than transformationalists have ever assumed, he is quite right. But we should not idealize away the possibility of innate or unconscious order simply because we don't know a priori what it might be. Conversely, we cannot idealize away history. Maher correctly objects to the mistake of assuming that all mutable traces and effects can be ignored by general fiat. At every point in the study of language, when we are dealing with individuation (individual words, individual uses of words, individual speakers, hearers, and occasions, etc.), we are necessarily involved in reality and history.

Maher is thus a useful astringent for a linguistic approach that focuses too exclusively on IDEAL, for he reminds us, like Bolinger, of the necessity for closer, more detailed analysis. The unnecessary irony: Chomsky's agenda can best be met by the relevant force of Maher's agenda, and vice versa as well.

3.3 INNOVATION

I propose that the distinction between synchrony and diachrony be taken as that between relatively slow change and relatively rapid change, with an implied continuum. Under this interpretation, IDEAL is a typical scientific idealization; it attempts to define the most constant factors of linguistic reality. SYNCHRONY is Gould's (1987) "deep time" or "time's cycle": the old and enduring, the seemingly eternal realities that do not change or change in a changeless way. DIACHRONY is "sequential time" or "time's arrow": change, especially the most idiosyncratic aspects of change. This is a distinction between (seeming) timelessness and time, with an implied continuum of relative immutability and relative mutability. (Obviously, linguistic deep time is not as deep as geological deep time.)

A synchronic grammar (so defined) is one that deals with those aspects of linguistic reality that are most invariant; more specifically, it may also have to include the variations that have considerable systematic effect (GB: "parameters"). A diachronic grammar is one that deals with all the variant details, including extralinguistic modulations. A diachronic grammar thus (by definition) includes at its "core" a synchronic grammar; more important, it includes the continuum of idealizations that represent more and more mutable aspects of linguistic reality. The language "of a particular time" is thus a complex: diachronic to the extent that it is highly specific to a time, and synchronic to the extent that it captures realities that hold across wide ranges of time.

These definitions may seem to severely twist the current uses of these words, but I think instead they manage to avoid a serious inconsistency. Consider: the word *meat* has changed both semantically and phonologically through time, and yet we assume that we should include it in a current, synchronic grammar. However, *meat* is also variable now. What TG assumes (and its critics deplore) is that a synchronic grammar not only ignores historical change but also ignores present variation. On the other hand, many critics try to ignore only the change and include the present variation. I think this latter enterprise is problematic; it misses the concrete similarities of both variations. It also misses the ABSTRACT INVARIABLES that contrast with the variations; these are what a synchronic grammar, in TG, tries to describe.

I am thus assuming that dialect and register variations are also diachrony: it includes what Anttila (1972: 21) calls the DIATOPIC. Such a reorientation is needed so that various degrees of idealization can be clearly delineated. The more concrete an idealization, the more it implies and includes variation; we are progressively trying to judge "degree of relative concreteness-abstraction". We move out of neutralized time concurrently as we move out of neutralized (social) space and occasion. What we call "synchronic" is not "pure present". We can observe sequential time at a single time: today's "dialect" is tomorrow's "standard". Labov (1987) observes linguistic realities in younger speakers that do not occur in older speakers, and infers that changes are taking place in time. Further, each present linguistic reality is in a particular stage of development: Eble, in addition to making this point with slang, shows (1982) that *else* is a dying word, now more restricted in its possible contexts than it was for Shakespeare.

There is an important converse caution: for a TG-style synchrony, all mutabilities must be neutralized or else presented in full variation. My reservations on TG (usually CTG) concern this point: the idealization is inconsistent, mixing the highly abstract with the relatively concrete. To repeat: the criterion for (relative) idealization must be (relative) degree of abstraction. Neither the current synchrony-diachrony distinction nor the pro- and anti-TG faultlines can be clearly aligned with this criterion.

Our pretheoretical heritage has conflated two quite different matters. As Harris (1980: 102ff) shows, the Greek tradition of "grammar" that has persisted to this day had its inception in the fact of variation: if people used different languages, then language was not "natural", but "conventional". If conventional, then it could be studied in itself. The (correct) discovery was that "language" (to some degree) constitutes an abstract autonomy of its own.

But that autonomy could not be correctly gauged. The immediate and greatest problems for the grammar tradition were the same variational facts that had been its inspiration. The solution for variation was the prescriptive one, the "Classical Fallacy": of all the variant possibilities, only one was considered "correct" and "standard". The grammatical tradition has thus been a blend of autonomous linguistic reality and prescriptivism to this day.

Yngve (1987) describes the whole grammar tradition as misguided, assuming that TG is simply a perpetuation, because of its prescriptive view of data and its idealized autonomy. But simple rejection leaves the complexities tangled, so they continue to mislead us in ways we don't notice. We need to look more closely at the reasons for prescriptivism.

For the grammatical tradition, the problem was that grammar became practical, pedagogical. To be practical, we must address linguistic reality in full concreteness, including "sequential time," diachrony. To be theoretical, we assume autonomies, "deep time," synchrony. The practical is not a straightforward "application" of the theoretical. The practical requires much that the theoretical never considers; conversely, much that is theoretically offered seems practically irrelevant. Theoretical concerns are more properly with "deep time," with realities that need not be taught because they allow us no choice: these realities are so pervasive and constant that we may not even suspect them. When first noted, they don't even seem "real."

The difficulty: to be consistently synchronic, assuming invariance, we can't deal with the whole language. The grammatical tradition mistakenly assumed that it could. It implicitly drew the bounds of linguistic autonomy in the wrong place, making too many things equally abstract, and thus it both overconcretized and overabstracted.

The grammatical tradition conflated theory and pedagogy so thoroughly that it compromised the possible corrective responses to it. Yngve renounces the tradition completely, and thus loses the insight of linguistic autonomy (though renouncing is never as full as one hopes). TG accepted the autonomy, and the equalization of abstraction, and thus was implicated, with no pedagogical need, in assuming a standard dialect. The constantly changing TG tradition has in effect been a disentangling of that ancient confusion.

While I obviously see value in the TG tradition, my present concern is diachrony. A more open idealization must deal (relatively) with the new and changing. However, in accord with scientific procedure, I approach diachrony from synchrony: I try to see what is constant about change.

Given "new" situations, a speaker must have Bolinger's "something like" [A1] possibility of innovating. Equally important, hearers must have the ability to recognize such innovations. To some extent, these two processes occur continually, and any speaker-hearer must have the relevant competences. At some point in the midst of continuing change (though not necessarily the optimal point for linguistic theorists) some innovations have a sufficiently differentiated effect, and we notice what we call a change.

To begin discussion, consider noun compounds. In Lees's (1960) early TG work, they were analyzed like this:

[9] mailman = someone who delivers mail
    fireman = someone who extinguishes fire
    salesman = someone who sells things

Such paraphrases can demonstrate differences between supposedly parallel formations, but they do so at the cost of highly specific additions. Further, these definitions do not capture the special social identities of the various people involved: not everyone who extinguishes fire is a fireman, and firemen have established duties other than extinguishing fires. The paraphrases introduce complexity and yet are inadequate.

We could say that the compounds are simple combinations of the constituent parts, perfectly compositional. Other than convincing no one, this falsely claims that the combinations (and all such) are perfectly transparent to speakers.

Or we could say that the compounds are no longer phrases, but single words, and like all words they are the equivalent of idioms. But this falsely claims that the phrases are mysterious to the language's users. Further, *busing* is a single word with the same double inadequacy: it underdescribes the situation it refers to and also cannot be applied to some situations where people are conveyed by buses. To avoid claiming that *mailman* and *busing* are unrelated to the rest of the language, it is more theoretically fruitful to assume a continuum with compositionals and idioms as two polar alternatives. (Bolinger proposes this in "Meaning and memory," but his examples, in my opinion, are all weighted too far toward the idiomatic end of the continuum.)

At the idiom pole, phrases are simply unanalyzable; they cannot be morphemically decomposed. We need this alternative for *breakfast*. We then allow degrees of possible analyzability up to the other polar alternative of full compositionality. The noun compounds of [9] are still relatively decomposable, since the parts relate to the full meaning. It is inaccurate to say that these words are on a par with *breakfast,* because they are much more readily analyzed; such a solution is an instance of underanalysis (and also of the often inappropriate analytic need to reduce many gradient choices to a polar distinction).

If "degree of compositionality" is the measure for our continuum, then we need to ask, "What composes?" Gleitman and Gleitman (1970) [GG] observe that a compound like *mailman,* while motivated and understandable as such, UNDERDETERMINES its meaning. Semantically, it is (p. 83) 'man-[some indefinite verbal relationship]-mail'. The language user is required to supply additional information pragmatically to specify the indefinite verbal relationship: not only that mailmen (and women) bring mail, but details about role and range of duties.

Noun compounding is one of the most productive parts of English syntax; as Lees and other linguists have noted, it is generally the case that the constituents of compounds rarely contribute the full meaning of the resulting word. GG's proposal suggests a condition that may seem startling at first:

[C] PRODUCTIVITY CONDITION
  Productive processes produce combinations whose parts underdetermine the whole.

Specifically, this is the initial status of such combinations, not the result of historical form-meaning slippage. This condition directly conflicts with the usual interpretation of compositionality.

Further, productive processes MUST underdetermine. In any situation where language is applied in some new way (which, specified enough, is every situation), there are a potentially infinite number of relevant "lexicalizable" factors. If many factors are crucially important (and many of these are not narrowly "informational"), the result is an extended explicit use of language; but even with painstakingly detailed discussion, there are important factors that must be left unlexicalized. Thus, we can additionally say that *the general condition of all language use is underdetermination.* As (merely) a special case, when we have an infinitely factorable situation condensed into a compound, even more details must be left out.

While this necessary condition of language use is hardly deniable, it is often forgotten, and with understandable reason. As we consciously attempt to understand what is lexicalized, we always see more than what the words contribute. If we have been trained to believe (and we have) that most of what we understand is conveyed by the words, then we naturally load those words with too much meaning. There are a sufficient number of "fully generated" expressions (like *eat the cookie, wash the car*) that seem to fully "mirror the reality" (though they don't). These confirm us in the belief that full linguistic compositionality is not only possible, but even the (desirable) norm. Further, when we do acknowledge underdetermination, we are too confident in our ability to determine what has been omitted: kind of cookie, meal or not, gulping or savoring, picnic or home, naked or clothed, fire alarm sounding or not, actual or pretense, habitual or nonce, slow-motion or normal, etc., until we are consciously exhausted, bored, or in need of a neat theory.

Consider, as another example, *the cat is on the mat*. Philosophers who cite this sentence give little indication of realizing how underdetermined it is; to actually use this in a particular situation, we may have to consider (for *cat*) if the cat is alive, asleep, cleaning itself, etc.; (for *mat*) if the mat is one the cat detests, really a mat or just a blanket used as one, etc.; (for *on*) if just the bottom of the cat's feet are touching, lying down, tail touching, etc.; (for place) if it is inside a house, in a wicked draft, with three mice playing alongside, etc.; (for time), if the cat is just crossing the mat, on it for only a few seconds, only one paw touching coming on or off, mat disintegrating at a rapid rate, etc.; (for medium) if in a picture or this real world that came into existence only a few seconds ago, etc.; (for etc.) if there is a significance in the rhyming words or in the relative shortness of the sentence, if God wanted this cat to be a punishment, a joke, etc. And if the answer is, "no, none of these, it's just a philosophic example," then how can and does it serve such a neutralized purpose? If we leave out all these factors, how many more should we leave unresolved before we understand the purely linguistic meaning of this sentence?

For words that are highly abstract (like *on, the, be*), it is not immediately clear what has been omitted. In fact, so much can be omitted that the words and their evoked effect in a particular sentence may seem to totally part company; we will see this more clearly later when we look at phrasal verbs.

The interpretive process that takes place in every use of language is most apparent to human awareness in those conditions where a word is shifted from one part of speech to another. An excellent study of such innovation is Clark and Clark's (1979) [CC] analysis of denominal verbs. As one example of many, in the following sentences the noun *siren* is used as a verb (all actual data):

[10] The fire stations sirened throughout the raid.

[11] The factory sirened midday and everyone stopped for lunch.

[12] The police sirened the Porsche to a stop.

[13] The police car sirened up to the accident.

[14] The police car sirened the daylights out of me.

They comment (I have changed example numbers):

> In [10] the siren's role is already indirect, since *siren* means
> 'produce a wailing sound by means of a siren'; and in [11]–[12], it
> is this sound that is critical. In [11]–[12], the sound is used as a
> signal—but the way it works in the two instances is distinctly
> different. In [11] it is a time marker, and in [12] a police warning;
> these two aspects are meant to be taken as part of the situations
> denoted. In [13], the siren's role is still less direct. To account for
> the police car doing something involving a siren up to the accident,
> one is led to the sense 'drive quickly accompanied by the sound
> produced by a siren'. The warning function of the siren here is less
> central. Example [14] is particularly interesting, for it is a syntactic
> blend of *siren* and the idiom *scare the daylights out of*. (p. 803)

CC note that an innovation must satisfy both intralinguistic and
extralinguistic context. *Siren*'s conventional category does not match the
syntactic position it occupies; it can occur there only if modulated by some
ambient condition. I propose:

[D] COHERENCE CONDITION

Given a syntactic or semantic requirement for X, some insufficiently
qualifying Y can fulfill the requirement if there obtain some pragmatic
means to modulate Y into X.

This is only part of a necessary, more general coherence condition, sketched
first by R. Lakoff (1971). She noted that a sentence such as *My grandmother
wrote me a letter yesterday and six men can fit in the back seat of a Ford*,
though it fulfills the well-formed standard of CONSISTENCY (no contradiction)
nevertheless seems odd unless there is some unifying idea that makes these
relevant to each other.[2] In general, a well-formedness standard of COHERENCE
still is compositional, and still consistent, but the composed elements are not all
(and not ever) explicitly lexicalized. Here, *siren* must be modulated to have a
form and meaning (the first easy enough in English) appropriate to the context.

The implicit ambience minimally involves the speaker, hearer, and relevant
actual situations. CC note (p. 786):

> . . . when a speaker utters such a verb, he intends his listener to
> see that the verb picks out a readily commutable and unique kind
> of state, event or process that the speaker is confident the listener
> can figure out—on the basis of the verb itself, the linguistic
> context, and other mutual knowledge.

Specifically (p. 787), they give the following:

[E] THE INNOVATIVE DENOMINAL VERB CONVENTION

In using an innovative denominal verb sincerely, the speaker means to
denote:

(a) the kind of situation
(b) that he has good reason to believe
(c) that on this occasion the listener can readily compute
(d) uniquely
(e) on the basis of their mutual knowledge
(f) in such a way that the parent noun denotes one role in the situation, and the remaining surface arguments of the denominal verb denote other roles in the situation

Extralinguistic context is especially crucial, for the glosses that CC provide (and correctly consider only approximate) cannot possibly be completely semantic, but must be inferential from the conventional meaning of the noun. It may be that 'sound' is already lexicalized in the noun; but even so, there is a metonymic shift attendant on a shift of noun to verb: in this case, a shift from the instrument (and its distinctive characteristic) to doing something with the instrument (parallel to the relationship of nominal and verbal *phone*). This shift is pragmatic; *siren* at this point is still a noun, which must be reinterpreted because it is in the position of a verb.

Thus, as is typical of innovations, the interpretation is both semantic and pragmatic; innovation necessarily goes beyond the word's inherent meaning. Eventually, after uses are more established, speakers may semanticize what is initially only inferential. This is the cutting edge of creative meaning in the language. To account for it, we must recognize that words must be open (A1); and for them to be open (or, Bartsch (1984), "tolerant"), the meanings of not only phrases, but even single words like *siren,* must be underdetermined.

CC are dealing with words that shift category with no formal change at all. Actually, even with such zero-affixation, inflectional endings (past and present tense) may give formal indications that *siren* is a verb. A derivational ending (*sirenize*) would make the category more obvious, less dependent on the context; it would, that is, preserve some redundancy. However, the meaning of *sirenize* would be just as mysterious as *siren*; it is important to know not only that it is a verb, but which kind of verb. That is the importance of CC's stipulation (f): we need to know the possible arguments and roles for the verb *siren,* so we can determine paradigmatic information. That is what CC imply in calling *siren* an instrumental verb.

Yet it makes a difference that we have the verb *siren* rather than *sirenize*; English is a language that has many zero-formations, which in effect shift information about paradigm to the context. With word order left to convey meaning that is morphological in other languages, English does less with individual words (at least, with words that are not heavily Latinate); meaning is more dispersed, from the figure to the ground. In general, that is, English reduces universally available formal redundancy (that possible in morphology) to ground rigidity (fixed word order).

CC are concerned with innovations already (but minimally) made; we can also predict possible further innovations, via PRAGMATIC GENERALIZATION. As an "instrumental" verb, *siren* can follow the path of *hammer,* as in (Green (1974: 221):

[15] He hammered the nail in with a shoe.

Like *siren, hammer* exemplifies the noun-to-verb metonymic shift from Instrument to Do-(Typical)-action-with-Instrument. But the doing need not be done with a hammer; a shoe can serve the purpose just as well. This is generalization following metonymy, as with *orange,* where the shift from fruit to color allows this color to be used generally, not just with oranges. *Hammer* has generalized even further, into abstracts (Green's examples):

[16] He hammered his point that the Russians were coming.
[17] He hammered into our heads the conviction that the Russians were
    coming.

Additional metonymies occur here: from the instrumental doing to the (typically insistent) quality of doing [16] and then to the (typically irresistible) quality of the result of doing [17].

    In parallel, it is possible through Pragmatic Generalization for *siren* to develop these possibilities:

[18] The policeman sirened me to a stop with a whistle.
[19] He sirened his point that the Russians were coming.
[20] He sirened into our heads the fear that the Russians would attack.

Here [19] and [20] represent the same sequence of metonymies (or generalizations). I have (for sake of illustration only) assumed that such extensions would emphasize 'warning' with siren (as opposed to something like 'insistence' with *hammer*); warning could be given either explicitly or implicitly, not necessarily loudly, but with an effect of totally gaining attention. Viewed as generalization, the shift would be from Doing-something-with-a-siren to Doing-the-same-sort-of-thing-as-with-a-siren: the metaphoric possibility Bolinger noted in [A1].

    With *hammer,* figuration has either already become or is becoming semantic. Although we need a larger database to make informed judgments, I would expect to find that the shift in category is established, along with the metonymic difference in meaning between verb and noun. Given the several metonymic shifts and the generalization, the full verbal meaning (some of which may be semantic, some pragmatic) may now be considerably removed from the noun, with their relationship soon to verge on homonymy. The figuration of *siren* seems still completely pragmatic; it is not yet an established verb.

    As CC stress, denominalized verbs represent a general process of word formation in English; this process is ongoing and progressive, by individual items. Not all the examples of denominalized verbs (nor all the examples of any formational process) are on a par in terms of conventionalization: *hammer* is more established than *siren,* and the meaning it conveys is thus likely to be more fully semantic, less dependent on other words or situational specifics. CC "tentatively propose six stages in this process, and illustrate each with examples from present-day English" (p. 804–805).

H. Clark (1983) pursues the point further. He considers the problems of machine parsers with respect to multiple meaning. These incorporate a "sense-selection assumption," an expectation that an ambiguous word will have a small number of distinct senses; the parser will then "select the sense the speaker must have intended." This is no small task in itself; however, there is a much greater problem (p. 298):

> The sense-selection assumption seems so natural, so obviously true, that it isn't open to dispute. Yet in the last few years, more and more evidence has been brought to the fore suggesting that it is in fact false. The problem is this. Not only can expressions be ambiguous, but they can also be *semantically indeterminate.* Many expressions, contrary to the assumption, do not possess a finite number of senses that can be listed in the parser's lexicon. Nor can they be assigned their possible senses by any rule. Each expression of this sort, instead, has only a *nonce sense,* a sense 'for the nonce', for the occasion on which it is used. It would be hard enough for traditional parsers if there were *any* such expressions, but, as I will argue, they are ubiquitous. No parser can avoid them, yet when traditional parsers meet them, they break down.

He illustrates this point with a column by Erma Bombeck, who uses *steam irons, stereos, Mr. Coffee,* and *electric typewriter* to refer to people who own these appliances; thus, in context, *stereos are a dime a dozen* doesn't mean what one would think. Yet indeterminateness may be more ubiquitous than even Clark thinks: as I tried to show, *bear* exhibits it in every use, including those established.

3.4 PRAGMATIC SPECIALIZATION

We don't need innovations of the type just illustrated to exemplify the openness of language; these are merely the innovations that are abstract enough to make a possible linguistic difference. Any use of language is innovative at some degree of relative abstraction. Those that occur while language remains constant are the subject matter of pragmatics. While words, sentences, etc. must have some quality of "repetition" to be recognized at all, each individuation is also "creative" by virtue of that individuation (though not "completely creative," as some Pythonic transformationalists overstated it). This type of openness is a necessary consequence of the fact that a language is not fully fixed in advance.

Underdetermination is always present, to some (varying) degree; any use of language involves modulation, which "alters" what the "bare language" contributes. As a general point, this "open texture" (Waisman (1951) is recognized by all linguists, but the details are too negotiable. Our understanding is tempered by pretheoretical inertia: like the notion of Simultaneity in physics, the notion of Full-Contribution-of-Language-to-Meaning is the stereotypic assumption made prior to any substantive evidence otherwise; it operates automatically in every noncritical moment.

The crucial question: how much modulation? My argument in this book requires the answer: much more than we usually think. I claim that a considerable part of alleged lexical meaning is actually supplied by other means; words are highly abstract in inherent meaning, often too much so for conscious understanding. It follows that all use of language is heavily modulated. The more diversely useful a language, the more it would have to be heavily modulated by other means to differing situations. If a species has the complex psychic capacity to develop a sufficiently rich cultural environment to provide highly complex modulations, it can have a communicational capacity that is highly abstract and remote from particulars: that is, highly underdetermining. A lesser species, with lesser endowment, would require more concrete communication, with much less underdetermining.

To develop this point, we can consider the modulations that I call Pragmatic Specialization. On individual occasions, individuals speak to individuals. The sentence *John was walking down the street* can be used to describe many different Johns, on many streets, and many occasions of walking. No one feels compelled to make lexical differences in meaning because of such differences, though we have no guarantees that we can safely ignore them. Data of use provide us access to this highly specific type of individuation.

However, there are other, more abstract specializations. With no additional context, hearers may infer that John is a male human being, likely adult, that he is awake (not sleepwalking), that he is walking at a normal rate (at which no one else takes notice), on a street in a real city, during the daytime. These assumptions are like those we made (in Chapter One) for *The thief took the jewels:* with no contrary evidence, we tend to assume a particular general set of circumstances. The reasons for this assuming are largely unconscious.

Negative assuming also occurs: John isn't leading an elephant nor carrying a hundred-pound weight, is not in a movie or a picture, and is not an arsonist looking for new targets. As interpreters, we (unconsciously) assume that if any of these possibilities were real, the speaker would be duty bound to state them.

Should *walk* have several meanings, one for sleepwalking? Should *down* have both horizontal and vertical senses? Is the presumption of "normal" walking part of the meaning of *walk*? Our answers depend on our theoretical assumptions and applications; and these depend on more tacit pretheoretical assumptions.

In CTG, the methodological exaggeration of (simplified) ambiguity and (simplified) paraphrase tended to affirm and even increase the polysemy of dictionaries. (Linguists were, in effect, commanded to find more and more examples of ambiguity and paraphrase.) If the goal of semantic analysis alone is to account for all situations in which two sentences mean the same, or one sentence has several meanings, then the inevitable result is that the syntagmatic will be excessively favored over the paradigmatic, unity of lexical meaning will be undervalued, and identity of meaning between words will be overvalued. In short, if too much meaning is viewed as semantic, there is no theoretical alternative to rampant polysemy.

One prevalent mistake is to attribute semantic status to what is habitually present in a particular context. In *The thief took the jewels,* the verb *take* can be pragmatically specialized as 'steal'; it may be almost automatic for *take* in this individual sentence. That is likely the reason dictionaries give 'steal' as one of *take*'s meanings. However, the uniformity need not have a lexical cause: the meaning comes not only from *take,* but *take*-in-this-context; it is the context that (quite heavily) suggests the specific taking that we call stealing. A word's semantics should concern what it contributes in all contexts.

Pragmatic specialization can be even more subtle. A good illustration of the degree to which we modulate (but don't realize it) is provided by Ziff (1972). He is exploring, as I am, how we understand what is said (pp. 127–33):

> I have in mind certain careless cases: in them communication
> proceeds succeeds readily easily: no one notices anything out of the
> ordinary, for nothing is, and no one seems to wonder. A case: a
> cheetah is a fast feline; such is the common conception, mine too;
> cheetahs have been clocked at eighty miles an hour; one says then
> 'A cheetah can outrun a man'. And is one apt to be understood? Of
> course! But how and why are hard to say or even see.

These are some of the difficulties:

> We put it to the test: a man and cheetah are turned loose in a field.
> The man lopes away while the cheetah sits lazily in the sun. But
> 'can' is not 'will'. The cheetah can even if it did not. We try
> again. This time we force the cheetah to run by beating it; but the
> man easily outruns the cheetah: the cat encumbered with an
> awkward two-hundred-pound weight moves sluggishly.
>   An encumbered cheetah is a cheetah. And I said a cheetah can
> outrun a man. Should I have said not that a cheetah can but, more
> cautiously, that some cheetahs can outrun a man, namely
> unencumbered cheetahs? But what about an unencumbered cheetah
> whose feet have been bound since birth? If we make provision for
> foot-bound unencumbered cheetahs shall we not also have to
> provide a place for three-legged cheetahs, drugged cheetahs,
> cheetahs forced to run after being force fed and so on and so on?

Further:

> These cheetah cases are not curious special or rare. Similar
> problems are encountered when one considers and ponders such
> comments as 'A tiger is a large carnivore': isn't a new-born tiger a

tiger and yet hardly a large carnivore? 'Skim milk is a healthful
food': isn't skim milk liberally laced with strychnine nonetheless
skim milk and hardly healthful? 'This car gets thirty-five miles to
the gallon': what about the leak in the fuel line?

In each of these cases a difficulty lies lurking in an absence of
specifications. One says 'A cheetah' and no further specification of
what one is speaking of is given; one says simply 'A tiger', 'Skim
milk', 'This car'. And as comments could occasion confusion, so
could commands and queries. There is, indeed, no lack of a variety
of cases exemplifying an evident absence of specifications, cases in
which, though a possible understanding lies lurking,
communication usually proceeds smoothly and easily and free of
difficulty.

The difficulties arise because Ziff deliberately involves REFERENTIAL
complications in the determination of sentence meaning; these complications are
always present, even when linguists are citing sentences "in isolation." That is,
Ziff addresses the problem of meaning under the same conditions that
semanticists usually do when they ponder the meaning of words like *tiger* and
chair, except he is facing the consequences of this more fully. The possibility
looms that we will not be able to explain the meanings of words until we
account fully for reality (as Bloomfield thought). Yet, as Ziff notes,
communication does not seem that difficult. What faulty assumptions create this
apparent paradox?

It could be objected that Ziff has forgotten his beginning comment: the
clocking of cheetahs at eighty miles an hour. This could serve as an "objective"
measurement and thus head off the impending possibility of an infinite number
of qualifications. But this test is similarly vague: was the tested cheetah
encumbered or not? How hungry was it? How old was it? Possibly very old and
infirm? Were all four of its legs in prime condition or did it have a slight limp
in one? Does it matter which leg? Appealing to an "objective" test merely
redirects Ziff's problematics to the test itself.

It could also be objected that Ziff's examples are all generic. But even if
that provided a solution (and it doesn't), I noted the same phenomenon earlier
with the sentence *John is walking down the street.* Is John adult or child?
Human or not? Awake or sleepwalking? On the sidewalk or in the street? One
leg partly paralyzed? And so on.

We might enumerate all the complicating conditions:

> Is it simply that further specifications are in fact implicit in the
> discourse? But can't what is implicit in the discourse be made
> explicit? Yet when one attempts to detail, to enumerate some set of
> specifications that would serve to safeguard the truth of a remark
> like 'A cheetah can outrun a man', the task seems impossible. It is
> not merely that such a set of specifications would have to have
> indefinitely many and anyway prodigiously many members but its

membership would have to be remarkably heterogeneous. If there
were any such set it seems that its vastness and heterogeneity
would preclude the possibility of an effective specification of
membership. (p. 131)

Ziff also bars another possible escape (one I used cautiously with pragmatic
rules for *bear*): the appeal to typicality or normality:

> The comment 'A normal cheetah can under normal conditions
> outrun a normal man' is merely obscure. Cheetahs don't ordinarily
> typically commonly or even normally race against men or for that
> matter against anything. They do chase after and catch antelopes.
> What are the normal conditions under which a normal cheetah can
> outrun a normal man? Is the terrain to be rough or smooth? Say it
> doesn't matter, that either rough or smooth is to count as normal.
> Then what if the lay of the land is such that it is slow rough
> broken uneven under the cheetah's feet, fast flat and easy beneath
> the man's feet? Are these to count as normal conditions? An appeal
> to normality is bound to be futile when it consists of nothing more
> than the invocation of a label. An appeal to normality would
> appear to be irrelevant in connection with the comment 'This car
> gets thirty-five miles to the gallon'. The vehicle in question might
> be used for commuting from Long Island to New York and thus
> typically operated in traffic jams. The relevant specification in this
> sort of case would require an appeal to optimum operating
> conditions and to some sort of ideal road conditions under which
> the vehicle is envisaged as being operated.

But these "ideal road tests" are notoriously difficult to specify fully, for the
same reasons. Should it be raining or not? Should the temperature be high or
low? What altitude should the tests be run at? How new should the car be? Are
all "new cars" (in some definitive terms) equally new? And so on. (Another
example: tests for the operating speed of computer printers calculate speed in
mid-line, not allowing for time lost in change of direction, change of page, etc.)

We can also note a point that Ziff omits: the cheetah does not have long-
range staying power. Given a sufficiently long course (a mile or two), a man
can outrun a cheetah; the "eighty miles an hour" obscures the fact that the
cheetah's speed comes at the expense of stamina. (Of course, this possibility
suggests a long race; most readers probably modulated Ziff's sentence
specifically as a sprint or chase.)

The problem in brief: (a) the Ziff sentences (and all sentences) need to be
modulated by additional details to be properly understood, yet (b) the necessary
qualifications cannot be exhaustively specified. The unconscious mind provides
a matrix of preclusions and expectations that we cannot fully assess; in trying to
assess them, the potentially infinite conscious mind, applying the sentence to
infinite realities, can find infinite complications. Moreover, (c) though it is
obvious that some meanings of the sentences are supplied by "understood"

qualifications, (d) it is not apparent which aspects of the meaning are "understood" and which are supplied lexically. Must the cheetah be alive, in good health, and adult? Obviously yes, but are these conditions part of the meaning of *cheetah*? How should the relevant adult-nonadult distinction be accounted for?

Also, we assume contexts where it is possible for the cheetah to run (not four feet of water or outer space). If possible-cheetah-running-places are specified in *outrun,* then it may be polysemic: different running creatures may require different running places. Many such questions await the linguist who is foolish enough to be consistent.

Ziff's sentence is a generalization of experience. But then, to varying degrees, so is every sentence. Also, Ziff's sentence is a specialization of experience, and so in varying degrees is every sentence. We can use any sentence in many different contexts, relying on pragmatic modulations to make both specific and general adjustments. This is common sense to all linguists. The problem, simply: in each particular sentence, what is supplied by words and what is supplied by other means? How can we determine the contribution of the words?

If we take Ziff's comments seriously, recognizing the lesser contribution of words, we discover a startling thing about *A cheetah can outrun a man*: it is the best answer to Maher's criticism of IDEAL. This sentence, and any sentence, idealizes to a considerable degree, providing a highly abstract "core" for many applicational modulations; this core can evoke many details but provides only a few. Of course, the core of any lexical item is much more specific than the core of a language; if the former is much more abstract than we thought, what then follows for IDEAL? Even the core of a more concrete word may be so abstract that it mystifies the conscious mind: necessarily so, if language is to provide its manifold resources.

Unfortunately, those who assume IDEAL have undermined its reality by adopting uncritically the traditional conclusions of polysemy. To make the words and sentence alone approximate more closely to the full intended message of *A cheetah can outrun a man* (both "information" and possible implied advice), we must make a number of words polysemic. Yet what are we assuming about human lexical ability, and language ability in general, if we draw our modular lines in accord with polysemic solutions? To make the multiple-meaning solution work at all, many details (if not runnable-places, then something else) must be ignored.

What, then, can a semantic analysis do? For determining intralinguistic meaning, I have already supplied a standard and method: comprehensiveness, a word's range in all its contexts; and the monosemic bias, the working expectation that a word has a single meaning, no matter how elusive (both initially and eventually) that single meaning might seem to be.

3.5 PRAGMATIC GENERALIZATION

Modulations are concretions; they take abstract meanings and specify, in many particular ways. If so, Pragmatic Specialization would appear to be the exclusive means, since the result is a specification. However, if a word is unspecified for either a specific or a general application, then Pragmatic Generalization would operate in a parallel fashion, though with an opposite result.

We can see this with Ziff's *cheetah* example, which has the force of a generic. As I have argued, words like *bear* are unspecified for concrete-abstract. Similarly, all words (even proper names) are unspecified for specific-general, token-type. *Cheetah* by itself means neither a particular cheetah (neither "actual" nor hypothetical), nor the species; these alternatives are all modulations (and similarly, *a cheetah* and *the cheetah*).

To establish this point, we can note first some sentences that are almost always modulated by Pragmatic Generalization. Proverbs are typical examples, and as such they create more difficulties for theories too strictly compositional and semantic. Makkai cites (1972: 176) *Don't count your chickens before they're hatched* as an idiom, because the words do not compose semantically to his presumed gloss: 'Do not celebrate in advance the anticipated favorable outcome of an undertaking or planned activity lest it misfire thus causing unnecessary disappointment and embarrassment'. However, this gloss makes the meaning of the proverb too sharply precise. We can get a better result by two steps: first, Pragmatic Generalization suggests a type-interpretation: 'Do not do the same thing that someone does in counting chickens before they're hatched'. Then further modulations specify "same thing" from individually variant knowledge of the world. (In contrast, a proverb like *out of sight, out of mind* is usually modulated by specialization.)

Another example of a phrase necessarily generalized is *he has his mother's eyes,* with the force 'her type of eyes'. Thus, Pragmatic Generalization is not limited only to expressions that have some "special" status, like proverbs.

Now consider the ongoing discussion in TG about the generic sense exhibited by such sentences as *The beaver builds dams, A beaver builds dams, Beavers build dams,* or *Man rules the earth.* Although this variation is sometimes taken as semantic, it has the earmarks of being pragmatic. Consider some other examples.

[21] Beavers in North America build dams.

[22] Beavers on my river build dams.

[23] Beavers in North America build the most intricate dams.

[24] Beavers in North America are industrious creatures.

With many such data, I think the "genericity" of a sentence will vary directly not with discrete and finite semantic properties, but gradiently and infinitely with perceived standards of what is considered a worldly-knowledge characterization of beavers and with the possibility that the sentence can be used to characterize. Characterizing is not only absolute or universal; relatively, even [22] can have a type-interpretation.

"Characterizing" is highly complex. Lawler (1972) considers the sentence *Garth drinks coffee*. (I am conflating his points in one of his examples to focus their collective force.) This sentence varies in meaning; what it describes can happen always (like the sun coming up in the morning) or occasionally (like a dog chasing cars). It can describe Garth's occupation. It can (varying by superordinate) describe the only thing he drinks or (variously) more. It can (varying by hyponym) describe one kind of coffee or (variously) more.

Dahl (1975) offers additional variations (I'm still using one sentence): it describes what has actually happened in the past, or what might possibly happen. It describes either an accidental characteristic of Garth or an essential one. It is a SUBSTANTIVE RULE about Garth, or a REGULATIVE RULE: either what he can't help doing or what he chooses to do. It might even describe, with no actual past events, what he might do (he is the type who . . .; he acts such that . . .). Obviously, for this sentence, some of these are more likely than others. Why?

Considering that these articles were written before any significant developments in pragmatics, these are impressive explorations, especially Lawler's. By theoretical demand, he assumes that all meaning is semantic; accordingly, he tries to reduce the complexity to expected finite proportions, proposing binary existential-universal distinctions. Yet, as he discusses sentence after sentence, he observes in disbelief that the most likely readings for different sentences vary in a seemingly random way; and there are more than two possible options.

Dahl, writing later, sees the two-value bind, but not the wholly-semantic bind, as this quote illustrates (my numbering):

> . . . the possibilities of interpreting an indefinite noun phrase as generic or non-generic often depend on the generic or non-generic character of the verb of the sentence. Consider, for example:
>
> **[25]** A dog is barking.
> **[26]** A dog barks.
>
> There is hardly any doubt that the natural interpretation of *a dog* is non-generic in [25] and generic in [26]. The restriction is clearly semantic. (p. 108)

However, the first can be generic (*A dog is barking at this moment in many places all over the world*) and the second can be specific (*at that moment, a dog barks*). Dahl is correct about what is "natural." Yet what makes it so?

Earlier (p. 107), Dahl says "the choice of a simple rather than a progressive tense necessitates a generic reading." This is standard textbook advice, and relatively sound (considering the practical purpose); but "necessitates" is too strong, as I have just demonstrated. Actually, all variants of the English auxiliary system can be both general and specific (the reader can work it out). What makes [25] and [26] pattern in a certain "natural" way are unacknowledged pragmatic modulations of unity and time, taken as the only possible modulations.

Modulation of Unity: consider *Garth was sleeping* and *Garth was hitting the table;* as often observed, the English progressive in the first seems stative (singular, one sleep), and in the second repetitive (plural hit). What about *Garth was knocking on the door:* one knock or more? *Knock on the door* can be stative (a unified process involves more than one knock), or repetitive (separate knocks); similarly for a dog's barking.

Modulation of Time: what does *now* mean? An instant, an hour, a day, a week, etc.? In geology, "now" is 11,000 years; in mathematics (*two plus two is four*) or religion (*God is love*), it is forever. Similarly, *here* (within a foot, a mile, a house, a neighborhood, a country, a planet) and *this (this time/place, these days/parts)*; semantically, these words have indeterminate range.

Yet, they have "natural" pragmatic specializations: with no contrary context, *now* is instantaneous, a "point" between the "lines" of past and future. Similarly with implicit 'now', especially in the simple present, but just as much with any time: a 'now' is always involved.

This specialization provides the "natural" interpretation. Once we see this, the sentences above become more variable. Sleeping can be repetitive, plural: *the years of insomnia were over; John was sleeping*. Rapid hitting is a process; in slow motion, hitting the table once takes quite a while. What if Garth through the night woke every ten minutes and went right back to sleep; does this count as one sleep or more? Stage directions: *a dog barks*.

All these possibilities are, admittedly, less "natural." But they are semantically possible. The pragmatic modulation of 'now' creates the singular or multiple naturalnesses. Similar pragmatic factors can be found in Lawler's and Dahl's other sentences as well.

Nunberg (1984) discusses some interesting variations in specific and generic in the following examples:

[27] Enzo drives *the same car* that I used to drive.

[28] Enzo drives *the car* that I used to drive.

[29] *Which car* is Enzo driving?

[30] Buick has come out with *the same car* that Toyota introduced last year.

[31] Otto has been reading *the (same) book* that he voted to ban in South Dakota a year ago.

The underlined phrases, Nunberg observes, are interpretable modularly as types. In [27–30], the car can be a specific car or a type, the latter if Enzo and I both drive 1983 Buicks or (more generally) Buicks. Even more generally, we can both drive cars with a similar or identical design. As [27] shows, the word *same* permits both interpretations (or rather, an infinite number of interpretations, since "sameness" is highly negotiable). *The* and *a* also allow the variation (*a* can occur in [28]).

In [31], the variation is between the book as type and the book as specific copy, the versions being chosen in accord with reality-adjusted modulation: it would be pointless to ban just one copy; and one reads a copy, not a type. Of course, Otto may use more than one copy to read "the" book, and in *People have been reading the book* we can have one copy or multiples; any modulations need not resolve this choice.

My argument implies that a sentence already modulated can be modulated again, even if the second cancels the first. Nunberg's sentences are modulated general or specific as circumstances suggest, but his examples, as we read them, are also modulated for generic isolation. Such multiple modulation can neutralize intervening effects. Nunberg's data have been so long overlooked because, in a modulation of "isolation," they do not self-evidently suggest a type interpretation; in actual discourse this possibility is more noticeable.[3]

The variant interpretations possible in these sentences are heavily dependent on the specific circumstances that they evoke. Put simply, they are not the reflexes of finite semantic options, but of infinite pragmatic possibilities. The reason a semantic interpretation sometimes seems successful is that the relevant data have been oversimplified.

Genericity and specificity are ends of a negotiable continuum. We use all the information relevant to a sentence and its context to decide which degree of specificity-genericity is appropriate for an interpretation. We do this not only for specific utterances (and specific written sentences), but also for the hanging-in-mid-air intuitional data that appear in linguistic articles. When I use *the thief took the jewels* in this book to illustrate a point, I do it with the expectation that my readers will not wonder which thief, which jewels, and which taking, but will see it as a "type", "independent" of any particular use. It is often thought that a sentence is thus presented in some "purely linguistic state"; yet for a sentence to meet a particular purpose in a particular context it must have a modulation appropriate to the desired interpretation. A sentence posing as "contextless" can do so only in a society, like ours, that has so highly abstracted educational institutions and training from immediate experience.

We thus have a new insight into supposedly "purely formal" logical validity. We are cautioned in logic books against the mistake of reasoning *Nothing is higher than Everest, anything is higher than nothing, and thus anything is higher than Everest;* we have changed meanings for *nothing.* But this is not just an occasional problem, turning on the accident of an ambiguous word; rather, the problem is ubiquitous and ineradicable. Consider, in the light of previous discussion, *All men drink coffee, Garth is a man, and thus Garth drinks coffee.* The validity of this is always dependent on a pragmatic modulation that provides coherent meanings for all the linguistic elements involved. (This even applies to *All A is B,* etc.) Such a modulation may be so "natural" and automatic that we forget about it, but it is nevertheless still operative.

With the foregoing discussion as a basis, I propose:

[F] OPENNESS CONDITION

Within a multidimensional mandatory context (lack of context is impossible), the inherent sense of a word or expression is always modulated pragmatically.

Openness is linked to MANDATORY CONTEXT; we will see the full implications of this in subsequent discussion.[4]

This condition defines (though minimally thus far) a more inclusive idealization, including extralinguistic dimensions, which I will call OPEN. As my remarks have indicated, I assume that OPEN has IDEAL as a "core" module. My goal: to show that OPEN is necessary for dictionary definitions, but that a more restrictive modularization of IDEAL is the optimal locus for defining those lexically inherent aspects of meaning that we call semantic.

Chapter 4

THE VERB *HIT*

Continuing to alternate chapters of general theory with analysis of particular words, I now turn to the verb *hit,* particularly as it occurs in some alleged idiomatic phrases. This verb exemplifies the points of the previous chapter, plus several related subjects: indirection; the status of "set phrases"; tacitly assumed "normal states"; and stereotyping.

4.1 INDIRECTION

If modulation is present in all language use, then to some degree in every application there is some degree of indirection: what is communicated is not solely what the words mean. The question in each use (however generally we conceive of "use") is how much? Given our propensity for oversemanticizing, some indirections in the last chapter were hardly noticeable, except for the proverbs. Recent research in Speech Act theory has discussed more obvious examples: how a promise can be made without an explicit indication of promising, and how a request can be made indirectly in "polite" imperatives. In addition, Grice (1975, 1978) has shown how, given a presumption of cooperation (or mutually understood enterprise), we can convey implicit information, quite removed from words uttered, by violating normative rules of appropriateness, adequacy, and relevance. Also, of course, an effect of indirection is present in figurative uses of language: metaphor, metonymy, synecdoche, irony, hyperbole and litotes, especially.

As a prelude to *hit*, I want to discuss the figure most indicative of indirection: METONYMY. While this can be a broad cover term for all the Speech Act and Gricean examples, I consider it here very narrowly, limited to words and phrases.

An often-cited example of metonymy is the noun *tongue*, which designates not only a human organ but also a human capacity in which that organ plays a conspicuous part. Another noted example is the change of *orange* from the name of a fruit to the color of that fruit. Since *orange* refers to all instances of the color, this change also includes generalization. A third example (Bolinger (1971a)) is the verb *want*, which once meant 'lack' and changed to the contiguous sense of 'desire'. In these examples both senses still survive; with *win*, 'desire' and 'strive' have been either supplanted by the goal of desiring and striving or marginalized (*winsome*).

Such examples are established; where several meanings survive, we have SEMANTIC METONYMY: the meanings are related and also independent of each other. *Orange* is a polysemic word, its two distinct and nondependent meanings metonymically related.

Metonymy is also a rhetorical and literary figure, where a nonce reference is made indirectly through something contiguous to the specified referent; a favorite example is *knives* to refer to 'warriors'. Even when used repeatedly, the contiguous meaning need not become established. The 'warrior' sense is dependent on (and partly predictable from) the first sense, so this is PRAGMATIC METONYMY. Adopting Richard's (1936: 96–97) terminology for metaphor, and applying it in parallel fashion, we can call 'warriors' the tenor of the metonym and *knives* the vehicle. Corbett (1971: 479–480) cites (his glosses) *crown* 'royalty', *wealth* 'rich people', *brass* 'military officers', *bottle* 'wine', and *pen* 'writer'.

Closely related are examples of SYNECDOCHE, the substitution of Part for Whole or vice versa; Corbett notes *silver* 'money', *steel* 'sword', *roofs* 'houses', and *hands* 'helpers'. I will follow the path of those scholars who consider synecdoche as a variant of metonymy, although synecdoche can alternatively be seen as a protofigure of both metaphor and metonymy. Corbett also cites these (pp. 481–482):

[1] In Europe, we gave *the cold shoulder* to DeGaulle, and now he gives *the warm hand* to Mao Tse-tung. (Richard Nixon)

[2] You can't read the history of the United States, my friends, without learning the great story of those thousands of unnamed women. And if it's ever told straight, you'll know it's the *sunbonnet* and not the *sombrero* that has settled the country. (Edna Ferber)

[3] *Capital* has learned to sit down and talk with *labor*. (George Meany)

In [1], we have as tenors 'rebuff' and 'welcome', in [2] 'women' and 'men', and in [3] 'managers' and 'workers'. Although (I would say) all of these are pragmatic meanings, not semantic, some such as [3] are given separate dictionary definitions. Dictionaries are more likely to list *cold shoulder* than *warm hand* [1].

Some other examples:

[4] You can even see *a bitter cup of coffee* on a man's face. (coffee ad)

[5] The road from Beverly to Salem is unusually busy this morning, and he [Rev. Hale] has passed a hundred rumors that make him smile at the ignorance of the yeomanry in this most precise science (study of witchcraft]. (Arthur Miller)

[6] I took *her poem* out of my pocket. . . . (Aldous Huxley)

[7] What will we do between now and *tea*? (John Cheever)

[8] Suddenly *the whole room* broke into a sea of shouting. (Langston Hughes)

[9] When *the dead man* got up and left, the other man followed him out. (*Columbo*)

[10] . . . if he was ever going to break *the four-minute mile* he had to stay in shape. (William Goldman)

[11] *His second shot* was batted out of bounds by Barry in a scuffle for the rebound. (David Dupree)

The metonyms in each example create apparent incongruity: not the coffee, but the man's reaction to it [4]; not the rumors, but the people who relate the rumors [5]; not the poem but the paper on which it is written [6]; not the tea but the time for drinking it [7]; not the room but the people in the room [8]; not the man who was dead *then* but who is dead *now* [9]; not the four-minute mile but the barrier it presents [10]. The last example [11] has a double metonymy: it is not on the shot itself but the rebound of the shot when the action occurs; and it is the ball and not the rebound that is batted out of bounds.

Metonymy is a useful device for saying something concisely when precision of reference is not necessary; the concise form has a more dramatic, less wordy effect, and the incongruities may not be immediately apparent, not even [9]. However, they would certainly become so for a linguist trying to account for each sentence's meanings. Since the above are not (fully) established patterns, they can be interpreted as nonce, and thus pragmatic. Anyone working in IDEAL could rightly ignore them, if only by default (as slang is ignored). But next we come to sentences more likely to seem established (such as *answer the door* and *Hanoi* in Chapter 3), where the uses cannot be considered nonce. First, more of Borkin's (1972) examples:

[12] I'm [= my car] parked at the corner.

[13] Sam [= Sam's body] weighs 250 pounds.

[14] Chomsky [= Chomsky's writings] is too complicated for freshmen to read.

[15] Turn up the hi-fi [= volume of the hi-fi].

[16] IBM [= its stock] is overpriced.

These exemplify the metonymic type Possessor for Possessed. As Borkin notes (p. 42), *IBM* "can refer to an organization, a building, IBM stock or the price of it, various factions of the people on the IBM payroll, and conceivably even a bowling team. . . ." It's even more open than that: a hotel room or dining table reserved for an IBM executive, a TV advertisement, a claimed "spirit of the age"—conceivably, anything that can be "connected" in some way with that company; "possession" must be taken rather broadly. Some further examples:

[17] . . . Gatsby informed Cody that a wind might catch him and break him [= his boat] up in half an hour. (F. Scott Fitzgerald)

[18] Mary got up and turned around so that Ma could unbutton her [= her dress]. (Laura Ingalls Wilder)

[19] It was an hour before the first shark hit him [= the marlin attached to his skiff]. (Ernest Hemingway)

[20] Vilas needed only 29 minutes to take the second set, breaking Nastase [= his tennis serve] in the third and fifth games. . . . (AP)

Some other examples, [21] and [22] from Borkin, [24] and [25] from Gleason (1972: 118), and [26] and [27] from Bolinger (1975: 204):

[21] The whole apartment house [= the people living in it] came down with hepatitis.

[22] This can [= contents of can] is contaminated.

[23] The day [= the events of the day, specifically a poor round of golf and a loss] took nothing away from 65 tournament victories, including nine major championships [= the personal record of 65. . .]. (Denne H. Freeman)

[24] Martha is peeling some potato salad [= potatoes].

[25] Jane is squeezing some lemonade [= lemons].

[26] Turn the cereal [= heat under the cereal] off.

[27] The statue of limitations has expired on that bill.

For the last, Bolinger says it is not the statute that has expired but "the period of time during which according to the statute of limitations the bill was legally collectable." Examples [21–24] illustrate the metonymic pattern Container for Contained. Reddy (1977) argues that much of our "language about language" is in terms of a "conduit metaphor" (actually, both metaphor and metonymy) which assumes language to be a formal container that has meaning as contents.

Warburton and Prabhu (1972: 36–41) present similar examples:

[28] After John had undergone a sex-change *he* became a nun.

[29] John tore the document to pieces and threw *it* into the fire.

[30] When a baby grows up, *it* becomes the mayor of the city.

[31] When a single cell has multiplied into millions, *it* becomes visible as a small lump.

[32] John dreamt that he was a woman and that *he* gave birth to twins.

In each of these, there is a rhetorical need to maintain a vehicle (or its pronominal substitute) as a topic, while the tenor undergoes a change that makes the vehicle inappropriate. It is possible to choose a vehicle that transcends the change, or to change to a new vehicle, but these options can lead to abstractness, wordiness, or disunity; the metonym solves the problem. To be concise and dramatic, or to maintain rhetorical unity—for these practical reasons, which need never be considered in IDEAL—pragmatic metonymy must occur in actual use.

The clipping of *kick the bucket* to *kick* is an example of SYNTACTIC METONYMY. Elliptical processes have been exemplified in transformational deletions, as in *one* implying 'one book' in the sentence *John bought two books and I bought one.* For linguists limited to IDEAL, syntactic metonymy is an alternative explanation, instead of polysemy or idioms; it was Borkin's solution. But Green (1969) considering the two possible IDEAL interpretations for [33] and [34], rejected the syntactic solution (deletion) for a semantic solution that makes *refuse* polysemic:

[33] He refused (to grant) my request.

[34] He refused (to accept) my offer.

Mutably, as we should expect, there is a continuum from syntactic metonymy to semantic metonymy, the first becoming the second in *private (soldier),* and borderline cases in *They're engaged (to be married), He was committed (to the hospital), He proposed (marriage), She's expecting (a baby),* and *I'll ask him on cross (= examination).*

Not all of these examples can be considered nonce or marginal. Whatever their status, they present a genuine problem, because a solution must acknowledge the indirect connection of form and meaning. This cannot be done in IDEAL; the options there all involve polysemy. The best recourse for IDEAL is to ignore the problem; the correct solution requires, in part, pragmatic information, and this by design is not part of IDEAL.

It is important to understand why this must be so. CTG assumed (in the positing of well-definedness) that linguistic knowledge is self-contained, internally complete and consistent, separate and independent of wordly knowledge. This strong systematicity implies two crucial notions: COMPOSITION and DIRECTNESS. If the meaning of a sentence derives compositionally from the sum of its syntactically ordered parts, and if all referential words refer directly and precisely to what they denote, then (possibly, though not necessarily) the sentence can be explained completely in semantic terms.

In other words, in IDEAL there is no need for the Richards distinction of tenor and vehicle, because these are always the same. If, however, sentences mean something different from the structured sum of their parts, referring indirectly either in part or whole, then we have evidence that natural languages do not exemplify IDEAL totally; as soon as the distinction between tenor and vehicle is significant, the system is no longer fully consistent, and we get collocational absurdities.

Does this reasoning invalidate IDEAL? Since I once thought so, I would like to dwell on this question awhile, if only for my own clarification. As I noted in Chapter 1, there are two basic considerations:

(a) Does IDEAL (plus an associated cline of progressively more inclusive idealizations) enable us most effectively to describe what we want to describe—whether or not that "what" corresponds in any significant way to the description?

(b) Does IDEAL in fact correspond to "what"? To say "yes" requires a large act of faith, since we still know little about the "what" side of the correspondence.

Though many linguists are happy with the "descriptive-convenience" justification of (a), Chomsky claims (b). I agree, with a more "realistic" condition: I suggest that a more specific form of IDEAL includes both innate and unconscious order, the latter less universal. By "unconscious," I refer to a mental capacity that defines primary categories and processes that enable the secondary categories and processes of consciousness. I assume that the order of the unconscious is often difficult for consciousness to understand. The unconscious is extremely abstract and strongly systematic; that is why IDEAL is well-defined in terms of Compositionality and Directness. However, Directness provides only the capacity for direct reference. Actual references (and the ill-definition that accompanies them) are not a concern of the unconscious at all; it is the function of the conscious mind to refer, and generally relate language to reality. One heuristic for noting this (a very useful general heuristic in the human sciences) is in the "breaking" of systematic relationships in some references: that is, in the conscious pragmatic operations of indirection.

The IDEAL properties of Compositionity and Directness are thus not merely descriptive conveniences. They are unconscious competences, which are (more often than not) overridden in various ways by conscious pragmatic means. The problem of lexical analysis (and definition), however, concerns the relative scope and effect of all means, not only (though including) Compositionality and Directness.

This perspective captures the truth of both sides in the Chomsky-Hockett disagreement over whether language is a well-defined system (Hockett (1968)). Hockett describes chess as well-defined and baseball as ill-defined because the first need not be referential (that is, complicated by relationship with external reality) while the second must be. Obviously, as Hockett saw, language-in-the-whole is not well-defined. The potential of consciousness is to be ill-defined, extralinguistic (extensional), open, atomistic, short-circuiting, overriding, undermining and inconsistent. However, to agree also with Chomsky, it is the inherent nature of unconsciousness to be well-defined, to be an intralinguistic (intensional), strong, automatic, closed system of fundamental options.[1]

4.2 SET PHRASES

We can now turn to *hit*. Again, there is no necessary or generally optimal place to start the analysis. I usually begin with another linguist's claim and weave my way from there. With *bear*, I took off from Bolinger's doubt that it had a general meaning, which sent me to the OED, which commented about opposed meanings in *bear up under* and *bear down on*. Here, I begin with alleged idiomatic phrases with *hit*. These were discussed by S. Robert Greenberg at an Annual Meeting of the Linguistic Society of America in an insightful paper (1966) which unfortunately was never published. I proceed with the two basic ingredients: the Monosemic Bias and many data.

There are many set phrases in English judged by linguists to be idiomatic, including *hit the road, hit the sack* and *hit the books*. I claim this is not their linguistic status, but rather another reflection of inadequate theory. Even if these are set phrases (which I need not question), they do not require that *hit* have meanings unique to these expressions.

Greenberg took these phrases as idioms and gave the usual justifications:

(a) *Hit* in these phrases does not have the basic sense of 'strike' or 'collide with'.

(b) The phrase *hit the sack* is ambiguous between a literal sense of physical contact and a metaphorical sense of 'go to bed with the intention of sleeping' or 'lie down to sleep'.

(c) Compositionality is violated; even if *sack* means 'bed', the phrase does not include the goal of sleeping.

(d) The phrases are syntactically frozen: if we make small variations, such as *hit the sacks, hit a sack, the sack was hit,* and *the hitting of the sack,* we get only a literal sense.

However, Greenberg felt that these phrases exhibit a degree of regularity. First, they follow a similar syntactic pattern. Second, and crucially, that pattern is productive. He noted that

> if your family were at the beach, and your teen-aged son said, "Let's *hit the surf,*" you would know what he meant. Again, if someone were telling you about the fall into decadence of a friend, and said, "Yes, first of all it was liquor, then pot, and then he began *hitting the needle,*" you would know that he was referring to injecting a drug such as heroin into his veins. You would be able to interpret this idiom on the basis of a very clear analogy with *hit the bottle,* just as your interpretation of *hit the surf* would be aided by your previous knowledge of *hit the road.*

To capture this degree of regularity, Greenberg proposed that the *hit*-phrases be considered a FAMILY OF IDIOMS. He suggested that any short word such as *hit*, referring to a simple action or object, and easily used in metaphorical extensions, could be considered "idiom-prone," capable of extensions of the same form that are also idioms.

Except for the claim of idiomaticity, I think Greenberg's observations are correct. But while he was on the right track, we need to go farther. Consistent with previous discussion, I argue as follows:

(a) The sense of 'strike' is not basic; that impression is a stereotype.
(b) The various apparent senses of *hit* are not extensions of a basic sense, but manifest a complete generalization of sense.
(c) Variation of meaning is not created by discrete semantic options, but is the result of contextually appropriate inference, which is a pragmatic continuum.
(d) Thus, *hit* has only one general meaning, and these phrases are not idioms.

Greenberg had the crucial insight: productivity. This in turn implies generality, which means nonidiomaticity. However, he seemed to consider productivity an occasional thing; rather, it is pervasive. He was unable to see this partly because he considered only a few phrases, an inadequate database. But, more crucially, he accepted and overextended IDEAL, which requires literal senses, compositionality, direct reference, and syntactic freedom. According to this standard, in regular (nonidiomatic) language, there can be no hyperbole, irony, metonymy or metaphor, nothing communicated by hint, omission or implication, and no set phrases, cliches, slogans, proverbs, etc. All of these are simply dismissed as exceptional. As Greenberg notes, his phrases are typical of informal register. The exclusionary requirements of IDEAL (as usually conceived) are best correlated with formal register, the register in which meaning more readily APPEARS to be solely linguistic.

The IDEAL standard of compositionality is inappropriate, and thus distortive, for many expressions whose perceived meanings come not only from the combined meanings of the words themselves, but from what those meanings and their possible referents suggest. That is, we must use Pragmatic Metonymy:

[35] I'm in a bar now near Columbus, Ohio, pausing before hitting the road again. (Bennett Kremen)
[36] More and more students are hitting the road instead of the books. *(Time)*
[37] ". . . I think the best thing for you to do is turn left, go through Titusville, and then hit the highway." (Carolyn Keene)
[38] "Latch, it'll be sooner if you hit the trail with that Leighton and his outfit," declared Carson bluntly. (Zane Grey)
[39] The President has been hitting the campaign trail again. . . . (Paul Duke)

[40] "The hounds hit a trail and went barking off on it." (Jim Kjelgaard)

[41] Ford Campaign Hits Rails . . . (headline, *Virginian-Pilot*)

[42] "Let's hit the grit, pardner." Quickly they mounted and crossed the little valley. (W. C. Tuttle)

[43] Finally I saw Levy come out and get into his car. I followed. He hit the outer drive and proceeded south. . . . (John J. Healy)

Neither language nor its use exists in a vacuum; in all speech, but especially informally, speakers rely on what their words suggest and evoke, assuming that certain information has been conveyed even if not expressed. This is the method of metonymy: a stated cause can suggest an unstated effect *(I struck the match)*, an intention its realization *(I decided to go to the movies)*, or an action its purpose *(We went to bed)*. Similarly, with *hit the road,* a means or medium of an action can suggest the action. It is not accidental that a sense of movement is evoked by expressions with *road, highway* and *trail.*

In fact, *road* suggests even more: travel as a necessity of work or duty, or as aimless wandering and restlessness, a life of searching open to new experiences. The *road* of [36] refers to college students looking for jobs *(hit the road)* instead of continuing their studies *(hit the books)*. These expressions are as good evidence as any that a language exploits, and exhibits indirectly, the ever-present extralinguistic background. IDEAL cannot and should not be the exclusive standard of linguistic regularity; its justifiably defined limits cannot be extended into a judgment that these expressions are idioms, a procedure that implies the odd conclusion that they are mysterious.

Now consider phrases related to *hit the beach* [44–54]:

[44] Junior asks Dad if he'd like to hit the beach. (Lawrence Maddry)

[45] Watch the weather reports and try to hit the beach before and after a storm, and even during it. (Joseph D. Bates, Jr.)

[46] To get yourself a bucket of clams, you ought to hit the beach at low tide. . . . (Peggy Payne)

[47] when the forces hit the beach. (W3)

[48] There was a splat of ocean breakers hitting the beach. . . . (Lawrence Maddry)

[49] "It's when we hit land that I'm worried about." (Mary Deasy)

[50] "Only thing to do on a day like this is hit the water." (Dan Wakefield)

[51] Brandy had already leaped over the gunwale and hit the water swimming. (Raboo Rodgers)

[52] Full pressure is applied the instant the lure hits the water. (Joseph D. Bates, Jr.)

[53] In another instant the car hit the water and dropped immediately out of sight. (Arna Bontemps)

[54] For some unexplained reason children develop a towel fetish the moment they hit the sand. (Erma Bombeck)

One of the problems with the idiomatic approach to such phrases, and all multiple meaning analyses in general, is that they underestimate the degree of polysemy that their principles entail. Consider the variation of *hit the beach:* people are swimming in [44] and fishing-clamming in [45] and [46]; these two activities are from inland, those in [47] and [48] from the sea; [47] concerns movement of humans, [48] of a natural force. Are these possibilities subsumed under one idiom? If not, how many idioms are there? How many more possibilities are not represented in these data? If we posit only one idiom, how do we capture the "synonymy" of *hit the beach* to both *hit the water* in [50] and *hit the sand* in [54]? An approach devoted to polysemy because of ambiguity, synonymy, or compositionality, should not balk at multiple meaning here, even if it threatens to be prolific. Conversely, if we assume such considerations are irrelevant here, then are they relevant elsewhere?

Following are more examples:

[55] He waited, until the fellow hit the shallows on the east side. . . . (Jackson Cole)

[56] Mid-depth trolling is comfort zone trolling, and the closer we hit the level preferred by the kind of fish we seek, the better our luck will be. (Joseph D. Bates, Jr.)

[57] But he kept on toward the north to hit the river as far upstream as he could go in one day's walking. (Ernest Hemingway)

[58] The half-completed canal had been planned wrong. Its upstream end let out of a backwater, where the current was unlikely to make itself felt, and the downstream end would hit the river at a spot the Confederates could easily reach with the guns at Vicksburg. (Bruce Catton)

[59] Just then the horse and buggy hit the curve, skidded widely, almost throwing the horse off its feet. (W. C. Tuttle)

[60] The truck hit suddenly a stretch of wide, hard road. . . . (Truman Capote)

[61] You'll be especially appreciative of a light [bicycle] frame when you hit that first hill. (Dick Teresi)

[62] I take the brick steps in front of the white Dutch Colonial two steps at a time and hit the walk like a hurdler psyched up for the hurdle. (John A. Martin)

[63] . . . then hardly 100 feet ahead Sideburns hits a wall of traffic himself . . . . (Tom Wolfe)

[64] I hit red lights at only four of nearly two-dozen controlled intersections. (Jim Schefter)

[65] The first photographer hits the scene. . . . (Jeremy Larner)

[66] ". . . this is the first place they'll look when they hear I've hit town." (James Tate)

[67] "It's generally close to 11 when Jody hits home." (Lloyd Shearer)

[68] I'd hit the house about four o'clock. (Connie Eble)

[69] He was running low on gas when he hit the Cape. (Mary Higgins Clark)
[70] About the time they hit Maryland, Profane decided to get it over with.
(Thomas Pynchon)
[71] The trucks hit Billings at the beginning of the afternoon rush hour.
(David Snell)
[72] As soon as Flamand hit California he was drafted. . . . (Jack Ludwig)
[73] They hit Urbana, Ill., on a Wednesday. . . . (Richard Dozer)
[74] So we went along like this and every once in a while we hit a tourist
hotel. . . . (Saul Bellow)

For all of these sentences, I assume metonymy. Except perhaps for [40], *hit* does have the supposed basic sense of 'strike'. Its minimal meaning is approximated by the more general 'meet' or 'arrive at' or 'join' (although each gloss has misleading implications). I also assume that these phrases imply a purpose for hitting the road, beach, etc.; this can be lexicalized as in [51] *swimming,* but usually it is understood. To repeat: these claims are based on the evidence of productivity, which is much greater than Greenberg thought.

Adam Makkai, in his *Idiom Structure in English* (1972), describes one of his idiom-types as TOURNURE (148ff): a fixed phrase of at least three words that appears to arbitrarily exhibit an obligatory and nonvariable word like *a, the* or *it*. Thus, while we have both *read the book* and *read a book,* we have only *kick the bucket.* A number of our *hit*-phrases also are limited in this way. A consequence of my approach is that a closed-class word like *the* cannot possibly be multiple in meaning or ever appear arbitrarily. While a few recalcitrant idioms might not undermine my argument, the appearance of an unmotivated *the* in a productive pattern certainly would.

The is sometimes required in the above examples, but not inexplicably. While all nominals with *the* are definite, some sentences require a Specific nominal and others a Generic. *Road* or *highway* is specific in [37], a type in [36], perhaps either in [35.] *Trail* varies between specific [40], (figurative) type [39], and either [38]. Not only *the* exhibits this variation: *a* is specific in [40], but it could be generic too (*All you ever want to do is hit a bar*); *that* is a type in [61], but can also be specific (*Be careful when you hit that hill up ahead*).

Similarly, *hit the sack.* This does not pluralize because *sack* is interpreted as a type. If the type were one of several, then *a* and plurality would be relevant. Conversely, the students hit *books,* plural, because the plural represents the type: students typically have more than one textbook. Admittedly, the variable conditions may seem quite messy to an enamored IDEAList (even an admirer-denier, like Makkai); but the patterns are productively motivated, even the "arbitrary" restrictions.

As I argued in Chapter 3, both specific and generic senses are modulations; words are unspecified for this distinction. Pragmatic generalization goes further in *Hit the road!* in the sense of 'get out of here' or 'leave'; this effect can be conveyed without the involvement of any actual road. This phrase can also generally indicate rejection, as also *go to hell, get lost,* or *get out of here.* Here, the metonymic shift is to an antecedent situation instead of subsequent: you will hit the road because you have been told to leave; and you have been told to leave because you've been rejected. The rejection sense is then usable in situations where you will not be using the road, or even for slight rejections (perhaps affectionately ironic), where you needn't leave. As noted in the last chapter, such a combination of metonymy and generalization can easily lead to a total form-meaning-function dislocation, creating an idiom. But in all the examples here, the extralinguistic situation and pragmatic connections are still relatively obvious. What distinguishes many of the phrases already noted is not that they are irretrievably set, but that certain simple patterns, most noticeably with *the,* are quite readily susceptible, by pragmatic generalization, to a type-reading.

4.3 IMPLICIT CONTEXTS

One effect of pragmatic rules is to evoke context that could alternatively be lexically supplied. Consider purposes. In [75–78], they are lexically supplied:

[75] [We] hit the refrigerator for provisions. . . . (Lisa Ress)
[76] . . . Raoul hoped to hit him for some bread. (John LeCarre)
[77] Later, Lange hit the hustings like a seasoned pol to push the movie. . . . (Cathleen McGuigan)
[78] Anytime a song resembled anything you could dance to, they would hit the sun deck to do their thing. (William Irwin Thompson)

Do their own thing (78) is pragmatically specialized to 'dance.'

The metonym *bricks* in [79–81] indicates a street, used by a cab driver [77], a policeman [76], and picketers [77], with implied purposes and activities for these various roles. Of course, the usefulness (or, relative obviousness) of such a metonym is highest in informal speech, where everyone is "in the know." A foreigner may have (relative) trouble with it, or any metonym; but foreigner's difficulty is not, as Makkai (1977: 475) believes, a reason for calling something idiomatic.

[79] "I gotta hit the bricks and make a buck." (comic strip, Steve Roper)
[80] . . . I hit the bricks and started cruising. . . . (Joseph Wambaugh)
[81] . . . a dispatcher told crews to "hit the bricks," and the firefighters went back to the picket lines. (AP)

Examples [82–99] also suggest purposes: *gas* 'to move' and *brakes* 'to stop' [82], *pool* 'to swim' [83], *auction block* 'to be sold' [84], *bank* 'to cash a check' [85], *supers* (a clipping of *supermarkets*) 'to shop for groceries' [86], *record stores* 'to see which songs are popular' [87], [bomb] *shelter* 'to survive bombing' [88], *fairways* 'to retire to play golf' [89], *sea* 'to fish' [90], and *slopes* 'to ski' [91]. Examples [92–99] suggest entertainment: *bars* 'to drink' [98] or 'to make a pickup' [99].

[82] Left turn, right turn, honk your horn, jump the traffic light, hit your gas, hit your brake, every action spawns whole galaxies of possibility. (Robert Silverberg)

[83] On the first day of fresh water everyone who hit the pool would yell, "Ice!" (Sam Ross)

[84] The items—182 in all—went on display Tuesday and will hit the auction block Thursday. . . . (Ann Blackman)

[85] "It's payday, kid! I gotta hit the bank and run a personal errand." (Steve Roper and Mike Nomad, comic strip)

[86] Well, the way is, let the missus here hit the supers [supermarkets] during the week. (Edward Hannibal)

[87] "It's just a matter of hitting the record stores, listening to the radio, and knowing what's hot," said James. . . . *(New Yorker)*

[88] The air was filled with barked orders. "Hit the [bomb] shelter, Pop." (Isaac Asimov)

[89] . . . Weaver volunteered to hit the fairways in Miami early. . . . (Ken Picking)

[90] ". . . they can't wait to get another boat and hit the sea again." (Gail Bolger)

[91] But that's all you need to hit the slopes. . . . (David Shelf)

[92] We ought to hit Baskin & Robbins before we go back. (Clayton Reave)

[93] . . . I knew it was time to eat. I couldn't decide whether to hit Chinatown or Little Tokyo today. (Joseph Wambaugh)

[94] . . . we decided to hit Gaslight Square because it was lively . . . . (William Goldman)

[95] One night in the spring of 1940 I did the town with Pep and Eileen, hitting the jazz joints along Hollywood Boulevard and the Sunset Strip. (Budd Schulberg)

[96] "Listen, let's hit the Tropics Club." (Dan Wakefield)

[97] "Honey, let's eat and hit the flicks," he says. (Vance Bourjaily)

[98] . . . he hardly ever hits the bars. (Cecilia Blanchfield)

[99] . . . she didn't feel like hitting the bars. (Judith Rossner)

More examples are *shuttle* 'to travel' [100] (note link to *road,* etc.), *trade mart* 'to trade players' [101], *whirlpool* 'for physical therapy' [102], *campgrounds* 'to camp' [103], and *phones* 'to make calls' [104]. (Some of these hardly refer to "places," and so 'arrive at' and 'meet' are no longer appropriate, although we are dealing with the same phenomenon.)

[100] The Mets will be hitting the N.Y.-Montreal shuttle pretty soon. (Dick Young)

[101] The Philadelphia 76ers and the Buffalo Braves were without first round draft choices, so look for both to hit the trade mart. (Bob Wolf)

[102] About the only thing Taylor is hitting these days, however, is the whirlpool in the Redskin training room. (Leonard Shapiro)

[103] Of course there are other excellent private campgrounds we just never got to; you can't hit them all in one season of camping. (Ray LaRoque)

[104] He leaves the capitol around 6 p.m., goes home and eats dinner, gets into bed and hits the phones again. (Marguerite Michaels)

More metonyms appear in [105–11]: *ice* for hockey [105], *floor* for basketball [106], *boards* for acting [107], *stair* for going to bed [108], *door* for quitting a job [109] and leaving [110], and *couch* for psychiatric help [111].

[105] At the start of their pre-game skate, the Red Wings hit the ice in single file. . . . (George McClelland)

[106] Smith played everyone rather extensively, and several new Tar Heel combinations hit the floor last night. (Carl Fincke)

[107] . . . [they] can't wait to get back on the road, to hit the old boards again, to sniff the grease paint. . . . (Edwards Park)

[108] As soon as his wife's footsteps hit the stair, he would take a rumpled pack of Camels out of his pocket and begin to smoke. (John Updike)

[109] I was about to quit a hundred times. Once I was just ready to hit the door, but I saw this satisfied smile on my foreman's face. (Bennett Kremen)

[110] "I've never been one to overstay my welcome. I wanted to hit the front door while they still wanted me to stay." (AP)

[111] "I was well into my thirties before I hit the couch." (*The World of Henry Orient,* movie)

Hit is usually defined as a temporal event, but [112–19] show a gradual generalization of time into abstraction [115–17] or purely spatial relationship [118] and [119]:

[112] . . . after he hit college . . . (BC)

[113] The slender young man hit the [golf] tour with the greatest impact. . . . (AP)

[114] "Spend it [money] like a kid the minute I hit civilization." (C. E. Scoggins]

[115] . . . do the same thing an expert does when he hits a slump . . . (Bill McKeown)

[116] "When he first hit the varsity," said coach Dean Smith, "I didn't think he'd ever play." (Bob Lipper)

[117] This means that a particular item *is related to* these "features', rather than 'picking them up' as it hits the semiotactics. (William J. Sullivan)

[118] A little skinny thing—he must have hit me up to here [waist]. (Janice Jacobi)

[119] The W [sports letter on a sweater] hit me along about a private part of my body; the bottom hung below my knees. (Winston M. Estes)

The objects of [120–24] are time expressions with various extra implications: [120] 'beginning of season', [121] 'late in the (football) season', and [122–24] 'getting old' (this gloss also needs specialization). These sentences relate then to other phases, stages and measurement expressions [125–45], of which [136–44] have an extra 'good' implication (Pragmatic Amelioration) and [145] a 'bad' one (Pragmatic Pejoration).

[120] "The Redskins need to hit the league season with everyone healthy. . . ." (AP)

[121] "You can't be going downhill once you hit Thanksgiving." (AP)

[122] "Face it, Lil, you're hitting the time of life when you need someone around. Someone solid." (Barbara Howar)

[123] I'd think she'd have found a husband before she hit middle age. (Mary Worth, comic strip)

[124] when you hit the middle sixties. (W3)

[125] . . . Chuck and his siblings began to get into trouble as soon as they hit puberty. (Alison Lurie)

[126] He's hit the stage of incredible enthusiasm. (William K. Riley)

[127] They hit the halfway mark in their schedule. . . . (Ian MacDonald)

[128] . . . they pulled away to a 40-27 advantage before hitting the half with a 52-39 lead. (AP)

[129] Once the pacers hit the stretch. . . . (Doug Gilbert)

[130] . . . the three-quarter mile post was hit in a sparkling 1:10.2. . . . (Shirley Povich)

[131] . . . the mercury never hit zero. . . . (Langston Hughes)

[132] A race is all the Dodgers would have needed in 1977 to hit three million. (Gordon Verrell)

[133] Motor-paced racers [bicycles] routinely hit speeds of 50 to 60 mph. (Dick Teresi)

[134] The panic of the alcoholic who has hit bottom. . . . (Gregory Bateson)

[135] The British pound sterling hit an all-time low today. . . . (Walter Cronkite)

[136] It is of course too early to tell whether Martinet's solution by way of functional classification hits the exact midpoint [between too precise or too vague a conception of universal grammar]. . . . (William Diver)

[137] . . . to hit the golden mean between too much ease and comfort and too little. (Albert J. Nock)

[138] The flowers of the dogwood, which are just hitting their peak . . . . (Durham *Morning Herald*)

[139] The rivalry hit its zenith in 1976. . . . (Frank Vehorn)

[140] Works on paper hit superb level (VP-LS, headline)

[141] Unemployment rate hits bright note (NO, headline)

[142] Attendance in Cleveland has not hit expectations. (Leo Monahan)

[143] Beaufort hit archaeological paydirt on his first landfall, Patara. . . . (Alfred Friendly)

[144] Boats Hitting Jackpot Off South Beaches (SFC, headline)

[145] Post-disaster evacuation also hits snags. (Wesley Marx)

Hit-objects can also indicate various elements of the communication media [146–55]; these relate in turn to the "markets" of [156–58]. Examples [159–63] show the metonymic versatility of *street:* 'for sale' [159–60], 'go outside' [161], *in search of jobs* [162], 'be a prostitute' [163]. *Street* in [159] and [160] can also represent all places of sale, another example of pragmatic generalization.

[146] [It] did not hit the newspapers until August. (John Dean)

[147] No wonder these stories hit the front page of *The New York Times*. . . . (Stephen Jay Gould)

[148] . . . *Time's* edition hit the newsstands. . . . (Carl Bernstein and Bob Woodward)

[149] . . . his revolutionary book hit the stands. . . . (Stephen Jay Gould)

[150] Helpful Cocktails Have Hit the Counter (LS, headline)

[151] ". . . the story hit the national wires. . . ." (Randy Galloway)

[152] Another aquatic series hits the air waves (LS, headline)

[153] . . . the ads hit newspapers, TV and billboards. . . . (Guy Friddell)

[154] . . . the bubble machine [Lawrence Welk Show] hit the big tube in 1955. . . . (Carol Burton Terry)

[155] This recording will hit the jukeboxes soon. (W3)

[156] Sweet corn hits the markets in New England in midsummer. (W3)

[157] Along with country music, identity crises and encounter groups, abstract art has hit the heartland. (Jean Stafford)

[158] One of the newest highs to hit the legal drug scene is actually one of the oldest. (Howard Smith and Leslie Harlib)

[159] It's [a best-selling book] made before it hits the street. (Kathryn Morton)

[160] . . . the first edition had scarcely hit the streets. . . . (Tom Wicker)

[161] When he hit the street he was exhausted. (Bernard Malamud)

[162] Some 200 CIA secret agents who have received pink slips in the first wave of a planned two-year cutback in covert personnel have been hitting the street in search of jobs. *(Time)*

[163] Clare, 16, having run away from home, met a pimp. . . . He persuaded her to hit the streets. *(Time)*

Some of Greenberg's examples follow. In *hit the bottle* [164], *bottle* is a metonym for drinking, as are also *sauce* [165] and *plum wine* [166], the latter showing that there is more productivity than Greenberg suspected (also: *hit the bubbly,* as a Bing Crosby character might say). These may be pragmatically ameliorative or pejorative. Of course, all that will make you *hit the skids* [167] and [168], which is solely pejorative. In *hit the sack* [169], *sack* is a metonym for sleeping, as in *pillow* [170] and [171] and *bed* [172]; this last sentence also

suggests physical contact. Examples [173–84] have "floors" or "grounds": in
hit the deck, deck is a metonym for lining up for inspection, getting to work, or
getting down out of danger. *Ground* parallels *deck* in this last sense [174], but is
more "literal" in [175] and [176]; 'point was lost' emerges from [175], 'dead'
from [176]. Although this may seem too obvious to mention, knowledge of
gravity and its effects plays a part in the interpretation of [176] and the *floor* of
[177]. *Dust* [178–80], *dirt* [181], *courtyard* [182], *sidewalk* [183] and *concrete*
[184] evoke more of a physical sense.

[164] "She hits the bottle pretty well. . . ." (John Updike)

[165] "He hits the sauce every once in a while, but nothing serious." (Carl
Bernstein and Bob Woodward)

[166] "I bet you been hitting plum wine again," she said joyously. (Hal
Bennett)

[167] But he must have hit the skids after that, drink being the reason. . . .
(Robert Penn Warren)

[168] Before the Sixers [basketball team] hit the skids, they pulled off a
major victory. (Jim O'Brien)

[169] After dessert, we placed the equipment under the tarp, and hit the sack.
(Roy Hunter)

[170] He had gone to sleep almost immediately after his head hit the pillow.
(Caroline Gordon)

[171] He hit the pillow and slept for a fragment of uneasy time. . . . (Dan
Wakefield)

[172] He switched off the light and felt his way across the room in the
darkness and hit the bed as if it were a tackling dummy. (Winston W.
Estes)

[173] "Sweeney Blue, hit the deck." (BC)

[174] "All of us hit the ground and stay there." (Robert Traver)

[175] At this moment the volley-ball hit the ground. (BC)

[176] "Three shots in that fella 'fore he hit the ground." (BC)

[177] In deadly earnest, the besiegers methodically stripped away portions of
the roof and tossed lighted rags outside, only to have most of them
stamped out by the women as soon as they hit the floor. (BC)

[178] . . . the attackers hit the dust in the face of the withering enemy fire.
(BC)

[179] The Ranger was out, Colt ready, boots hitting the dust of the road.
(Jackson Cole)

[180] The scout went on past them at a gallop and Josh could hear the
black's hooves ring on the bridge planking, then quiet as he hit the
dust of the road on the west bank. . . . (Jessamyn West)

[181] I braked hard, hit the dirt, cut my own light and U-turned. (Ross
Macdonald)

[182] . . . he hit the courtyard on the balls of his feet. . . . (William Styron)

[183] Steps hit the sidewalk and I went over to the front door and opened it. (Raymond Chandler)

[184] Something tugged on my trouser leg and spun me. I got a tight grip of air and hit the concrete like a sack of sand. (Ross Macdonald)

4.4 CONTACTS AND IMPACTS

The sense of physical contact becomes more pronounced in [185–99], but this apparent discrete sense is not as simple as our definitions make it. Example [185] describes a physical contact, but it also has an implied purpose 'to open the lock', and appears to be a form of understatement for literary effect. That effect is to lead the reader to supply part of the meaning, and thus be engaged in the story; this involvement through indirection or incompletion is an essential feature of both informal speech and literary enactment (as opposed to exposition). Physical contact is present in [186–93], but not essential; we again have the general sense of 'meet' or 'encounter'. It is not until examples [194–99] that we get the direct "head-on" type of hitting that comes to everyone's mind when this word is considered in isolation.

[185] I'm mopping near the ward door when a key hits it from the other side and I know it's the Big Nurse. . . . (Ken Kesey)

[186] I sat in my seat and didn't even breathe until I heard Reverend Carson's big feet hit the bottom step. (Anne Moody)

[187] But Bob's bad leg dragged a little and his foot hit a crack. (Robert Arthur)

[188] The Lone Wolf smashed through the opening, kept rolling as he hit the porch, and rolled off onto the dirt. (Jackson Cole)

[189] Just past the entrance there was a wet spot on the pavement. The speeding car hit it and spun out of control. (Ernest K. Gann)

[190] Instead, straddle the edge, get back with a sharp turn and quick return to the straight-ahead steering position the moment the tire hits the pavement. (Jim Liston)

[191] . . . my right front wheel hit a pothole. (Lawrence Maddry)

[192] When a sinker hits a shoal the area can be probed for its size and shape. (Joseph D. Bates, Jr.)

[193] But in a few feet he [dog] hits the sheet of ice rimming the lake and starts sliding. (Bill Tarrant)

[194] . . . the thud of darts hitting the board. . . . (Inglis Fletcher)

[195] . . . [he] heaved it [mousetrap] down the passageway. It hit a bulkhead and went off with a loud snap. (Thomas Pynchon)

[196] In a minute a quarter came shooting out under the deck. It hit the wall and spun around on the floor. (Earl MacRauch)

[197] This time [as he was digging] Joe's spade hit the object that had been buried. (Franklin W. Dixon)

[198] . . . on her [ship] first run of the season up to Goose Bay, she had hit ice and sunk. (Tim Severin)

[199] Muskies are attracted by the propeller and the wake to the extent that many have been hit by the blades. (Joseph D. Bates, Jr.)

But physical reality is more than agents and sharply defined surfaces [200–09]:

[200] . . . the wind hits the steep cliffs and flies up over them. (Anthony Bailey)

[201] . . . the spitting crackle of the flame hitting the water drops on the coffeepot. (Nancy Pellitier Pansing)

[202] Two boys were killed during the Cleveland storm when they were hit by lightning. . . . (UPI)

[203] The strong current hit my knees and thighs. . . . (Johnny Greene)

[204] The first [taste] occurs when the wine hits your lips. (Creighton Churchill)

[205] When she pushed the door open, warm air and cigarette smoke hit her face. (Leslie Silko)

[206] The evening air hit us like a blaze. (James Baldwin)

[207] Gusts of beery breath hit my face from six inches range. (James Herriot)

[208] ". . . his voice hit my ears. . . ." (Austin Clarke)

[209] . . . water hit him from another angle. (Ruth Rendell)

Sometimes it is hard to decide how much the "physical" is relevant: *fog* in [210] and *rain* in [211] are physical, and in [212] and [213] *air* and *wind* are agencies, but the sense of encounter is more prominent than the physical. This diffuseness of the physical reveals that *hit,* like *bear,* is unspecified for concrete-abstract; the distinction becomes more tenuous as an absolute distinction when we investigate physical realities other than objects. If we take *hit* as unspecified, the variants of [215–23] are more understandable. *Air* suggests 'go outside' in [215], like *street* in [161]; it is more physical in [216] and more abstract in [217], where it is metonymic for 'be heard' or 'be realized'. (If *hit* is unspecified, the creative appearance of [181] is not the effect of breaking any limits of meaning but of exploiting an unused possibility already within the rules.)

[210] . . . 12 miles out [at sea], we hit fog. (Ed Neal)

[211] ". . . we went through [in a plane] at eight thousand [feet] and only hit a little rain. . . ." (Ernest K. Gann)

[212] The night air hit them like a clean bath. (Dan Wakefield)

[213] It [dry wind] hits the Plains and comes across Alberta and Saskatchewan like the breath of a blowtorch. (Wallace Stegner)

[214] . . . at that moment the plane hits an air pocket. (Piers Paul Reid)

[215] As soon as I hit the open air, Madrid was all jewelry and art to me. . . . (Saul Bellow)

[216] Steam emerging from scores of safety valves turned into vapor as soon as it hit the cold air. (Joseph Kraft)

[217] But the man who creates the music is hearing something else, is dealing with a roar rising from the void and imposing order on it as it hits the air. (James Baldwin)

[218] Trains passing appeared to emerge from a tunnel of trees and, hit for a second by the cold sky, vanished terrified into the woods again. (Flannery O'Connor)

Light is also an "agent":

[219] The light hit his face. (Sterling Hayden)

[220] "But he sure sat up quickly when the beam of the flashlight hit him." (Peter Matthiessen)

[221] A monument stood shining in the distance, hit by a ray of sun. . . . (Ayn Rand)

[222] The flash of light that hit her had no source. (Ayn Rand)

Hit is often made polysemic in dictionaries because of intuited differences in agency. These are usually stereotypic: hitting with one's hand or a bullet are cited in definitions, both implicitly and when *hand* or *gun* are explicit. Again, this process of analysis, if adhered to consistently, has no hope of closure short of absurdity. *Hit* can have a number of implicit instruments: hand [223], shoe [224], part of body [225], car [226], motorcycle [227], hammer [228], bullet [229], airplane [230], voice (when speaking) [231], and fingers [232], the last having the same understatement effect we saw in [185].

[223] . . . I pulled into Dot's Dixie Gas Station and hit the horn. (Stuart Kaminsky)

[224] "These leather heels are awfully tricky. I hit an ordinary piece of wax paper in the street the other day and went down." (Saul Bellow)

[225] Going out, he stumbled over a rug, and trying to recover himself, hit Lousia's waste-basket on the table, and knocked it to the floor. (Mary E. Wilkins Freeman)

[226] Marvin hit a car on the way to his parents' house that night. . . . (Joan Kerckhoff)

[227] "She was riding a motorcycle, hit a wet spot and went off the road." (Rex Morgan, comic strip)

[228] "Barbara did the carpentry. You should hear her swear when she hits her thumb." (Robert A. Heinlein)

[229] "He only meant to shoot out a tire." "Yes, but he hit the windows." (Saul Bellow)

[230] . . . I hit the trees and my airplane twisted and somersaulted . . . . (Richard Bach)

[231] Always hit the message-bearing words firmly. (W3)

[232] Somebody was paying him to hit those letters [on the typewriter] and make words. (Edward Hannibal)

Greenberg suggests that the direct object can sometimes be a 'target'; this is also a pragmatic inference. It is inferred in [232–255] in many guises, both concrete and abstract; these examples blend into [256–61] where 'target' weakens. Note that *stride* [259–61] is both concrete and abstract. In a very productive subpattern, the notions of agent and target combine with implied instruments and purposes in examples [263–77].

[233] "Yossarian, did the bombs hit the target?" (Joseph Heller)
[234] That [flight] of Lindbergh stands out preeminently because he went absolutely alone and squarely hit his objective. *(Scientific American)*
[235] The crew said that they had approached from out of sight of land, and without any knowledge of navigation, had hit the island dead on. (Horace Beck)
[236] When bass hit a topwater lure, the fun is fast and furious. (Joseph D. Bates, Jr.)
[237] The shark closed fast astern and when he hit the fish the old man saw his mouth open. . . . (Ernest Hemingway)
[238] The poet William Cowper called Newton a 'childlike sage' for that quality, and the description perfectly hits the air of surprise at the world that Einstein carried in his face. (Jacob Bronowski)
[239] "Actually, those sermonizers never did hit the basic facts about me." (Sara Harris)
[240] None of these analyses seem quite to hit the main characteristic. (R. D. Ellmann)
[241] Yes, that was surely the "summation" of the play and Tertan had hit it, as he hit, deviously and eventually, the literary point of almost everything. (Lionel Trilling)
[242] As in other things, when we *deliberately* try to hit a subtlety that is new to us, we find it very hard. (Paul Goodman)
[243] writing that hits the public taste precisely. (W3)
[244] . . . if William could hit precisely the right promotion note. . . . (BC)
[245] advertising techniques designed to hit the subconscious mind. (W3)
[246] Also, if they [gamblers] hit the number or scored heavily with the bookie. . . . (Gay Talese)
[247] He's the kind of guy that goes to the track, hits the daily double . . . . (Milt Moss)
[248] He doesn't hit all the notes [on an instrument]. (Charles Beaumont)
[249] . . . a soprano hits her high notes. . . . (Dwight Bolinger)
[250] Prew nodded and hit a tentative chord. . . . (James Jones)
[251] The guitar hit a lovely A-minor chord. . . . (Jean Shepherd)
[252] "Shell those peas in the pan!" she ordered. . . . "I can't hit the pan, Mommy!" (Augusta Stevenson)

[253] Wherever the oilmen drilled, east and west, north and south, they hit oil. (Nathan M. Adams)
[254] spent years in prospecting without ever hitting gold. (W3)
[255] Even before he hit big money, he had begun buying modern paintings. (BC)
[256] [It] took him some time to hit the better magazines [publish]. (W3)
[257] Each year, almost routinely, Americans read about how the average score of students taking college entrance tests has hit a low. (Kevin P. Phillips)
[258] . . . the second half of August, just around the time when the Greek sun hits its fiercest heat. (John LeCarre)
[259] . . . the Patagonian camels plunge, dip their necks, and appear to stumble violently before they hit their stride. (George Gaylord Simpson)
[260] But after a couple of years he hit his stride. (Tom Buckley)
[261] They [basketball team] hit stride midway through the first half. . . . (Dan Collins)
[262] Anyway, I thought I still might be able to hit my quota. . . . (Evan Hunter)
[263] Racing out the door that cold, blustery morning, you hop into your car, buckle up, hit the starter, and—nothing. (Michael Lamm)
[264] As the cashier hits the alarm, the woman fled. (AP)
[265] . . . Thorn hit the gearshift, gunning the car backward. (David Seltzer)
[266] He hit the radio button. (BC)
[267] At 200 feet, the pilot hits the switch to retract the wheels. (VP)

Obviously *hit* can stereotypically imply 'vigor', which Greenberg also notes as a sense; intense impact or drastic effect can be achieved in several ways. In [268–73] the modifier *hard* and related forms are explicitly stated, and in [274] *deeply*. The subject noun describes something with known drastic effects in [268–94], though in [291] it is hyperbole; all effects are pejorative except [292]. In [295–308] the effects are less drastic, because the subjects are less drastic; the suggestion of impact comes from understanding the significance of the situation being described. Examples [309–313] present various mental impacts; [308] and [310] relate directly to *It hit me that. . . . Home* is ego-reflexive in [312] and [313].

Throughout all these examples, the intensity of *hit* is variable (just as with *bear*), and all share some sense of being relatively sudden and unexpected. Examples [280–94] show variants of inferential 'attack': 'penalize' [280], 'criticize' [281–83], 'attack militarily' [284], 'rob' [285] and [286], 'bomb' [287], and 'kill' [288]; contextual information (*thieves* in [285]) specifies interpretation. Examples [289–94] evoke a weaker imposing, with purpose sometimes expressed in a *for*-phrase [291–94]; imposing is from mild [289] to harsh [294]. Some examples show that *hit* is a favorite word of headline writers, because it is so short and versatile in meaning.

[268] Runnstrom's companies were hit hard by Florida's construction slowdown. . . . *(Forbes)*

[269] Hooks said he is aware that increased energy costs resulting from deregulation would hit poor families disproportionately hard. (William Raspberry)

[270] A blizzard came up four days before that primary, but it didn't hit that state half as hard as that TV blitz and the Anderson campaign. (Tom Wicker)

[271] A deep depression hit me so hard that even my physical movements became leaden. (Jeb Stuart Magruder)

[272] A year later the energy crisis struck, hitting hardest those poorer nations lacking both oil and fertilizer. . . . (Thomas Y. Canby)

[273] The people hardest hit by this suspicion are, of course, Christians on the mainland of China. (BC)

[274] The loss of that factory crawler hit him more deeply than it should have. (Frank Herbert)

[275] The dizziness hit him momentarily when he stopped to lift the canvas flap. . . . (Fred Bodsworth)

[276] A kind of panic hits him, a kind of sickness. (Wendell Berry)

[277] "But I came home one day, reached up for the light switch to turn off the light and the pain hit my elbow." (Art Spander)

[278] Slow decompression is necessary to keep a man from being hit by the diving disability called the "bends." (Jack McKenny)

[279] And six months later Schaller wrote me that distemper had hit the pack [of dogs], leaving only nine survivors. (Robert Ardrey)

[280] That fall, a rabies epidemic hit the fox population. (Laura White)

[281] . . . just beyond Denver, they got hit by a blizzard. (Laura White)

[282] ". . . the tornado struck two or three years ago and hit a barn north of Lowry." (Luther P. Gerlach)

[283] Floods Hit First Leg of Safari Rally. (SFC, headline)

[284] . . . we know the location of at least one other buried house apparently hit by the same mudflow. . . . (Richard D. Daugherty and Ruth Kirk)

[285] Many of the roads also were hit by an unusually severe winter. (BC)

[286] Our present inflation problem stems from a series of special shocks that hit the economy. (William E. Simon)

[287] It [inflation] hits the new car buyer from all directions, but mainly in fuel costs and new car prices. (John Lamm)

[288] . . . [he] strapped himself down [in space ship] and relaxed as the acceleration hit him. (Robert A. Heinlein)

[289] . . . the most surprising series of upsets ever to hit the four major bowls in one day. (New York *Times*)

[290] Mortgage Blues Hit More Homes. (VP, headline)

[291] The invasion of Italian movies that hit the United States in the fifties and sixties. . . . (Alvin Toffler)

[292] At home, where success first hit them, they were mildly delighted. . . . (Dylan Thomas)

[293] During the meat shortage in the summer of 1973, a flood of deer hunting applications hit the Springfield office. (Art Reid)

[294] There is always a danger in a democracy when a wave of nationalist feeling hits the people. (Max Lerner)

[295] My laughter hit them like cold water. (Howard Breslin)

[296] In short, Schoenberg, both the man and the musician, had hit his opponents' feelings at a very profound level. . . . (Donald Mitchell)

[297] In the West, the influx of coal miners and construction workers and their families has already hit towns like Gilette, Rock Springs and Green River, Wyoming. . . . (David Sheridan)

[298] He saw the quick anger flash in her eyes and knew he'd hit a nerve. (Harold Robbins)

[299] To Buchanan Rabbit says, "How much for the drinks? Wow. They're just hitting me." (John Updike)

[300] He could see her eyes brighten as the dope hit her. (Harold Robbins)

[301] "Boy, they can rave when their pocketbook's hit." (John Updike)

[302] Profit Taking Hits Market (VP, headline)

[303] Probably the hottest thing to hit the Dallas investment community in years was the Martin Foods stock issue. . . . (BC)

[304] And mixed feelings are the way events like the Little Miss Virginia Pageant hit us. (Tony Stein)

[305] In fact, debate about limiting the right to use the public lands and waters has already hit the courts. (VP)

[306] "Wait until some kind of reform Judaism hits this land. . . ." (James A. Michener)

[307] Occasionally one [religious synthesizer] will hit the public imagination. (Wayne C. Booth)

[308] Then he stopped as a sudden recollection of tradition hit him. (Isaac Asimov)

[309] I was on a jet returning to New York when a thought hit me. (Alex Haley)

[310] When Short brought them [surveying instruments] to Lincoln it hit him as another surprise in his young life. (Carl Sandburg)

[311] ". . . it hit me what a comical scene it all really was. . . ." (Wendell Berry)

[312] It was finally hitting home, the foolishness of it. . . . (Michael Douglas)

[313] "This hits home," he said. "People understand attempts to tamper with public opinion." (Bernstein and Woodward)

[314] "The only time our juries hit physicians is when they've been negligent. . . ." (Anne Smith)

[315] Kissinger Hits Panel on Data Misuse (VP, headline)

[316] Schultze hits GOP tax plan. (NO, headline)

[317] No prime minister in our history has been hit so hard by a biographer who knew him. (W3)

[318] In one wave after another, these people [Huns] hit the Rhine and Danube frontiers, which crumbled. (Paul Johnstone)

[319] Horse thieves hit the place a week ago, making off with a 10-year-old mare in foal. . . . (VP)

[320] We recently learned that Abrams hit up the Sultan of Brunei for several million dollars. (Elizabeth Drew)

[321] On August 16, Notaro's house was bombed, and by then Hale had drawn up lists of other locations to be hit. (Gay Talese)

[322] The authorities took elaborate precautions to keep their organized crime witness from being hit in jail. (John Dean)

[323] The first sawmill he hit hired him. (Sterling Hayden)

[324] . . . having to hit the last of their savings to do it. . . . (Edward Hannibal)

[325] hit the company education fund for a year in technical school. (W3)

[326] The vagrant hit me for a dime. (AH)

[327] ". . . I'll hit the next trail boss for a job. . . ." (Zane Grey)

[328] McAdoo confirmed that he had been fined by the club. Asked how much he had been hit for, he said, "I don't know." (AP)

4.5 UNITY AND DIVERSITY

My claim is that apparent specific meanings of *hit* are determined by pragmatic inferences of metonymy, specialization, generalization, and amelioration, pejoration, hyperbole and understatement modulating a single general sense to produce a potentially infinite number of variations. An implication of this view, exemplified several times, is that a word or phrase with a single meaning can nevertheless be highly ambiguous. Another illustration is the phrase *hit it* in (329–34). *It* evokes 'high speed' in [329] (i.e., they're going fast), 'the ground' in [330] (i.e., "someone's shooting at you; get down"), and 'older age' in [331] (i.e., they're getting old; also *they're hitting that time of life*). *It* is liquor in [332] and a target in [333] and [334]. Since the meanings of *hit it* are so variable and seemingly unpredictable from the two words, Makkai should find many tournure idioms, all of them mysterious to a speaker who doesn't know English and American society fully enough.

[329] They [boats] were hitting it. (David L. Shores)

[330] "Mike. Hit it." (*Streets of San Francisco,* TV show)

[331] . . . those women are hitting it. (Rosary Eble)

[332] "Two double Scotches," Lambert ordered.
"Double! You're hitting it hard!" (Simone de Beauvoir; tr. Leonard M. Friedman)
[333] . . . Winkler finally hit it big in Hollywood. (Pamela Swift)
[334] He [broadjumper] hit it right on the money. (Keith Jackson)

To summarize: the point of view I am proposing has the following advantages:

(a) It explains why all these senses can be represented by *hit*.
(b) It assumes less irregularity in the language.
(c) It accounts for a wider range of data.
(d) It integrates a wider range of linguistic abilities.
(e) It makes linguistic and extralinguistic knowledge highly interdependent.
(f) It implies a simpler theory of mental processes (without making those processes simple).

The usual point of view, taken by Greenberg and Makkai, must posit discrete meanings (and more than they think if they want consistent applications), and yet pragmatic abilities are nevertheless still needed to disambiguate all supposed semantic differences. Thus, positing discrete senses is a complication, considering the number that would realistically be involved.

But, perhaps most important, my point of view, through pragmatic processes such as metonymy, also

(g) provides a basis for linking historical change with current variation and figurative uses.

Those who have followed IDEAL need to avoid figurativity; but as these examples show, it is too pervasive and too subtle to be ignored by sweeping edict. The possibility of a mental correlate to IDEAL is actually strengthened if we carefully explore how particular figurative modulations work.

There is another subtle assumption that we need to criticize. Consider examples [335] and [336]:

[335] "Only when I said that, she hit the roof." (Thomas Pynchon)
[336] I mean he didn't hit the ceiling or anything. (J. D. Salinger)
[337] "You're too modest." "Al, you've hit the nail right on the head," Caldwell said. (John Updike)
[338] The leader of one factional clan in politics had been hit below the belt and had hit back—below the belt. (Carl Sandburg)

These sentences are the last resort of the idiomatic view, apparently the most resistant to explanation. Obviously, set phrases are involved; but I have not denied that earlier. Nor could I deny that some figurativity is involved.

However, neither of these two ingredients is sufficient cause to call these idioms. A necessary question: why are these phrases used in the way they are?

If there is no apparent reason for the words at all, nothing but an arbitrary connection of form and meaning, then we could justifiably call these idioms. But their use is quite clear, at least figuratively. Examples [337] and [338] operate metonymically, evoking 'accuracy' [337] or 'unfairness' [338]; both show pragmatic generalization too.

It may even be preferable to consider some of these expressions literal. Figuratively, *hit the roof* [335] and *hit the ceiling* [336] indicate rising anger; *roof* and *ceiling* symbolize, with perhaps a touch of hyperbole, a very high intensity of anger. There may even be a psychosomatic reason that makes these phrases more apt: an angry person needs more surrounding space. We must ask: what human state is assumed for literal meanings?

Lowen (1958), whose approach to psychotherapy stresses the relationship of body rigidity to (supposedly purely) mental disorders, observes that *kick* 'complain', as in *I can't kick,* has a psychosomatic aptness: people unable to complain literally have little strength in their legs and cannot kick. He also notes that expressions of duty, responsibility and burden using *on (It's on me/my back/my shoulders/my shoulders)* also have somatic correlates: people unduly burdened have rigid torsos, as if they were weighed down.

Lowen's interpretations should ring an alarm: they show that we have certain presumptions of "normality" and "reality" in our theories about language that may not be respected directly by the language. When we talk about both innateness and experience it is all too easy for us to forget that human beings are complex creatures, much more intricate and diversified than we usually consciously recognize (no matter how much we may "scientifically know").

4.6   STEREOTYPES

Put another way, the "literal-figurative" distinction is sometimes STEREOTYPIC, based on a highly selective view of a human being as a sober, mental, detached, "objective" creature, a picture enabled by the limitations and vanity of the conscious mind. Stereotyping is modulation that isn't recognized as such: we think we are seeing wholly when we are seeing only in part. This conscious limitation was my major concern in Chapter 1 when discussing data: a theory based solely on minimal intuited data is going to be stereotypic. By taking account of conscious limitation, we can address a key unresolved problem in this chapter: why, when confronted with the word *hit* "in isolation," do we think first of strong physical contact?

This supposed "basic" sense of *hit* is its stereotype. Stereotypes are "favored" pragmatic inferences; sometimes they are triggered by lexical contexts (the 'steal' sense of *take* in *The thief took the jewels*), and sometimes they seem to operate "in isolation": in the latter, they are the possibility that springs first to mind when we think of the word. There is always a context, and thus no word "means" in isolation.

To demonstrate this point and also review the chapter as a whole, we can consider the sentence *John hit the house.* What does this sentence mean? How do we account for this meaning?

John and *house* can refer to many people and houses. The verb indicates an action that can occur many times. There can be many different conditions that allow the choice of the definite article. Accordingly, this sentence can be used on different occasions. Such variations are assumed by all linguists to be pragmatic.

On the other hand, the following variant factors are usually considered semantic:

(a) Is this deliberate or accidental on John's part (or any other possibility)?

(b) Is John the agent of the action or the instrument (for example, his body dropped from a plane)?

(c) Is John using part of his body as an instrument (fist, for example)?

(d) Is John using some other instrument (rock, gun, baseball bat, bomb from hand, bomb from airplane, etc.)?

(e) Was the whole house hit or just part (and which part)?

(f) How intense was the hitting (a pebble bouncing off or a bomb totally destroying)?

(g) Was the hitting assumed in (a–f) a physical contact? Other possibilities: arrival at a house (returning home, stopping for a rest, reading gas meters, robbing the house), reaching someone at the house (a telephone survey, door-to-door selling, trick-or-treaters, etc.).

As we evoke different means, purposes, and other attendant circumstances (involving other people or not), the different total meanings seem so diverse that we feel compelled to make *hit* polysemic (and perhaps *John* and *house* as well).

I have argued that this is a mistake, for several reasons:

(a) the possibilities are highly numerous, if not infinite;

(b) any attempt to categorize these possibilities will likely ignore some of the data.

It is simpler, and more explanatory, to say that all these details (and many more) are provided by pragmatic means, by knowledge of the world. Even if the variants can be finitely specified, this is not sufficient reason to claim a semantic difference. One caution is

(c) the extrapolated consequences may be catastrophic.

What if, for example, we want to claim that a certain word, such as *teacher,* is (without formal distinction) polysemic with respect to sex; we must then, consistently, make all such words polysemic, a highly complicating consequence, when the alternative is to make all such words simply "relevant to but unspecified for sex", and then have, as a separate pragmatic condition, the two sexual possibilities for all relevant words. Or consider a proposal for polysemy that seems to lack dire consequences: Bolinger (1977b) claims that the verb *regard* is discretely and comprehensively ambiguous between *look (up) to* and *look at*. Even if his claim is correct and this applies only to one word, extrapolation is still involved: Bolinger implies that all general terms should be *n*-ways ambiguous when they have *n*-ways discrete and jointly comprehensive hyponyms. A better general principle is that a general term can be pragmatically specialized to mean any of its hyponyms.

What Bolinger must additionally show for *regard* is that a generalization is impossible. To claim semantic variation without formal variation, we need more justification than the citing of multiple specifics.

Consider another example of stereotyping: *father*. Upon hearing this word, we are not likely to think first of fourteen-year-old or 114-year-old fathers; they are fathers nevertheless. For me, the word triggers an image of a man from 25–40 years of age, about the age range when one is a child and knows one's father. (Since my father died when I was young, and I have few memories, my image cannot merely be from him.) In other words, the stereotype of *father* chooses EXPERIENTIAL SALIENCE. Similarly, with *hit:* movement, suddenness, vividness, intensity, noticeable effect, and human action are more salient than their opposites. More generally, what is concrete is more salient than what is abstract. For both *father* and *hit,* the conscious mind (perhaps almost exclusively) recalls the salient possibilities. In short, even though the word *hit* has a wide general range, our conscious awareness is of only a small part of that range.

Context can also become stereotypic; an expression can be specialized only for a certain purpose. This is RITUALIZATION. Eble (1983) shows how expressions that are motivated can be misapplied; for example, *Good morning* serves as an appropriate greeting in the morning, but its metonymic status as a greeting can cause it to be used generally, even when it is not morning. As Fillmore (1984: 98ff.) notes, such ritualization can create an erosion of the form: children reciting a pledge they understand only as a pledge saying *and to the Republic for Richard Stans.* Similarly, *for all intents and purposes* becomes *for all intensive purposes,* or *take it for granted* becomes *take it for granite.* (As one of my students wrote, *it's a doggie dog world.*) Fillmore cites these as evidence that form is independent of meaning, but I see it as a more limited pragmatic effect; the ritualization has minimized the need for distinctiveness, allowing shifts to mere phonological similarity.

Hit-phrases can be caught in ritualization: *we have to hit the road* serves the ritualized need of farewell, spoken by a visitor who need only walk down the street or even down the hallway of an apartment house. I've even heard *We hafta hit it.* These expressions can also serve as ritualized commands to get (back) to work, like *let's get this show on the road.*

It is possible that ritualization can make such an expression an idiom, but we must ask if it is such solely because of ritualization, or for some other, less superficial reason. *Good morning* and *Good afternoon* have motivated content: their words are appropriate to the meaning. Of course, they underdetermine the meaning, not overtly indicating greeting; but then, few greetings or farewells are as overt as *I bid you greetings/farewell*. As Eble argues, our semantic theories should note when productive processes are working. Even *How (do) you do* has words appropriate to its message; we can also get (slang) greetings minimally variant with it, as *How (are) you coping?* If stereotyping and ritualization are misanalyzed as semantic realities, rather than more specific pragmatic variations, we must posit more multiple meaning and more idioms.

A stereotype need not be a unified thing; more than likely, that of *hit* is a combination of several different factors, all or most of which should be correlated with conscious partializations. Given a semantic range over both concrete and abstract, *bear* and *hit*, we will stereotype to the concrete, treating the abstract as an extension. Similarly, when a word covers the full range of agency, we will stereotype to agent as a separate and conceptually prior category.

What also enables these partializations is the tendency for POLAR EXTREMES, which reduces a continuum to two (or a minimal few) possibilities. Thus, we tend to notice first (and to explicitly provide for in our theories) only the fully concrete or fully abstract, and the fully agentive; as a polar complement, the reagent given first status is the Object, the fully passive recipient of an action. We even tend to stereotype to extreme forms of agency: agents must be conspicuously "acting" (the verb *act* is stereotyped to conspicuous action), with the most notable impact. Even when we depart from these extremes, under the pressure of data discovered "later," we do so in polarized subdivisions.

Consciousness cannot hold all the possibilities at once, and thus must selectively partialize. We know unconsciously, but we consciously forget, even things we are able to know and recognize immediately when they are explicitly noted. If we knew in advance, of course, what particular stereotype we were succumbing to now, we would avoid it; but if we had that ability in general, my claim here would clearly be wrong. We are always noticing first the "misleadingly obvious," but we don't know it is misleading or why it is obvious.

Similar to stereotypes in their communicational effect are what Rosch (1977b) calls PROTOTYPES. When people are asked to substitute a more specific term for *bird*, they are more likely to choose *sparrow* or *robin* rather than *turkey* or *penguin*; likewise for *fruit, apple* is more likely than *watermelon* (p. 255). Rosch argues that categories are organized around such prototypic and peripheral terms; children appear to learn a category by learning its prototypes first.

Are these organizations semantic or pragmatic? Fodor (1981: 296) notes that such meanings don't compose:

There may, for example, be prototypic *cities* (London, Athens, Rome, New York); there may even be prototypical *American cities* (New York, Chicago, Los Angeles), but there are surely no prototypical *American cities situated on the East Coast just a little south of Tennessee.* Similarly, there may be prototypical *grandmothers* (Mary Worth) and there may be prototypical *properties of grandmothers (good, old* Mary Worth). But there are surely no prototypical properties of, say, Chaucer's grandmothers, and there are no prototypical properties of grandmothers most of whose grandchildren are married to dentists. Or, if there are, it's clear that knowing the prototypes can't be required to understand the phrases.

Using Rosch's experimental methods, I would likely discover that the prototype for *hit* is intense physical contact. Thus, prototypes are also stereotypes, pragmatic and not semantic; it is thus not surprising then that they do not strictly compose, since various combinations evoke different realities. Prototypes are no less valuable for being stereotypes. Rosch's experiments give us insight into conscious and even unconscious selectivity. Prototypes are certainly relevant in discourse analysis; someone using *bird* in a sentence would likely mean to convey, and be understood as conveying, a prototypic robin rather than a turkey, unless accompanying context indicated otherwise.

The key point: prototypes, and stereotypes in general, reveal meanings conveyed in minimally explicit contexts. They show us implicit modulations: *bird* doesn't come to us in semantic nakedness, but invisibly clothed in its prototype. Similarly, an isolated intuitional sentence is not semantically pristine either. Unfortunately, Fodor's test has rarely been applied to these. *Mrs. Smith wanted to go, and so he went* seems ill-formed, but not following *Mr. Smith said he'd go with his wife:* a modulation makes us "find" as many antecedents as we can. Similarly, Reddy (1969: 240) notes that a sentence that seems "literal" in isolation (like intuitional sentences) can in particular contexts become "metaphoric"; each status is a modulated one, not purely semantic, and the literal sense is the stereotype-prototype, the one we "naturally" think of first.

Prototypes and stereotypes reveal the invisible modulations of supposedly context-free language. They are (in computerese) "default values," which specify implicit domains, conditions, structures, eligibilities, responsibilities, expectations, etc.: thus, we have all the various frames, scripts, procedures, speech act conditions, conventions of communication, etc. of current pragmatic research. Each of these relevant ambiences (or ambient relevancies) serves to modulate the autonomous language, creating a more concrete meaning, an interpretation.

Though I will return briefly to *hit* later, here and there I barely begin an adequate study of this verb; a full treatment would require a book or more.

There are many remaining problems: I must confess, as one problem, that I have found no sufficient explanation for *hit it off,* as in *They hit it off* and *John hit it off with Fred.* My collected data thus far show no closely related expressions. It may turn out that this is either an idiom or a "near idiomatic" expression; that is, an expression that is only barely related to other *hit*-expressions.

I will grant this possibility: even with words that are monosemic, there may be a few phrases that are only remotely relatable. If *the bucket* is an idiom in *kick the bucket,* then this is one example at least of *the* not being generalized with other uses (though originally, when the phrase connected with reality, *the bucket* was interpreted as a type, and so *the* was exclusively appropriate). It is likely (though I will admit it only once) that no word is completely monosemic: all words can get caught in phrases, sentences and discourses that become, pragmatically and then semantically, laws to themselves. This is a consequence of both the infinite openness of the conscious mind and its limitations: stereotyping and forgetfulness. However, we can rightly call *hit it off* an idiom only after we have given *hit, it,* and *off* the full study they require, with an adequate database. It is time to stop being gullible victims of our stereotyping intuitions.

Chapter 5

FORM AND MEANING

The Monosemic Bias implies that form and meaning are highly congruent. Yet, they are not completely so. What is the nature of this partial congruence? To a striking degree, what we call "form" tends to be more abstract (more remote from reality) and what we call "meaning" is more concrete (more directly related to reality). In this chapter I will argue that (gradiently and relatively) form is closed abstract meaning and (gradiently and relatively) meaning is open concrete form. The degree of congruence is what we should expect from any abstract-concrete relationship: (more) abstract unities relating to (more) concrete diversities. Put simply: syntax is abstract semantics, and semantics is concrete syntax. Pragmatics is then even more concrete, relating with (our partly created) reality.

This claim is not meant as a "discovery"; it is more a programmatic proposal. I assume the possibility that some linguistic details described currently as "syntactic," "semantic," or "pragmatic" may not be placed (in some "correct" way) in the most appropriate domain. What I am minimally saying is that our definitional practices point in a particular direction, so it would be fruitful if we recognized the tendency, applied it consistently, and drew both practical and theoretical consequences.

5.1 SYNTAX, SEMANTICS, PRAGMATICS

In one view (essentially that of Morris (1971: 301–03)), we have the following definitions:

SYNTAX: the relations of signs to SIGNS
SEMANTICS: the relations of signs to THINGS
PRAGMATICS: the relations of signs to USERS

This view of Semantics makes it extralinguistic, like Pragmatics, and so excludes the possibility that so-called semantic relationships such as synonymy, hyponymy, and antonymy can ever be solely sign-to-sign relationships. In the Fregean view (1892), however, Semantics is both sign-to-sign and sign-to-thing, respectively SENSE (intensional-intralinguistic) and REFERENCE (extensional-extralinguistic). As Quine (1953: 130) notes, these are "two provinces so fundamentally distinct as not to deserve a joint appellation at all"; he distinguishes them, respectively, as Meaning and Reference. Obviously, any systems found in a theory of reference would involve more than just language. The difference is reflected in two different kinds of definitions (Robinson (1954)): NOMINAL DEFINITIONS, which are of words, say of *tiger* (thus, in principle, intralinguistic), and REAL DEFINITIONS, of reality, of tigers (thus extralinguistic).

It is a commonplace that the syntax of a language is more constrained (fewer categories, more general regularities) than the semantics. Given a particular syntactic category like Verb, there are many verb subclasses. When we distinguish subclasses we initially use syntactic notions ('transitive', 'intransitive'), but further distinctions are semantic: "instrumental verb" or "verb of motion". This is a general condition, for all syntactic categories. While the feature [+ Verb] seems clearly syntactic, the feature [+ Causative] seems semantic; the more specific the feature, the more meaningful it appears. This is the point of McCawley (1968: 132–34), who questioned the "syntactic" status of features such as [+ Animate] and [+ Human].

It is also a commonplace that a semantically interpreted sentence can be used in a potentially infinite number of situation-specific applications. In other words, we have a continuum: syntax is most constrained and least diverse, semantics is less constrained and more diverse, and pragmatics is least constrained and most diverse, this last diversity created by extralinguistic modulations. Of the three, the categories of syntax are most closed, those of pragmatics most open. With syntax we are exclusively in language (or almost so); with pragmatics we are closely linked to reality.

If we consider form to be the most abstract meaning, then we have a continuum of meaning, from the most general and abstract to the most specific and concrete. Semantic "categories" are hyponyms of syntactic categories, and pragmatic categories are hyponyms of semantic. Other linguistic realities also reflect this scale. Languages have both major and minor classes, "lexical" and "grammatical" morphemes, open and closed classes. These pairs are not identical, but they show the same contrast; or rather, each contrast reveals a continuum, from that which is closed, abstract, formal and strongly systematic (Saussurean mutuality), to what is open, concrete, meaningful and weakly systematic (modularity). I propose that this manifold continuum, which I will describe simply as Closed to Open (and Language to Reality), is a universal design characteristic of language.

The (gradient) relationship of abstract to concrete also applies within each of the three divisions. Noun can syntactically specify to Noun Phrase [NP], *dog* to *the dog,* both specify semantically to *collie* and *the collie,* and the phrases pragmatically specify to the animal I am pointing to, or more specifically that animal as it trots across the lawn.

Further, in English, Noun Phrases can more specifically be Nominatives, which can be Subjects; and Subjects can be Agents. From this perspective, the currently debated question of whether Grammatical Relationships (Subjects, Objects, etc.) are "primitive" or "derived" takes on a different cast: Grammatical Relationships are more abstract than Semantic Roles (Agent, Patient, etc.) and more concrete than Syntactic Categories (Noun, Verb, etc.).

In principle, a category on one level of abstraction might be fully derivable from one on another (perhaps not generally), given that all the distinguishing attributes of level difference can be exhaustively stated. That is what Chomsky attempted to do in *Aspects* (1965) by defining Subject as the NP immediately dominated by S [Sentence]. If, however, some attributes are not minimally definable, as the Accessibility Hierarchy suggests (Keenan and Comrie (1977)), the relationships take on independent importance; all three levels—categories, relationships, and roles (three stages from abstract to concrete)—must be studied in their own (but highly interrelated) terms. (Marantz (1984: 1–12) also argues for three independent phenomena, on other grounds.)

Another complication is cross-classification: Experiencers are a subclass of Subjects, but they may also be a subclass of Direct Object. Cross-classifications on the same level of generalization (say, Proper and Count) must be distinguished from those on different levels (say, Direct Object and Experiencer).

The subject matter commonly called Semantics thus lies in a "middle" range of meaning. It is more specific and concrete than the subject matter called Syntax, whose meanings are so abstract that we do not comprehend them consciously, and thus rarely consider them meanings at all. On the other hand, Semantics is more general and abstract than the subject matter called Pragmatics, which can be highly complex, various and specific, and which may seem not to be meaning at all, but rather merely "what is."

Why does this middle range appear to be what is distinctly "meaningful"? Rosch (1977a) makes a pertinent observation. Given three words such as *animal, dog* and *terrier* (ordered most general to most specific), children learn the middle term, *dog,* earlier than the other two. She proposes (p. 213):

> . . . of the many levels of abstraction at which any given thing can
> be classified, there is one basic level of abstraction at which the
> organism can obtain the most information with the least cognitive
> effort. That is, in so far as categorization occurs to reduce the
> infinite differences between stimuli of behaviorally and cognitively

usable proportions, two opposing principles of categorization are operative: (a) On the one hand, it is to the organism's advantage to have each classification as rich in information as possible. This means having as many properties as possible predictable from knowing any one property (which, for humans, includes the relevant property of the category name), a principle which would lead to formation of large numbers of categories with the finest possible discriminations between categories. (b) On the other hand, for the sake of reducing cognitive load, it is to the organism's advantage to have as few classifications as possible, a principle which would lead to the smallest number of and most abstract categories possible. We believe that the basic level of classification, the primary level at which 'cuts' are made in the environment, is a compromise between these two levels; it is the most general and inclusive level at which the categories are still able to delineate real-world correlational structures.

As category continua, "animal-dog-terrier" and "syntax-semantics-pragmatics" differ drastically in scale, but I think Rosch's explanation has a parallel application: in both, the middle category is the "easiest" to comprehend, because it represents a balance between the unified, but highly abstract first category and the concrete, but highly diversified third category. Put another way: consciousness functions best in a "middle range" of categorization, even though it has (and needs) the additional abilities of highly abstract unconscious unity and highly concrete experiential particularity. This "best" range applies not only to the particular circumstances Rosch describes, but also to language-in-the-large.

The middle ground is also the favored stereotypic range of consciousness, at which our limited awareness works best. Both more abstractly and more concretely, we must make a special effort to comprehend consciously; often we fail, and usually we simply do not notice. The middle range contains the words that are most commonly distributed and easily understood; it is the one that we take automatically as (stereo)typical of words. Words that are too abstract for this middle ground are either "function words" *(the, that, and)* or are defined with high polysemy *(bear, take, hit)*. As *dog* illustrates, we favor words that "point" to reality, though not too specifically. Our foremost conscious preoccupation concerning "meaning" is in the direct relationship of word and thing, as Morris reveals in making it the defining characteristic of semantics.

To develop these comments further, we need to explore how we think: to ask why (as insufficiently reflective linguists) we look for certain favored categories and then treat these categories as basic, and even exclusive and complete. I suggest that the human mind is also a continuum, from closed unconscious to open consciousness. The crux of all theories of semantics (and of language-in-the-whole) is the underlying view of unconscious and conscious. We must now look at how we misconstrue the linguistic reflexes of these two aspects of mind.

5.2 CONSCIOUS DISTORTION

Anyone who surveys the range of semantic theories should be struck, if not surprised, by the preoccupation with nouns. In particular, the most appropriate starting point in theorizing seems to be nouns designating visible objects *(dog* or *tiger)* or social roles *(bachelor)*. Why are such nouns considered the best place to begin a theory?

One possible reason for this preoccupation is heuristic: words like *tiger* and *bachelor* are easier to assess than *take* or *of* or *nevertheless,* or nouns like *flood, shadow, gratitude,* or *perpetuity. Tiger* represents a real object with well-defined borders, and thus we have the sense of having available (nearly) all the information we need to assess its meaning. *Bachelor* represents (as Bolinger (1965: 566) notes) a CONSTRUCTED complex of meanings where we (apparently) need only factor out what we earlier factored in. Yet, since such conditions are not widespread in the language, how valuable and ultimately useful is such a starting point?

Another reason is that nouns are "basic", so that we need an understanding of *tiger* before we can deal with the other words noted above. Yet, how are such basics determined? An equally good (perhaps better) case could be made for verbs. And what is it that makes *tiger* more basic than *flood?* Are concrete objects more basic? Can we formulate a general theory of what is basic, such that verbs are next most basic, and then adjectives, etc.? An atheoretical claim is little more than a hunch.

Another reason is that nouns, especially of the favored type, represent real-world phenomena that are more salient, more demanding of our attention. But salience and even "reality" may not be central criteria. Making them such leads us to exaggerate the scope of salient details (as Aristotle did with horse-drawn motion) or to believe that scientists merely "describe" reality, without any interpreting medium.

I think all these factors contribute to the prominence of nouns in theorizing, but the crucial reason is one I have already noted: most semantic theories are centrally concerned with the problem of reference, how language relates to reality. As Morris's classification reveals, some theories apply the term "semantic" to the relationship between language and reality.

Admittedly, much of "reality" is in some complex way "created" or "defined" by language. Yet, as *of* and *thus* make clear, there is a significant difference between language and reality, at least in how we understand the latter. (We could, of course, say that *of* represents a highly abstract aspect of reality.) My arguments concerning *bear, take, break,* and *hit* have been to the effect that these words are more abstract and centrally linguistic, and thus more remotely referential, than words like *tiger;* dictionary definitions of these words are polysemic because they are erroneously made too concrete and too precisely referential.

By beginning with words like *tiger,* a word that (I will eventually argue) can be only minimally defined in solely linguistic terms, we tend to make all words just as concrete, and thus run the risk of conflating the order of the language with the order of reality, the same type of unnecessary complication Maher creates in conflating the iron with its particular magnetic field. This preoccupation with reference needs an explanation. I suggest that it derives from and continues to justify the mistaken but hardy belief (often, but only ritually, renounced) that words are "labels" and that language is (or should be made to be) a "mirror" of reality.

This belief carries over into a confusion about what is considered "scientific." A desired goal of scientific research is that scientific language should be as direct a mirror as possible of the reality being described, serving to make all distinctions and generalizations that the reality requires. It is debatable to what extent this can be achieved (it implies that language can be a transparent medium). But even rashly granting that language can serve such a purpose (and that this is, or ought to be, the basic purpose of language), when the reality to be studied is language itself, there often develops (especially by philosophers) an attempt to "improve" the language, and then to claim that the improvement is the intended object of study. It is, of course, both possible and desirable to change one's language to make it more useful, for scientific and other reasons, but not when language is the subject matter of investigation; in that event, the language is imperialized into something it "ought to be." Among linguists, this often occurs with linguistic expressions that seem to mystify us: idioms.

A telltale indication of what I mean is that exemplar words like *tiger* are usually studied narrowly and individually, with little investigation of all their contexts or their semantic fields. The goal of analysis seems always to be a relatively concrete quasi-ostensional "its meaning is THAT!" The Ogden-Richards (1923) theory of meaning reflects this: one-to-one relationships between word and concept, and concept and reference. In a strong Saussurean system, such a one-to-one pointing solution may not be possible.

We need not look far to find a language-derived system that effectively refutes Ogden-Richards: mathematics. Numbers are not defined referentially, nor are seconds, minutes and hours, or inches, feet and yards. These must be related to each other first. It is not relevant to the system that adding one drop of water to another results in yet another one drop.

It can be objected that while mathematical "entities" are strongly systematic, language is not necessarily or exclusively systematic in this way. As Coseriu and Geckler (1974: 140) note, some parts of a vocabulary are NOMENCLATURES, which do serve as labels referring directly to reality. But, they additionally warn, such subvocabularies give us little insight into the organization of a full vocabulary. For them, distinguishing language and reality is the first essential task for a semantic theory. Of course, we must not overgeneralize in the opposite direction; we must explain why vocabularies are heterogeneous, containing both highly abstract systematic words, remote from reality, and also reality-specific nomenclatures. In short, we must respect both of Rosch's principles.

In fact, mentioning mathematical systems is misleading for a different reason. While we actually understand such systems, and can "account" for them with our features and logics, any other strong systems in the language are likely to be mysterious. Mathematical systems seem unique not because they alone are strongly systematic, but rather because they are the most thoroughly known.

Words that are remote from reality, such as *of* and *take,* are likely to be in closed classes, to be highly systematic, and to be indicative of unconscious categorizing. Words that seem more directly referential, such as *tiger,* are likely to be in open classes, to be less systematic, and to be more indicative of conscious categorizing. But it is important to note that all words belong to classes that in fact are closed, though some are potentially open; words, that is, are more closed, systematic, and unconscious than sentences (although even these, as we saw with Ziff, are hardly concrete).

A preoccupation with referential words reveals an exaggerated reliance on what I will call the 'methods of conscious thought.' These can be seen in the usual minimal consideration of relevant data and the subsequent slighting of paradigms. As we consciously attempt to discover order in language, we are confronted with systems and categories that are largely unknown, and perhaps unknowable in conscious terms. The habit of consciousness through many centuries has been to impose its narrow range of systems and categories on the whole language, with any resulting deficiencies of theory (such as widespread multiple meaning) attributed to the language itself.

Conscious thought partializes; it operates by separating something from context and treating it as self-contained. Its awareness is that of a spotlight; it sees figures better than grounds, divisions better than continuities, brief and dynamic events better than lengthy and static conditions, the mid-sized rather than the very small or very large: it stereotypes, treating parts as wholes. Thus, consciousness fixes on nouns (the stereotypic "basic" word class), particularly those that refer (the stereotypic use of language) to the mid-sized type of discrete and movable objects (the most stereotypic reality). Further, consciousness is analytic (the stereotypic kind of knowing), with unbounded potential; within the consciously isolated self-contained entity can be found an infinity of parts, conditions, processes, and attributes. When context is acknowledged, it appears disguised as these various parts (thus: overloading), but its inclusion is piecemeal and random, its full influence minimized. The context most slighted is that provided by unconscious thought, on which conscious thought depends.

Conscious thought is oriented to reality, but in a narrow way. Spotlight awareness simplifies perception; things become more easily obvious and understandable. It is necessary, in an often turbulent reality, to make quick decisions and act on them. As a consequence of its limitations, when dealing with language, consciousness will be first concerned with reference, the fit of language and reality. Of course, "literal" meanings will be considered basic to (largely ignored) figurative and "stylistic" meanings. The differences between linguistic order and natural order, while they can hardly be ignored, will be accorded secondary status or deferred, because rigorously "formal" theories (as consciousness conceives them) cannot handle everything initially and must put "secondary" things aside. Even if nonreferential words are granted close to equal importance, referentials will be viewed as providing a phenomenal base for epiphenomenal abstractions and purely "grammatical" or "logical" words.

Conscious thought also tends to be atomistic and mechanistic, proceeding with the explanatory expectation of basic isolated elements that are combined by simple processes. Thus, its "reality" will be based on discrete elements (perhaps physical sensations) that are amalgamated, each amalgamation possibly receiving a linguistic label; other amalgamations, and more complex linguistic notions, are built from these. The general processes require the inclusion of puzzling words like conjunctions, but these will be simpler than the conjunctions of actual languages. Consciousness will overemphasize and make exclusive the "rational" standards of direct reference and compositionality, and will tend to favor the syntagmatic over the paradigmatic. Conscious deductive logics will always be much more consistent in these respects, compared to language, and this will lead some to feel that language is too messy and vague, and probably in large part a baggage of discrete historical accidents.

5.3 UNCONSCIOUS DISTORTION

In spite of conscious attempts to ban or ignore it, the unconscious cannot be excluded, merely belittled and displaced; we have the disguised "return of the repressed."

As an example, recall our previous discussion, with *bear,* of agency. Originally in Case Grammar, it was proposed that agency could be handled by the two "cases" agent and instrument, the first the animate and initiating cause, the second the inanimate and immediate cause, used by the agent. Then it was recognized that (say) hurricanes were initiating but inanimate, and so a third category was established, force. But it was evident in discussions of agency that this third category worried some linguists, because it threatened a "proliferation" of cases. The usual view expressed was that it is desirable, even necessary, that cases be strictly limited.

Why? What is the reason for this desirable necessity?

It might be that these "cases" (or, currently, thematic roles) are actually formally differentiated. Yet, while they are morphologically explicit in some languages, they are not in English; they must be invoked as covert categories. However, considering the usual minimal attention to data, such covert distinctions may be only the artifacts of a mistaken theory.

In addition, a claim for covert categories on "universal" grounds is too weak, because too selective: we should then be able to claim that, since earlier

English had Singular, Dual, and Plural divisions of Number, Dual is now a covert category. It could be claimed that Cause-relationships are more important than Number, and so must be universally recognized. But then how is "importance" determined and why should it be a criterion?

It could be claimed that a theory requires minimal categories, or that we need to explain how an infinite language can be based on finite means. But, again, such claims can too easily be imperialistic. If the language is based on finite means, then those means should be in the language and discoverable; why must we invoke distinctions that are not apparent? Why not also require in advance that plurality be divided into several different subdivisions? Unless we can find evidence for finite means, why is there a need to require them?

There is a supposedly reliable means of justifying binary distinctions which lack formal reflexes: analytic tests. These "tests" are perhaps the most dubious part of current theorizing, and they illustrate how even an explicit and formal theory can protect itself from hostile data. One test is that of prohibited co-occurrence: *John and the key opened the door is ill-formed, it is claimed, because agent and instrument cannot be conjoined. If, so the argument goes, there were no such distinction, the prohibition could not be stated.

However, this test is incomplete. For one thing, it doesn't guarantee that the prohibition is semantic; a pragmatic lack of coherence (R. Lakoff (1971)) is equally explanatory. Second, the prohibition may simply involve animacy. Third, as Kuno (1987: 5) notes, the data are not all supportive: what about *The bandits and their smoking guns terrorized the town?* Or, joining force and agent, *The hurricane and the looters devastated the town?* (Of course, we could give *and* a special meaning to cover these cases, creating more polysemy.)

Another test is that of context: we have *John deliberately broke the window* versus *John accidentally broke the window,* which indicates greater agency in the first sentence. But while the sentences are certainly different, why attribute difference to the subject or verb, which don't vary?

Yet another test is that of ambiguity: *John broke the window* is ambiguous between the two possibilities. But does this sentence have only these two possibilities? Why can't we use this sentence when we don't know whether John acted deliberately or not? If this sentence can be unspecified for agency, and also represent many degrees of agency, then a two-way distinction distorts in at least these two ways.

Linguists who invoke these tests often do not ask a more basic question: have the tests themselves been tested? Do they do precisely what is required, for the reasons supposed, and what is their implied full range of application? Linguists in the TG tradition should be especially wary, given Chomsky's well-founded suspicion of oversimplifying tests.

The oversimplification comes from the unconscious: we invoke closure, a finite set of choices, where the language in fact does not exhibit them. We overanalyze, but in a constrained way: by dividing a unity into a few parts, we fail to realize that the unity implies an infinite number of specifics. We in effect make what is both unified and potentially open into something closed, something infinite into something finite.

Thus, each test must be measured by a meta-test: Are we applying this test-for-distinction and its reasoning consistently throughout the language, and is there a principled end to the divisions the test finds? It is much too easy to invoke distinctions by "context", because this method can be used to give a word as many meanings as it has distinguishable contexts. The reason the test appears reasonable is that the testers fail to do the extrapolation that the test requires.

A caution must be made about "universals": it is too easy to find universals in a language if the only requirement is the ability to find multiple interpretations. With such unrestraint, anything linguistic can be found to have multiple meanings. Even if we assume that the same highly differentiated set of "atomic" meanings are available to all humans, regardless of the organization of their languages, the analytic question is still: at what degree(s) of abstraction does *this* language enable *this* differentiation to be made?

The system of unities and distinctions claimed for a language should give primary and overriding importance to its system of formal distinctions (and lack of distinctions), for these are the distinctions that the language represents (or doesn't) on its most abstract levels; these are "foundational" meanings, the fundamental categories from which additional categories stem. It is distortive to approach a language with a predetermined (and supposedly universal) notion of (say) Cause and then "discover" that the language's "surface structures" radically obscure its "deep structure" meanings.

Semantic distinctions can be correlated with formal distinctions, but they must be established first, by paradigmatic test. Even a large-scale formal distinction such as transitive-intransitive need not imply two meanings for a verb (like *break*) that appears in both patterns. A-word-in-its-(concretizing)-contexts is always more diverse than the word itself.

The problem with the tests is that they do not by themselves reveal at which level of abstraction a distinction is made. Thus, as evoked, their effect is to stereotype: to simplify the degrees and ranges of abstraction in language and make them more manageable. The model (unconsciously) assumed is that of a system with both minimal unities and minimal diversities; in effect, by minimizing unity (though apparently preoccupied with finding it), we also minimize diversity, and vice versa. Language is thus seen as complex, but not too complex; it is heterogeneous, but not too heterogeneous. We create a stereotype of language, one whose prime attribute is that it can be understood consciously. To counter this stereotype, I may seem to be taking a contradictory course, yet it is one that must counter both minimizations: to discover the unities of words, I have to reveal their infinite range of (more concrete) possibilities.

The proposal I made for agency with *bear* recognizes that the possibilities are endless and thus are not lexically determined. Such infinities are more frequent that we usually think. Even the lengthy divisions of sense for *take* and *break* in the OED are not necessarily the complete story; they are simply the limits of the data on hand, or of the persistence of the investigator, who knows that an end must come sometime, if only for economic reasons. As a methodological necessity, closure must be demonstrated, not merely assumed or achieved by neglect. We too often expect finite possibilities, and then our hasty commitment to several supposedly evident, "important" or "salient" (stereotypic), uses makes us reluctant to look further. As a result, we do not recognize how often an alleged polysemy is in fact infinite, and thus not polysemy at all, not semantic, but pragmatic.

Why do we feel the need to posit finite distinctions? Why do we expect to find them, to the extent of fooling ourselves about the appropriateness of our proposals and tests? The answer: there are genuine, formally evident examples in the language. That is, a language has closed classes, and these can be discovered, not invented. Closed classes are evidence of the unconscious, and accordingly mysterious; conversely, the open classes are proportionally conscious, and accordingly easier to understand. Even the stress in our theories on rational standards such as direct reference and compositionality comes from unconscious order. These reflect a pure systematicity (IDEAL) that we routinely supersede and complicate when we consciously interact with reality.

We have this irony: by inappropriately invoking and applying oversimplified standards, we actually underestimate our conscious abilities. Anyone with minimal intelligence, for example, knows that human intentions are highly variable, with questions of intentionality often hard to determine. Sometimes, as an often unsatisfactory practical necessity, we must reduce intentionality to "did he do it or not?" (as in law); but even the legal system allows for qualifications of this stark alternative. Thus it should strike us as bewildering to find linguists claiming that a sentence like *John broke the window* is exactly two ways ambiguous, between full intention and full accident, though it shows no formal variation for the choice.

When we look for a small set of relevant factors or features, we are following the model of the unconscious, reacting to our unconscious need to have finitely differentiated foundations and frameworks. We do what Bateson (1972: 445) calls "short-circuiting": we notice only isolated parts of an intricate unconscious-conscious system and impose on these our own consciously created design. We reduce the mind's diversity, using the finite categorizing of the unconscious to invent bogus closures, thus also underestimating our open and infinite conscious capacities.

5.4 CONTEXT

To review so far: I am assuming a continuous scale of abstraction, from the most abstract, autonomous, mutually (i.e., strongly) systematic, and well-formed level (IDEAL) to the empirical, most concrete, non-autonomous, modularly (i.e., weakly) systematic, and ill-formed level. Roughly, this is the continuum from Language to Reality: from language as a (nearly) autonomous closed system to an experientially open system directly involved in and influenced by externalities. The different levels of abstraction are distinguished, essentially, by their degree of specific context.

In his book *Search for the Real and Other Essays,* the artist Hans Hofmann (1967: 41) suggests the following exercise:

> . . . take a sheet of paper and make a line on it. Who can say
> whether this line is long or short? . . . But when, on the same
> sheet of paper, you make another short line, you can see
> immediately that the first line is the longer one. . . . Was it
> necessary to enlarge the first line to make it the longer one? We
> did not have to touch that line to make any change. We gave it
> meaning through its relation to the new line.

Where did the sense of "longer" come from (or "shorter", "left of", "right of", "above", etc.)? This is the famous (or notorious) problem called EMERGENCE: something new seems to arise "out of nothing". The whole appears to be greater than the sum of its parts.[1]

Hofmann notes another emergent relationship:

> But is that all that happened when you made these two lines? . . .
> Certainly not! The fact that you placed one line somewhere on the
> paper created a very definite relationship between this line and the
> edges of your paper. (You were not aware perhaps that these edges
> were the first lines of your composition.)

Actually, there is no emergence, merely a confusion about different levels of abstraction. All the relationships of the line to other things are already there. They are missing simply because the line has been viewed abstractly, in isolation. Abstracting involves omitting the same properties that, when we concretize, seem to emerge; emergence is the reverse of abstracting. The line does not exist in isolation; it is necessarily bound to contexts. Recall the Openness Condition and its mandatory context:

[A] OPENNESS CONDITION

Within a multidimensional mandatory context (lack of context is impossible), the inherent sense of a word or expression is always modulated pragmatically.

Hofmann correctly notes why this might be surprising: we are not fully aware. We need to state the following, as a general condition of conscious human knowing:

[B] ABSTRACTION-EMERGENCE CONDITION

To the conscious mind, the whole will always seem to be greater than the parts; the parts exist "in isolation" only because they have been detached from more concrete wholes. Consciousness typically puts the parts and the whole on the same level of abstraction, making the relation of part to whole problematic (emergence): the whole is reduced (but never successfully) to the compositional sum of the abstracted parts, and the abstracted parts are interpreted as if they were concrete, "basic" elements.

Holism is not a congenial perspective to consciousness, which prefers (and, even when knowing better, reverts to) an atomistic-compositional perspective. But even "holism", as we conceive of it, is distorted by conscious limitation; the above condition implies that, because of our limited range of (actual and possible) awareness, "emergence" and "greater than the sum of the parts" will always seem like illusions; they are created by our ability to abstract and then made mysterious because we do not allow for the implications of abstraction.

In systematic terms, the whole is not greater than the parts; in fact, the whole and the parts cannot be compared in a way that makes such a notion sensible. "Greater than" is apparent only because we misunderstand the parts: Hofmann's line is not an isolate; it is itself-in-all-possible-(infinite)-contextual-wholes. Put alternatively, it is a particular subsystem (figural) focus implying many systems; "things" and "parts" are holograms.

A word is thus an IMPLEX: not merely an isolated entity, but also all its constituent relationships; unconsciously, it includes all its possible specificities. Consciously, we are unable, even with great effort, to think of all these specificities (though we can recognize one unconsciously or consciously when the opportunity arises, as our usage shows); expressing an implex as a theoretical generalization gives us only partial understanding.

While this may seem mystifying, I am trying to explain my continual surprise, when collecting many uses in context of a particular word. I discover that "yes, I knew we could say that, but I probably wouldn't have thought of it"; I wonder "how could I have ever realized this possibility without this example?"; and I conclude that "this word is both more diverse and unified than I had imagined, than I *can* imagine." When we talk, we are not putting boxcars together (in fact, that isn't as simple as it sometimes intellectually seems either), nor even merely building particular hierarchical structures. An image of Stratificational Grammar [SG] seems more apt: with each linguistic choice, we are creating "spreading activations".

The theoretical impasse, then, is that we consciously see "parts" merely as isolates. The purpose of an idealization is essentially to mimic the abstracting of the language, factoring out the variable particulars of context; but it cannot factor out context itself. That was my point about stereotypes and prototypes. Although this appears to make idealization impossible, in fact the only effect is to correct our faulty assessment of the level of abstraction. Idealization is the natural and unavoidable strategy of the (fully functional) human mind (especially the unconscious). As we saw earlier, once we correctly assess the context of IDEAL, we find that it accounts for less, on a more abstract level. The problem with CTG transformations is that they actually did not treat sentences as isolates; they thus conflated several levels of abstraction and claimed generalizations on too low a level of concreteness.

Hofmann's first line, and any other humanly created "isolated" thing, is an abstract generalization of all its potential contextual diversifications; that is, it unites an infinite number of concretions. So too do words and sentences, which are also human creations. A language is a matrix theory; it is much more extensive than scholarly theories because it uses more fully the resources of the unconscious. Words, sentences, theories are all idealizations. The realities they abstract will always have "emergent" characteristics; that is the reverse implication of abstraction. Thus, *The thief took the jewels* and *The editor took my article* appear to have quite different *take*'s: the realities evoked are much more detailed and complicated than anything that the words and sentences contribute. The difference between sense and reference is this difference between levels of abstraction.

The general problem is one that Whitehead (1925) described as the Fallacy of Misplaced Concreteness: "the expression of more concrete facts under the guise of very abstract logical constructions" (p. 52). Whitehead locates the source of the fallacy with an observation that parallels Rosch's:

> Classification is a halfway house between the immediate
> concreteness of the individual thing and the complete abstraction of
> mathematical notions. (p. 30)

This follows from the mutability of human experience:

> Apart from recurrence, knowledge would be impossible; for
> nothing could be referred to our past experience. Also, apart from
> some regularity of recurrence, measurement would be impossible.
> In our experience, as we gain the idea of exactness, recurrence is
> fundamental. (p. 33)

From this perspective, R. Hall's (1978: 38) exclusively "real" idiolects seem fundamental only because he tacitly conceives of them as context-free. The concept of "idiolect" is already a highly abstract notion. To be fully faithful to his reductionist purpose, Hall would have to count as real only particular speech events that occur in contexts that can never be duplicated. But, as both Rosch and Whitehead imply, such possibilities are not even conceivable without the use of the abstract generalization. That is why Hall's idiolects are also, in his perspective, "fictions."

Whitehead notes that some of our basic scientific notions stem from faulty assumptions about what is "fundamentally" real. Consider the notions of "simple location", "quality" and "substance":

> Of course, substance and quality, as well as simple location, are
> the most natural ideas for the human mind. It is the way in which

> we think of things, and without these ways of thinking we would
> not get our ideas straight for daily use. There is no doubt about
> this. The only question is, How concretely are we thinking when
> we consider nature under these conceptions? My point will be that
> we are presenting ourselves with simplified editions of immediate
> matters of fact. When we examine the primary elements of these
> simplified editions, we shall find that they are in truth only to be
> justified as being elaborate logical constructions of a high degree
> of abstraction. (p. 53)

Consider several complications in the most minimal requirements of
IDEAL. First, the "basic elements" (words) are not as unproblematic as we
require. IDEAL is abstract, and these basic elements must be correspondingly
abstract. I am arguing that, individually, they vary in their degree of
abstractness and direct relationship to reality. Certainly, as they are defined in
dictionaries, they have properties that are too concrete for IDEAL. If we commit
Whitehead's fallacy and make IDEAL too concrete, individual words will seem
to be more fully part of it, but we will then be unable to capture the
generalizations that IDEAL was designed to make.

In mathematical and logical systems, "basic" elements can be stipulated as
relatively homogeneous (at worst, representing a few classes whose members
are minimally variable); but the morphemes and words of natural languages are
much more heterogeneous. Further, the details of this heterogeneity are not
given in advance, but are a major part of what must be discovered; if we
stipulate homogeneity as a methodological axiom of our system, we also
stipulate away the subject of our investigations.

We should expect, given the systemic linguistic reality I am arguing for,
that on a highly abstract (syntactic) level heterogeneity is more minimal. That is
what the hypothesis of X-bar theory (Jackendoff (1977)) attempts to capture, by
factoring out what is common across categories; the "isolated" notion of 'head'
(contrasted with 'modifiers') captures more generally (for the parts of speech
included) the necessary relationships of a word to its context. The traditional
part-of-speech distinctions, assumed in CTG, obscured higher unities because
they conflated (like CTG transformations) different abstract levels. But, even
with (what we call) syntax, things get too complex; in the less abstract company
of nouns, verbs and adjectives, and the even more concrete reality of semantic
subclasses, the diversity of basic units effectively makes irrelevant the stipulated
simplicity of artificial languages.

We struggle with confusions that cause us to think too concretely at one
point and too abstractly at another, and perhaps both simultaneously. In order to
extend IDEAL as if it were an artificial language, to formulate the required rules
or constraints, we are not able to take the actual diversely abstract words of
language as "basic", but must either oversimplify their (more concrete)
complexity or decompose them into (supposedly) "more" basic (actually, more
abstract, "de-emergent") units, or both. To handle the increasing complexity

attendant on (more) concrete diversification, we resort (necessarily) to more highly abstract building blocks, but then—forgetting we have "lost" something by abstracting—we often misinterpret the building blocks to be as concrete as the reality they abstracted.

As we move out of the middle range of language that is the limited home of consciousness, these "basic" elements become more mysterious (or, even worse, tediously detailed and unenlightening). We confront the main design flaw of mechanist philosophies: the supposed basic elements, far from being settled and well-defined, are more unruly than the complexities they are supposed to build. The basics are not as fully abstract as they should be; consciousness cannot see clearly what is concrete and what is abstract.

A sentence is more concrete than its constituents, because each constituent is potentially all the sentences in which it can occur. By starting with the sentence and then dividing it into parts, TG moves from (relatively) concrete to (more) abstract. With each phrase structure rule, something is lost. Further, the sentence is more abstract than all the discourses of which it can be a part. If, as in TG, we take the sentence as axiomatic, we must expect that with each discourse, something is gained. In both instances, we must resist the temptation to make word, sentence and discourse equal in degree of abstraction; when we do this, the inevitable result is polysemy.

We need, then, a full, not merely postulated, theory of "performance" to supply the full particularities and their relationships, for IDEAL cannot, especially with the sentence as an axiomatic center. The supposed isolated sentence is actually a holographic abstraction of discourse: it represents what is (abstractly) common to all discourses in which it can occur. (It then also follows that a word, on an even more abstract scale, is also a holographic abstraction of discourse.)

5.5 THEORIES AND PEOPLE

Language, by the process of abstraction, unifies: it idealizes and homogenizes. In our research, we try to discover at what level of abstraction a particular unity is achieved. At the next lower level, moving toward reality, we find the diversity that the unity abstracted. I am claiming that diversification often occurs more concretely than our theories assume: it is pragmatic, not semantic.

I can illustrate this point by showing how some diversities of meaning are not intralinguistic, but rather correlate with the complexity and individuality of people. Referring to the IDEAL conception of "competence", Hymes (1979) makes some pertinent observations about human individuality (p. 41):

> We know, of course, that the abilities of individuals are both more
> and less than was implied by Chomsky's notion: more, in that they
> comprise more than grammar, more often than a single variety or
> indeed language; less, in that it is in the nature of the social

division of labor and the contingency of experience that the
systematic potential of the language as a whole exceeds the
command of any one person. What a person is able or not able to
do, after all, is at the heart of much of the interest in the subject,
where individual differences as a social problem are involved. And
when we are forced to reflect on our assumptions about ideals of
speech and an ideal speech community, it is about an ideal
distribution, or organization, of competencies that we must think.

Hymes questions using terms such as "competence" and "ideal" for
theoretical purposes that are so abstractly removed from, and perhaps
antithetical to, their uses to describe more concrete realities. This would not be
a problem if we were consciously able to fully recognize and accurately assess
shifts in abstraction; but, through our inept direct applications of such abstract
conceptions, short-circuiting and the fallacy of misplaced concreteness run
rampant, usually to human detriment. However, as Korzybski (1933) noted, this
is a problem of all language: we are always illegitimately assuming that
(abstract) words refer directly to reality, like labels. If this were not so, even
among scholars, there would not be so persistent an attempt to ground linguistic
meaning on reference.

However, even granting all that Hymes says, I don't think he invalidates
IDEAL. The difference he notes is the same as that between a highly theoretical
and a highly practical approach: each in effect emphasizes what the other
diminishes. This is not a fault of either, merely the territorial imperatives. Two
aspects of individual difference must be included in OPEN; although these
contrary aspects seem to undermine IDEAL by cross purposes (making it both
too weak and too strong), they instead imply both the necessity of IDEAL-type
knowledge and its limits: "necessary" because scholars dealing with variation
will reach abstractions very slowly, and "limits" because the high abstractions
are simply that: abstractions.

The problem: while CTG posited uniformities on too concrete a level,
Hymes seems to be making them too abstract, underestimating human
similarities. Everyone who speaks English has knowledge (say) of *take;* we
would be astonished to find someone who otherwise spoke English, yet did not
know this word. On the other hand, if someone lacked (say) *elicit,* we might
conclude a limited education, but not be surprised. Also, it would be surprising
if someone knew *take* and yet found odd and never used the phrase *take a drink.*
On the other hand, some people use the expression *take and do something,*
while others do not. Some *take decisions,* while others *make decisions.* What
these observations show is that some words are common knowledge, while
others are not; and, even with a common-knowledge word, some of its contexts
are common and some are not. That is, we have both unity among all speakers,
and on a fairly specific level, and also diversity, by dialect, idiolect, register, or
otherwise.

I am claiming that some knowledge of a language is shared by all speakers of that language. More generally, some highly abstract knowledge will be common to speakers of all languages. This is the point of Chomsky's observation (Paikeday (1985: 49ff)) that GB is not really about language: that is, not about the diversity found in actual languages, but about what is common to all languages, and thus innate. More concretely, we have the differences which make different languages (where "a language" is admittedly a highly variable thing), yet no language is ever totally differentiated from other languages. In short, an IDEAL scholar can readily grant Hymes's theoretical modulations, if the claim is accorded its correct degree of abstraction.

When some aspect of language is made either too abstract or too concrete (and these often go hand in hand), one likely result is bogus polysemy. Taking people as individuals, and thus a diversifying factor, we can explore the consequences of ignoring (that is, overidealizing) their differing involvements. Consider several examples of lexical analysis.

The first is from Stockwell, Schachter and Partee (1973: 728) [SSP]. They note that for three nouns representing three biologically bisexual species— *neighbor, horse, fruitfly*—the permitted pronouns vary (my sentences):

[1] My neighbor is fascinating, but he/she/*it is also unreliable.
[2] The horse is beautiful, but he/she/it is also unmanageable.
[3] The fruitfly seems to be dead, but *he/*she/it may only be resting.

SSP observe that there seem to be three different systems of pronouns at work; they accordingly propose a solution which makes each of the pronouns inherently ambiguous: *he,* for example, sometimes contrasts with *it* and sometimes doesn't. If this were the best solution, it would undermine the hypothesis of monosemy, because closed-class words such as pronouns should, most typically, be monosemic.

We need to note several excellent qualities of the SSP solution. First of all, it takes systematicity seriously; it analyzes related words together, and the (hardly desired) solution is dictated by systematic considerations. Second, the data invoked are often overlooked in overhomogenized analyses; they are the data a Bolinger delights in finding. Thus, in these two respects, it is a model of semantic research. The only weak point is the implicit assumption that the semantic content of the pronouns alone accounts for the differences. By assuming that linguistic order is more concrete than it is, SSP place the individuating factor on too abstract a level and thus create polysemy.

In some earlier comments (Ruhl (1975: 86)) I suggested that the difference could be attributed to a pragmatic principle with the effect of, "The higher in the order of animals, the more necessary it is to make sexual distinctions." Except for infants, I noted, it is necessary to make distinctions with humans, but optional with horses, and usually impossible, unnecessary, or overparticular with fruitflies. On this interpretation, the pronouns have consistent, systematic meanings; it is only the pragmatic application of these words that creates the lack of parallelism.

However, while I still agree with this solution, I think it doesn't stress enough the individuating factor. Obviously, most horse breeders would never call a horse *it,* and some biologists would carefully distinguish male and female fruitflies. What occasions the *it* (and for babies too) is individually varying degrees of ignorance or indifference: some people in some situations can't distinguish male and female and they're not expected to. Thus, the individuation is on a more concrete level than semantic: it arises out of different experiences of different people with humans, horses and fruitflies.

A key point: inherent linguistic meaning does not have to mirror reality. It is a mistake to assume that if in reality a fruitfly is female, then a pronoun used to refer to it must have 'female' or some other specifically adjusted sense as one of its inherent meanings, or that the choice of *it* over *she* diminishes the 'female' status of *she.* Language and reality do not match in such a simplified way, and any idealization that forces such an assumption is asking for trouble. One might equally well insist the opposite: that if I call a fruitfly *it,* then it actually is neuter. (Actually, this mistake is perhaps more common than the first.)[2] Both claims confuse language and reality, giving both equal degrees of abstraction.

Now consider the following data and comments from Cohen (1979: 67) (my renumbering):

[4] It wasn't an insult because it was not intended as such.

[5] It was an unintentional insult.

> Clearly the word "insult" might be described by a compositional semantics as occurring in a sense that is + INTENTIONAL in [4], but not in [5]. But such a description chooses what I have called the method of cancellation. It supposes that the occurrence of the adjective "unintentional" in [5] has canceled the + INTENTIONAL feature in the occurrence of the word "insult," (because the retention of that feature would render the sentence self-contradictory). We need then, for the description of [4] and [5], just one lexical entry for "insult," alongside some general set of rules for semantic feature-cancellation in the process of composing sentential meaning. Correspondingly both [4] and [5] are ambiguous.

Cohen claims that *insult* is semantically different in [4] and [5], but not because *insult* is polysemic. He rejects (and so do I) positing two different verbs, one marked + INTENTIONAL, the other − INTENTIONAL, because this would, if extrapolated to its implied full range in the vocabulary, create unnecessary multiplicity. He also rejects a possible pragmatic solution:

> . . . there is not a third—quasi-Gricean—possibility. It will not do to say that "insult" never has the feature + INTENTIONAL but carries with it, in normal contexts, a conversational implicature of intentionality, which happens to be canceled in [5]. The reason

why this possibility is not available is because it cannot explain the
force of the "because . . ." clause in [4].

Rather, Cohen takes the innovative step of making not the word, but the
cancellation rule, semantic. The analytic test he uses is that of prohibited
co-occurrence: if sentence [4] is to be considered well-formed, we must account
for the assumption in the *because*-clause that *insult,* without modification, is
taken as intentional. Another use of cancellation rule is exemplified in the
following (pp. 67–68):

[6] I tried to warn him but he didn't hear me.
[7] I warned him, but he didn't hear me.

> The method of cancellation would describe the word "warn" as
> occurring in a sense that is + UPTAKE in [6] but not in [7]. . . .

Again, we must note the strengths of this approach. The "strongest" (most
abstract and general) solution for such data would seem (other than the
obviously wrong syntactic solution) to be the semantic one SSP and Cohen seek,
because semantics, being more closed and abstract, imposes more constraints. A
pragmatic solution seems an encouragement to "anything goes"; it is looser and
vaguer than the systematic semantic features that Cohen so precisely specifies.
A pragmatic solution is too easy and exemplies a common dodge: discarding
troublesome data to the relevant "garbage heap" (adverb, idiom, parole,
performance).

The Monosemic Bias, however, is an alternative standard for "strongest
solution": monosemy is theoretically preferable to polysemy. Of course, this
does not automatically put a pragmatic solution in a better light; both Cohen's
hypothesis and mine are on trial. The merits must be determined by linguistic
realities. Consider these additional data for the verb *insult:*

[8]   Mary insulted John, . . .
[8a] . . . and he strenuously objected, but she hadn't meant that.
[8b] . . . hoping to rile him, but he was too dumb to notice.
[8c] . . . or so Bill claimed, but neither of them realized it.
[8d] . . . which appalled me, but neither of them realized it.
[8e] . . . or so John claimed, but he had to be pretty touchy to consider *that*
      an insult.
[8f] . . . and they quarreled about it, but their kind of peevish exchange
      hardly qualifies as an insult.

Unnoticed by Cohen, "uptake" by the patient (or reagent, in my terms) is
also necessary with *insult,* as [8b] shows. Do we really have an insult, even
when intended, when the reagent fails to be insulted? What if neither agent nor
reagent view it as such, but rather some external party [8c and d]? What if one
external party views it as such, but another doubts it [8c]? What if the reagent,
or both agent and reagent consider it an insult, but the external party does not

[8e and f]? If intention is relevant in the way Cohen suggests, then these factors are too. And these considerations are not necessarily all the possible factors: do the same criteria apply when agent or reagent is drunk or in great physical or emotional pain, when social status of agent and reagent are quite different, when rational Mr. Spock or a judge is the reagent, etc.? It is misleading to consider only intention, because other aspects of the situation can create equivalent inconsistency.

Cohen seems to tacitly assume that because the word *insult* is used, there really is an insult. Again, the fit between language and reality is made too direct. An insult is not an immediately obvious thing: it is an evaluation, a judgment, and different evaluators can differ without contradiction. Thus, Cohen's solution ignores the crucial individuating factor: it is the independence of involved people that creates the apparent variation in meaning. Further, involved parties can recognize this (in [8e and f]), acknowledging that others may view it as an insult, but judging it not themselves. Cohen has treated a reality-complicated situation as too purely and too simply linguistic.

Perhaps for the word *insult* to be used at all, someone (including the speaker or hearer of the sentence) must view something (and this can be quite subtle) as such, but the possibility of two points of view (at least speaker and hearer) is always present. What the data show is that people can call something an insult both with intention (agent-judgment) and without, and with uptake (reagent-judgment) and without. Thus, *insult* is simply unspecified semantically for these factors, with modulations determined situationally. Also, since evaluations are concerned, these determinations cannot be final in the sense that Cohen seems to make them, unless finality is determined by the speaker. (The overhearers-of-the-sentence, including Cohen and me, can also add determinations.) Accompanying unspecified nouns for *insult* will also be pragmatically specified as agent and reagent.

There are a number of other explanatory possibilities, depending on the level of abstraction. I am assuming that the presumption of intentionality is stereotypic: fully pragmatic, a result of the conscious mind's narrow awareness of all the possibilities. (Cohen's selective data show as much.) Another possibility: we may discover that *insult* (either alone or with other psychological words) is best seen as assuming "full involvement" of intentionality and uptake, biased toward full agency and full reagency. A BIAS may serve as the most likely pragmatic assumption, the DEFAULT or SCHEMATIC EXPECTATION; if so, it might be difficult to decide whether intentionality or uptake are semantic or pragmatic. If semantic, a bias would not require "canceling," even if the reality so indicated, because its semantic status would not change; the cancellation would be pragmatic.

A bias, as I define it, is a stereotype that has been conventionalized; a stereotype in turn may also be a bias that has been deconventionalized. This is also a continuum, implied by the recognition of an open present, with words at different stages of development; along this continuum, pragmatic processes of specialization and generalization can have semantic effects. We may even have individual differences: speakers who make intentionality and uptake as simple as do linguistic theories would likely sympathize with a polysemic view; as they learn more about human nature, they might sympathize with Cohen; learning more, they might have intentionality and uptake as biases, and then as stereotypes. That is, the more they knew about human variation, the more abstract they would make the word *insult*.

More reflexively abstract, the bias may generally follow from the psychological nature of the verb. Even more reflexively abstract, it may turn out that we bias toward this bias, unless there are reasons otherwise. We must note all of these possible solutions because they are potentials of the multiply-reflexive human mind; the best solution for any particular datum may be any of them. Unfortunately, in our attempt to explain too much maximally in narrowly synchronic and semantic terms, we in effect create the language of an unreflective moron.

Now consider *warn*. What does *try to warn* mean? Did I yell to get his attention, but fail? Did I scream *"That car . . ."* and then despair because I knew he couldn't hear? Did I get out the whole *"That car's going to run you down"?* Did he actually nod, but not react appropriately, so I knew he didn't hear me? Or, I concluded he didn't hear me, since I didn't think he intended to commit suicide or thought himself indestructible. Did I just scream *"Watch out?"* Did I wave my hands, knowing he was deaf, or knowing that the sound of the waterfall would drown out my warning?

Probably not the last, but the others are all possible, given this particular sentence. Now what about simply *warn?* As far as I can see, all of the above possibilities (again, except the last) still hold. There need be nothing different in the external reality; what the *try to warn* variant does is make explicit the attempt, and thus pragmatically suggest failure. But when only *warn* is explicit, pragmatic rules can supply both attempt and failure, so that both *try to warn* and *warn* in this situational context mean effectively the same. That is, two different senses can have the same reference (for the degree of accuracy that is contingently required). Thus, we are not obligated to explain semantically why *try to warn* and *warn* are sometimes equivalent (like *remind* and *strike as similar*), a move which requires oversemanticization.

Cohen's phenomenon is much wider than he thinks. Some additional examples:

[9] John won the race, but he was disqualified. Those Russian judges won't let the Americans win anything.

[10] A: Dickerson fumbled the ball, but the referees missed it.
B: The instant replay official overruled the referees.
C: Yeah, but the television announcers said he didn't really fumble.
A: But you can *see* on the replay that he did.

In sports, what *happened* (in obscure situations) used to be what the referees on the field said it was; in pro football now, with instant replays, even that old conventionalist verity is not always true. A semantic theory that must fully account for the varying status of *win* and *fumble* in [9] and [10] is going to get very complicated: how can you both win and not win a race, or have three distinct, potentially contradicting, criteria for fumbling? Significantly, the variation will parallel our full awareness of the (apparently) intended message(s) and the complexity of the involved human evaluators.

To repeat: my general point in this discussion concerns degree of abstraction. A linguist using the NORMAL framework is likely to push too hard for individuation, foreclosing systematic possibilities; a linguist using the IDEAL framework is likely to push too hard for systematicity, ignoring individuation. If (say) "intentionality" is posited generally as a semantic fact, then what for some words is a fairly concrete variable will be implicitly overabstracted; some words that are unspecified for degree of intentionality will then be analyzed as polysemic.

Another complication: individuation does not stop with individual human beings. The two "individuals" who differ on *insult* or *fumble* may be the same person. Like words, people are not merely unities; they also are contextually variant. People can change their minds or be indecisive without misusing the language; in fact, the language allows them to be so.

Thus, also, an utterance that is inherently contradictory can nevertheless be a well-formed utterance, because human beings are renowned for even the most blatantly obvious contradictions. A direct and immediate change of mind or contradiction can be easily classified as performance, and thus pragmatic; but if the data are slightly complicated, as in Cohen's examples, we can be fooled into believing that something more linguistically distinctive is responsible. We formulate our intuitional sentences as abstractions, to factor out such complications; but when we then judge a sentence as well-formed, are we successfully eliminating people in all their complexity?

People can also fill different social roles; we have noted one example with *bear*. Compare *I bear you greetings* and *The Queen bears you greetings*. Both appear to be examples of greetings, a kind of explicit speech act with distinctive appropriateness conditions. There is one small problem: the second greeting does not include the first-person pronoun. Further, it may have several different permissible speakers: the Queen, a delegate of the Queen, or even a humble peasant who presumes, if only out of politeness, to speak either for the Queen or the country she is sovereign of. Obviously, also, a Queen uttering the first (or even a representative of the Queen) will imply different appropriateness than the peasant. And what about the variations possible when the same person (the Queen) utters the first sentence as Queen, as individual person, as functionary just going through the motions, . . .?

For this small special case, things are already complicated, and all these possibilities involve what Speech Act theorists Austin and Searle would consider "serious" utterances. What other possible complications lie in wait, especially when we unconsciously assume them in trying to judge a sentence on IDEAL standards? I suggest that we want the sentence in abstraction to mean "only" what it means in all uses, no matter how complex those uses.

Cohen's proposal seems to give us the possibility of precise, limited variation without the need to make a word polysemic. Yet does a lexical difference need to be noted at all? Cancellation rules are significant advances in method, as possible explanations. They are likely to be correct for some phenomena of meaning; the issue is whether they apply in particular instances. (I also have no quarrel in principle with Bolinger's comments about idiomaticity, only their relevance to some of the particular examples he cites.) With their posited minimal finite possibilities, Cohen's solutions assume the closed-class, intralinguistic nature of semantic factors. I see the variations of *insult* as more open, and thus empirical.

In these examples, my proposals may create a sense of "incompleteness". I have left too much of the "full" meaning of a sentence unaccounted for, at least by current standards. It may seem (and for some readers, probably has seemed so for *bear* and *hit*) that I am missing something essential.

This brings me back to the point I have been stressing throughout this chapter: the need for us to recognize that words and sentences are much more remote from reality than we have believed. We have been continually guilty of Misplaced Concreteness. Any act of reference is much more complicated than simply putting a highly specified label on a concrete object or situation. That is the conclusion I have reached by assuming monosemy as my initial hypothesis.

Chapter *6*

IDIOMS AND PARTICLES

The Monosemic Bias makes a significant difference for two classes of words: simple prepositions *(to, of, from, on, in, at, off, out, by, with)* and the most common general verbs *(be, do, have, go, come, take, give, put, make, let,* etc.). All of these words exhibit multiplicity in dictionary definitions. Some uses even seem "empty" of meaning: *of* usually; *to* in infinitives; *be, do, have* as auxiliaries; and the verbs in *take a walk, give a shout, have a drink, make a bid,* etc. As with *bear* and *hit* earlier, I claim that all these words are semantically abstract and monosemic; concrete senses include pragmatic modulations.

Since common verbs and simple prepositions are highly general, they contribute only minimally to the meaning of larger expressions, especially so when they combine, as in *take off;* when no obvious modulation can be read into them, they are treated as idiomatic, two-word "verb-particle constructions" or "phrasal verbs". I claim, instead, that *take* and *off* always have a single meaning; *take off* is semantically a combination of *take* plus *off,* the preposition being intransitive. To substantiate this claim, I have to address more closely the standing notion of idiom, especially those that involve "particles".

6.1 IDIOMS

A good starting place is Makkai's *Idiom Structure in English* (1972), a book that both in thoroughness and explicit statement makes clear what is often only implied in semantic analyses, regarding idioms and otherwise.

Consider first two relatively minor, but revealing, points. Makkai cites an English sentence *Kim drives at sixty miles an hour* and comments that in French, German and Russian the preposition would correspond to English *with* rather than *at;* he then reaches the puzzling conclusion that by using *at* here English speakers "conform to an *a-logical* construction whose existence is justified by a majority of speakers" (p. 57, my emphasis). Such a direct comparison of isolated sentences from several languages, while a common practice, mocks the idea that languages are systematic. Makkai neither gives nor appeals to a complete treatment of *at* and *with.* The claim: a language is a-logical if it is out of step, in some immediately evident way, with other languages.

Elsewhere, Makkai discusses certain expressions with apparently empty *take,* such as *take a train, take a bath,* and *take a hint.* He observes: "Even *cursory investigation* reveals that they fall into neatly classifiable categories. . . ." (p. 56, emphasis mine). Although he later considers his classification tentative, it is surprising for someone to announce conclusions that were the result of cursory investigation. He could do this only if he believed that semantic facts can be directly taken from selected data, and expected his readers to believe this too. Yet it is quite possible that additional data would show that his categories overparticularize a larger category.

Makkai's objective is to provide Stratificational Grammar [SG] with a large body of interpreted data, since it is partly the lack of such that put SG at a disadvantage with TG. Idioms are a strategic choice of subject, because they are the best examples of discrepancy of form and meaning, and thus can exploit fully the SG distinction between 'morpheme' and 'lexeme,' the former of which is only a form and not directly related to meaning. Makkai is willing to grant *kick* in *kick the bucket* a morphemic status, since it has the usual morphological variations of *kick (kicks, kicked, kicking),* but he denies it lexemic status: it seems to contribute no meaning to the phrase.

Makkai distinguishes between ENCODING (the *drive at* example earlier) and DECODING idioms, the latter both LEXEMIC *(kick the bucket, hot dog, red herring)* and SEMEMIC (proverbs such as *Don't count your chickens before they're hatched).* Decoding idioms create DISINFORMATION: interpreters are misled if they try to compute the parts. This criterion is determined by his definition of IDIOM, which (SG technical language aside[1]) is simply: *an expression whose full structured meaning is not equal to the sum of its parts.* Ironically, this implies that "free syntax", supposedly the overstated mistake of TG, is the sole linguistic norm; it also assumes that compositional computation never, or only very superficially, involves pragmatic factors.

Makkai correctly notes the inadequacy of some attributes that are often considered criterial for idioms. Regarding frozen or formulaic forms, he cites a number that are not idiomatic: *assets and liabilities, man and wife, each and every, facts and figures,* and others (p. 316). Also, while idioms are often figurative, a figurative expression is not necessarily an idiom. Makkai notes: "*Go down* in the sense 'sink, perish' as said of ships is . . . not an idiom, because a simple metaphorical extension of each constituent lexon will easily suggest the meaning" (p. 142). (I don't consider either word figurative, but I accept the general point.) By stipulating that each word of an idiom must occur elsewhere with a meaning, he also eliminates constructions involving uniquely occurring words, as *kith* in *kith and kin,* because they do not create disinformation; he calls them PSEUDO-IDIOMS (p. 123).

Makkai's treatment is extensive and carefully reasoned; but his overcommitment to compositionality creates the idioms he describes. The problem (as I see it) is not the SG model he assumes; though he considers his book a confirmation of SG and refutation of TG, I find the claim irrelevant. Neither SG nor TG rises or falls because of his arguments; his intuitive judgments of idiomaticity could also be those of someone in CTG.

Nor is the problem primarily due to Makkai's strange assumption, in his standard of Disinformation, that pedagogical and theoretical grammars can be the same. Obviously, a foreigner has trouble to the extent that language-in-the-whole (with pragmatic modulations) is not a self-contained entity with immediately evident systematicity. The foreigner's major handicap is, in fact, no different from the native's, or the intuitional linguist's: the stereotypic conscious mind. Proceeding from oversimplified, overconscious expectations, Makkai implies in his definition of compositionality that non-idiomatic expressions *should* exhibit unfettered generativity and that contributing contextual effects *should* be irrelevant.

Nor does the problem concern the word *idiom* as such. Obviously, it can be (and is) used for various different kinds of individuation: a speaker, a dialect, a style, a language, etc. Admittedly, all of Makkai's phrases present some degree of idiosyncrasy. My question is simply: at what level of abstraction does a phrase individuate? By giving constituent words morphemic, but not lexemic, status, Makkai judges the individuation to be relatively abstract, intralinguistic. For some phrases, this may be correct. My claim is, however, that for (most if not all) "phrasal verbs", the individuation is pragmatic, extralinguistic; thus, in the SG framework, constituent words should have both lexemic and sememic status.

Assuming then that "idiom" should apply (for present purposes) only to phrases that are intralinguistically idiosyncratic, we need this definition: *an idiom is an expression whose words occur elsewhere but never with the same (inherent) meaning as in this expression.* This definition allows what Makkai assumes must be denied: the possibility that constituent words may contribute semantically to an expression, yet not account fully for its perceived meaning (a circumstance we noted often with *hit*). Not only words, but also combinations of words, are open to modulation of meaning. By adopting a less strict definition, we can avoid Makkai's handicap: the belief that compositionality must be accounted for totally by lexical means.

My suggested definition does not deny the possibility of disinformation nor eliminate the problematic nature of Makkai's examples; but it does allow their explanation. Nothing is gained by the usual tactic of treating as idiomatic every phrase that is strange to conscious intuition. As a consequence of my definition, idiomaticity cannot be directly, immediately and obviously judged; rather, it should be concluded only after an exhaustive, and finally futile, investigation that finds no linguistic unities.

The defects of Makkai's view of compositionality are revealed by Makkai himself; he is his own inadvertent and conscientious critic. At the end of his book he organizes idioms by frequent meanings they exhibit, and notes (p. 308) that four idioms with *up* (*build up* 'increase', *build up* 'exaggerate', *lay up* 'accumulate', and *mark up* 'increase prices') share a sense of 'increase', a sense that *up* exhibits in other expressions also. Makkai must conclude that "this is not sufficient reason to regard *up* as literal here and disqualify the idioms *qua* idioms, because the total paraphrases remain nondeducible from the constituent parts" (p. 310). Because of misconceived (and thus misapplied) compositionality, it must be denied that the *up* here is the same lexeme that occurs elsewhere, though its semantic role is evident even to the linguist who denies it.

Also, a number of idioms with the meaning of 'decrease' and 'diminish' contain the word *down* (p. 308: *die down* 'decrease', *cut someone down* 'deflate ego', *mark down* 'decrease price of', *play down* 'deprecate', *talk down* 'minimize importance of'), yet these are unrelated to each other or to other uses of *down*. Seven different idioms with *get* share a sense of 'success, attainment' (p. 308: *get along* 'succeed', *get along with* 'have successful relation', *get by* 'barely succeed', *get away with* 'succeed in perpetuating illegal act or mischief without punishment or repercussions', *get something over with* 'render accomplished', *get on* 'succeed', *get in with/on* 'succeed in obtaining desirable position or association'); a number of idioms referring to speech have words such as *speak, tell, talk* and *answer* (p. 307: *speak up* 'speak louder', *tell someone off* 'blast, tell honest opinion in anger', *talk over* 'discuss', *answer back* 'retort disrespectfully', *talk back* 'reply sassily'); and yet, because compositionality is lacking, none of these words can be related to other uses. Although Makkai's appendices diligently show these semantic links, there is no place in his theory to accommodate them. Such conclusions should indicate that something is wrong with his definition of *idiom*.

A startling aspect of Makkai's analysis is that he ignores (solely on the strength of principle) even the most transparent relationships. Equally startling is the total faith he has in his glosses; they sometimes create the differences he finds. The examples just quoted give evidence. *Play down* and *talk down* are closely related, yet the glosses 'deprecate' and 'minimize importance of' needlessly blur the relationship. *Get along* and *get along with* differ in parallel to *succeed* and *succeed with*, yet Makkai obscures the use of *with* by glossing the latter as 'have successful relation'. *Answer back* and *talk back* are obviously linked, but the glosses 'retort disrespectfully' and 'reply sassily' seem to imply greater distance.

These examples also show the critical role of glosses in overconscious treatments. Although glosses are presented as evidence, faithfully and accurately representing meaning that form obscures, they are rather akin to propaganda, serving external judgments that have been made in advance. We have a typical process of conscious distortion. First, an expression appears puzzling to the conscious mind. Then, instead of researchers admitting they are puzzled, and thus suspending judgment while they gather a wider range of data, they rush to a conclusion, based on paraphrase and compositionality. The conclusion is disguised because it is formulated as a gloss. The researchers then proceed to analyze, not the expression, but the gloss. There are no established guidelines for glosses, and so they can be slanted or subtly rephrased to support any prior theoretical claim. While it is assumed that the glossed expression is misleading, the gloss is taken as accurate, at least to the degree that it makes no difference in the analysis. The researchers then draw the conclusions that are inherent in the gloss. Whatever results is an irrelevancy, because the original data have been eliminated from the proceedings.

English is not Makkai's first language, so he relied on informants rather than his own intuitions; but informant judgments are also intuitions, and suffer from the selective awareness of consciousness, which has little insight into paradigms. A number of other idioms Makkai cites also have closely related expressions. He gives *look back on* 'reminisce about' (p. 222); there is also *think back on*. He gives *fly in* 'arrive by airplane' (p. 230); there is also *fly out, fly by, fly over*, as well as *come in, drive in, motor in, ski in, jet in*, and others. He gives *come again* 'repeat what you said' (p. 216); there are also *send that by me again, run that by me again, let me have that again, give me that again, give that to me again*, and *put that to me again*, data that not only establish the non-idiomaticity of *again*, but provide evidence for possible relationships between *come, send, run, have, give* and *put*. These expressions do not allow immediate, obvious conclusions, for they are all problematic; but they are data, not glosses, and they demonstrate sufficiently well that quick judgments of idiomaticity are highly suspect.

However, my comments thus far are at best only suggestive, and thus as cursory as Makkai's judgments. As one extended illustration of my point, consider the expression *take off*, a typical "phrasal verb" or "verb particle construction". Of course, even Makkai would concede that *take off* sometimes is compositional, as in *I took the dish off the table*. W3 provides for such possibilities in the following (though it is given as a definition of *take off* in combination):

[1] to remove from a position on something or the condition of being attached to a part of something (as by lifting, pulling, cutting or breaking off or by subtracting or deducting)

W3 also lists these more idiomatic meanings:

[2] **a.** to draw or conduct away
   b. to go away; depart (used reflexively)
   c. to kill, as an assassin, disease, etc.
   d. to make a copy or likeness of
   e. to leave the ground or water in flight, as an airplane; HENCE
   f. to start
   g. to imitate in a burlesque manner; mimic

Makkai gives *take off* two idiomatic meanings, 'become airborne' and 'parody', thus agreeing with [2e, g]. His failure to cite the others doesn't imply that he would consider them non-idiomatic; rather, neither he nor his informants apparently thought to consult dictionaries. (The conscious mind can be very overconfident about its comprehensive powers. Even the order of the W3 definitions illustrates a severe lacking in conscious awareness: why weren't (d) and (g), which seem to be related, at least listed adjacently?)

To the intuitional mind, the meanings of [2] may seem irreconcilably diverse and unrelated to any senses of *take* and *off* separately. But are the definitions correct? In Chapter One, I presented evidence (sentences [1–9] above) to show that both horizontal and vertical movements are described by *take off,* so 'become airborne' and [2e] are overspecific. To continue that earlier discussion, consider the following:

[3] I dumped the law thing for good and took off for L. A. (Whitney Balliett)

[4] A great many of the young Bostonians leave town, often taking off with a sullen demand for a freer, more energetic air. (Elizabeth Hardwick)

[5] The zealous leftfielder took off in mad pursuit of a fly ball. . . . (A. J. Carr)

[6] Ronnie Lott caught the ball, then tossed a lateral to Tom Holmore, who took off down the field. (Lowell Cohn)

[7] . . . running in and then reversing his field on Reggie Smith's two-base hit which sailed over his head. "The ball took off and I couldn't change directions," he said. (AP)

[8] . . . some who caught the spirit of the modern movement but took off in their own private ways. . . . (Russell Lyens)

[9] Here the trail took off toward the west through this notch. . . . (Dudley Cammett Lunt)

[10] The jukebox took off in stratospheric answer to her question. (Herbert Gold)

[11] But about 1935 highway departments began planting the kudzu along rain-washed banks throughout the South. The kudzu took off. (Guy Friddell)

[12] Once in a while he'd take off to show his skill with a piece of rope in knot tying. . . . (Saul Bellow)

[13] It was at that point that the dog director program really took off. (Robert Barndoll)

[14] After 1900 sculpture took off in so many directions that it is impossible in this space to give even an elliptical outline of its progression. (Russell Lyens)

[15] That is the pace of evolution; once it takes off, it goes as the ratio of the two numbers goes. . . . (J. Bronowski)

Unlike [1–9] in Chapter One, [3] and [4] do not specify means of movement, nor is the movement as concrete. 'Departure', suggested in [3] and [4] of Chapter One, is missing in [5] and [6]. Movement is both concrete (Chapter One, sentences [3–6]) and abstract (Chapter One, sentences [7–15]), parallel to movement with *bear*.

As a definition, [1] has both virtues and shortcomings. It recognizes that a general meaning can be both concrete ('remove from position') and abstract ('remove from condition'). But 'remove' is minimally different from 'draw or conduct away' ([2a]); further, 'go away; depart' ([2b]) is the intransitive variant. Though using *from* to define *take off*, [1] ignores (though exploits) the shared meaning of *off/from/away*. While [1] recognizes that the method of removal ('lifting, pulling, cutting, breaking . . .') is irrelevant, its *hence* in [2e] pinpoints only one of several metonymic possibilities. Actually, 'start' is part (like 'remove') of a more general CHANGE-OF-STATE that either encompasses or metonymically suggests the 'develop, accelerate, proliferate' possibilities [10–15] that both W3 and Makkai miss.

It might be objected that I am twisting or contorting data to get the answer I want. But is the possibility of monosemy here farfetched, or just strange? Contortion is obviously apparent to anyone who assumes that the glosses are correct. Yet that is exactly what is at issue. How can glosses be correct when they fail to note that [2e] is a specialization of [2b], and when they ignore the concrete-abstract distinction in some respects and make it criterial in others? Also, does *take off* need to be cited as a separate combination in [2a], where *draw* in effect defines *take,* and *away* in effect defines *off?*

My claim is that the divisions of [1] and [2] show the limits of the conscious mind, which doesn't consider enough relevant data and so doesn't comprehend all that is involved in what we call "defining". This is not a criticism of W3; [1] is actually an exemplary definition for current dictionaries, given their working assumptions. Rather, I am trying to make more evident a general human condition. Before Newton, it would have seemed a contortion to generalize the movements of planets, wagons and falling apples. Physics has developed ways to go beyond the limits of concrete, conscious awareness; we have nothing comparable in lexicography or semantics. Like Aristotle, fixating on the need for impetus to keep the wagon moving, we get distracted by immediate, but misleading, impressions.

To continue with data: as with *bear,* the above intransitives relate to transitives that have a reflexive as direct object:

[16] The birds had taken themselves off to feed in the brooks. (Virginia Woolf)

[17] ". . . I will take myself off to bed." (Joan Aiken)

[18] . . . that excellent officer had to take himself hurriedly off. (Michael Innes)

These relate to transitives with non-reflexive objects:

[19] "Come, Rose," Nancy broke in, and took the girl off for a swim. (Carolyn Keene)

[20] He sighed, and took her off on a conducted tour of the building. (Fred Hoyle and John Elliott)

[21] The revolutionists have taken off all the cattle and sheep on my father's ranch, and left it bare. (Langston Hughes)

[22] Otherwise, we would take the crew off [the ship]. . . . (Lowell Thomas)

[23] He supervises an unmatched collection of the devices that have taken Man off the surface of his planet. (Edwards Park)

Examples [21–23] bring a systematic element into prominence: *off* is the opposite of *on;* the cattle and sheep that were on the ranch [21] are off as a result of the taking, and similarly for [22] and [23]. (*On* in [20] plays another role). 'On' is hardly suspected in sentences [1–19] of Chapter One, being there an implicit AMBIENT, whose object is a PLACE or LOCATION ('on the ground/spot/ . . .').

"Locations" can be smaller or abstract; the following are only a small selection:

[24] They ate slowly, taking glazed white paper off huge white sandwiches. . . . (Katherine Anne Porter)

[25] The bronzed mates are busy everywhere, taking fish off hooks and rebaiting. . . . (Carl and Nell Craft)

[26] She could take off her shoes in his apartment; he could take off his jacket and tie in hers. (Maury Allen)

[27] Eventually, we were forced to take him off research of any kind. (Isaac Asimov)

[28] . . . Mondale took a year off to head the student arm of the liberal Americans for Democratic Action. . . . (Albert Eisele)

These are the examples that seem to be straightforward combinations of *take* and *off* (both concrete and abstract). The systematic contrasts of *off/on* are obvious here to the conscious mind, and this makes the roles of *take* and *off* more distinctive. The problem is that we consciously expect the system always to be this clear cut. Yet (as I noted at the end of Chapter Three), for this to hold, the pragmatic modulations must be consistent, with all concretions keeping *on* and *off* parallel. When they don't (because a particular message and domain must exploit their individuations more unevenly), we think we have different words or meanings.

Several brief points: (a) in the examples thus far, the pragmatic rules of Concretion and (Re)agency are in effect; *take* and *off* can range over all possibilities; (b) in [28], *duty* (or *job*) can be an implicit object of *off*.

A *from*-phrase, indicating a "source", is also possible:

[29] The first model aeroplane to take off from the ground and make a successful flight. . . . (Peter W. Brooks)

[30] And Maggioni had outdone himself [in a painting] with a pair of pintail ducks taking off from the water in their characteristic backward-jumping, splashing way. . . . (Margaret G. Nichols)

[31] "I'd have to take off from work." (John Updike)

[32] It was from this concept of impeachment that American thinking and experience took off. (Theodore H. White)

[33] When she had a grief she didn't play it with any arts; she took straight off from her spirit. (Saul Bellow)

[34] It was not until the twentieth century, however, that research took off from the launching pad prepared by Boole. (Anatol Rapoport)

[35] Settled agriculture creates a technology from which all physics, all science takes off. (J. Bronowski)

[36] The third conversation took off from a speculative question about the political vision motivating the women's movement. (Barbara Charlesworth Gelpi and Albert Gelpi)

[37] Just as Fielding took off from Richardson, so Hemingway takes off from Sherwood Anderson. . . . (Harry Levin)

[38] "*Pi* will only describe a sphere once formed, and a sphere moreover idealized because static. But the generation of forms is described by vectors." To take off from there let's say *pi* is the point of view of art as static and measurable. . . . (Ronald Sukenick)

[39] . . . A. A. Hill takes off from Bloomfield's argument, and defines style. . . . (Karl D. Uitti)

Consider now [2c]. *Take off* is neutral to concrete-abstract; that is, it is highly abstract, with all specific concretions supplied pragmatically. Thus, it is possible for disease to be agency and death to be implicit destination (W3 example):

[40] . . . disease appeared . . . and without respect of persons or neighborhoods, took off young and old. (*American Guide* Series: Delaware, W3)

If we do semantics too realistically (too concretely), compounding semantic and pragmatic, this example readily invites a status of figurativity. Yet, for *take off*, it is simply one abstract possibility; any figurativity must be supplied pragmatically, personifying disease or death. The impression of indirectness is euphemistic, a commonplace with death. Of course, we can have *The epidemic took my parents*, with even 'off' implicit.

Consider finally the two remaining senses in [2]: 'copy' in (d), 'mimic' in (g). For the examples thus far, we have made another subtle (pragmatic) assumption: that X can (schematically speaking) be in only one "place" at a time; thus, when X is taken off Y, X is no longer on Y. But with copies, this is not true: the original X remains on Y, while the copy proceeds on its own (possibly independent) course. Thus, using a copying machine, we can *take off a copy of the report* (although *off* can be omitted, and *take* is usually British, *make* being preferred by Americans). One type of copying is "continuing" or "following," using something as a starting point [32–39]. Mimicry is a specific form of copying, and parody and burlesque are specific forms of mimicry (as described by *take off*). 'Burlesque' and 'parody' are thus overspecific glosses:

[41] . . . let Lou Magee recite the funny piece where she took off a lady going to the dentist. (Maureen Howard)

[42] She could take off people until you fell down laughing. . . . (Reynolds Price)

[43] He [Stanley Baxter] only takes off people he respects and admires. (Jeremy Britt)

[44] He [Mailer], too, is a spoiled child, with a partiality to his own family that permits him, like Pound, to take off on the world at large whenever he likes. (Alfred Kazin)

Makkai also cites the noun *take-off* with the sense of 'parody'. Strangely, some linguists seem to assume that if a verb has an associated nominal with only a portion of its range, this means that the verb should have a separate sense that directly parallels the noun. As general knowledge about derivation should tell us, there is no necessary reason why a nominal should (or can) duplicate the verb; such an expectation too easily eliminates the difference between categories. Further, a phrase of two words, verb and preposition, is related to a single word, a compound; compounds typically depart from their source forms, as we know from such as *black bird* and *blackbird*. There is also a general tendency for verbs to be more general than formally related nouns, regardless of the direction of derivation: *give* is more general than *gift*, and verb *hammer* more general than the noun. In short, the status of *take-off* as a noun has no necessary relevance to the status of syntactically combined verb *take* and preposition *off*.

This noted, however, we should not trust our conscious awareness for the meaning of nominal *take-off* either; this compound can attend to more than just flight and parodies. As the following show, it duplicates a good deal of the range we have seen with the verb-preposition:

[45] The aircraft, which would ride along this takeoff rail. . . . (Tom Crouch)

[46] You have to worry about your hands slipping on take-off [in pole-vaulting]. (Bob Seagren)

[47] Many pro-football players who feel uncertain about the instant take-off from speed use Black Beauties. (Neil Amdur)

[48] . . . the phase is not likely to be prolonged much beyond the period of industrial takeoff. (Lawrence Stone)

[49] So it has always been in French Guiana, a country long habituated to being poised for take-off to greatness. (Gary MacEoin)

[50] . . . it [information theory] represents one of the take-off points within Western science. . . . (Sigmund Kvaloy)

[51] Using a take-off on an old Casey Stengel line, Kiner said he felt he would have been elected [to the Baseball Hall of Fame] sooner except that "many who saw me play are dead at the present time." (Jack Lang)

[52] Another example is Descartes' *cogito, ergo sum*. The number and kinds of take-offs on this sentence are quite varied and have permeated many languages and eventually assumed the set form *I X, therefore I am*. (Makkai (1972: 170–71))

Makkai's use of the nominal in [52] is obviously more general than 'parody'.

Of course, even more data are needed; my purpose here is to make reasonable the possibility that *take* and *off* might have their usual meanings when they appear to be idiosyncratically combined. This claim does not deny the possibility of idioms, even with my definition. It is likely impossible to relate *white elephant, red herring,* and *trip the light fantastic* semantically in any significant way to the rest of the language.

However, most of Makkai's examples are "phrasal verbs," a general, productive pattern. Why should a productive pattern like phrasal verbs be so pervasively idiomatic? My answer is that these phrases merely underdetermine the apparent full meaning, and thus they are not idiomatic. Makkai's resort is to deny semantic motivation (except as only one possibility), proposing instead that language users make new combinations of words with total disregard for present meanings. But even *white elephant* and *red herring* were initially motivated; Makkai implies that the form-meaning correlation can be typically unmotivated right from the start.

The problem: even if not initially predisposed to argue for idioms and lack of motivation, Makkai's assumptions left him no choice. In conscious, realistic, what-you-notice-is-all-you've-got terms, no sense of *take* appears motivated in *take off*. Therefore, productive processes need not exhibit motivation. Yet, outside of the data under consideration, motivation is the norm: very little (though some) new word-formation is due to outright coinage, and words are rarely given inexplicable new meanings. Makkai resolves the dilemma by abandoning motivation.

I resolve it by claiming that motivation can be unconscious. We can make systematic innovations without knowing why or wondering if they are motivated. Actually, there need not be any lexical innovation. Words can be used with the same meanings but in different contexts; these contexts, with all their extralinguistic implications, may be radically new, even though the lexical meanings are not. When we view enough data, and allow more relevant factors to contribute to meaning, *take off* does not seem so mysterious. In the context of many uses, a unity emerges, one that is highly abstract and social, though not likely to be consciously known. This, I am claiming, is the linguistic reality of closed-class words.

6.2 PARTICLES

The notion "phrasal verb" includes another bogus discrepancy of form and meaning: the so-called "particles" (*in, out, on, off, up, down, through* and *across,* etc.). These words have a curious status in descriptions of English. When followed by nominal objects ([53–60]), they are called Prepositions:

[53] He walked *in the door.*
[54] He walked *out the door.*
[55] The dog jumped *on the table.*
[56] The dog jumped *off the table.*
[57] Jean climbed *up the ladder.*
[58] Jean climbed *down the ladder.*
[59] He walked *through the room.*
[60] He walked *across the yard.*

Without an object ([61–68]), they are called Adverbs or Particles, the latter when they seem to lack one of their usual meanings and form an indivisible, idiomatic unit with the preceding verb ([69–76]); this is the Phrasal Verb:

[61] He walked *in.*	[69] The soldiers fell *in.*
[62] He walked *out.*	[70] The store closed *out.*
[63] The dog jumped *on.*	[71] They led him *on.*
[64] The dog jumped *off.*	[72] The lane took *off.*
[65] Jean climbed *up.*	[73] The girl spoke *up.*
[66] Jean climbed *down.*	[74] The wind died *down.*
[67] He walked *through.*	[75] Our plans fell *through.*
[68] He walked *across.*	[76] He put a point *across.*

I claim, supporting and extending the arguments of Emonds (1972) and Jackendoff (1973), that these words are always prepositions; thus, in [61–76], they should be considered intransitive prepositions. When not followed by an object, these words have a prominent syntactic feature: they can occur either adjacent to the verb ([77]) or after its direct object ([78]). Scholars usually observe that *my hat* in [77] cannot be the direct object of *on,* since real direct objects cannot shift as in [78]. It is rarely mentioned that there can be a direct object; both [77] and [78] can be elliptical for [79] (though *my head* is favored):

[77] I put *on* my hat.
[78] I put my hat *on*.
[79] I put my hat on my head/the bed/the pile/the table . . .

Most transformationalists have taken the verb-adjacent order as basic, deriving the other by a transformation called Particle Shift. Thus [77] is basic and Particle Shift moves the particle after the object to get [78]. This transformation needs several special conditions: it is obligatory when the object is an unstressed pronoun ([80] and [81]), and likely to be blocked when the noun phrase becomes complex ([82] and [83]).

[80] *I put *on* it.
[81] I put it *on*.
[82] I put *on* the old gray tattered hat that Uncle Fred gave me.
[83] *I put the old gray tattered hat that Uncle Fred gave me *on*.

Emonds, however, proposes exactly the reverse: the non-adjacent order is basic, and Particle Shift operates, with opposite conditions, to move the particle adjacent to the verb. Thus, [78] is basic, and Particle Shift moves the particle before the object to get [77]. This solution implies that all prepositional phrases within the verb phrase, both transitive or intransitive, occur in the same basic syntactic position, after any direct object. Accepting this view, Jackendoff (1973: 354) proposes the following PP-rule [PP-prepositional phrase]:

[84] PP → P (NP) (PP)

For anyone interested in capturing generalizations about syntax, Emonds's claim has a number of surprising virtues—especially surprising in that they have gone unacknowledged so long. If these words are always prepositions and if their basic syntactic position within the verb phrase is always the same, both word classes and syntax are simplified, in a way that accords directly with apparent form and structure.

These generalizations are not the result of some involved theoretical argument, built on a number of dubious other claims, but rather regularities drawn from what is directly and consistently apparent. Linguists who can ignore category differences when directly relating verbal and nominal forms (as noted with *take off*) have difficulty in seeing *on* as the same thing with and without an object. The reason is that while the formal parallels are obvious, the semantics seem all askew. The difference of *take off* as verb and as noun appears minimal compared to that between a phrasal verb and its constituents.

Such is the appearance on the relatively concrete, semantic-pragmatic level that is the favored field of the conscious mind. Trusting intuition (and limited databases) too much, many scholars easily embrace the possibility of rampant idiomaticity and polysemy and then argue for highly dubious regularities or conclude that languages are largely hodgepodges.

What is most surprising, the prevailing view has no virtues at all. In addition to its spurious complications, its theoretical justification is merely a combination of Latin prescriptivism (prepositions always have objects in Latin, so English prepositions must too) and a shallow overconfidence about meaning and how it is realized. The claim of idiom for some V + P combinations has been often asserted, repeated and illustrated, but it rests on untested intuitional judgments of meaning and has never been sufficiently challenged by an alternative perspective.

Moreover, relating to the original Particle Shift, even if certain combinations are idiomatic, it must further be demonstrated that linguistic descriptions should require the parts of idioms to be adjacent: discontinuous idioms like *to pull X's leg* are currently proposed. As far as I can see, the only proven virtue of the prevailing view is its familiarity and popularity in dictionaries and linguistic theories.

One possible misunderstanding must be noted. As [84] shows, Emonds's proposal does not imply that with all intransitive prepositions an object has been "deleted" or understood. Sometimes, especially in elliptical discourse, an object may be understood; and often transitive and intransitive may be closely parallel, as I made them in [53–68]. Similarly, some transitive verbs (like *eat*) can also look intransitive, with an understood object. But like many intransitive verbs, some intransitive prepositions simply stand by themselves. There need be no great mystery what they mean: at worst, precisely what they mean as "adverbs". A different part of speech is no more needed here than with verbs; the need is an artifice of prescriptivism.

However, a complication in Emonds's view must be corrected: his reversed but equally arbitrary rule of Particle Shift. If this rule is part of a more general and motivated phenomenon, the whole argument can be strengthened. The necessary insight comes from a neglected source: Yngve's (1960) Depth Hypothesis. Yngve claims that, because of limits on short-term memory, syntactic complexity must be concentrated later rather than earlier in sentences. Some proposed transformations exhibit this: they shift complex noun phrases "rightward", either partly (Extraposition) or completely (Heavy NP Shift). Yngve proposes (p. 458) that the variant orders with "particles" come from this shifting of complex noun phrases. Thus, [78] is basic, and Heavy NP Shift moves the object beyond the preposition to get [77].

Since studies of phrasal verbs generally assume verb-adjacency and particle shift, and account for variations from this perspective, it is important to appreciate the different requirements for Yngve's hypothesis. Assuming post-object position as basic [78], this hypothesis can fail in two ways: either if a non-heavy object occurs after the preposition, or if a highly complex object need not move. The set [80–83] provides the testing data. In [80] the unstressed pronoun cannot shift because it is no heavier than the preposition. In [83] the highly complex noun phrase must shift because it puts a strain on processing. These two "boundary" examples demonstrate what Yngve's hypothesis predicts, and they follow naturally as consequences. Between these two boundaries, since prepositions are typically short, it will be possible for a noun phrase either to stay in its basic position or shift later in the sentence; that is, when the object is neither too light nor too heavy, both orders can occur, unless other conditions impose additional requirements.

But there is a further requirement on Yngve's hypothesis. Since its claim encompasses more than prepositions, shifting of object noun phrases should occur generally, as long as the noun phrase is more complex than phrases which follow it. This also is confirmed: objects can occur after adjectives [85–87], adverbs [88] and [89], and prepositions with objects [90–94]:

[85] Bermuda grass was at work breaking *apart* the seven cracked driveways. . . . (Doris Betts)

[86] . . . intestinal mucus, which has the protective effect of breaking *open* bacteria that attempt to invade the body. (Horace Freeland Judson)

[87] Let's take those companies and trash them—maybe rip *apart* their equipment. . . . (Richard Cohen)

[88] Further, I have difficulty taking *seriously* the notion that most stars in the sky harbor advanced malevolent societies. (George Greenstein)

[89] "For that I bore *patiently* the burden of work, of disappointment, of humiliation. . . ." (Joseph Conrad)

[90] . . . nevertheless there broods *over them* a mythological identity of cosmic proportions. (Theodore Roszak)

[91] "You do not take *into consideration* the time element!" (Robert Ludlum)

[92] Valerie got out, and took *from her purse* the sheet of St. Regis stationary with the Air Force telephone number. (Robert Ludlum)

[93] . . . who wants nothing so much as to rip *to shreds* the pretensions of the heros. . . . (Joyce Carol Oates)

[94] . . . Adrian is to bear *on his frail shoulders* a tremendous symbolic burden. . . . (Joyce Carol Oates)

Neither the variant syntactic order nor its explanation is limited to phrasal verbs.

In addition, with phrasal verbs there are also Extraposition [95] and [96] and Extraposition from NP [97] and [98]:

[95] I didn't make it *up* that John skipped town.

[96] He gave the news *out* that Fred won a car.

[97] He took the boy *in* who had lost his parents.

[98] He saw the matter *through* that had caused him so much anxiety. . . . (Yngve, p. 458)

Bolinger (1971b: 39ff.) observes that stressed pronouns can occur in final positions (his attested examples; my numbering):

[99] The lady bade her take away the fool; therefore, I say take her away. — Sir, I bade them take *away* YOU.

[100] I knew that the school board contemplated throwing out Spanish in order to throw *out* ME.

[101] You may give up society without any great pang, but severe are the mortifications and pains you have if society gives *up* YOU.

[102] Fancy taking *on* HER.

The conclusion I draw is that stressing the pronoun makes it heavy enough to shift, while leaving it unstressed does not. However, Bolinger, assuming basic verb-adjacency, concludes that [99–102] make the fixed position of unstressed pronouns unimportant. Listing (1971b: 55) the next five sentences (I add [108] and the pronoun variants) to illustrate various alternative stress patterns with a noun object, he fails to note the predictable limits on pronouns:

[103] How can they put NIXON *over?*   . . . put HIM *over?*
[104] How can they put *over* NIXON?   . . . put *over* HIM?
[105] How can they put Nixon *OVER?*   . . . put him *OVER?*
[106] How can they put *OVER* Nixon?   *. . . put *OVER* him?
[107] How can they PUT Nixon *over?*   . . . PUT him *over?*
[108] How can they PUT *over* Nixon?   *. . . PUT *over* him?

To summarize thus far: the Emonds-Yngve solution accounts for the boundary conditions in a simple and motivated way. The prevailing view of particles and basic verb-adjacency, with its attendant complexity of word classes and syntax, would have to present some impressive compensatory advantages to justify its convolutions. Yet, even if pardoned for this complexity, the verb-adjacent view still cannot account for the boundary condition of [80], except arbitrarily as in Particle Shift. Moreover, an analysis positing alternative orders as basic also fails this requirement. These other solutions would have to be clearly superior in dealing with the many complications that occur within the boundary conditions; yet, as I will now show in part, the Emonds-Yngve view fares at least as well.

The essential requirement is a definition of HEAVINESS. Since heaviness is a matter of degree, we are also defining its opposite, LIGHTNESS. As we might suspect, prepositions are usually light. I propose the following:

[A] HEAVINESS CONDITION
Assuming a basic, unmarked order, determined by phrase structure (or dependency) rules, the sequential ordering of phrases in a sentence may be overridden by "heavy elements", so that these are shifted later in the sequence.

Although the choice in some context of shifted or non-shifted variant must be pragmatically motivated, the heaviness may be conditioned by factors on different levels of abstraction: that is, either syntactically, semantically, or pragmatically. Since on all levels of abstraction the result is still a grammatical sentence, all three kinds of heaviness are to some degree intralinguistic. Since the shift is pragmatic, all three variations are to some degree extralinguistic. Thus, this is a wide-ranging condition, involving all levels of abstraction.

The measure of SYNTACTIC HEAVINESS, the most abstract and intralinguistic, is complexity of form, realized either in length (of string) or depth (of hierarchy).

The measure of SEMANTIC HEAVINESS, which is less abstract, is degree of content, realized either in specificity (of hyponyms) or contrast (of antonyms). (To the extent that words evoke pragmatic modulations and thus create pragmatic content, some specificity and contrast may be pragmatic.)

The measure of PRAGMATIC HEAVINESS, the most concrete and situation-specific, is evaluation of newsworthiness (Bolinger (1971b: 51)), realized either in accenting (of focus) or deaccenting (of redundancy).

While problematic, syntactic complexity is relatively clear; the other two types of heaviness require more discussion. With semantic content, general words like *thing* or *someone* are less heavy than specific words like *table* or *girl*. Bolinger observes (1977b: 166) that the more specific *travel* sounds better than the more general *went* in the frame *He _____ far; far* is so general that it would usually be chosen with a heavy verb, and *went* in this frame by its generality indicates that its information is unimportant. *Travel* and *a long way* have heavier content than *go* and *far*. Words in minor, closed classes (articles, pronouns, conjunctions, prepositions) or in major subclasses (verbs such as *be, do, have, run, get, set, take*) are inherently light in content; one indication of their closure is that they have a limited number of (equally general) contrast partners.

A major barrier to understanding prepositions has been the belief that concrete senses are more basic than abstract senses. To make matters worse, this contrast is usually additionally defined as literal versus metaphoric (Makkai's analysis of *go down* describing a ship sinking). Thus, for prepositions the "directional" senses of [53–68] are considered basic, while the "aspectual" senses (Bolinger (1971b: 96ff.)) of [69–76] seem mysterious, arbitrary and idiomatic. Linguists typically note that the former group can all freely occur in some context and make a difference; thus they can be considered separate words, prepositions or adverbs. The latter group seem to occur in restrictive contexts and often make little or no difference; thus they are considered merely "particles," part of the "phrasal verb."

According to my Concretion Condition (Chapter Two), the most abstract sense is the inherent sense; pragmatic modulations make prepositions concrete. If we consider the "aspectual" meanings basic, we can explain their apparent arbitrary nature: they are the meanings of highly general words, whose mutual contrasts are unconscious. Within specified domains like "direction", however, they are interpreted more specifically, so their contrasts are more understandable consciously.

This view takes seriously the special characteristics of closed classes. If such a class is used over a number of domains, each with differing characteristics, then the words will keep consistent apparent meanings only if the domains are all systematically parallel. Even in related domains like time and space, the dimensions differ, and so prepositional roles in the two domains cannot be neatly and directly paired. What is needed is a full-scale study of closed classes that starts with the assumption of monosemy. Works on "idioms" such as Makkai's by implication assume that all classes should be open classes: free substitutability with copious contrast possibility is taken as the exclusive norm.

Pragmatic heaviness involves the ongoing evaluation of information by a speaker concerning what information is old or new, familiar or strange, easily inferrable or not. Generally, the contrast is between what has lesser need to be said or made much of and that which has greater need. According to Bolinger, this contrast is in part indicated by accent and position after accent. If the syntactically determined unmarked accent occurs on a final element of an expression, it automatically becomes the new information, with no implied status for other elements; but if the accent occurs before the final element, then what follows is specified as old or redundant. In the following comments, Bolinger (1971b: 55) applies this perspective to [103–108]. (Although he takes the particle to be part of the verb, I accept the other implications of his argument):

> By putting the particle at the end and accenting it, we recapture the power to make the verb the high point without explicitly degrading anything else. By putting it there and not accenting it, we are able to make the verb explicitly redundant. In addition, nothing is sacrificed. . . . The first [103] occurs in a setting where acts of political maneuvering are familiar (*putting over* may or may not actually have been mentioned). The second and third [104] and [105] approach the political maneuver from outside: they could be spoken by someone broaching the whole question of politics, the difference being in the relative newsworthiness of the person or action. The fourth [106] treats Nixon as redundant. The last [107] is an instance of rectification—the accent displaced onto a syllable that would be meaningless if interpreted as highlighted in its own right implies "How can such things be?" "How can they be thinking of such a thing?"

According to the Heaviness Condition, we can say the following about Bolinger's sentences. In them, the preposition *over* is slightly heavy semantically, with a slightly modulated directional sense; it has as contrast partners (at least) all the prepositions noted in [53–60]. *Nixon* is highly specific, with numerous contrast partners, but not complex. Taking all heaviness into account, we can explain the full degree of variation shown in [103–107]. When we accent any word, we make it rhetorically heavy; but given the specificity of *Nixon, over* is not heavy enough to block object movement even when accented

[106], although it could if the PP were more complex and specific: *over on the country*. In general, *Nixon* is heavy enough with respect to *over* that it can move regardless of the accent pattern, yet not sufficiently complex that it has to move.

Him as object changes the conditions. Pronouns are rhetorically less newsworthy, primarily because they are semantically general, with limited contrast partners. Thus, the inherent heaviness of prepositions (though not great either) is sufficient to block movement unless the pronoun is accented [104]. Even when accented [103] and thus movable, the pronoun does not have to move. Pronouns and prepositions are about equally light (the former perhaps lighter), so without accent the pronoun cannot change original position.

Consider now the relative strength of the three types of heaviness:

[B] HEAVINESS DOMINANCE PRINCIPLE
Given relevant conditions of heaviness on several levels of abstraction, if there is a conflict of conditions, the more concrete level will override the more abstract: semantics will override syntax, and pragmatics will override semantics.

Bolinger illustrates the latter override while discussing his Definite Noun Phrase Test (1971b: 61):

[109] They took *along* a couple of old newspapers.
[110] They took *along* the newspapers.
[111] They took *with them* a couple of newspapers.
[112] *They took *with them* the newspapers.

He notes (p. 64):

> These examples show that an adverbial adjunct to a verb is not
> normally allowed to precede a simple definite object noun phrase
> [112]. The exceptions—the phrases that behave like simple verbs in
> this respect [110]—are defined as phrasal verbs.

However, heaviness suggests another interpretation. The difference between [110] and [112] is in the syntactic complexity of the PP's; the difference between [111] and [112] is in the complexity of the objects. But if we simplify [111] to *a newspaper*, we still have the factor that Bolinger intended to isolate: why can an indefinite phrase move when a definite can't, given comparable complexity? (Again, I think the difference is relative, not absolute as his asterisk indicates.) While the definite is semantically more specific because anaphoric, the indefinite is rhetorically heavier because its information is newer. This pair provides a minimalized comparison of specificity and newsworthiness, showing that (other things equal) the latter has more weight, Again, there is no need to create a new formal category like Phrasal Verb to explain the variation.

As Bolinger illustrates in his discussion of [103–108], Heavy-NP shift can subtly alter (modulated) meaning. When V and P are adjacent, the action of the verb is emphasized; when they are separate, the effect indicated by the preposition is emphasized. As he demonstrates, this effect applies to other adjuncts too: *They made clear their intentions* ('clarified'), but *They made their intentions clear* ('unmistakable') (p. 82). His point is well taken, even though the glosses suggest that the difference is semantic. Rather, the sequential positioning determines different pragmatic modulations: the relative value and novelty of information.

This variant meaning suggests caution toward the strategies of TG scholars who use tests based on movement transformations to define or classify phrasal verbs. It is an overemphasis on paraphrase to assume that alternate positioning of elements should make no or negligible difference. One such test involves fronting; since we get *Down they sat* but not **Down he broke* (Bolinger (1971b: 116)), the first *down* is considered an adverb, the second a particle. This reasoning ignores the purpose of fronting, which is to make certain information prominent and thus shift the relative pragmatic values of lexical meaning. Obviously, very abstract meaning (which has not been concretely modulated) will never need to be fronted. The first *down,* interpreted within the domain of directions, is eligible because it is pragmatically more specific and thus heavier.

But fronting is also conditional on what is left behind. Consider the following:

[113] They traveled *off.*   *Off* they traveled.
[114] They ran *off.*   *Off* they ran.
[115] They went *off.*   *Off* they went.
[116] They took *off.*   ?*Off* they took.

Data such as these can be used to argue that *take off* is an idiom; but all four expressions describe the same type of event, with *off* playing the same role, so the difference must be with *take.* An argument by semantic heaviness would go as follows. Examples [113–116] show decreasing specificity with regard to movement; *travel* is most specific, and *take* hardly specific at all, needing the link to *off* to be modulated for movement. The verb left behind in fronting must have enough specificity to indicate the intended meaning without the close presence of the preposition: *travel* easily qualifies. I claim that *run, go* and *take* are all highly general, monosemic words; their differences in meaning are reflected in their different applicability to a particular domain. *Run, go* and *take* can all be used in movement contexts, but while *run* and *go* can specify directly to concrete movement, *take* requires the help of adjuncts. Because *take* is more dependent on context in this particular domain (to have this full effect), the fronting of *off* is more problematic.

The syntactic, semantic and pragmatic properties I am claiming here are not merely obscured by conclusions of idiomaticity; their discovery is actually precluded. Bolinger shows this in commenting on verb phrases where alternative orders are impossible (1971b: 114): ". . . the entire verb phrase is frozen. Theses are 'idioms.' They are worth exemplifying, but no more."

These are some of his phrases, the first column with V-P adjacent, the second column separated:

[117] to put *on* the dog

[118] to take *up* arms

[119] to let *off* steam

[120] to choose *up* sides

[121] to shut *up* shop

[122] to keep one's hand *in*

[123] to put one's foot *down*

[124] to cry one's eyes *out*

[125] to talk his head *off*

[126] to keep one's shirt *on*

It is important to note that even if all these expressions (plus others with the same properties) were found to be idioms, they would have no effect on my argument in this book. Precisely because they were idioms, they would be unrelatable to the rest of the grammar and thus irrelevant. Oddly, those who argue for verb-adjacency often seem to be using the supposedly "irregular" data of [117–126] to establish regularities. This practice could be justified only if all V-P sequences were idiomatic. But then, any variation in order (or lack of it) could be explained purely ad hoc; why would idioms have to be treated in a parallel fashion, if they are really idioms?

A thorough investigation of [117–126] would take seriously the properties of closed classes. Fixed word order may reflect relics (as *kick the bucket*) or social commonplace *(salt and pepper),* but it can also indicate limited choices available (perhaps only one) in the verb, the object, the preposition, or any combination; *put up with,* for example, may require those three particular words because no other choices are available to convey the intended meaning. Only a thorough study of each word can supply an informed conclusion.

Some expressions aren't as fixed as advertised: Bolinger also lists *to put on airs* to parallel [117], and W3 cites *put a saintly manner on* and also *put it on* 'exaggerate'; there is also Hamlet's *put an antic disposition on.* Poses or manners can be put on just like clothes. These data suggest that [117] is stereotyped because of the unusual use of *the dog.* Of course, anything having to do with appearance can be deceptive, as the verbs *act, look, sound, feel, taste* and *appear* all pragmatically suggest, and also *put on* 'affect, pretend'.

Heavy-NP Shift is optional, up to a point; the apparently fixed patterns of [117–126] indicate that the object is less important. My intuition is that the prepositions of [117–121] have heavier content than those of [122–126], and that the metaphoric status of the objects (not the whole phrases) makes them correspondingly weaker. But only full investigation of the involved words can establish legitimate conclusions.

The major problem with Makkai's work, as impressive as it is, is that idiomaticity is reduced to a simplified Either-Or. In "Meaning and memory," Bolinger notes that idiomaticity is a gradient, and in general I agree, quarreling only with his and Makkai's placement of specific examples. On a more continuous scale, we can fully grant the relatively concrete idiosyncrasies of Makkai's examples. We can also show, I hope, that these individuations are not the whole story: that in a network of more abstract systems, they are not exceptions to, but essential parts of, a language's highly heterogeneous order.

Chapter 7

DEFINITION

How should linguistic theories use the notion "definition"? We can apply it narrowly to a word's semantics, its Sense, which is linguistic, intensional, systematic, non-modulated, and non-referential. Alternatively, we can apply this term widely to (some of) a word's pragmatic diversification, its Applications (or Uses), which add the extralinguistic, extensional, non-systematic, modulated, and referential. While this assumes a clear distinction of sense and applications, semantic and pragmatic, we have no prior assurance that this is correct.

I am arguing that we cannot discover the sense(s) of a word without fully gauging its applications. Dictionary definitions, especially of common words, highlight a few applications, which implicitly deny a unified sense, and thus underestimate the full range of applications. This typically, even inexorably, happens because stereotypical applications suggest discrete senses, and because the unified sense is too abstract, inexpressible, and practically (i.e., consciously) useless. Thus, for heuristic and pedagogical reasons, it is probably best for linguists to keep the more inclusive notion of definition, including both "dictionary" and "encyclopedia".

7.1 THE SHAPE OF A VOCABULARY

Thus far, I have argued that common verbs and prepositions are all monosemic, having a homogeneous (semantic) sense, with all heterogeneity attributable to pragmatic inferences. But the whole vocabulary is not as abstract. We must now consider words that more closely relate to reality, and which as a consequence can also be figurative.

Polysemy is often claimed for a word because its implied range appears too varied to be covered by a single meaning; that is the motive for many proposed distinctions based on contrasts like abstract-concrete and causative-noncausative. My counterarguments for monosemy have assumed the following:

[A] RANGE CONDITIONS

1. The range (or comprehensiveness) of a word (and thus its set of actual and potential hyponyms) is not necessarily homogeneous to any factor.
2. It is possible that the range of a particular word is not expressible by any other linguistic means.

In general, a word's hyponyms will only partly cover its full range (thus, "potential" in A1), or some or all of the hyponyms will not be limited merely to the word's range. But even if there are hyponyms that only and exhaustively cover the range, there may be no other word or expression in the language (other than a conjoined listing of the hyponyms) that can characterize that range except that word. Thus, complete paraphrase is often, perhaps usually, impossible.

COMMON HYPONYMS share the same SUPERORDINATE; these are also called ANTONYMS, in the expanded range of that word assumed by linguists. Antonyms, of course, will be heterogeneous (perhaps in many ways) with respect to each other. A superordinate with its hyponyms is a SEMANTIC FIELD; I will refer to the most general term of a field as the ROOT. Like "superordinate", this is a relative notion; what is a root with respect to some words will be a hyponym with respect to another word.

An essential fact about human vocabularies is that a superordinate and its hyponyms can sometimes contrast, appearing at times to be contextual antonyms. This is part of the general phenomenon known as MARKEDNESS. For illustration, suppose we have in a language two systems, one of which is a subsystem of the other, as in [1] and [2]. In a certain DOMAIN (a set of contexts), the elements in [1] exhaust all the possibilities, thus creating a three-way contrast; in another domain, the fuller set in [2] is required to account for all the possible contrasts:

[1] lik, fot, rud
[2] lik, fot, rud, hum, vit, slaf, cobor, rimarta, simoka

How are the sets related? In strict systematic terms, the elements in [1] cannot be identified with their counterparts in [2] because the contrast possibilities are different. Nevertheless, they can be equated under two conditions: (a) if *lik, fot* and *rud* relate comparably to each other within the two systems; and (b) if we can consider these three elements to be superordinal to the other elements. Superordinals are those of a set that are used in domains where contrasts are limited, and finer distinctions are unnecessary; they thus serve as "unmarked" terms.

We have a clear example: the number system. The positive integers form a superordinal set of numbers, on which the negative integers, fractions, etc., are elaborations. In addition, we can also consider the round numbers (10, 20, 30. . . .; 100, 200, 300, . . .; etc.) even more superordinal, since they are used in limited domains where only round-number information is needed. By "strict" standards (where contrasting elements are by fiat considered equally abstract), these would all be different systems; but mathematical relationships between the elements are constant, no matter how limited a part of the system is used, and so our two conditions hold.

Though references of a set of elements may have some degree of systematicity, there is no requirement that they should; the notion of system in linguistics applies intensionally. Linguistic systems do not reflect properties of the external world, but of the human mind. The difference is very clear with mathematics. If we intend the meanings of numbers to be extensional, then we have different subsystems: in practical instances where we round off, 100 may refer to anything from about 95 to 105; in more elaborated situations it may mean anything from about 99.5 to 100.5; and in still more elaborated situations, it may mean precisely 100 and nothing more or less.

A similar variability applies with the word *number*. In a *Blondie* comic strip, Dagwood is asked to guess a number between one and ten. The answer is 6 ¼; as most people would, he considers only integers and thus cannot guess correctly. However, this does not require that *number* be semantically ambiguous (not even when *a number of* implies a large number). It is the root of a heterogeneous system, subsuming and neutralizing all domains. For it and its hyponyms, we specify the following:

[B] DOMAIN CONDITION
   A semantic field can specify to various contextual domains, each of
   which (perhaps without parallel) systematically proportions the meaning of
   member words to that domain. Any particular word/phrase/sentence/etc.
   may be interpreted differently under different domains. The distinctions
   within the domain may be semantic or pragmatic; the interpretive choice
   of domain must be pragmatic, determined by all relevant factors.

We have another field with similar characteristics: colors. Paralleling the variability of *100*, we have several apparently polysemic or idiomatic uses of *white, black, red* and *yellow:*

[3] white/black/red/yellow skin
[4] white/red wine, white/red grapes
[5] red hair

Consider the Berlin-Kay (1969) [BK] hypothesis about colors. They claim there are eleven basic color terms in the world's languages; the most primitive system has only two colors, *white* and *black;* if a third color is added, it is *red.* The fourth is either *yellow* or *green,* the fifth, the other; etc.

[C] IMPLICATIONAL ORDER: COLORS

black		yellow					purple
	→ red →		→ blue →	brown →	pink
white		green					orange
							gray

Other terms are not considered basic by BK because they are either specializations of one of these (like *maroon* to *red* in English) or apply only in a limited domain (such as *blond*).

The implicational order of (C) is not merely an empirical generalization across languages, but a hypothesis about the human mind. As such, it relates even to languages which have all the basic terms, like English. The domains of [3–5] (skin, wine, hair) are domains of limited color distinction. Limited domains require fewer contrast partners, and thus effectively enlarge the extensional range of each primary color. (Similarly, in a situation where the only animal is a dog, it can be referred to as *the animal*.) Since *red* is the finest distinction that needs to be made with respect to hair in a certain color range, it is applied to a color that could not be called red in a more elaborated range. Limited domains allow the modulation of "unmarking" to a more superordinal (unmarked) word; skin color can be represented as if the language had only four color terms. This shift is negotiable, for strongly inappropriate terms are not used: we skip *black* for wine; we use *white, black, red* and *yellow* for skin color, then *brown,* not *green* or *blue.* What is extensionally puzzling and inconsistent is intensionally systematic. A polysemic treatment of *red* focuses too concretely on extensional range and leaves unexplained why the word is used in strikingly different ways.

As with *number, color* can vary in different domains, including 'white but not black', 'black but not white', 'both black and white' and 'neither white nor black'; but these variations are attributable to the domains, not to *color*.

We can expand and sharpen BK's hypothesis with the following set of ordered classes, where (D1–3) incorporate (C). The terms "primary" and "derived" are from Kay and McDaniel (1978) [KM]:

[D] ORDERED CLASSES: COLORS
   0. Root: *color(ed)*
   1. Prime: *black, white*
   2. Primary: *red, yellow, green, blue*
   3. Derived: *brown, pink, purple, orange, gray*

4. Hyponym: *maroon, violet, indigo, chartreuse, . . .*
5. Specific: *blonde, brunette, . . .*
6. Secondary: *cinnamon, maize, lime, turquoise, . . .*

SPECIFICS are non-general color terms, applying only in certain domains. SECONDARIES are words with non-color meanings; the color meaning is thus pragmatic, metonymic. Some details are questionable: (a) *gray* may be more primitive than BK supposed; (b) there may be no clear distinction between (D3) and (D4) (KM, pp. 640–41); and (c) the order of (D4–6) may be variable.

The colors of (D) are ordered by superordinality, from the most abstract to the most concrete. The PRIME class is minimally closed and maximally remote (in this field) from reference: these polar terms are like "proto"- or even "pre"-colors. In languages with just these two, they contrast 'dark-cool' and 'light-warm' (KM, p. 616). PRIMARIES provide the basic full-fledged color class, but this class is still highly abstract; as just noted, primes and primaries appear to have conflicting references. As we add (D3,4), the system becomes more open and the terms become more consistently concrete in their application to reality; and with (D5,6), the real-life exemplifications are as important as the color itself, if not more.

As the class grows (opens), the mutual (strong) system becomes modular (weak), more and more attuned to referential needs; highly autonomous linguistic order opens to nomenclature, according more directly to the order of reality. Another point of evidence: when a word starts as a secondary and then abstracts to a more closed class, the color meaning becomes independent of its motivation and more arbitrary; the pragmatic meaning becomes semantic. This applies not only to *orange* (in lesser degree, also, to *turquoise* and *lime*), but with even greater effect, earlier, to *white* and *green*.

Why are color terms implicationally ordered in this way? I suggest the following general condition:

[E] HOLISTIC CONDITION:
The human mind operates holistically, in orders of progressively expanded closed classes that eventuate in open classes.

Any holistic order will exhibit markedness.

I have claimed that syntax-semantics-pragmatics is a continuum from abstract to concrete: from maximally arbitrary linguistic order and minimally realistic order to minimally arbitrary and maximally realistic. So too the vocabulary of a language: broadly, some words (aptly described as "grammatical" or "formal") are highly abstract and remote from reality; other "content" or "lexical" words are more concrete. Some words are fully within language, as shown by their membership in minimal closed classes; others, in more open classes, look outward, linking directly to reality. Yet there are not merely these polar classes, but many gradations.

Now to extrapolate: the whole vocabulary of a language can be seen as a (partially) ordered set, from the "primitive", grammatical, closed-class words, to the "elaborated", lexical, open-class words. This is the Vocabulary Principle that I mentioned briefly in Chapter One:

[F]   VOCABULARY PRINCIPLE:
   The vocabulary of a language is ordered in accord with the order of the
   human mind. Closed minimal classes in a language reflect primary,
   unconscious order, remote from reality. Open maximal classes in a
   language reflect secondary, conscious order, related to reality. There is a
   continuous cline from closed to open, from unconscious to conscious.

The color system shows that this principle applies on a graduated, continuous basis.

However, colors are not a wholly apt model for the whole vocabulary; the set of colors is more motivated by, and more closely linked to, reality than a verb like *take*. KM argue that there are perceptual reasons (reality limits) why the primes and primaries are ordered first, and this also makes the class of colors less arbitrary, more natural. Yet, even within this relatively concrete domain, there are strikingly different degrees of abstraction, an indication of complex and varying unconscious-conscious ordering.

I will call this PRIMARY ORDER. PRIMARY WORDS are those that rank relatively early in the implicational scale of the full vocabulary. They have the following characteristics:

First, they are highly abstract. These abstractions are unconscious and strongly systematic. We usually conceive of abstractions one concept at a time, and thus most of our conscious abstractions tend to be atomistic (non-systematic). For example, someone insisting that red hair be called orange, bronze or the like is making an atomistic abstraction. Typically, the abstractions we make deliberately are strongly systematic only when correlated with mathematics. The uniqueness of mathematics may be attributable to our high degree of conscious ignorance about other strong systems.

Second, primary words are the most intensional of words; their connection with extensional uses is remote. Thus, the apparent meaning of a primary word is highly variable in context. An extension may be totally the contribution of the context and its related domain. The sense tends to be formal and schematic, like an L-shape that in various contexts can be a nose, an intersection, a slice of pie, or the letter L:

Third, primary words will not be definable by paraphrase. A proposed paraphrase (typically, a word that is more domain-specific) will overspecify and undergeneralize. In a particular context, a paraphrase may in fact be accurate, but only because the differences are neutralized: the paraphrase will be more specific than the primary word, but the context may allow or require the primary word to take on a more specific meaning; the other uses of both the paraphrase and the primary word will not be relevant in the particular context. (These are familiar facts to all linguists, but they must be deliberately noted, and not merely assumed, in a linguistic climate where paraphrase has had an inflated value.)

Words may be primary in their own field (like *red*) or/and primary in the vocabulary as a whole. Prepositions, conjunctions and articles are obviously primary words with respect to the rest of the vocabulary, as indicated by their membership in closed classes and their multiple uses over quite different domains. Verbs like *bear* and *hit* are also (relatively) primary verbs; a (referential) noun such as *ice* is not. *Bear* and *hit* are highly intensional, *ice* highly extensional; *bear* and *hit* must be highly modulated to be referential, while *tiger* and *ice* are relatively direct. Yet (a necessary constant reminder), these are not polar opposites, but rather alternatives on a continuum. There are words more primary than *bear* and *hit* (*be, do* and *have*) and there are words less primary than *ice* (proper names).

The more primary a color word, the more ordinal closed classes it will be part of, and there will be more possibilities for the apparent polysemy that *red* exhibits. How should we account for this multiplicity? What is *red*'s meaning? It seems to me that both these questions are answered by the primary order of colors. *Red*'s place in this order is its semantic definition. What is semantic is essentially a word's place in its field, and the more primary a word is, the more it will vary accordingly to its varyingly relevant contrast partners.

If a word's semantic status is linked in a strong system to its contrast partners, then obviously primary words like *red* will exhibit a type of semantic heterogeneity. However, I suggest that variation because of markedness should still be considered a type of monosemy, not polysemy.

Of course, for such a definition to be practical, it must be pragmatically augmented by information about the domains: we need to note that when color terms are applied to hair, the more primary colors are preferred. Again, this is not binding: if people dye their hair green, purple, sky blue, cinnamon, etc., it is possible for all colors to be applied. But hair color typically uses first the more primary colors.

I am proposing, then, that the AXIOMATIC SHAPE of a (sub)vocabulary is a systematic series of progressively opening classes. The semantic status of a word in such an order is its rank, which implies a system of relationships (antonymic and hyponymic) to other words.

As the variant inclusions and exclusions of *black* and *white* in *color* indicate, the Primes of a class might not be enough to establish the class; alone, *black* and *white* can be (virtually) equal to *dark* and *light,* with the class of colors emerging as a distinctive class only when other members are added. Primes and Primaries are more domain-variant (because they are more domain-free) and thus are PRIMARILY VARIANT (yet monosemic) in the full class. In domains requiring a more primary class, the contrast partners are few, and meanings are broadly applicable; in domains requiring a more expanded class, the contrast partners are many, and the meanings are more narrowly applied.

7.2   SEMANTIC-PRAGMATIC

The boundary between linguistic order and natural order is the difference between a word's semantic and pragmatic status. Semantically, a word contrasts with other words systematically; pragmatically, it relates, complexly, to an infinite number of particular circumstances.

This boundary is not the same for all words, because some are more concrete and thus more realistic; these words also relate less systematically to other words. The more concrete a word, the more directly it is linked to external order, and thus the more "obvious" its use. A concrete word like *tiger* relates only minimally to other words (its relationship to *lion* is more empirical than linguistic), and its semantic status is thus correspondingly minimal. Dictionaries largely (and correctly) give a pragmatic definition, of tigers, rather than of *tiger,* not a "nominal", but a "real" definition.

As Schwartz (1979: 301–302)) reminds us, the traditional view assumes that "the intension of a term is a list of descriptive properties" which are "necessary and jointly sufficient" and which serve as "a set of criteria for application of the term." The extension then "is the class of things to which the noun applies." The goal of semantic research, so characterized, is simply to find the descriptive properties of each word, the intension. This is semantic, arbitrary, conventional, and linguistic; it will be noted in a dictionary. The extension, on the other hand, is a class of objects, "correctly called by the term," which are natural, empirical, and real; any further properties such objects may have will be noted in an encyclopedia.

Like me, Schwartz does not quarrel with this approach in its basic outline; he objects primarily to the implicit assumption that all words are "abbreviations" of listable descriptive properties. His objection is part of a development in philosophy of the notion of "natural kind", which he chronicles as editor of the collection *Naming, Necessity, and Natural Kinds* (Schwartz 1977), including articles by the philosophers Donald Davidson, Saul Kripke, Hilary Putnam, W. V. Quine, and others. The point of the notion "natural kind" is to make the rather startling claim that some words have very little, or no, intension at all. That is, they have little semantic content.

Extending the insights of Putnam (1978) and Kripke (1972,1977), Schwartz argues (1977, Introduction) that proper names have no intensional properties, and that other words (natural kinds such as *tiger, gold,* and *water*) have much less semantic content than is usually assumed. Dictionary definitions of natural kinds are often scientific (atomic weight for *gold*); but if scientific status is the "best" standard for descriptive properties, then we have the curious implication that some people (without scientific knowledge, thus even whole cultures) can (in some effective way) know what gold is without knowing the meaning of the word that refers to it.

Schwartz thus concludes that the atomic weight of gold has merely empirical status, not linguistic. Further, since things that are not gold can have its color, weight, shape, etc., these more experiential properties cannot be the criteria for defining gold either. What we know about gold is tempered by highly mutable "real" factors; we lack any distinctive property of gold to qualify for the "necessary and sufficient" requirements of traditional definitions or for the "arbitrary" status supposedly indicative of semantics.

Like Schwartz, I think the notion of natural kind is one of the most significant intellectual discoveries in semantics. However, like Greenberg with his insight about the productivity of *hit*-phrases, Schwartz (in both 1977, 1979) doesn't note a broader implication of his argument: that, in general, for every word, we have likely attributed too much "encyclopedic" information to dictionaries. He concludes with a simple division (only slightly complicated) of words into Natural Kinds and Nominal Kinds, the latter of which do meet traditional requirements. His discovery is short-circuited because he doesn't question an even more basic traditional assumption: the guiding principle that language should mirror reality, that all of a language should be highly nomenclatural, directly referential, relatively homogeneous, and relatively concrete.

This assumption is reflected in the chronic problem of the traditional view that I noted earlier: it is too stereotypically concerned with concrete nouns. They are also Schwartz's only preoccupation. Do either "natural kind" or "nominal kind" apply to *of, take*, and *hit?* The notion of "descriptive property" is likely too concrete to help with such words (thus, they seem meaningless, unless defined by more concrete words like *related, steal*, and *crash.*)

We must keep returning to the unacknowledged "wild card" in all our theories: what do we mean by "reality"? Jackendoff (1983) argues that we should not claim reality for our concepts, but only perceived or conceived reality; #tiger# (in his notational scheme) is what we mentally fashion, not what is "really there". While proposing this move, Jackendoff worries that it may appear solipsistic; but, in fact, it is too modest. As long as we are trying to explain in words, theorizing in words, we remain in language, not in reality, and not even in some independent conceptual reality; we do not somehow mysteriously escape language as long as we are using it.

The details of, and the relationship between, language and reality, to the extent that we try to describe these in language, are thus a part of language. "Concepts" too are usually other words, phrases, sentences. What I am calling pragmatic, uses of language, are not "out there" conditions, but also linguistic:

the pragmatic, to the extent that we can note it at all, is linguistically more specific, more diversified than the semantic.

This does not deny any reality external to our thoughts. We also know that we cannot be solely in language either; we never only think, interpret and theorize in language.

To reorient: I propose that a language is an implicationally ordered system, rooted in highly abstract, closed, strongly (mutually) systematic classes, diversifying into less abstract, more open, weakly (modularly) systematic classes. The (inclusive, more concrete) definition of each word is a mix of semantic and pragmatic information, a combination of both its status within the linguistic system and the "real world" properties of the word's references.

For the most primary words, like *of,* the definition is almost totally linguistic; as a member of the closed class of prepositions (and a primary of that class), its "value" is in effect not to refer but to set a framework. Its dictionary status is thus high, its encyclopedic status low. On the other hand, for a word like *tiger,* the linguistic status will be minimal; what is most crucial are the properties of tigers, extralinguistic facts. Thus, *tiger'*s definition will be largely pragmatic. As a "natural kind word", its "value" will be to refer. Its dictionary status will be low, its encyclopedic status high.

These are but two relatively polar extremes of a continuum; the mix of semantic and pragmatic information will vary for each word, depending on its systematic status. Those that are highly systematic will be correspondingly part of closed classes; those that are minimally systematic will be part of open classes.

For many linguists, the dictionary-encyclopedia distinction seems increasingly artificial; the reason is that the boundary has been sought in the wrong place. The belief has been that out of the purely pragmatic properties of referents we could find some minimally characterizing information that would be, in some way, markedly different from all the additional information we could consider as less essential; but the only relevant semantic information is that which designates a word's systematic, contrastive place in its vocabulary.

Semantic "features" (I am claiming) have often been part of what should be pragmatics. Giving (say) *tiger* the semantic feature 'animal' is misleadingly appropriate, because the order of language and the order of reality for such highly referential words may be (or seem to be) rather close: the relationship of *tiger* to other animal words can be highly similar to the relationship of tigers to other animals, and thus 'animal' can be both a semantic or pragmatic fact. This homology, for such words, likely inspired the traditional agenda of finding descriptive properties for each word, and kept that enterprise plausible, but it is only a limited phenomenon of nomenclatures; extrapolated to the whole vocabulary, it makes a science of semantics impossible.

Further, word class has usually been considered a syntactic feature, yet it is just as much a particular word's more abstract semantic property; its field relationships will be based on its part of speech. Even "mass" and "count" are just as much semantic as syntactic. In fact, if we see the relationship of syntax and semantics as one of degree of abstraction, then there is no need to ponder excessively which label should apply.

Syntax and semantics are (I am arguing) a linguistic continuum, but pragmatics is extralinguistic; yet pragmatics relates to semantics as a more concrete extension of a continuum of thought. In principle, (at least some of) what is pragmatic can be put into words; otherwise, we wouldn't be able to consider it theoretically at all. Semantics has been "pushed" into pragmatics primarily because it has never been accorded its correct degree of abstraction. The vocabulary of a language is as a whole relatively closed and abstract compared to its more open and infinite set of sentences. Obviously, then, phrases/sentences/discourses will be more concrete, though still to a highly abstract degree.

A possible objection can reveal the degree of abstraction: *black cat* is more concrete than *cat,* as I claim, but what about *alleged cat,* which "denies" *cat,* and thus seems more abstract? (Any negation makes the same point.) This objection is based on a false assumed meaning of *cat.* We usually say that *black cat* "implies" *cat* and *alleged cat* does not, but this "implication" is not of the phrases as such, but rather a presumption of "reality" that we have illegitimately smuggled into *cat:* we read *cat* as *real cat. Alleged cat* is more concrete than *cat* because we do not know with *cat* alone whether the cat is real or not (we stereotypically can make it real); even with the former, we don't know if this is allegedly our friend's cat, a linguist's example, bad luck, a secret code, etc. Language is a "free logic", free itself of reality claims, though providing the infinite means for making such claims.

My point here is the one I make in my discussion of Ziff's sentences. Actually, all of the above phrases are quite remote from reality; and Schwartz (1979) gives the reason. A distinctive characteristic of "natural kinds" is that they vary and change. With cats, there is a developmental sequence: being born, growing, maturing, aging, dying. The word *cat* abstracts from all that (and more), although in our sentences and discourses we can describe all those variations in increasingly concrete degree. (Recall that age was one of the problems in Ziff's *A cheetah can outrun man.*)

As abstract as *cat* is, *take* and *of* are much more abstract. Compared to such words, *cat* seems more linked to reality; such a word is part of a language because a salient reality occasions it. *Take* and *of* do not seem similarly motivated. According to my reasoning, *cat* should be part of an open class; a test for this is that the loss of this word would have minimal systematic effects, in contrast to the loss of *take* or *of.*

In short: while all words are abstract, remote from the flux of reality, some words are less remote than others. There should be a cline of words from less remote to more remote. Words can even change their position; initially *orange,* when its color sense was still pragmatic, was closer to reality than it is now.

A word may differ in abstraction in different domains, for different purposes, or different people. That is, the variation of a word will also involve the communicational variations of interlocuters, intentions and uptakes, time and place, etc. Schwartz gives the example of *continent* (1979: 315). According to the scientific theory of plate tectonics, a continent like Australia has a history, a pattern of development, and this has the effect of making the word seem more "natural". Australia isn't a continent because of some arbitrary principle that excludes Greenland; rather, it lives like a continent (but of course so does Greenland, so the arbitrariness is even more apparent).

Since a conscious failing is that of reducing continua to their polarities, the two extremes of vocabulary seem to imply contradictory theories of what a language is. The more concrete words are more closely linked to reality (proper names closest of all); their reference is less problematic (but much more complex than we think); they seem to adapt to reality; language is naming. We are highly consciously aware of what we mean; with these words, as common sense tells us, we speak language.

The more abstract words are remote from reality (the primaries most of all); they don't refer in any clear way (unless we heavily modulate); they seem to be purely linguistic, formal, and they dictate to reality and us. We are highly unaware of what we mean; with these words, as Heidigger (1971) saw, *language speaks us*.[1]

Of course, in every sentence, both conditions hold simultaneously. The abstract words define our more concrete lexical freedoms. The finite, more abstract vocabulary underlies our infinite, more concrete sentences. The Sapir-Whorf Hypothesis is both obviously right and obviously wrong, and a considerable bit of in between. The abstracts lead us to believe that rules are substantive, empirical (Chomsky); they describe what we actually automatically do. The concretes are more regulative, normative (Itkonen 1978); although we recognize them as rules, we violate them often. Chomsky and Itkonen are both right, for different parts of language. Neither is exclusively correct; a vocabulary, and a human mind, is not that homogeneous.

Thus also, it is a mistake either to think that a language is fully autonomous or that is fully non-autonomous. Rather, it is autonomous in gradient degree. Chomsky argues that syntax is autonomous, but is dubious about semantics. As a gradient judgment, this is correct: syntax, being more abstract and remote, more closed, is thereby autonomous to a high degree, especially syntactic principles that are universal. Within semantics, the most primary words are more autonomous, the less primary less so. Autonomy is correlated with strong systems: mutuality. When a system becomes weaker, modular, it becomes correspondingly analogous to whatever externality is dictating the system. Yet it never becomes a perfect mirror.

7.3 THE NOUN *ICE*

How can we distinguish the semantics and pragmatics of a highly concrete and referential word? Consider the noun *ice*. This word will also illustrate another property of such words: they can be figurative.

To repeat an earlier caution (and despair): any one individuation is less than fully adequate as an exemplar, even for any generalization it exemplifies. As I earlier complained, my model for primary ordering, the individual set of colors, is more concrete as a set than the whole vocabulary and thus to that extent deficient as an exemplar. The idiosyncrasies of an individuation always complicate analysis; as I noted with *bear* and *hit*, there is no (apparent) optimal place to begin the analysis of a particular word.

Ice is no exception; it is (I have found) best approached by a seemingly circuitous route, through a word that maps more clearly some of its territory, especially the figurative: the adjective *cold*. The earlier *break the ice* examples fit here.

This requires another delaying comment: except for brief remarks on numbers and colors, this is my first attention to a semantic field. Considering the claims of this book, this is a large irony. *Bear, take,* and *hit* are in what I am assuming to be closed subclasses of verbs, subclasses that are strongly systematic, which should exhibit more completely the properties of a field. *Ice* is the most open-class word I have addressed, and should be least affected by a field.

This irony is unfortunate, but it is implied in some of my other claims. I confessed to having only minimal insight into which verbs are most closely related to *bear*. It was difficult to plot *bear*'s domains, but finding its field is even more difficult (and so, I did not really find its meaning). Even though by my principles *ice* should not be part of a strongly systematic field, it is also easier (for the reasons Rosch and Whitehead noted) to see which other words are related to it.

In the most detailed dictionary treatment, W3 lists a number of definitions for "figurative" *cold*, but they are poorly integrated. I propose they be organized as follows (with *W3* definition numbers in parentheses):

[G1] very negative emotion, active
      feeling: fearful, renouncing
      affect: angry, hostile
[G2] very negative emotion, passive
      feeling: frigid, inhibited (3b)
      affect: dispiriting, discouraging (5a)
[G3] negative emotion
      feeling: isolated, reserved (3a, 3c)
      affect: chilling, unfriendly (3a, 3c, 5b)
[G4] no emotion; emotion should be present
      feeling: apathetic, indifferent (3d, 3e)
      affect: stale, uninteresting (10)
[G5] no emotion; emotion should be absent

feeling: deliberate, sober (3f, 3g)
affect: factual, impersonal (11)
[G6] no motion or change
feeling: immobile, dead (6)
affect: certain, assured (6, 14)

This scheme is only suggestive. It overdistinguishes both in degree of emotion and in the split of feeling and affect; the latter distinction is rather strained in (G5, G6). Many English words, such as *angry* and *impersonal,* do not clearly distinguish between feeling and affect. *Cold* ranges over all degrees of negative and "neutral" emotion, so the distinctions of (G1–G3) overspecify; *impersonal* can also differ in emotional intensity in different contexts. W3 does not recognize the extreme range of (G1), but the following data illustrate it.

This scheme is a flow chart of pragmatic possibilities, not fixed semantic distinctions. The crucial transitions are (G3–G5). Negative emotions blend with another negative state, the lack of emotion when it should be present; this in turn blends with another state, now positive, where emotion should not be present. This in turn blends with a lack of motion, a semantic unity also reflected in the morphology of *motion* and *emotion* and in the range of the verb *move.*

The following are ordered from (G1) to (G6). I have not categorized them precisely because some of them could fall into different categories. It must be kept in mind that *cold* does not gloss as 'angry', 'reserved', 'terror-stricken', 'dead', etc., but rather describes a quality associated with these states.

[6] I lay there in the dark, feeling the cold emotion of renunciation. (Floyd Dell)

[7] But when my aunt asked me whether I could not manage a little more I refused with cold dignity. . . . I carried my outraged feelings into the drawing room. (W. Somerset Maugham)

[8] They talk, but only to make ill-tempered demands and cold refusals. (Lewis Thomas)

[9] She took in the immediate scene with one cold glare. . . . (William Faulkner)

[10] His voice was cold with anger. (Harold Robbins)

[11] Some people, like my sister Harriet, even found him cold. But I suspected he was simply reserved, perhaps inhibited. . . . (Louis Auchincloss)

[12] He looked up at me with a cold annoyed stare. (Ursula K. LeGuin)

[13] The cold implacability was still in his voice. (Harold Robbins)

[14] Did I think that I would be choosing, irrevocably, the cold loneliness of that afternoon if I went on? (Betty Friedan)

[15] . . . his small voice had been cold and full of authority. (Irwin Shaw)

[16] His father spoke for the first time, his voice cold and harsh, level, without emphasis. . . . (William Faulkner)

[17] . . . She looked at him, trying to appear a little cold or at least disinterested. . . . (Theodore Dreiser)

[18] his cold, mean selfish policy toward those whom he liked to segregate and hate as his enemies (W. A. White, W3: 3c)

[19] His voice was cold and expressionless. (Harold Robbins)

[20] He finds the people of his village cold to this noble and time-honored sentiment. (Arthur Knight, W3: 3e)

[21] the cold, correct, regular, narrow poetry of Pope. (A. L. Kroeber, S3: 3a)

[22] a cold traffic of mind and ideas and, for all the melodrama, not a clash of living people. (J. R. Newman, W3:10)

[23] competing on the basis of sheer cold efficiency (T. W. Arnold, W3: 11)

[24] a cold calculated punishing punch in the mouth (John Steinbeck)

[25] It is spread with cold deliberation to other countries. (Meyer Berger, W3: 3g)

[26] She was cold sober. . . . (Peter Taylor)

[27] . . . the best way for him to counterbalance the cold, almost inhuman objectivity of his nature. . . . (Louis Auchincloss)

[28] I was pretty pleased with myself, but of course a cold assessment of the case would show only one thing—that I had done hardly anything from start to finish. (James Herriot)

[29] the cold neutrality of an impartial judge. (Edmund Burke, W3: 3d)

[30] In cold fact the Hula of the Old Way was a shambling, dreary, and very boring dance. . . . (Eugene Burdick)

[31] Remember the good old days when bands were cold and impersonal. . . . (Erma Bombeck)

[32] lay cold in his coffin. (Margaret A. Barnes, W3: 6a)

[33] The actors had their lines cold a week before the opening night. (W3: 6b)

The (G) scheme also maps the figurative range of *ice,* though it can indicate more severe negative states than *cold:*

[34] I felt that ice in my guts again, the dread I'd felt all afternoon. (James Baldwin)

[35] A patch of ice formed in the pit of Maxwell's stomach. (L. P. Davies)

[36] Kid Sampson's cry turned Yossarian to ice. "Is something the matter?" he [Yossarian] yelled in horror. (Joseph Heller)

[37] . . . very different from the terrifying menstrual ice of her rages. (Saul Bellow)

[38] The ice of his manner betrayed his dislike of the new ambassador. (RH)

[39] Somewhere beneath the load of the emotion-freezing ice which my life had conditioned my brain to produce, a spot of black anger glowed. . . . (Ralph Ellison)

[40] "When you're with her," Yolles said, "you sit there wondering what's under all the solid ice. Is it a woman? Does she feel about the way her

husband died? . . . No warmth, no tears. Just her head tilted up, that way she has, and that haughty look she gives you." (Arthur Haley)

[41] . . . the light from the windows gave their faces the look of inimical coldness, of ice. (James McCormick)

[42] I made a joke about linguistics, and ice fell on the meeting. (H. A. Gleason, Jr.)

[43] I may not have ice instead of blood in my veins the way Croft has. . . . (Norman Mailer)

[44] He arrived at ideas the slow way, never skating over the clear, hard ice of logic. (Ursula K. LeGuin)

[45] It was the knowledge of that I, not safe in her head, but in her gut, the ice of its inevitability, its no way back. . . . (Mary Lee Settle)

The *I* of [45] is a noun, modified by *that*. In [42], the joke produces a negative reaction that ends the conversation.

We can add examples of figurative *ice-cold:*

[46] Even though the sun was beating down I felt ice-cold. I guess I was in a state of shock. . . . (H. R. Haldeman)

[47] . . . he was a total expert who only dealt in established clinical fact and ice-cold logic. (Bill Knox)

[48] The nihilist now appears as an ice-cold business conspirator. (Michael Polanyi)

[49] Then their shooting [in basketball], which had been near perfect, went ice-cold. (AP)

Alternately, we can say in [49] that their shooting went "dead". The adjective *icy* shows the same range:

[50] His icy terrors were all his own. (Harriet Frank, Jr.)

[51] . . . [I] froze in icy shock against the wall. . . . (George MacDonald Fraser)

[52] An icy tentacle of uneasiness wrapped around him. (Clive Cussler)

[53] . . . [he] quickly stated his name and title in tones icy with disdain. (Tom Wicker)

[54] "I?" she repeated in tones of icy outrage. (Gordon R. Dickson)

[55] . . . looking me up and down with an icy loathing. (Marjorie Kinnan Rawlings)

[56] She directed an icy stare at the intruder. (James Herriot)

[57] . . . Griscom replied with icy irritation. (James A. Michener)

[58] Koplin shot Donner a disapproving air, his tone icy. (Clive Cussler)

[59] The voice throbbed with icy authority. (Ralph Ellison)

[60] . . . Howe, whose head had become icy clear in the nonsensical drama. . . . (Lionel Trilling)

[61] His lips refused to move; his tongue felt icy and inert. (Richard Wright)

[62] Or to be cold and clean. This has the advantage of icy, barren virtue. (Daphne Athas)

[63] . . . Judy rose with perfect, icy grace. . . . (Kristin Hunter)

[64] Maybe each commonplace reassurance I gave her helped temper the icy wind of truth. (Samuel Yellan)

The verb *freeze* and related forms cover the same semantic range:

[65] "What if," someone asked a ranger, "a climber freezes in fear and can't continue?" (Robert Paul Jordan)

[66] Softly, frozen with anxiety and fear, she turned the door handle. (D. H. Lawrence)

[67] Hardesty was frozen with accumulated anger, annoyance, disbelief and disgust. (Mark Helperin)

[68] They froze helplessly, rage and hostility seething through their every pore. (Clive Cussler)

[69] Ashley Fleming's face froze in a mask of indignation. . . . (Clive Cussler)

[70] And the pain frozen on the faces of those who have attended kindred dead. (William S. Ellis)

[71] The sight that greeted them stunned each of the men into frozen positions. . . . (Thomas Page)

[72] . . . a silent frozen loneliness takes over. (Katherine Kuh)

[73] Then she tells me a story which almost does freeze my blood. (Lewis Nordan)

[74] . . . this feeling of being suddenly frozen, this dryness inside his mouth came from facts, not little-kid fancies. (Paul Darcy Boles)

[75] Mr. Dumbleby's big frame froze suddenly into immobility. (James Herriot)

[76] If we leave aside those formerly empirical sciences whose theories have frozen into definite mathematical form. (Stephen Toulmin)

[77] . . . the printed word was inflexible, permanent . . . This embalming process froze language. . . . The word became a static symbol. . . . (Edmund Carpenter)

Both *ice* and *freeze* stress category (G6), where things are immobile, solid and static.

The following examples expand the semantic field with words morphologically related to those already noted and also other words having some sense of 'cold':

[78] I shook hands with him rather coldly. I wished I had not come. (W. Somerset Maugham)

[79] We can afford, emotionally speaking, to be coldly objective in judgments of athletic ability. . . . (John Gardner)

[80] . . . I was careful to smile with the right degree of coldness so that she would realize I had survived her attempts at interference with ease and despised her for prying into my personal affairs. (Susan Howatch)

[81] an icily unenthusiastic audience. (Mollie Panter-Downes, W3)

[82] . . . she recovered quickly, a warm smile replacing the iciness. . . . (A. J. Russell)

[83] I felt a chill of horror. (James Herriot)

[84] Laura feels a slow chill, a purely physical sense of danger. . . . (Katherine Anne Porter)

[85] . . . he continued in such a dead, equable tone that she felt a slight chill fall over her shoulders. . . . (Joseph Conrad)

[86] He showed a rather chilling detachment. . . . (Louis Auchincloss)

[87] . . . his lawyer's aplomb, a kind of iciness that removed him, like a surgeon, from the human pain of his client's distress. (Paul Olsen)

[88] And now Peter was chilled by despair. . . . (Ron Faust)

[89] perceptibly chilled by the ice in his voice. (W3)

[90] "You may seek my damnation as often as you wish," said Axel, cool as ice, the faint flavor of contempt lingering in each syllable. (Susan Howatch)

[91] A pair of cool, unemotional eyes considered Thane thoughtfully for a moment. (Bill Knox)

[92] I displayed a cool indifference, freezing them out of my life. . . . (Cathy Mitchell)

[93] But when I run into her, most of the time she's quite frosty. (Nancy Hunt)

[94] The name was a sharp cut, ice cold. It was incredible how, after all these years, the memory of Cavanaugh and his frigid rejection of *The Last Magic* still had a power to chill him. (N. Richard Nash)

[95] "He bowed frigidly but did not stop to speak to me." (Lawrence Durrell)

[96] "Will you be so kind as to explain to me what this is all about?" he then said, with what frigidity he could muster. (Conrad Aiken)

[97] The Tsar had received him with glacial frigidity. . . . (George F. Kennan)

The verbs *melt* and *thaw* are part of a larger field:

[98] "Our job, and the job of all small countries, is to melt the ice between the superpowers." (John Darnton)

[99] And, with that sound, my frozen blood abruptly thawed. . . . (James Baldwin)

[100] Austin believed that this slovenly imprecision had frozen philosophy into an unscientific non-cumulative state. He wanted to "thaw the life of ages, by unflagging application of the intellectual, and make philosophy a cumulative science." (John Stewart)

[101] thawed a little of the ice that held his lady's heart. (Robert Murphy, W3)

[102] I thawed out my fear and got to him just as he began to move. (Hunter Kay)

This field also includes figurative *flow*, which stands for life and change, in contrast to the solidity and deadness of ice.

7.4 LEXICAL SHAPE

These are not the only figurative meanings of *ice*, but they can serve, before we turn to additional data, to define what I will call LEXICAL SHAPE: the axiomatic minimal characteristic of every natural language word. Following Bolinger's requirement, this shape must allow for Openness. As a starting point, we can take a highly detailed definition for *ice*, provided by W3. Since *ice* is a natural kind, the best definition is (almost) totally pragmatic, a description of ice:

> W3.1a: water reduced to the solid state by cooling and when pure constituting a nearly colorless brittle substance that in freezing expands about one eleventh in volume, that has a specific gravity of 0.9166 as compared with 1.0 for water at 4 degrees C, that under normal atmospheric pressure is formed at and has a melting point at 0 degrees C or 32 degrees F, that occurs in the common form as hexagonal crystals, and that in large masses is classed as a rock—compare BLUE ICE, FROST, SNOW; HEAT OF FUSION.

This is intended as the literal meaning; under the same number, W3 adds this:

> W3.1b: the layer of frozen water covering a surface (as of a road, rink or body of water) <broke through the ice>: the surface of a sheet of ice <slipped on the ice> <skated down the ice> <an ice carnival>.

This is pragmatically different from 1a, not semantically: it specifies different embodiments of the material. Given this special treatment, there should also be (but isn't) a definition for relatively small-sized pieces of ice: icicles, ice cubes, blocks of ice. (*Icicle* and *ice cubes* are hyponyms of *ice*.)

Much of W3.1a need not be known by someone to use *ice*. The parallel, shorter definitions from WNW are limited to only the knowledge more readily available:

> WNW.1: the glassy, brittle, crystalline form of water made solid by cold; frozen water. WNW.2: a piece, layer, or sheet of this.

WNW.2 notes the possibility of "piece". WNW.1 gives more directly (yet still tangentially) a detail only slightly acknowledged in W3: that ice is cold. Considering the figurative data we have just seen, this is a surprising minimalization; it shows how distortions can occur when definitions become too scientific. While scientific classifications are legitimate for their own purposes, they are not reliable guides for assessing linguistic realities. They tend to omit or diminish an essential ingredient: lived, immediate human experience.

AH is even more concise, but adds 'mass'; it also makes the rink a special case:

> AH.1: water frozen solid. AH.2: a surface, layer or mass of frozen water. AH.7: the playing field in ice hockey; rink.

W3 and WNW account for our figurative data above, but AH does not (excepting an entry for *break the ice*):

> W3.2: the quality or state of being emotionally cold (as from formality, embarrassment, or hostility) <perceptibly chilled by the ice in his voice> <thawed a little of the ice that held his lady's heart—Robert Murphy>—compare BREAK THE ICE. WNW.4: coldness in manner or attitude.

However, these do not cover the full range of (B): fear [34], horror [36], *hard ice of logic* [44], and *ice of its inevitability* [45]. The emotions, manners and attitudes are more diverse than a reader might conclude from these definitions.

Another definition specifies appearance:

> W3.3: a substance resembling ice in appearance or solid form <these hydrogen ices might well be retained in meteoritic particles—P. M. Millman> *specif:* ICING.

> WNW.3: anything like frozen water in appearance, structure, etc.

> AH.3: anything resembling frozen water.

These differ in the implied scope of generalization; *ice* usually applies only to frozen hydrogen and carbon dioxide. If WNW and AH were correct, *ice* would have a more general meaning.

Closely related are these:

> W3.4a: a sweet frozen food containing a fruit juice or other flavoring and usu. served as a dessert or refreshment; *specif:* one containing no milk or cream (as a fruit ice or water ice). b: *Brit:* a serving of ice cream; specif: ICE CREAM CONE.

> WNW.5: a frozen dessert, usually made of water, fruit juice, egg white, and sugar b: *Brit:* ice cream. 6: icing; frosting.

> AH.4: a dessert consisting of sweetened and flavored crushed ice, distinguished from a similar dessert made with milk or cream. 5: Cake frosting; icing.

Notably, WNW and AH make a special case of icing.

For discussion, let us assume that AH's 'water frozen solid' is the minimal (most abstract) literal definition of *ice*. A literal meaning need not be solely semantic, if at all; we will turn to the semantic-pragmatic distinction shortly. How do figurative meanings relate to 'water frozen solid'? A necessary ingredient for definition, as Bolinger noted, is that a word must have the capacity for definitional change. The Openness Condition provides this dimension; that condition does not require all changes to result in the homogeneity that I argued for with *bear*. We need to define the lexical condition that allows for conventionalized meaning which has not been fully subsumed under a single meaning:

[H] AXIOMATIC LEXICAL SHAPE [ALS].

The inherent meaning of any word has the axiomatic shape of a "core" and a "periphery", GROUND and FIGURE respectively. In the more concrete OPEN idealization, both of these can be changing in accord with figurative processes such as metaphor, metonymy, generalization, specialization, and others. The ground is that aspect of meaning which is fully ARBITRARY; figural meanings, in contrast, are PARTIALLY PREDICTABLE or MOTIVATED, because they can be derived by the same figurative principles from the ground. (Cf. Lakoff 1987:204 on extensions of his "radial structures.")

Some implications of ALS:

(a) The ground is that part of a word's meaning that must be learned outright; the figure will likely be learned outright too, but should seem to the user as appropriately extended (thus motivated) from the core. That is, the ground (partially) enables us to find the figure or recognize it as such.

(b) Semiotically, the (arbitrary) ground is SYMBOLIC; the figure is ICONIC (paradigmatic-metaphoric-generalized: "something like") or INDEXICAL (syntagmatic-metonymic-specialized: "something with").

(c) These figurative PROCESSES can become figurative RELATIONSHIPS; however, because of possible reanalysis or eclipsing change, synchronic relationships may not reflect diachronic processes. Diachrony is both evolutionary and revolutionary, both continuous and discontinuous.

(d) The figure may be empty. While all words have a ground-figure shape, the ground of some words may be so inclusive that there is little room for figurativity. This is what I have argued for the most primary words. There is a direct proportion between a work's openness for figurativity and the openness of the set it belongs to: the most primary words, in the most closed sets, have corresponding minimal chance for change. Since they are also the most abstract words, they also lack the link to reality that occasions most (or all) figurative change.

(e) The (unconscious) knowledge of a particular user of a language might not reflect the "maximal" organization of figure and ground. As we noted with *hit*, a user may have a STEREOTYPED SENSE (something such as 'intense physical contact'), that would then not permit available figurative principles to motivate other meanings. Or a user may not (unconsciously) make full organizational use of figurative principles. In either case, the user may have more than one arbitrary meaning, and the word will seem to be homonymic. Of course, a speaker may have maximal organization unconsciously (as evidenced, say, by a wide range of uses for *take off*) and yet have a minimal organization consciously (being aware of only a few isolated and unrelatable uses of *take off*). In general, such diatopic variation can be both temporal and (socially) spatial.

(f) Extended meanings are only partly predictable; they are also in part arbitrary. This is the condition of all indexical and iconic signs: indices (such as pronouns, or tense markers) do not sufficiently indicate and icons (such as a map) do not sufficiently resemble without the help of other enabling factors. Generally, an arbitrary sense (and anything linguistic) cannot be a sufficient ground; there must be additional interpretive processes, both linguistic and nonlinguistic, both conscious and unconscious, both thought and practice. A linguistic ground is in fact another figure, with its own grounding (including its paradigmatic fields, and even the vocabulary and language as a whole). Figurative meanings are those whose ground includes at least two figures: the language used, and the referential reality that it figures.

A sense remains figurative because the implied process is only partial. Assuming *ice* as 'water frozen solid', 'water' is only partly generalized to 'chemical element or mixture', if *ice* describes only the frozen states of hydrogen and of carbon dioxide. 'Water' is also partially metonymized-generalized to 'chemical mixture of something with water', so the *ice* can describe frozen confections like icing and ice cream. These are partial generalizations because they do not apply to all elements, compounds, and mixtures; if they did, 'water' would be too specific to include in the ground.

Partializations of process may not be singular; there may be systematic constraints. There may be reasons ("the normal range of human experience") why only water, hydrogen and carbon dioxide are considered ices when frozen. If so, 'water frozen solid' would be a stereotype, not the semantic status of *ice*.

There are other systematic possibilities. We have just seen how *ice* fits into the field of *cold*, sharing its extensions. *Cold* has been extended thus: if something is physically cold, it will be felt as cold; the physical is fully or partially generalized with the perceptual and psychological. For some words, this generalization may be full, with 'physical', 'perceptual' and 'psychological' now simply pragmatic modulations of a single semantic sense: a word like *sensation* is unspecified for these distinctions. I suspect *cold* is also unspecified, or well on its way; that is, it is more an intensional word like *bear* and *hit*. This possible unity inspires again my repeated caution: the factors that determine the semantic status of a word, and its range of applicability, may be undiscoverable or unimaginable if the relevant data and considerations are too narrowly conceived.

Ice may not be as generalized as *cold,* because it more immediately relates to a real-world referent. Without completely denying a strong systematic influence, we can continue to explore the possibility that 'water' is part of *ice*'s ground and thus that the use of *ice* for frozen hydrogen and frozen carbon dioxide is figural (in my sense, including generalization and specialization).

One generalization of range must be noted. *Icy* and *ice cold* can describe some temperatures of water and air, so they do not imply '32 degrees or less'; their senses are either generalized, metaphorized ('like ice') or metonymized-metaphorized ('feel like ice'): these need not be distinct exclusive choices.

Not all figurations come from 'water frozen solid' and 'cold'; they can draw on more obviously pragmatic realities. Ice is a crystal; *ice* is used for other crystals, especially those that reflect or gleam. *Ice* can mean 'diamonds' [103–105]; emeralds are called *green ice* (FW). Further, the appearance ('shiny, translucent') of diamonds can suggest ice, as can also glass [106–109]; ice can in turn suggest diamonds and crystals [110]. (Scientifically, glass is not a crystal, although it is often taken as such.) The association led to further figurative use in [111].

[103] "An old pal . . . is bringing me a two-caret hunk of ice." (Major Hoople, comic strip, FW)

[104] "Along comes a guy . . . a piece of ice in his tie that made Tiffany's front window look like a hardware exhibit." (George Bronson-Howard, DU)

[105] fenced the ice for the gang. (W3)

[106] . . . a glittering icy chandelier for the dining room. . . . (Anne Tyler)

[107] Clawing at space, he seemed to suspend there for a moment in mid-air, before gliding with white floundering legs and arms across the hood of the car toward me, shattering the windshield in an icy explosion of glass. (William Styron)

[108] "That's what gives Waterford [glass] its weight—and its icy sparkle." (John Scofield)

[109] . . . the glass [of the lamp] is thick and clean, with icy lights in it. (James Agee)

[110] "All the trees sparkled with diamond icicles, and crystal prisms on the shrubs." (V. C. Andrews)

[111] His sharp glance had a glint—icy; crystal—of humor. (James Gould Cozzens)

(DU cites *ice palace* 'a high-class brothel'. According to Godfrey Irwin, it is "from the many mirrors and cut glass chandeliers found in these resorts.")

Ice, diamonds and glass are colorless, translucent, and capable of shining or glittering. These are properties that even water can have:

[112] There, in fact, stood the four glasses, brimful of this wonderful water, the delicate spray of which, as it effervesced from the surface, resembled the tremulous glitter of diamonds. (Nathaniel Hawthorne)

'Shininess' also shows up in *ice plant,* a tropical plant so called because its leaves glisten (W3).

Most of the ground (the arbitrary sense) seems to be pragmatic. If we insisted that all figurativity has a semantic base, we would then have to include in the ground something about the physical appearance of ice. Further, ice is brittle (noted by W3 and WNW), a property implied in the figurative phrase *(skating) on thin ice* [113] and [114]. This phrase is not rigidly fixed: *thin* can be modified by *very* [115] and the phrase can be varied [116, 117, 119]. A word with a similar sense can replace *thin* [118] and [119].

[113] I nevertheless persisted in the practice of skating on thin ice. (Bertrand Russell)

[114] For a few days, Bruce and Ellen skated on thin ice, each being overcareful not to aggravate the other. (Dorothea Bennett)

[115] I was on very thin ice and I backed away a little. (Ross MacDonald)

[116] "We had better not rush things at this stage. The ice gets thinner as we get farther out, you know, and the shore in less easy to reach. I've a feeling we ought to play doubly safe." (Helen MacInnes)

[117] "We've skated on thin ice for so many years. Colonel, this is going to break!" (Zane Grey)

[118] His mind skated on the brittlest ice. . . . (Norman Mailer)

[119] "It seems his widow didn't receive all she was entitled to," Donner said, skating onto unsure ice. . . . The ice parted and Donner fell through. (Clive Cussler)

We pragmatically (metonymically) infer 'brittle' from the reference of *thin ice,* and this inference can in turn be metaphorized. Further metonymy is possible: the sense of risk or danger; in addition, [113] implies (metonymically) that by courting danger Russell was being intellectually daring, and [114] implies that the two people are being careful as if (metaphorically) there was a danger.

Given these relationships, neither *break the ice* nor *(skate) on thin ice* should be considered idiomatic. Similarly, we have *cut no ice* and *(put) on ice. Cut* and *put,* like *break,* belong to closed subclasses of verbs; they are highly abstract, intensional and systematic, so they need not (but can) be viewed as part of the figure. *Cut no ice* [120] has the variant *cut little ice* [121]: other modifiers with similar import also seem possible. The phrase implies metonymically that there is no influence or success:

[120] That argument cuts no ice with Bavas. (Norma Quarles)
[121] The eight New Hampshire delegates would cut little ice at the Republican convention. (*Time*, DA)

(Put) on ice is glossed by dictionaries as 'in reserve' [122], 'in safekeeping' [123], 'in jail' [124], 'in abeyance' [125], 'assured' [126], and 'dead' [127]. These glosses are too specific; *ice,* as we have seen, implies 'lack of motion or activity':

[122] kept the invention on ice for 10 years. (W3)
[123] put you on ice quietly until they've had time to settle up their affairs. (Dorothy Sayers, W3)
[124] on ice pending his appearance in court. (*Front Page Detective,* magazine, W3)
[125] Wilde, with his galloping sense of self, as Attila of the drawing room, kept his heart on ice and his speech on fire. (Robert Mazzocco)
[126] With their lead they had the game on ice. (W3)
[127] Potter said irritably, "Jesus Jenny, Phil, he ain't dead. You're talking about him as if he was on ice." (Paul Darcy Boles)

Also, we have the pragmatic inference of 'preserve'.

An example of a larger figurative phrase:

[128] In general he was as independent as a hog on ice. (Gerald Carson)

7.5 SEMANTIC UNITIES

We now must ask: How much of the meaning recorded by dictionaries is semantic, intralinguistic? Obviously 'noun' is a linguistic category, and 'mass' (but *ice* can also be 'count'). But these "features" are highly abstract (syntactic) and provide very little meaning. Limiting ourselves only to the literal meaning, the most minimal thing we can say is 'water frozen solid' (the AH definition), or some variant ; these could be the semantic features, all others pragmatic.

Yet 'water frozen solid' describes ice. Even this minimal information is just as much about ice as about *ice.* Given this double status, it suggests that all our knowledge should be part of semantics. Or, conversely, even the least "meaningful" thing we could say about *ice* is something related to its reference. What is "semantic" seems to have disappeared into what is "pragmatic". This apparently reveals a deficiency in any argument that assumes a semantic-pragmatic distinction.

However: if this is factual information about the world, then it is also information generalized and differentiated in this language. Not every language has *red* as a distinct, unified color, and even fewer have *cinnamon.* English, like some Eskimo languages, could lack a general word for ice, but divide the "reality" into several different words. Or, like some African languages, it may have one term that covers snow, ice, hail, etc. It is certainly a linguistic fact that English patterns the world in just this way.

Couldn't we then justify 'cold' and 'shiny' and 'brittle' as semantic too? These are realities, but they are also realities as figured by English. Accepting this line of argument, where would semantic end and pragmatic begin?

What about the figurative extensions? There is nothing in reality that dictates them; figurativity seems to be a decidedly linguistic phenomenon. On the other hand, reality supplies a large part of the motivation for the extension: solid related to liquid, cold, shiny, brittle reality, not just language. So where does pragmatic end and semantic begin?

Putnam (1975: 165) says that he doesn't know the difference between *elm* and *beech*. He knows only that these are English words, nouns, and different kinds of trees. We might grant that he knows the linguistic facts (or does he?) but doesn't know much about trees (the reality). What if he thought (or thought possible) that these are just different names for the same tree, synonyms? What if he knew only that they were English nouns? Or only English? Or wasn't even sure of that? We would be less and less likely to credit him with linguistic knowledge.

Reverse the procedure: if he didn't know these were names of trees, does that mean he has no real-world knowledge? No, he might know these trees very well, but not as beech or elm or trees. That is a limited kind of knowledge, isn't it, if he doesn't know the words to describe what he knows? Note: it is an arbitrary fact about English, and not just a reality, that elm and beech are two kinds of tree, because English has (and some languages do not) the word *tree*.

Given this maddening ambivalence (both confusions and distinctions of semantic and pragmatic), I return to the question I posed earlier. Is the assumed semantic-pragmatic split a deficiency of theoretical reasoning? The answer is both yes and no. We are delivered from madness when we realize that we have posed the problem in a way that makes it unsolvable. Under the influence of the traditional approach, we have imagined a set of meaningful features, conditions or properties, and tried to divide them into semantic and pragmatic. As we have just seen, this is impossible. Rather, with a word like *ice,* the linguistic (semantic) and pragmatic (reality) have fused so that we cannot distinguish them in that way.

Yet, we can distinguish them, and in fact have been doing so in the above paragraphs. When we look at *ice* and see the arbitrary way it represents reality, we see its semantics; when we see the natural way it reflects reality, we see its pragmatics. Systematically, *ice* is a word in English related to other words; English might have other possible words and relations, but it does not: this system is intralinguistic, semantic. Systematically also, what *ice* "means" corresponds very closely with what we "know" about ice: this is pragmatic.

This system is intermodular (language and reality), pragmatic. The systems are clearly different, yet it is a difference that is obscured by features.

In effect, the features-conditions-properties, as well as the traditional approach and the dictionary definitions that antedated them, have been a theoretical hindrance. Yet, it is a very subtle hindrance. After all, such methods use the systems of synonymy, hyponymy and antonymy that are part of the subject matter of semantics. That is the key point: these systems, especially for the most concrete words, are both semantic and pragmatic. Assuming them to be solely semantic, yet trying to make an exclusive, across-the-board division in advance between language and reality, we begin a theoretical path that leads inevitably to rampant polysemy. Real-world factors intrude on the "linguistic" system from the start, not annulling that system but creating another. The arbitrary-linguistic and the natural-realistic are mutually "two sides of the same coin."

The close semantic-pragmatic intermodulation with highly concrete, referential words is a possible reason for Saussure's insistence that Signifier and Signified are closely linked; the coin analogy is his. The Signifier is linguistic, a word. If the conceptual is equivalent to semantics plus pragmatics, as Jackendoff suggests (1983: 95ff.), then the Signifier is the more concrete extralinguistic reality evoked by the word.

The relationship, like that of form to meaning, is one between an abstraction and all that it implies: an implex. In the primary vocabulary, the implex is largely a framework, a grid imposing on and ordering reality; in the nomenclatural vocabulary, the implex is largely an identification, a label, a means of organizing and recognizing reality. The more concrete the implex, the more language and reality seem to fuse.

The semantic-pragmatic distinction is more marked with primary words, at least if they have the monosemic status that I have argued for. While *be, do* and *have* can be correlated with reality, it is usually in polysemic and stereotypic fragments; they are so abstract that their realistic link is highly tenuous, though it nevertheless is there. However, they could be equally serviceable in a range of markedly different realities.

If my observations here are correct, they occasion a Saussurean irony. Two of his basic ideas were the strong system and the signifier-signified mutuality. In a vocabulary, these conditions hold in inverse proportion. Saussure's notion of 'Strong System' applies intralinguistically, exemplified in the primary vocabulary; but in the nomenclatural vocabulary, we have only a weak system. On the other hand, the Signifier-Signified link for Saussure is a strong link between word and reality, exemplified in the nomenclature, and less so in the primaries.

Strong systems apply to closed-class words, those abstract and remote from reality, but not to open-class nomenclatures. Conversely, the close signifier-signified link applies only to nomenclatures, not to primaries. Language-language relationships are mutual for primaries, modular for nomenclatures. For language-reality relationships, the inverse holds: modular for primaries, but mutual for nomenclatures.

Nomenclatures are not only more concrete, they are more consciously grasped. They are thus also more variable, mutable, and open to the full range of human experience. *Ice* may be known differently by different people, as ice is known differently. The more one knows about ice, the more one knows about *ice*.

In the traditional approach, we say that a particular word has features *A, B* and *C*. For a natural kind word, all three are likely to be pragmatic in "content". What is semantic is the choice and combination of these three features for this word, when the choice and combination could be otherwise. Since semantics is more abstract than pragmatics, it is more formal than pragmatics, as syntax is more formal than semantics.

Parallel remarks can be made concerning "reference". Noting that many expressions are non-referential, Jackendoff (1983: 94) remarks on the "illusion that the purpose of language is to describe the world":

> If, on the other hand, one takes the view that the purpose of
> language is to make one's internal structures projectable to others
> as #sounds#—i.e., to express thought—then there is nothing at all
> puzzling about non-referential expressions. It is just that some
> internal structures correspond directly to experience and some do
> not, a conclusion that should come as no surprise in any
> contemporary theory of mind.

Jackendoff affirms Chomsky's formalist claim that language is fundamentally an expression of thought, in contrast to the functionalist claim that language is fundamentally a tool for communication. The difference is semanticist to pragmaticist, a view from language versus a view from reality.

Jackendoff shows how we project form upon the world; we dictate the order of reality. Thus, reality is always projected reality. *Ice* is 'water frozen solid' because we have projected *ice, water, frozen, solid* as particular English categorizations.

And yet, these projections are not total. They can create many "real" objects that might seem to others to be illusionary, but "reality", beyond our projections, intrudes and dictates that if we project *ice,* it will have to correlate with what we project as *water, frozen* and *solid.* Perhaps reality intrudes most effectively when our system of projections is most diverse, and we can exploit the system's versatile possibilities to approximate more closely to that elusively independent external modularity. But no matter how we manipulate, our systematizing is constrained by something nonlinguistic. This is the character of highly concrete, referential words.

The "semantic" search for features-conditions-properties creates two significant problems. First, it diminishes the importance of a word as a unity. So much attention is focused upon the word's variable content that the word as a feature itself gets lost. Second, simple difference is overlooked as a semantic property: *red* and *green* are different colors, and there need not be any paraphrasable "content" that distinguishes them.

The most serious complication is the inappropriate expectation of minimal features, etc. Semantic research is often a search for such "primitives" and "general relationships". What is often overlooked is that each word is a primitive: posited primitives are often simply English words. Jackendoff (1983: 172ff.) takes BE, DO and GO as primitives, and thereby develops significant insights; he succeeds because these are primary words of the language, and he demonstrates how other verbs are more specialized. The minimality is appropriate, because these primaries are a minimal closed class. But these must be seen as English words and their abstract potential fully assessed.

If, on the contrary, we are told that a feature CAUSE is not *cause*, then we have only a promissory note and often an imperialist imposition on a language that doesn't quite reflect the imputed correctness of the feature. I doubt if anyone has tried to determine comprehensively what the word *cause* can do in English; such a study must include its relationship to *do* and *make* (which are more primary). Although CAUSE is intended as an improvement over *cause* (perhaps a universal innate concept), it is likely when applied in an analysis to be merely a stereotype of *cause,* a typical overconscious short-circuiting.

Recall Bolinger's warning about overhomogenizing. Seeking "important" generalities, we erroneously assume that some notion of "cause" ranges widely over the vocabulary, always at the same degree of abstract arbitrariness. In principle, some highly abstract relationships must be quite widespread, but they are likely to be as elusive and illusive a goal for intuitionists as were the assumed wide-ranging transformations of CTG, and for the same reasons: a language is much more heterogeneous than we deductively hypothesize, and one language may be individuated in a way that obscures any universals.

The most widespread abstract relationship is also the most overlooked: immediate exclusive difference, minimal antonymy. It is the minimal linguistic knowledge that Putnam had of *beech* and *elm*. This is a significant "bit" of knowledge, a different thing to know than that they are the same or that their mutual status is undefined. Such difference may be describable by some "concept" (i.e., word in the language), but it need not be.

Simple difference is in fact the solution KF proposed to distinguish colors: the difference between two colors such as *green* and *blue* had to be in the idiosyncratic distinguishers, not in the systematic features; the only such feature for these words is (Color). In Katz (1977) the difference between *green* and *blue* is pragmatic, not semantic, leading Jackendoff (1983: 117) to comment (my numbering):

> This means that in this theory [129] is contradictory (false by virtue of its semantic structure) but [130] is not; rather [130] is only false by virtue of encyclopedia information.

[129] Green things are not colored.

[130] Green things are blue.

But Katz is right: the semantic reason [130] is contradictory is only that *green* and *blue* are antonyms (and thus immediately exclusively different); the specifics of difference ("content") are pragmatic.

The point Jackendoff is making is instructive: there is no difference between semantic and pragmatic if we view language from CONTENT, from diversity. Semantics must be viewed from FORM, from unity. This granting is not easy and obvious; we cannot simply make each word a unity. We must still determine homonyms such as *bank* and polysemes such as *orange*. However, given my suggested procedures, multiplicity will not be easy and obvious either. We break out of our minimality trap, and thus can discover new kinds of unity and also new kinds of diversity.

7.6 SEMANTIC AND PRAGMATIC DIVERSITY

We proceed with a flexible view of what a diversity can be; it is pointless to restrict ourselves to the traditional notion of an exhaustive set of necessary and sufficient conditions, usually homogenized. There is no theoretical necessity or desirability to simplify, minimize or homogenize; the unity need not be discovered "out there", for it is already given. Rather, we search to discover what it is that motivated such a unity.

In effect, the traditional view has limited us to one analogy: the diversity of a file cabinet. Reality offers many possibilities: a cat is a unified thing, though its parts are diverse and heterogeneous . Or consider a body of land unified and connected at low tide, but cut into islands at high tide. Or consider Wittgenstein's analogy of a rope, no individual strand of which extends its full length.

Wittgenstein (1953: 31f) advises:

> 66. Consider for example the proceedings that we call "games." I mean board-games, card-games, Olympic games, and so on. What is common to them all?—Don't say: "There must be something common, or they would not be called 'games' "—but *look and see* whether there is anything common at all.—For if you look at them you will not see something that is common to *all*, but similarities, relationships, and a whole series of them at that. . . .
> And the result of this examination is: we will see a complicated network of similarities overlapping and criss-crossing: sometimes overall similarities, sometimes similarity of detail.
> 67. I can think of no better expression to characterize these similarities than "family resemblances"; for the various resemblances between members of a family: build, features, colour

of eyes, gait, temperament, etc. etc. overlap and crisscross in the
same way.—And I shall say: 'games' form a family.

This famous quote by Wittgenstein reveals a hidden preclusion: the word
common pulls us into a homogenizing, minimizing, oversimplifying trap. If this
is a mandatory prerequisite, our success is doomed; it is the problem with
traditional approaches. We need also to emphasize what Wittgenstein doesn't
mention but seems to assume: that *game* is a unified notion because English says
it is. We now need to find what that unity implies. Of course, if we find no
"network of relationships", we have homonymy.

The trap involves another word, which Wittgenstein also mentions:
similarity. This precludes the aptness of his rope analogy, which suggests the
relationship of CONTIGUITY. As Jackendoff notes (1983: 128ff.) at great length,
human "preference rules" favor both similarities and proximities; this is the
difference between metaphor and metonymy, between paradigm and syntax. It
is also cross-modal, as Jackendoff demonstrates by perceptual and musical
examples.

If Jackendoff is right, semantic unities may have contiguous parts, and only
contiguous parts, so that there are no general similarities to capture in features.
Such preference rules will also be prevalent in unconscious organization.

Yet Jackendoff himself misses a contiguity, and in the very same book.
Intending to illustrate how Wittgenstein's advice applies to verbs also, he
considers *see* (p. 150ff.). He offers the following intuitional data (my
numbering):

[131] I must have looked at that a dozen times, but I never saw it.

[132] I must have seen that a dozen times, but I never noticed it.

[133] Bill saw into the room.

[134] Bill saw under the table.

[135] Bill saw the flying saucer from his living room.

[136] I saw Bill.

Jackendoff notes that [131] and [132] suggest two different senses of *see*.
That of [132] seems like '*x*'s gaze goes to *y*'; *see* appears to be a movement
verb, as also in [133] and [134]. The "destination" *into* of [133] is paralleled by
the "source" *from* of [135]. This sense, Jackendoff observes, "says nothing
about whether the subject of the sentence has derived any information from his
gaze." In contrast, the *see* of [131] has the sense of '*y* comes to *x*'s visual
awareness'; "it is precisely this awareness that is not necessary" for [131].

Jackendoff presents these data to argue against the traditional assumption
that all the supposed semantic "features" of a word must apply in every use of
these words; if not, under traditional reasoning, the word must be made
polysemic. He proposes instead that there are TYPICALITY CONDITIONS, and that

a word need meet only some of them. Instead of two different *see*'s, "directed" and "aware" there is a normal type of seeing including both [136], and two less typical types in which only one applies. This analysis captures the "family resemblance" and is a better solution than polysemy, which leaves unexplained why the same word is used for supposedly different meanings.

However, the relevant data are underrepresented. *See* has a much wider range than just simple visual experience; it also involves understanding *(I see your point)* and planning *(I'll see that he reads it)*. We have no assurance, lacking analyses governed by the Monosemic Bias, that these are distinct; they too may be part of a set of systematic typicality conditions. Though departing from traditional treatments, Jackendoff makes the same polysemic judgment. Understanding, planning and visual experience are not similar, or similar enough, to warrant a unified meaning; multiplicity is declared by preclusion.

Even for Jackendoff's permitted data, a unity has been compromised. *See* is monosemic for a more comprehensive reason than that typicalities can coincide. *See* describes a human experience with diverse possibilities: we can see "immediately" with no need of effort, or not; we can see by directing our eyes in a certain direction, or not; we can be aware of what we see, or not; and we can see a real external thing, or not. There are also variant grades: for all four factors, the choice is not polar, but a continuum.

A language need not have a word that unifies these; but in English, *see* does. What I find most intriguing is that the language, in this word and likely many others, ignores the (gradient) difference between consciousness and unconsciousness (and also differences of intentionality).

As Jackendoff notes, his "conditions" are stereotypic; they make prominent what is favored by the conscious mind. Effort, Movement, Awareness, and Realness are noticeable and important; a superordinate unity of all the varying degrees is not. Following our conscious interests, and equipped with our conscious penchant for analysis, we "discover" differences in something that doesn't differ. The differences are certainly genuine, supplied by something, but not by *see*. For someone to understand *see* in a particular sentence, the context must supply sufficient clues to motivate the appropriate pragmatic modulation.

It might be argued that Jackendoff's solution is required for a different reason: to account for the different syntactic frames of *see*. It has been a common practice (traditional, lexicographic, and TG alike) to use syntactic frames as reason for positing multiple meanings: *break,* for example, is given at least two meanings because it occurs in both transitive and intransitive contexts. Yet, as I have asked repeatedly, why does a distinction made elsewhere have to be duplicated in an unvarying word? The syntactic context helps to specialize the meaning, but the specialization need not be inherent in the word.

Words like *break* and *see* can appear in differing contexts because the diversities are contiguously related. Effort and movement are (sometimes) necessary for sensory perception; to show their relevance we put *see* in a context appropriate for an effort or movement verb, leaving the perception to be inferred. Or, *see* can be put in a simpler context, from which we infer that effort or movement were not needed. The verb *see* is thus a striking confirmation of one of Jackendoff's preference rules.

Why are such unities so difficult to see? Culler observes (1981: 188ff.) that metaphor has long dominated metonymy; it has been considered *the* figure, the one most revealing of meaning and truth. Traditional necessary-sufficient conditions, favoring similarity and generalization, by implication have precluded unities with proximate, contiguous diversities.

Jackendoff suggests three types of diversities (p. 121):

(a) NECESSARY CONDITIONS
These are still possible, though not exclusive: *red* has *color* as a superordinate. On the other hand, necessary conditions obviously do not apply with *game* (as far as we presently know), or any proximate-contiguous unity.

(b) CENTRALITY CONDITIONS
These provide a focal value: e.g., pragmatically, certain hues of red are more red than others. This implies that boundaries between unities may not be discrete, but fuzzy.

(c) TYPICALITY CONDITIONS
"Conditions that are typical but subject to exceptions"; while a tiger typically has four legs and stripes, we can still recognize something as a tiger with three legs and stripeless.

For all three types, especially the latter two, we do not require "completeness of meaning", for these reasons:

(a) Given the limited nature of consciousness, we may never be able to understand a word fully, especially a verb like *bear*. Even consciously, but especially unconsciously, we can project a unity whose full applications cannot be surmised, either in advance or ever. This is a formalist insight, affirming the unity of language, as opposed to a functionalist view in which unities are inductively developed from reality.

(b) Some highly referential words are open because our knowledge of reality is open (given our standards of knowledge). This is certainly the case of diseases for which we only have symptomatic knowledge, and words like *syntax, semantics* and *pragmatics*. This is a functionalist insight, affirming the diversity of reality, as opposed to a formalist view in which everything is fully sufficient in advance.

(c) Some words imply realities that are, or sometimes can be, gradient, more-less rather than yes-no, as Labov (1973) demonstrated with his cup-dish experiment. Semantically, *cup-dish* and *day-night* are discrete, exclusive, determinate categories; pragmatically, in their real-world applications, they can be continuous, non-exclusive, and indeterminate.

(d) The more concrete a semantic unity, the more it is likely to vary, along all the dimensions of variability. Words/phrases/etc. may have differing pragmatic diversities, and may even have different semantic unities; each of these differences may have larger scale unities or not, describable in words or not.

(e) Some words are negotiable, in social dispute: is abortion murder? (This can happen even to fairly established words, as I have demonstrated with *synchrony* and *diachrony*.)

The latter two points also allow for a factor that I can note only in passing. When we try to understand language, we must include POWER. We can see this additional modality in the W3 definition of *ice,* couched in detailed scientific language. A person can know ice very well and use *ice* effectively, and yet not know ice-*ice* as W3 describes it. W3 is using an ideology. Granted, science is now so established an ideology that it seems to most people (although not all) to be an embodiment of truth itself. But it is a limiting choice of truthway nevertheless, an additional kind of human interpretation.

When Bloomfield (1933: 139) suggests defining *salt* as NaC1, lamenting the lack of scientific knowledge for many lexical items, and when Putnam talks of experts who know meanings better than most people, they are not talking just about system (language) and truth (reality), but of a particular mandated method of interpretation, a prescriptivism. The scientist in our society, by accepted fiat, "knows" *ice*-ice "better" than the workman who handles ice every day intimately; that is how we define and value language-related meaning. So too, our scientific society "knows" language-reality better than primitive societies because we do not consider their knowing as equal to ours. We thus create an anomaly, noted by numerous scholars: how can primitive people talk at all if they don't know proper meanings?

Chapter 8

THE VERBS *KICK* AND *SLAP*

Thus far, my examples of monosemic words with no semantic figure have been verbs (*bear, hit*), while the one with a semantic figure has been a noun (*ice*). I have claimed that words with semantic figures are likely to be words that readily refer, having fairly delineable referents. Nouns are thus more likely to be figural than verbs; but verbs can also refer fairly precisely to reality. Two likely candidates: *kick* and *slap*.

These two verbs also offer new perspectives on the complexity of syntax. On first impression, they appear to be fellow hyponyms: *kick* an action of the feet, and *slap* an analogous action of the hands. Their parallel syntax seems to confirm this status. However, on detailed inspection, their syntax has slight but significant variation, which puts them in different fields: *kick* is a movement verb, *slap* a contact verb. Further, *kick* clearly has figurative senses, *slap* probably not.

8.1 LITERAL *KICK*

Anyone who likes semantic puzzles should love *kick*, which presents such figurative enigmas as *kick the bucket, kick the habit, kick up a fuss, alive and kicking*, and others. But the challenge comes not only from exotic data as these, for *kick* also presents puzzles when it refers "literally" to an action of the foot and leg.

Dictionaries and linguistic treatments note the contrast of intransitive *kick* in [1] and transitive *kick* in [2–9].

[1] You have to kick rapidly when using a crawl stroke. (Random House)
[2] He kicked the door again, louder. (Richard G. Brown)
[3] . . . a few men went over to admire its [car] fittings and kick its front tires. (Tom Wicker)
[4] . . . they were standing around the back door, kicking the steps. (Flannery O'Connor)
[5] Tillotson drew back his right boot, then drove it forward, kicking Gideon's temple. (John Jakes)
[6] "Not even a plum seed," said Virgil, kicking the grass. (Eudora Welty)
[7] Maybe she wrote another one, he thought, and kicked some sand. (Norman Mailer)
[8] . . . he began to hit and splash and kick the filthy river. (Flannery O'Connor)
[9] She kicked the air. . . . (Kimon Lolos)

The transitive is usually defined as 'strike with the foot or leg', implying that 'foot or leg' is an inherent part of the meaning and that a blow has been landed on the entity named by the direct object. A blow seems obvious in [2–5], but less so in [6–9], where the entity is not a solid object (*grass, sand, river, air*). Intransitive *kick* is usually defined 'strike out with the foot or leg', implying an attempted blow, but this definition confuses inherent meaning with contextual meaning; intransitive *kick* indicates only a movement, with additional information supplied by prepositional adjuncts as in [10–21]:

[10] A soft body came in contact with his toe. He kicked out viciously, and the room was full of yelping. (Edith Wharton)
[11] As O'Niel regained his grasp on the strut with both hands he kicked up and out. (Alan Dean Foster)
[12] Haskel kicked through the remains of the bonfire. (Jerry Bumpus)
[13] He got one leg loose and kicked at Pete, hitting him in the stomach. (Donald Honig)
[14] Suddenly I let go of my knees and kicked powerfully toward the ropes. (Stanley Elkin)
[15] He turned around on his hands and knees and lowered himself backward off the roof, kicking blindly for a foothold on the window frame. (George Cuomo)
[16] Soon the young men were in a frenzy, leaping and slapping the ground, clapping their hands, then springing and kicking into the air like acrobats. (Henry Bromell)
[17] Someone kicked against the chair across the table. . . . (Hunter Kay)
[18] . . . Pa suddenly kicked out at the row of pokers. . . . (Donald Honig)
[19] I started kicking around in the snow. (W. H. Gass)

[20] Gardener kicked down savagely at his face. (Ngaio Marsh)

[21] I took a breath and drove my head into the cold, kicking down and against the current that swept me back. (Hunter Kay)

These adjuncts indicate 'direction/path' (*out* [10], *up and out* [11], *through* [12]), or 'target/goal' (*at* [13], *toward* [14], *for* [15], *into* [16], *against* [17]) or a combination of these (*out at* [18], *around in* [19], *down at* [20], *down and against* [21]). Transitives can also include prepositional adjuncts [22–25], which indicate a specific location on the direct object (*in the rump, between the legs*):

[22] The eyepatch man had kicked Harry Beecher in the rump. (Jerome Charyn)

[23] One student rises, marches to the front, kicks each of them firmly on their behinds. (Geoffrey Stokes)

[24] . . . [he] Kicked the conductor at the shins. (Paul Horgan)

[25] He kicked the robber between the legs. . . . (John Jakes)

"Instrumental" phrases can occur with both intransitives [26–32] and transitives [33–38]. The instruments include *leg* and *foot*, and also *knee* [27], *force in leg* [30], *toe of slipper* [31], *heel* [33], *boot* [34], *instep* [35], and *toe of shoe* [37]:

[26] She smiles when she sees him [lamb] open his big innocent eyes and kick with his strong legs. (Jesse Stuart)

[27] . . . then, kicking with his knee and forcing his antagonist's head down with his hands, he loosened the grip on his waist. . . . (H. G. Wells)

[28] The kid kicked out with his left leg. . . . (Bob Ottum)

[29] She kicked at the dirt with a bare foot, sending a spray of it in front of her. (George W. Cornell)

[30] . . . he had kicked at Yussie's face with all the force in his leg. (Henry Roth)

[31] She kicked at it with the toe of a high-heeled slipper. (John P. Marquand)

[32] . . . I spin on my left foot and kick backwards with my right for the nerve complex. . . . (Frederick Busch)

[33] "Giddyap," she said, kicking him with her bare heel. (Elizabeth Spencer)

[34] Disgusted, the actor kicked the other character with his boot. (Phil Roura and Tom Poster)

[35] . . . [he] kicked her buttocks with the instep of his foot. . . . (Peter Matthiessen)

[36] He sat in the middle of the sofa, kicking it with his heels. (Flannery O'Connor)

[37] He stopped once to get his breath and then began again, kicking the

door frenziedly with the blunt toe of his heavy work shoe. (Flannery
O'Connor)

[38] . . . Tom Ruffin kicked the horse with his bare feet. (John Jakes)

All of these instruments are clearly connected in some way to the leg or
foot, and imply that the leg or foot moved as well, but it is not clear if this range
of instruments can be specified semantically or rather pragmatically. Another
question these adjuncts raise is whether 'with foot or leg' is part of the inherent
meaning of *kick* or rather a highly predictable context. In the context of Case
Grammar, Fillmore (1970: 120) assumes it is part of the context and argues that
some arguments of some verbs (such as the instrument of *kick*) are part of our
understanding of these verbs, needing to be lexically specified only if they
require modification or are not fully expected by the hearer, otherwise serving
like a zero morpheme. In Fillmore (1975, 1976), this is part of *kick*'s frame.

Is 'with feet' semantically understood? Actually, there are more involved
factors. A kick is usually assumed to be a forward movement of the foot and
leg; when not, it can be lexicalized as in *backwards* [32] and *with heels* [36].
Also relevant is the position of the body: if a person is standing upright, with
weight on the legs, it is difficult to kick with more than one leg, and so a kick
would be understood as involving only one leg. But if one is lying down,
suspended in air, or in water, then both legs can be kicked, and an unrealized
instrument could be understood as plural. Plural is assumed for the
suspended-in-air situation of [15] and the water situation of [1]. A plural is also
possible for a four-legged animal standing upright. Even human upright position
can be understood as plural if the kicking is continuing, as in [8], [12] and [19].
The forward-backward contrast is not fully specified in all situations; [3] and
[15] allow backward kicking. All of these factors contribute to specifying the
implied instrument; their referential diversity indicates not semantic knowledge,
but pragmatic.

With the data thus far, we may be tempted to give phrase structure rules for
intransitive and transitive; this would be premature, because instruments can
also appear as direct objects in the intransitive pattern, as in [39–64]. The
instruments include singular and plural of *foot, leg, toe, heel* and *boot.*
Directional adjuncts include *back, out, across, over, through, in one direction,
up* and *backwards;* goal adjuncts include *against, into, at, in* and *on.* Adjectival
adjuncts are also possible: *high* [62] and [63] and *deep* [64]. Backward
movement occurs again in [40], [42], [47], [50], [54], [60], [61]. *Kick one's leg*
is thus ambiguous between a movement sense and a contact sense. (I include so
many of these examples because some linguists have expressed doubts to me
about the movement possibility.)

[39] . . . he wasn't kicking his feet, stroking his arms. (Wayson S. Choy)

[40] It [the horse] scampered up the rise with the others, kicking its heels and
snorting. (John Sayles)

[41] . . . he tossed his head, kicked his front and back legs. (William L. Franklin)

[42] He kicked his feet back and pulled himself forward. . . . (Margaret Gibson)

[43] . . . kickin' out my toes . . . (John Dos Passos)

[44] The little boy kicked his feet against the underside of the dashboard. (Toni Morrison)

[45] . . . he kicked his toes against his heels to stir the blood in his numbed and sodden feet. (Neil Bell)

[46] She kicked the top of her shoe against the brick column that supported the table top. (Flannery O'Connor)

[47] . . . he was shouting with the others and kicking his heel violently against the rung of his chair. (George Orwell)

[48] Haze turned suddenly and kicked his foot into the front tire. (Flannery O'Connor)

[49] Morose, he trailed along behind, kicking his toes into the cracks between the [marble tiling] squares. . . . (Nancy Hale)

[50] . . . [she] kicked her heels into her horse's sides to keep it running. (Cecelia Holland)

[51] . . . kicking his boot into the dog's rear. (Thomas Sanchez)

[52] ". . . he laughs hard and kicks his thin legs into the air. . . ." (Leon Rooke)

[53] She stepped forward, stepped back, and kicked one leg across the other, her arms extended. (Cecelia Holland)

[54] . . . donkey named Nancy, kicking her heels at a yapping dog. (Joseph Judge)

[55] She kicked her foot over the furrow. (Eudora Welty)

[56] They kicked their feet through the dying but raucous leaves. (Daphne Athas)

[57] She took two or three slow steps in one direction with her knees bent and then she came back and kicked her leg slowly and painfully in the other. (Flannery O'Connor)

[58] . . . causing one of the younger men to lie down on his back and kick his legs up in the air for joy. (Peter Matthiessen)

[59] The child began to scramble up the steps on his hands and knees, kicking his feet up on each one. (Flannery O'Connor)

[60] . . . [she] threw her arms around him, kicking one leg back in the air. (Dan Wakefield)

[61] He kicked his foot backwards on the can and a hollow boom reverberated in the alley. (Flannery O'Connor)

[62] . . . Jenny shied away, kicking her heels high. (Richard Wright)

[63] . . . the male stood kicking his front feet high in the air. (William L. Franklin)

[64] . . . [he] proceeded to kick an imaginary foot deep into my crotch. (Norman Mailer)

There is a further complication in that instruments can occur in subject position with both intransitives [65–70] and transitives [71]. The varying position of Instruments was one of the inspirations of Case Grammar, and their analysis one of its strengths. A simply intransitive-transitive distinction is unable to deal fully with the possibilities.

[65] The boy ran in the air, legs kicking. (Joyce Carol Oates)

[66] The cat's legs kicked and reached. . . . (Andre Dubus)

[67] . . . his hands tied behind him and one leg kicking out. . . . (Donald Honig)

[68] His foot kicked out and struck one leg of the other's chair. (Ellery Queen)

[69] . . . Tosca's red-satin high heel kicked in the empty air. (William O'Rourke)

[70] His boots kicked and fists tore and smashed on the bark. (Michael Rothschild)

[71] He kept watching his foot kick the suitcase. (Flannery O'Connor)

The solution I propose comes from another observation by Fillmore (1970: 127). He notes that the verb *tie* occurs with three quite different direct objects in the sentences *He tied his shoestrings, He tied the knot,* and *He tied his shoes.* He comments:

> The act of tying things can lead to fastening things, and so an extension of the verb *tie* to uses proper to a verb like *fasten* and *secure* has occurred . . . the verb *tie* continues to describe the original activity, but it has been extended to take in the results of the activity.

That is, in tying shoes, one produces a knot, which serves to fasten the shoes to the feet.

There are (at least) three solutions for this extension to 'fasten'. We can say that *tie* has a new meaning. The first solution makes the fastening meaning independent, so *tie* is polysemic. The second solution makes the fastening meaning a figure of the first, so *tie* is still monosemic, in the same way as the noun *ice*. Obviously, I would prefer the latter choice; this requires that the second sense be dependent on the first.

But there is a third solution. We can say that *tie* remains the same in meaning, but that since its context is appropriate to a verb like *fasten,* the puzzling context (how can shoes be tied?) leads us to infer that fastening has taken place. This inference is possible because fastening is a natural consequence of tying; *tie* is contiguously (metonymically) linked to *fasten.*

Kick also illustrates this metonymic contextual shift. There are three different general contexts (domains) for *kick*. The first, *kick*'s GROUND DOMAIN (A), is that appropriate to a MOVEMENT verb; the domain includes both intransitive and transitive patterns. (FOOT represents all instruments; the angled parentheses in (ii) mean that only one of the two possibilities, direct object or instrumental object, can occur. AdjP-adjective phrase):

[A] i. FOOT kicks   (AdjP)   (PP*)
      ii.   X kicks   <X-FOOT>   (AdjP)   (PP*)   <with X-FOOT>

   i. The foot kicked high into the air.
   ii. She kicked her foot high in the air.
       She kicked high in the air with her foot.

In (ii), when FOOT is a direct object, it is viewed as "the thing moved" rather than an instrument; *all the force in his leg* [30], an instrument not indicating movement directly, is unlikely as a direct object.

   Another domain is (B), one appropriate to a CONTACT verb. ((AdjP) is possible, but I have no data for it or for (PP) in (i).)

[B] i. FOOT kicks Y   (AdjP)   (PP-part of Y)
      ii.   X kicks Y   (AdjP)   (PP-part of Y)   (with X-FOOT)

   i. The foot kicked the dog flush on the mouth.
   ii. He kicked the dog flush on the mouth with his foot.

The (i) and (ii) variants are parallel in (A) and (B), but only in (A) is this an intransitive-transitive contrast; also, in (A), the (ii) variant can be either intransitive or transitive.

   If (A) is *kick*'s ground domain, then it is a specific kind of movement, a hyponym to *go* and *move* (assuming *go* is the primary verb of movement, and *move* the primary of verbs that take instrumental objects). Our experience tells us that movements can lead to contacts; in fact, some PPs (with *on* and *against*) will provide contact as the goal of the movement. The relationship of movement and contact is metonymic. *Kick* can, by a metonymic shift, assume a context (B) appropriate for a verb like *hit* (B). This is the difference between *kick (one's leg) against the table* and *kick the table*. Conversely *hit* (and *strike*) can shift metonymically in the opposite direction and take the context of a movement verb. This is the difference between *hit/strike the table* and *hit/strike out at the table*. (Fillmore notes the contrast *hit the table with the stick/hit the stick on the table*: more on this later.) *Kick* has the same movement sense in (B); the contact is inferred from the movement and the context. In a ground domain, the context is redundant to the sense of the verb; in a shifted domain, the context discrepancy requires an inference (the Coherence Condition).

   The third pattern for *kick* is (C):

[C] i. FOOT kicks Y   (AdjP)   (PP)
      ii.   X kicks Y   (AdjP)   (PP)   (with X-FOOT)

    i. The foot kicked the ball high into the air.
   ii. He kicked the ball high into the air with his foot.

Here, PP is a directional, not a location as in (B). But this is not the original movement, of FOOT, but of something affected by the contact [72–100]:

[72] I found her muttering and kicking an empty carton about fiercely. (Ann Copeland)

[73] . . . he had to keep kicking the ball around. . . . (E. B. White)

[74] At the entrance he kicked aside an empty beer can. . . . (Norman Mailer)

[75] It was easy to imagine the police vice squad kicking in a door. . . . (Patrick F. McManus)

[76] The magpie walked the fence, kicking off snow. . . . (Max Schott)

[77] Larry moved his hands to the handlebars and kicked up the footstand. (Andre Dubus)

[78] John kicked it [knife] at Emmett. (Jay Neugeboren)

[79] He kicked a few scoops of dirt against the long body. . . . (Paul Horgan)

[80] . . . kicking stones down the slope. . . . (Kaatje Hurlbut)

[81] . . . she moved quicker and kicked the knife under the table. (V. C. Andrews)

[82] She kicked loose dirt on the snake. (Paul Horgan)

[83] He kicked a piece of wood in the fire. . . . (Kent Nelson)

[84] I kicked a stone into the river. . . . (Wayson S. Choy)

[85] Psin kicked his horse into a faster trot. (Cecelia Holland)

[86] . . . Eddie Stanky's kicking the ball out of Phil Rizzuto's glove in the 1951 World Series. (George Vecsey)

[87] He went back to the other burning magazines and kicked them away from the wall. . . . (Frederick Busch)

[88] . . . kicking the chair back into place. . . . (Norman Mailer)

[89] Abruptly Tshant kicked his horse forward toward the cattle herd. (Cecelia Holland)

[90] He caught up with her and kicked her over onto her back. (Cecelia Holland)

[91] . . . kicking her cosmetic case ahead of her across the marble floor. . . . (Charles Newman)

[92] . . . she kicked open the baggy screen door. (Daphne Athas)

[93] He kicked a stone loose. (Margaret Gibson)

[94] The dun horse swerved violently, and Psin kicked him straight. (Cecelia Holland)

[95] Stiffly, they dismounted, kicked their donkeys free to find their own shade. . . . (James A. Michener)

[96] The Abbot kicked a stone clear of the path. (Brian Moore)

[97] If I found the bottle I'd kick it deep under the snow. (W. H. Gass)

[98] . . . he kicked the top board up with his foot. . . . (Wilson Lucas)

[99] He kicked some of the snow into the air with the toe of his shoe. (Sylvia Fromberg Schaeffer)

[100] Halleck kicked the door shut with one heel. (Frank Herbert)

Metonymically, the contact leads to another movement; note that this movement can have another contact as goal in [79]. This shift is possible both for contact verbs like *hit* (thus, *hit the ball to the outfield*) and *kick*, which has been shifted once already. We have a metonymic scheme (C), which enables the shifts in (D) (brackets indicate shifted domains):

[D] MOVEMENT $\rightarrow$ CONTACT $\rightarrow$ MOVEMENT

[E] *hit*: [move] contact [move]
     kick: move [contact] [move]

Pattern (C) is not simply an optional variant of (B); the direct objects have different status. It may seem obvious that if X kicks Y to Z, then X kicks Y; while this is often the case, it sometimes fails, as in [86], [93]. In addition, real world limitations show the difference in two sets of data. In the first, the first object names something that cover's X's body or legs. In [101–104], where the covering is a sheet or blanket, the inference may still hold; 'off body' is assumed in [101], with *off* 'body' in [102] and *off legs* in [103] and [104]. However, in [105–11], the direct object names a piece of clothing, which cannot be kicked; there is *off* 'foot' in [105] and [106], 'off feet' in [107], *off* 'body' in [108], and *off feet* in [112].

[101] . . . I kicked the sheet straight up. . . . (William Hoffman)

[102] He always kicked the covers off in the intense, private struggles that dominated his dreaming life. . . . (Sue Miller)

[103] He kicked the blanket off his legs. (Robert Penn Warren)

[104] Granma kicked the curtain off her legs. . . . (John Steinbeck)

[105] Jared kicked off his shoes. . . . (John Jakes)

[106] One of the crew had kicked off his boots. . . . (Barbara Reiff)

[107] Soon I kicked away my boots and breeches. (Brian Aldiss)

[108] . . . he kicked off his shorts angrily. (Tabitha King)

[109] Slowly he walks to the house, kicks the loose snow from his boots. . . . (Jesse Stuart)

[110] . . . they kick the snow from their shoes on a wooden platform. (John J. Putnam)

[111] She kicked her shoes free of her feet. (Francis Irby Gwaltney)

[112] . . . [she] kicks the shoes off her swollen feet. . . . (Joan Colebrook)

An attempt to characterize this set solely in semantics runs into a problem already noted: even if shoes and the snow on the shoes [109] can be connected with feet in a semantic notation, how can that notation indicate that it is impossible to kick shorts [108] when one is wearing them?

The second subset of data has a reflexive as a direct object [113–15]; the

inference of (C) to (B) fails here too. Further, the reflexive can be omitted
[116–25].

[113] . . . he kicked himself backward and away. (Peter Matthiessen)
[114] They ran aft and kicked themselves free off the screw. . . . (Richard
McKenna)
[115] On his back he kicked himself under the bed. (William Hoffman)
[116] Together they started the long swim to the bank. Ben kicked along on
his back, resting, recouping his wind. (Raboo Rodgers)
[117] . . . face partners and kick up to a handstand. (Charles A. Pease)
[118] The spider surged away from the shore, and an underwater frog kicked
up to examine the spectacle. (Franklin Russell)
[119] Then I perceived Buliwyf kicking down into the depths of the sea.
(Michael Crichton)
[120] Lear pulled himself along by handholds, kicked off from walls . . . .
(Larry Niven)
[121] Up the stairs Momma stumbled, clasping Cindy, who was still trying to
kick free. (V. C. Andrews)
[122] [underwater:] . . . the creature wheeled toward him in a rage. Colin
neatly kicked out of its way. . . . (Arnold Federbush)
[123] Rabbit kicks out of the bedcovers and hunts in the dark for his clothes.
(John Updike)
[124] I kicked free of my tangled trousers and shorts. (William Hjortsberg)
[125] With 330 yards to go, Baker kicked into his final sprint. (William J.
Buchanan)

There are thus two quite different syntactic situations in which an intransitive is
really a pseudo-transitive: (A) patterns that omit the instrument, and (C) patterns
that omit the reflexive.

There is more syntactic complexity. First, some adjuncts indicate not
movement but destruction of the entity of the direct object [126–31]. These can
be generalized with (C), since change of place and change of existence are often
treated in parallel: *turn into the driveway* and *turn into a spoiled brat.*

[126] He kicked apart his dormitory bed. . . . (Jack Ludwig)
[127] ". . . you stay here and kick the fire out," said Oscar. (Paul Horgan)
[128] . . . he's got on boots gray and dusty and heavy enough to kick a man
in two. (Ken Kesey)
[129] . . . kick a boulder into a thousand glittering shards. (Ron Faust)
[130] Psin kicked three fires to pieces. (Cecelia Holland)
[131] . . . Vespasiano Gonzaga kicked his only son to death. . . . (Aldous
Huxley)

Also, the direct object can be a result: hole [132], a cloud of dust [133],
haze [134], double-step [135], cancan [136], and way [137–39]. This result is
similar to *knot* and *He tied a knot.* There are EFFECTED OBJECTS; earlier

objects (and *shoestrings* in *tie shoestrings*) are AFFECTED OBJECTS. Effected objects are quite widespread: almost every verb can take an object like *way;* a "destruction" verb can have an object like *hole,* a "performance" verb an object like *cancan,* and a "creation" verb a wide range of created objects. The relation of Affected to Effected object is also metonymic; the direct object position is variable between these two possibilities, often for the same verb (*break a window/break a trail*).

[132] . . . [he] kicked a hole in the slush. . . . (Michael Rothschild)

[133] They whirled like spinning tops, kicking up the dust. (Zane Grey)

[134] A horse going by used to kick up a sweet-smelling, stifling little haze. (Paul Horgan)

[135] The two lines [of dancers] shimmer forward, legs kicking out an emphatic double-step. . . . (David M. Schwartz)

[136] . . . the great gleaming hams of a line of ponderous danseuses kicking up a cancan. . . . (Jerry Bumpus)

[137] One sees a man swimming or flying it may be, stretched out belly-down and furiously kicking his way along the wall at about shoulder level. (Alexander Eliot)

[138] Then he flung outward, feet first, with a swish
Kicking his way down through the air to the ground. (Robert Frost)

[139] She is tall, quite young, and was probably once one of those long-legged beauties in cowboy hats who kick their way through southwestern football. (Nancy Chaikin)

8.2 FIGURATIVE *KICK*

If we assume that kicking involves the leg and foot, then a use of *kick* without this contextual specific will involve figurativity. We have three possibilities:

    (a) the figure is pragmatic, not yet conventionalized (as the use of *door* to refer to a communicating person);

    (b) the figure is semantic, and can be inferred unidirectionally from the ground (as the use of *ice* to refer to diamonds);

    (c) the figure is semantic, and could be the ground for the other sense, the inference being bidirectional, and so each sense being independent (as with *orange*).

I have argued that only with (c) should a word be considered polysemic; with (b), we still have monosemy, the variation in meaning following from the definition of axiomatic lexical shape. Of course, there is a fourth possibility: that there is no figurativity at all, kicking not being specific to legs and feet. I will presently claim this last possibility for *slap* (which is not limited just to hands), but I conclude from the following data that (b) is the correct assessment for *kick*.

However, to support (b), we must do more than contrive glosses that allow such a solution. One indication for (c) (or even homonymy) would be syntactic patterning that differs in unpredictable ways from ground to figure. Thus, I need to show that (A–C) carry over into figurative meanings. To review, these are the three patterns of SYNTACTIC ground and figures:

A'. Ground Domain: "move leg or foot', adjuncts indicating direction and goal: *I kicked (my leg) (high) (up) (against the fence).*

B'. Figural Domain, shift from movement to contact: goal as direct object, adjunct indicating place on goal: *I kicked the fence (at the top).*

C'. Figural Domain, shift from contact to movement or change of state of something affected by contact, adjuncts indicating direction and goal: *I kicked the fence to pieces.*

These also occur figuratively in [140–43] respectively; [142] and [143] show the two adjuncts (movement, change of state) for (C):

[140] As the time wore on the sea began kicking up. . . . (Lowell Thomas)

[141] But now the wind was kicking up 12-foot seas. . . . (Curtis and Kathleen Saville)

[142] The war in Europe was kicking prices up. (John Dos Passos)

[143] Religion in our Christian land was mostly puerile fiddle-faddle until science kicked it apart. (Philip Wylie)

The possibility of the direct object being a result is exemplified in [144]:

[144] . . . the bullets kicked up sprays of snow ahead of me. (Derek Lambert)

As another indication of parallelism between ground and figure, some sentences can be taken either literally or figuratively, with the effective message remaining the same [145–50]; that is, while the action can be performed by the foot, it need not be to get the same result:

[145] "Think of your daughters, left to kick their heels in the carriage." (Georgette Heyer)

[146] "I'm sure you all saw Dennis Morgan kicking George Raft out upstairs as you came in. . . ." (Mark Goodman)

[147] The astounded dog finds himself kicked into the damp outdoors. . . . (Jesse Hill Ford)

[148] . . . they kicked open the safety valve. . . . (Richard McKenna)

[149] . . . the Duke kicked on the jet brakes? (Frank Herbert)

[150] He poured himself a little tequila into a mug, drank it off, kicked off the light, and went to sleep. (Olivia Davis)

The parallelism of syntax for both ground and figure assures that we are justified in seeking a monosemic status for *kick*.

To recall: the Ground-Figure distinction I am assuming is semiotic, reflecting the difference between arbitrary and non-arbitrary signs. The Ground is arbitrary (symbolic), while the Figure is non-arbitrary (iconic and indexical), in some way predictable from the Ground. Icons are metaphoric, based on similarity, resemblance; indices are metonymic, based on contiguity, juxtaposition.

Metaphorically, we can use *kick* in the Home Pattern to describe an action that resembles that of the leg and foot [140]. Or we can use *kick* in a Shifted Pattern to describe an effect of contact or movement that resembles that of kicking [141–144]. Metaphor is the open "something like" quality of lexical meaning that Bolinger noted.

Metonymy, however, is "something also" (literal) and "something instead" (figurative). Literally, metonymy provides something cooccurent in a situation, a cause to an effect, a motive to an act, a part to whole, or vice versa for each. As we saw with *hit,* this cooccurent part of the message is the real point; though the words contribute to the meaning, the contribution is irrelevant. Figuratively, since the specified part is irrelevant, it can be absent.

With metonymy as explanatory means, we can describe the indifference of [145–50] to literal and figurative distinctions. Example [145] implies a feeling in the daughters of impatience, boredom and protest, which can be actualized by a (conscious or unconscious) nervous act of kicking. The main point of the message is the feeling, not the act; the act is not essential. But the act reveals the feeling so well that the words describing the act can be used to indicate the feeling, even when the act does not occur.

Examples [146–50], when figurative, combine metonymy with metaphor. An act and its result are metonymically related. The point of [146–50] is that result, so any action resembling kicking in results can be described with *kick.* in addition, kicking a person or dog implies disrespect, so in [146] and [147] *kick* can be used metonymically to convey disrespect, whether a kick occurs or not.

Metaphor and metonymy interact is complex ways, so it is sometimes difficult to differentiate them. Since anything human has considerable metonymic potential (purposes and goals, for example), we need non-human examples to best isolate metaphor. Kicking is a large-scale, all-or-nothing act, lacking the finer human traits of subtlety and delicacy, so it can be easily adapted to non-human circumstances. As dictionaries see it, *kick* as figure suggests vigor and forcefulness, with jerky and erratic movements and effects that are striking and decisive. By discarding the requirement of foot and leg, the foot-movements and goal-movements are conflated. Thus, while some examples may seem to stress agency [151], the usual dictionary treatment is to consider intransitive objects [151–160] reacting as if kicked, rather than actually doing the kicking; this is especially clear in [159] and [160]:

[151] The bomber's engines kick with a 350,000-pound thrust. (W3)

[152] The gun kicked in Matt's hand. . . . (Andre Dubus)

[153] . . . it [motor] would kick back against the compression and begin
reversing. (E. B. White)

[154] His stomach kicked. (John Updike)

[155] The press kicked. Tonto screamed and pulled back his hand. (Tony
Ardizzone)

[156] The jumping jack kicked about on the floor until it ran down. (W3)

[157] an engine that kicked a good deal. (W3)

[158] . . . that sump pump had suddenly kicked back on again. . . . (Charles
McGrath)

[159] MacBean watched the dust kicking around the ports as the machine gun
fired. (Oakley Hill)

[160] The rifle fired, and the bolt kicked free. . . . (Bruce Palmer)

I suspect that by conflating the two movements, the figure of *kick* creates a drift,
as yet fairly minimal, which could make this verb eventually an intransitive-
transitive verb like *break*. That is, *I kicked the ball* would relate to *The ball
kicked* in the same way that *I broke the window* relates to *The window broke*.

Without human agency, the message in transitive examples [161–166] also
appears to be concentrated on the goal:

[161] . . . you could see shot charges kicking up the dust on beyond the
target. (Nash Buckingham)

[162] He took the rifle by the muzzle and flung it, and they watched it
cartwheel slowly in the air and kick up snow 30 feet away. (Charles
Fox)

[163] A bullet kicked adobe dust from the wall. . . . (Oakley Hall)

[164] . . . this might have caused a surge of gas to kick the [perforating] gun
up to the top of the lubricator. (Wallace Stegner)

[165] This injection tube kicks the protons produced in generator into the
actual accelerator. (*Smithsonian*)

[166] "We don't know if comets formed in the cloud [Oort Cloud] or formed
in the solar system and were kicked out to the cloud by the giant
planets," Yeomans said. (Thomas O'Toole)

Metonymic potential is more apparent with examples involving humans. In
literal examples [167–179], *kick* indicates simply being alive and doing
something [167], even if only for the sake of doing [168]. More specifically, in
tune with metaphoric potential, *kick* indicates acts that are sudden and decisive
[169] and [170], crude and clumsy [171] and [172], and displaying negative
feelings of dissatisfaction [173] and [174], opposition [175–77], and anger
[178]:

[167] "My mother says I started kicking inside her when Hiroshima
happened." (Mary McCarthy)

[168] She herself, when she was a girl, used to kick a stone home from
school. (Gertrude Friedbreg)

[169] He kicked back his chair and leaped upon me. . . . (John Barth)

[170] Ryan kicked the door open and stepped inside. . . . (David Westheimer)

[171] Bundling the telephone into the pillowcase, he kicked it under the bed. (Tabitha King)

[172] . . . someone might kick a wire loose in the semidarkness. (John P. Wiley Jr.)

[173] In the corner the baby kicked and cried. (Joanne Greenberg)

[174] . . . she went dignified up to her room and lay on the bed and brooded, and kicked pillows around. (Wallace Stegner)

[175] Danny tried to kick against them. (Paul Horgan)

[176] . . . Sidaci tired to kick him away. . . . (Cecelia Holland)

[177] The major-domo and portiere caught up with him and dragged him, kicking and struggling, back to the hotel. (Bernard Malamud)

[178] . . . he heard her kick the refrigerator and then the dishwasher. "I hate you broken-down, fucking, second-rate appliance!" she cried. (John Cheever)

Like the inferential meanings associated with *hit*-phrases, these metonymic meanings are pragmatic; they become semantic, and part of *kick*'s figure, when the lexical meaning no longer contributes any meaning, but merely serves to indicate the inference. Figuratively, the "alive" inference becomes liveliness [179–80], effectiveness [181–82], and simply currency, the last usually with *around* and *about* [183–86]. The sudden decisive quality can imply tough-mindedness and no-nonsense [187–190]. Crudeness and clumsiness imply failure [191]. The negative qualities are evident in a range of belligerent states [192–99], with *row* or *fuss* serving as result expressions [200] and [201].

[179] "Well, how's old March?" Nathan says . . . "Still kicking around?" / "Still kicking." / "He must be eighty-five, or something." (Joyce Carol Oates)

[180] . . . an active and kicking liberal wing of the Democratic Party. (Roger Mudd)

[181] "You kicking?" / "Still." / "But not too high, huh?" (Reynolds Price)

[182] "Call me back after this ballot if you're alive and kicking." / "We'll be alive and kicking so hard nobody will have to tell you." (Tom Wicker)

[183] So we kicked the idea around for a while. (David Eddings)

[184] an old chair that kicked around the house for years. (W3)

[185] He's kicked about a good deal before settling down. (RH)

[186] It was the tale trying to take form that kicked about inside the tale-teller at night when he wanted to sleep. (Sherwood Anderson)

[187] . . . to remind us and to kick the crutch from our complacency. (Hannah Green)

[188] For thirty minutes I sat before the typewriter, battling inside myself, trying to kick the panic away. . . . (Les Whitten)

[189] . . . the tough Marine who has vowed to kick the corps into better shape. (George C. Wilson)

[190] The story was kicked out — without regrets. (Eric Frank Russell)

[191] "I hate to say it, Woody, but you kicked this one. . . ." (Gerald Green)

[192] "I can depend on him not to kick up at the wrong time." (Mildred Savage)

[193] . . . with this Berlin blockade and the Commies kicking up, you know perfectly well we're going to be in another war. (Otis Carney)

[194] kicking at neighboring countries to distract their own people from internal problems. (W3)

[195] For in childhood this great disciplinarian had kicked against all discipline. . . . (Edward Crankshaw)

[196] "Then, when he gets your bill, he will not misunderstand or kick." (Sinclair Lewis)

[197] tends to kick against authority. (W3)

[198] . . . the waiters kicked at the rule. (FW)

[199] The ham spread was a bit watery but nobody kicked. (John Sayles)

[200] The two dogs, left locked up in the apartment, kicked up a tremendous row. (RH)

[201] "Well, the old girl found out, and kicked up a big fuss." (J. G. Ballard)

Anger indicating reproach or punishment can be expressed with some kind of conditional statement [202–204], but it can also be fully figurative [205]; such reproach can be addressed to oneself [206–207]. When a human is a goal or closely associated with a goal, *kick* can indicate treatment that is casual [208], rough [209–210], dehumanizing [211], inconsiderate [212], disgraceful [213], and rejecting [214]. The expression *kick upstairs* [215] gives the rejection an ironic twist. *Kick the habit* and related expressions [216–219] also indicate rejection.

[202] "I could have kicked her head in." (Philip Roth)

[203] "I felt like kicking them in the face. . . ." (D. H. Lawrence)

[204] "I told him I'd kick him in the backside from here to Hayden if he doesn't come. . . ." (Catherine Cookson)

[205] You don't kick people like Sheppard in the butt without them trying to kick you back twice as hard. (Alan Dean Foster)

[206] He could have kicked himself. (Francis Clifford)

[207] He kicked himself all the way into London for being a coward. (Irving Stone)

[208] His case had been kicked around the press as a political football. (Stanley Kauffman)

[209] . . . he felt compassion for these black innocents so violently kicked into freedom. (Elizabeth Spencer)

[210] Their faces as the bullets kicked them to one side were surprised. . . . (Derek Lambert)

[211] . . . his [Washington] ragtag army had been kicked all the way across the state by Lord Cornwallis. (Jim Hartz)

[212] Business was so good he felt he could kick the customers around a little. (W3)

[213] . . . he got kicked off the team for smoking. (Fred Setterberg)

[214] took to drink after being kicked in favor of a rival. (W3)

[215] Of course, he'd been kicked upstairs after the fracas in Cairo. . . . (Joseph Hone)

[216] "He wrote about kicking the drug habit. . . ." (Saul Bellow)

[217] The addict thrown into a cell and left to kick the drug cold-turkey. . . . (Ellery Queen)

[218] "We've got to kick this addiction." (John McPhee)

[219] Ex-Blue Devil Kicks Cancer, Saves Career. (headline, Durham *Morning Herald*)

The quick, no-nonsense all-or-nothing quality of the act is also prominent in other examples where it may not be as obvious [220–223]. The basketball example [222] has the hands as instruments, but the message concerns the decisive suddenness of the action. All-or-nothing lends itself very easily to any mechanical gadget that can be either "on" or "off" [224] and [225]; any gadget allowing a more varied and delicate setting would be inappropriate. I suspect a similar quality is implied in *kick in* and *kick back* examples also [226–230]; the message concerns the completion of the action, not any subtlety involved in it.

In short, *kick* suggests an action which is clear-cut, requiring or allowing no deliberation. It lends itself with *off* to certain types of beginnings, such as those in [231–36]; even though kicking is literally part of [231] and possibly [235], it is the intended crisp, unfuzzy start which makes *kick* appropriate. This quality, of course, has been drawn from *kick*'s literal reference; figurativity uses the details of reality.

[220] kicked his car into the lead. *(Newsweek)*

[221] Houston kicked its lead back to 20–13. . . . (Larry McMillen)

[222] I therefore fixed myself a scotch, kicked life into the living room fire, and began to enjoy the quiet. (Shirley Ann Grau)

[223] [Basketball:] "Our job is to give them one shot and then get the rebound," Jones said. "That's our whole game, to get the ball and kick it out." (AP)

[224] When the burner kicks on, warm air rises in the furnace by convection. (W. Clyde Lammey)

[225] . . . half the circularity fused, alarm bells went off, the sprinkler

system, and a couple of 002 cylinders kicked in. . . . (Thomas
Pynchon)

[226] "He kicked in big for Hunt's campaign." (Tom Wicker)

[227] asked to kick in a dollar for a present for the boss. (W3)

[228] forced to kick back out of every paycheck. (W3)

[229] The baseball strike was 12 days old yesterday, but today, when it hits
13, the owners' considerable strike insurance kicks in. (San Francisco
Chronicle)

[230] "You don't turn things around in your farm system overnight,"
Kenneday said. "Ours, in fact, didn't really start to kick in until last
season. . . ." (Joe Goddard)

[231] The Giants won the toss and elected to kick off. (RH)

[232] For January kicks off the new year's sport and outdoors vacation show
reason across the South. *(Southern Living)*

[233] In October, events kick off with Leif Erickson Day in Jensen Beach.
(Bill Clark)

[234] The campaign kicked off at Chicago in July. . . . (Carolyn Bennett
Patterson)

[235] I kicked off, and the canoe slid into the darkness. (Jerry Kambites)

[236] [Driving:] . . . we kicked off into the windy, blue space of the Golden
Gate. (Janus Crumley)

These general figurative conditions are accompanied by a number of special
cases. Although feelings with *kick* are usually negative, it is possible to get
'happiness' as in [237] and [238]; both can be either literal or figurative. The
literal action implies the feeling, and so can figuratively indicate it.

[237] "When I get on land I shall kick up my heels just as poor Daisy [a
cow] will when she gets to pasture." (Dorothy Eden)

[238] It [moonshine] will make you kick your heels high. (Jesse Stuart)

Examples [239–243] are a sampling of figurative expressions including
kick. Like single words, phrases can pragmatically suggest, and then become
institutionalized as phrases, conveying the figure semantically. With [239], the
figure is likely pragmatic, calling on current cultural information. Examples
[248–250] indicate personifications. While showing part of the figurative area
that *kick* claims, all of these examples are too specialized to reveal general
characteristics.

[239] The lawyers continue to kick up dust around the regional water crisis.
(*Virginian-Pilot*)

[240] "Well, you sure kicked over a bucket of worms with that one." (Ben
Haas)

[241] "It'll kick over a dozen applecarts, but it's necessary." (Margery
Allingham)

[242] "Don't kick a dead horse," said Burt. (Ellery Queen)

[243] He's tired of being the 98-pound weakling who gets sand kicked in his face. (Ira Miller)

[244] . . . kicking the window shut with the heel of his hand. . . . (J. L. Powers)

[245] . . . the driver opened the door into him and kicked him from the running board onto the hard pavement. . . . (Mark Smith)

[246] . . . he lapsed into what seemed certain sleep./But in less than a minute his chin kicked the air. . . . (Reynolds Price)

[247] . . . Macalister's boy had caught a mackerel, and it lay kicking on the floor. . . . (Virginia Woolf)

[248] . . . [it] is an idea that has been kicked in the head. (William Safire)

[249] Fate began drawing back her leg to kick him. (Flannery O'Connor)

[250] Kicking its white-water heels through sparsely populated hills as tough and worn as a farmer's overalls, this frisky calf of a stream . . . . (Harvey Arden)

What about *kick the bucket, kick off, kick in, kick it,* and *kick,* all meaning 'die'? An example like [251] suggests that *kick* describes a type of death in which the person dying makes a kick, literally or figuratively, as a protesting action or as a last-ditch effort for life. A circumstance like this could integrate these examples into the figurative field we have been exploring. But the connection seem tenuous; I suspect that this *kick* is now sufficiently distinct so that the form *kick* is homonymous.

[251] The shotgun caught Norm Lilly full in the chest. Lilly kicked once and died. (Larry Niven and Jerry Pournelle)

8.3   THE VERB *SLAP*

While *kick*'s ground domain is movement, with figures on subsequent contact and secondary movement, *slap*'s ground domain is contact, with figures on preceding and succeeding movement. I have condensed the variants in the following scheme: X = agent, Y = instrument, Z = goal, R = result, and p = preposition.

In (F), Contact, I list six basic patterns. Example sentences are enumerated in two columns, which reflect two ranges of instruments. If *slap* paralleled *kick,* the literal instrument would be a hand or palm, as in examples in the first column [252–66]; in (e,f), 'hand' as instrument is understood. Most dictionaries, however, recognize a wider range of instruments: 'flat object'; these are exemplified in [267–81].

[F] CONTACT

	'hand'	'flat'
'Instrument':		
a. Y slaps Z	[252]	[267–72]

b. Y slaps Z p-Z   [253]   [273]
c. X slaps Z with-Y   [254–59]   [274–77]
d. X slaps Z p-Z with-Y   [260]   [278–79]
e. X slaps Z (with-Y)   [261–63]   [280–81]
f. X slaps Z p-Z (with-Y)   [264–66]
[G] MOVEMENT BEFORE CONTACT   'all instruments'
a. Y slaps p-Z   [282–86]
b. Y slaps p-Z with-Y   [287–90]
c. X slaps p-Z (with-Y)   [291–95]
d. X slaps Y p-Z   [296–318]
[H] MOVEMENT AFTER CONTACT
a. X slaps Z R   [328–38]

Patterns (a,b) of (F), in [252] and [253], have the instrument as subject; in (b), an added PP indicates specific location on the goal (p-Z). Patterns (c–f) have the agent as subject; (d,f) have locative phrases. An instrumental adjunct is present in (c,d), implied in (e,f). Although commonly expressed by *with*, adjunct instruments have variant pronouns. In [257] the preposition is omitted, in [258] it is more elaborated, and in [261] and [262] it is in an external phrase. Example [263] mentions the instrument by describing its action.

[252] His hand whips out and slaps the side of my head. (Terry Davis)
[253] A heavy hand slapped him on the back. (John Dos Passos)
[254] Once she slapped a fly with her bare hand. (Walker Percy)
[255] The old woman slapped their little haunches with her open palm. (Katherine Anne Porter)
[256] Angelo slapped Fidelman's face first with one fat hand, then with another. (Bernard Malamud)
[257] I began to hit him then, slapped his face forehand and back. . . . (Kelly Cherry)
[258] . . . to slap it [shell] back and forth with its [cat] paw. (Shirley Ann Grau)
[259] She slaps the pillow hard, with a flat yellow palm. (Anne Tyler)
[260] The sheriff slapped her straight across the face with his open palm. (Richard Wright)
[261] . . . he drew back his hand and slapped Howard's face. . . . (Paul Olsen)
[262] Using the flat of his palm, he tried slapping the beef. . . . (Alan Dean Foster)
[263] . . . [he] slapped him in two motions, palm and back, of the same hand. . . . (William Faulkner)
[264] Croft slapped Martinez on the shoulder. (Norman Mailer)
[265] They were men and women mostly with two first names who slapped me on the back. . . . (Hunter Kay)
[266] "Sometimes I wanted to slap her in the face. . . ." (Stephen Schmidt)

Sentences [267–81] exemplify the wider range of instruments; heels, slippers, feet, rope, towel, ruler, whip, check lines and envelope can all be flat objects. In [274] a fish uses its flat body as instrument. 'Bat' is assumed in [280], and *a paddle* is mentioned externally in [281]. More dubious as instruments are waves, wind and snow [271–73]. I see no reason to limit literal slapping just to hands and feet, when the expansion to flat object is so general. These sentences show that *slap* has inherently a more general meaning than *kick*.

[267] . . . his heels slapping the stone. . . . (Henry Bromell)
[268] She walked away from him down the chapel, her slippers slowly slapping the stone floor. (Barbara Rieff)
[269] He walked on, and heard her bare feet slapping the path behind him. (Ellery Queen)
[270] The planks sprang beneath the step, slapping the river. (Ken Kesey)
[271] He listened to the waves slapping the bow. . . . (Smith Kirkpatrick)
[272] . . . a sandbagged main gate with a flagpole on it that slapped its frayed ropes in the scalding wind and never flew a flag. (John LeCarre)
[273] The snow slapped him in the face. . . . (Cecelia Holland)
[274] . . . [a fish] slapping the sand with its tail, flanks, belly, and head. . . . (Edward Bonetti)
[275] ". . . Cousin Ella was slapping my face with a wet towel." (Dorothy Canfield)
[276] Every day the nuns slapped them with rulers. (Rose Rosenblatt)
[277] . . . [I'd] slap his skinny rump with the backside of a fork full of manure. (W. H. Gass)
[278] He slaps the mules on the rump with the leather check lines. (Jesse Stuart)
[279] . . . she slapped me across the chest with the envelope. (James Crumley)
[280] A pinch hitter slapped the ball. (Vic Wall, W3)
[281] I slapped the water, angling my paddle, sending a shower in her direction. (Donald L. Gold)

With (G), Movement before Contact [282–318], (a) has the instrument as subject, (b,d) the agent; the instrument is an adjunct in (b), implied in (c), and a direct object in (d).

[282] Then he ran back down the beach, his canvas sneakers slapping against the hard-packed sand. (Ellery Queen)
[283] [skipping rope:] . . . the rope slapping against dirty-fresh girl flesh. . . . (Robert Hazel)
[284] Above him, the bullets hissed, slapped into the trees. . . . (Willi Heinrich, tr. Richard and Clara Winston)
[285] . . . the grass slapping at his knees. . . . (L. Woiwode)
[286] Rain slapped at the stained-glass window. (Berton Roueche)

[287] Fencer began to slap at him blindly with his free arm. (Robert Stone)

[288] He slapped with the palm of his hand on the table. (W3)

[289] . . . [she] removed a clean handkerchief from her cuff and began to slap at her eyes with it. (Flannery O'Connor)

[290] Sebastian yelled, spun around, slapped at her with the spade. (Hal Borland)

[291] He slapped at his right thigh. . . . (Larry Niven)

[292] Here their mother again slapped at the air. . . . (Catherine Cookson)

[293] . . . the cat slapped at his hand. (Cecelia Holland)

[294] . . . the full-leafed branches slapping at us as we went by. . . . (Donald Honig)

[295] The water slaps at the dock and the moored boats. (Gordon Weaver)

[296] Mildred slapped her hand down on the journal page. (Barry Targan)

[297] Casement slapped a palm on the desk. (John Jakes)

[298] She slapped her right hand into her forehead. . . . (Charles Baxter)

[299] . . . slapping the back of an open palm into his other hand. . . . (Noel Hynd)

[300] He drew in his mouth reflectively and slapped a hand to his knee. (Martin J. Hamer)

[301] He slapped one hand against his neck. (Jean Toomer)

[302] The boy slapped his palm against his leg. . . . (Jack Matthews)

[303] . . . the click of metal as travelers' coins are slapped upon the thick table. . . . (Agnes Sligh Turnbull)

[304] . . . she slapped the knife into Bob's palm. (Frank C. Slaughter)

[305] He slaps his cup against the saucer. (Norman Mailer)

[306] . . . he stood slapping his soaked hat against his thigh. . . . (Ken Kesey)

[307] She got out a knife and began to slap peanut butter and jelly on slices of bread. (Doris Miles Disney)

[308] . . . she idly slaps the shortened length of rope on her thigh. (Wright Morris)

[309] "Oh, brother," says the cop, slapping his nightstick in his palm. (Steve Katz)

[310] . . . I slapped the covers over my face. (Corinne Demas Bliss)

[311] . . . [he] slapped the quilt over her buttocks. (L. Woiwode)

[312] . . . [carved a] bun into three horizontal slices, slapped two beef patties between them. (*Time*, W3)

[313] The angrier he got, the slower and harder he slapped his paint brush across the walls. . . . (Terry Schultz)

[314] . . . a beaver slapped his tail on the water. (Sally Wood)

[315] . . . [waves] would greedily slap their tops over the gunwale. (Dudley Cammet Lunt)

[316] The rain came now in sheets so dense that the wind slapped them against the building. . . . (Barry Targan)

[317] A ricochet slapped some more dirt on top of them. (Norman Mailer)

[318] The clerk slapped on a stamp and tossed the letter into the canvas wheeler. . . . (George Cuomo)

Not shown in (G), but part of it, is the possibility of additional directionals like *up* and *down* [319–27]:

[319] His voice is clear and strong slapping up against the cement and steel. (Ken Kesey)

[320] . . . her arms came slapping down to her sides. (Philip Roth)

[321] . . . [he] slapped both hands down on his knees. (Ken Kesey)

[322] . . . she slapped one hand desperately down into the other on her lap. (Mark Schorer)

[323] He cut them [grapes] with his manly knife and slapped them into the crude sack. (John Cheever)

[324] . . . I slap the case of beer down on the couch. . . . (Hugh Allyn Hunt)

[325] Alice slapped the paper down on the grass. . . . (Peter de Vries)

[326] And he took out his solitaire deck, shuffled the cards loudly, slapped them down. (Tillie Olsen)

[327] . . . an irritable clerk slapped down a key. . . . (Agatha Young)

With (H), Movement After Contact, [328–338], all my examples have the agent as subject, although an instrument is possible: *A hand slapped the book across the room.* Results can be movements [329] or a new state [335], expressed as either AdjP [334] or PP, the latter transitive [328] or intransitive [331].

[328] . . . slapping the ball over the makeshift net. . . . (Austin Clarke)

[329] Graber extended the magazine he had been reading to arm's length and slapped it violently to the floor. (John Mayo Goss)

[330] . . . she saw the lady slap a slice of coconut out of the hand of her illustrious son. (Francis Gray Patton)

[331] Finally, Baby Suggs slapped the boys' hands away from the bucket. . . . (Toni Morrison)

[332] She stood up and slapped powder from the sofa cushions. (T. Gertler)

[333] "I'll slap that stupid smirk right off your face myself!" (Thalia Selz)

[334] . . . I put the bottle back in the drawer and slapped it shut. (Ken Kesey)

[335] . . . they had covered his burns with grease and slapped him almost sober. . . . (Cecelia Holland)

[336] I was slapped awake as if I were new-born. . . . (Mary Lee Settle)

[337] He slapped it [newspaper] open on the table. (Henry Roth)

[338] Underhanded, he chucked it onto the fire and slapped clean his palms. . . . (Michael Rothschild)

In short, *kick* and *slap* occur in the same three contexts. Why, then, do I claim they have different ground domains?

Consider: *kick* can occur with only an instrumental direct object; *slap* needs an additional adjunct. That is, *I kicked my foot* is ambiguous between movement and contact, but *I slapped my hand* cannot mean merely 'I moved my hand'. When *slap* is intransitive as in [339], it is pseudo-intransitive, with an implied goal; *I kicked*, however, need not have an implied goal. In these respects, *slap* is like *hit*: we can get *hit my hand on the table*, but not *hit my hand* 'move my hand'.

[339] The mosquitoes were back again. Walt slapped and reached for his cigarettes. . . . (Madison Jones)

As further support, note [340–43], where the context of *slap* explicitly or implicitly includes a sound resulting from contact; there is no parallel with *kick*:

[340] As the screendoor slapped behind her. . . . (Tom Wicker)
[341] . . . the book slaps shut with a loud pop. (Patrick F. McManus)
[342] Clothes slapped warm and dry with wind and sun. (Janet Frame, W3)
[343] The piston was slapping in the cylinder. (W3)

Examples [344–47] present interesting combinations: *slap palms together* [344] combines movement and contact; [345] coordinates and [346] and [347] parallel contact and movement patterns. If *slap* is assumed to be polysemic, then [345] would be an example of zeugma.

[344] Whiteside slapped his palms together for emphasis. (Noel Hynd)
[345] Hand slapped his sides and up his legs. (Bruce Palmer)
[346] Before him the windshield wipers slapped back and forth quietly, slapping the melting snow to stream trailing to the sides. (Theodore Weesner)
[347] . . . now she was pushing and slapping at the young man who slapped her right back. (Joyce Carole Oates)

With *slap* a more general verb than *kick*, its figurative possibilities are more limited. I have two examples of metaphor [348] and [349], the first 'movement like a slap', the second 'effect like a slap'; but both of these seem phrasal to me, not merely figures of *slap*, both also pragmatic. Metonymic examples also seem phrasal and figurative: in [350–67], additional information informs us of the purpose of the slapping; and in [368–76], the purpose and wider significance is implied.

[348] I slapped the barrels [of the gun] on him [woodcock] and pulled. (H. G. Tapply)
[349] "Your wife?" bellowed Dad, his astonishment so clear it slapped me too. (V. C. Andrews)
[350] to slap a child for disobedience. (WBED)
[351] I don't like being slapped on the back as a greeting. (OALD)
[352] . . . he slapped the deck down for Prew to cut. (James Jones)
[353] Holden slaps his pocket for a match. (Walker Percy)

[354] I slapped my hand over the receiver to hide my laughter. (Joyce Carole Oates)

[355] . . . sometimes he slapped his left chest with the flat of one hand as if to awaken his heart. (Doris Betts)

[356] . . . she felt like slapping her to bring her back to earth. (Simone de Beauvoir, tr. Leonard M. Friedman)

[357] Bill slapped down his badge on the first of January and made room for Roger Straws. (Jerome Charyn)

[358] "Let's make sure," the policeman said, and he began to slap Francis' clothes, looking for what—pistols, knives, an icepick? (John Cheever)

[359] This same baby girl would not miss her, she whose hand she had slapped more than once. (Margaret Gibson)

[360] He races out of the door of the elevator. Slaps the elevator button. (Joe McGinnis)

[361] "You lying little devil!" I said, itching to slap her defiant face. (V. C. Andrews)

[362] I scowled, then slapped Jory's hand when he reached to take my slice of pie. (V. C. Andrews)

[363] Mosquitoes whined around. One bit his cheek. He slapped it fiercely. (Madison Jones)

[364] He slapped himself several times on the belly happily as a baby. (John Dos Passos)

[365] . . . the child, slapped and crying into life. . . . (Arthur A. Cohen)

[366] . . . [he] said nothing and his hand did not acknowledge mine. I would rather he had slapped me. (Cynthia Marshall Rich)

[367] . . . she had been able to control W. O. in his cups, slapping sense into him. (Andrew Turnbull)

[368] He had been slapped down badly in a committee hearing, by a consummate pragmatist. (Willie Morris)

[369] . . . found himself divorced and slapped in jail for nonsupport. (James Crumley)

[370] ". . . I said come back or I'll slap a reprimand on you. . . ." (Jay Neugeboren)

[371] What sent its mayor to the boiling point was a damage suit Adam slapped on him. . . . (Tom Wicker)

[372] slapping new taxes on farm collectives. (G. E. Cruikwall, W3)

[373] slap a quota restriction on foreign imports of fur. (*New Republic*, W3)

[374] slap an additional fine on the violator. (J. M. Flagler, W3)

[375] slap certain academic critics. (Dudley Bitts, W3)

[376] slap him with a summons. (W3)

Syntactic patterns are parallel in literal and figurative examples for both *kick* and *slap*. As far as I know, this parallelism has rarely been noted or expected by the many scholars who study figurative language (though

Marantz (1984: 25ff.) not only notes the parallel, but implies unified meaning). Here, too, scholars have been content to consider isolated examples and build elaborate theories on meager data.

Some brief, incomplete comments can be made on the movement-contact variation. Fillmore (1977: 18) has noted, in his Frame Semantics approach, the capacity of certain verbs to present the same "scene" from several different "perspectives" (my numbering):

> Languages, and lexical items, differ in interesting ways in the options they present in taking particular perspectives on complex scenes. Consider, for illustrating this point, a scene of a person taking something and causing that thing to come into abrupt contact with something else.
>
> The English verb "hit" allows either of two perspectives on such a scene. One is that of the actor and the manipulated object; the other is that of the actor and the affected object. Illustrating the first of these we have a sentence like [377]; illustrating the second we have [378].
>
> [377] I hit the stick against the fence.
> [378] I hit the fence with the stick.

He also notes that only the second of these can be a minimal transitive: *I hit the stick, I hit the fence.

This is the same variation we have seen with *kick* and *slap*:

[379] He kicked his foot against the table.
[380] He kicked the table with his foot.

[381] He slapped his hand on the table.
[382] He slapped the table with his hand.

In parallel, *slap* does not allow a minimal transitive in [381]; *kick* does in parallel [379], but that shows that *kick* is a movement verb, not a contact verb like *hit* and *slap*.

Fillmore also notes:

[383] I beat the stick against the wall.
[384] I beat the wall with the stick.

Fraser (1971) supplies more examples (some of the following are mine, using his general formulas). The verbs in parentheses are his also; I will refer to them presently.

[385] I sprayed paint on the wall. (put)
[386] I sprayed the wall with paint. (fill)
[387] He loaded the goods on the wagon. (put)
[388] He loaded the wagon with goods. (fill)
[389] She stuffed the clothes into the suitcase. (put)

[390] She stuffed the suitcase with clothes. (fill)
[391] The workers planted trees in the garden. (put)
[392] The workers planted the garden with trees. (fill)
[393] I cleared the dishes off the table. (take)
[394] I cleared the table of dishes. (deplete)

Fraser lists other verbs with similar variation: *clear, drain, empty, trim, prune, stock, stuff, wad, emboss, engrave, pack, stack,* and others. He supplies the alternate verbs to illustrate that they are limited to only one pattern: *put* or *take* for the first of each pair, *fill* or *deplete* for the second. Noting the occurrence of *with* in the second of his pair, he calls these "device" patterns; the first of each pair has a prepositional phrase giving a "location." With minimal theoretical comment, he essentially agrees with Fillmore that the variants offer different "perspectives." But of what?

One proposed explanation is that the first sentence takes "partitive" view and the second a "holistic" view; Fraser notes these contrasts:

[395] He crammed/stuffed/wadded a pencil into the suitcase.
[396] *He crammed/stuffed/wadded a suitcase with a pencil.
[397] *He packed clothes full into the suitcase.
[398] He packed the suitcase full of clothes.
[399] *He loaded up the goods onto the wagon.
[400] He loaded up the wagon with goods.

[397, 399] imply 'fill' or 'up' even if they are not explicit.

However, Jeffries and Willis (1984) show that a holistic effect, though widespread, is hard to formulate; also, the *kick, slap* and *hit* sentences do not have this effect, though they exhibit the same variation.

A clue to the perspective difference is provided by Fraser's insight that sentences like [395, 397, 399] can include something like *one-by-one,* while the second pattern cannot. I suggest that the first sentence takes a DURATIVE PERSPECTIVE while the second sentence takes a PUNCTUAL PERSPECTIVE; movement and continuing activity are subspecies of the first, and contact and completed activity are subspecies of the second.

What is confusing is that the two patterns sometimes seem to produce almost synonymous sentences. But I think that is misleading in the same way that the border of two adjoining states or countries might make us think that they are both the "same". Since the movement pattern of *kick* allows a prepositional goal (*kick my foot against the table*), it appears to be synonymous to the contact pattern (*kick the table*); yet (as Fraser shows) the full ranges of the syntactic possibilities are quite different.

These alternative syntactic contexts (or perspectives) are metonymically related: thus, the involved verbs need not be considered polysemic, unless we are bound by traditional views that require unities to be based on similarity and not on contiguity.

Chapter 9

SUMMARY

These are some of the positions taken in this book:

1. Hypothesis
   A word has a single general meaning.
2. Method (Monosemic Bias)
   Assume that any meaning that is not present in all contexts of a word is
   not part of the word's inherent meaning; if this fails, assume distinct
   meanings are figuratively related.
3. Limits of Dictionaries
   Definitions confuse inherent lexical meaning (semantics) with meaning
   provided by context (semantic and pragmatic).
4. Limits of Paraphrase
   The more general a word's meaning, the less likely it can be paraphrased
   by other words. At best, dictionaries will define it by hyponyms; but
   these can be hyponyms of several words, and thus introduce irrelevant
   meaning. Since many hyponyms diverge from each other, the impression
   is created of a highly polysemic word.
5. Data
   Neither intuition nor usage alone is sufficient as a source of data.
   Theories require intuitional judgments, so usage is insufficient; but

consciousness always underestimates the relevant evidence, so intuition is insufficient.

6. Compositionality

Words contribute less meaning to sentences than usually assumed. The meaning of a sentence is always more than the structured semantics of its parts.

7. Systematicity

Language is systematic, both strong and weak. Weak systems exhibit modularity: dependence on other modularities, but with relative autonomy (so idealization is possible). Strong systems exhibit mutuality, lack of autonomy: a change in one systematic element requires a change in others (Saussure). Where the linguistic system is strong, it is maximally autonomous of other modularities (though never completely); where it is weak, it is minimally autonomous.

8. Idealization

The Chomskyan idealization [IDEAL] is a highly abstract "core" of strong systems, which are modulated by external concretions, with the effect of weakening systems, to full realistic linguistic variability: diachronic, referential, figuratively open, specific languages/dialects/registers/idiolects. All linguistic realities are enabled by modular combinations; each reality must be described by the appropriate idealization. The more abstract an idealization, the more likely it will mistakenly include realities explicable only on a more inclusive, modulated idealization.

9. Closed-Open

Strong systems are realized by closed classes, weak systems by open classes.

10. Unconscious-Conscious

The fundamental unconscious capacities are relatively immutable, strongly systematic, and closed; these extend progressively to conscious capacities that are mutable, weakly systematic, and open. A word's general meaning may not be definable in conscious categories (other than by itself); however, with abundant data, consciousness can infer the range and limits of the meaning.

11. Individuation

In highly complex systems, modular combinations produce many unique individuals, which nevertheless are parts of systems. All words are individuals; thus, it is dangerous to generalize from a single word. Those words in closed classes are unique according to intralinguistic systematicity; those in open classes are unique according to systems both intralinguistic and extralinguistic (external realities, cultural beliefs, etc.).

12. Semantic Fields

A field of related words exhibits a closed-to-open continuum, paralleling unconscious-conscious: e.g., colors diversify from primes *black* and *white,* through primaries *red, yellow, green,* and *blue,* and eventually to secondary colors like *cinnamon.* The field is potentially open, but rooted in series of closed classes.

13. Vocabulary
The full vocabulary of a language is a semantic field, rooted in closed (minor, grammatical) classes. Each open (major, lexical) class of words roots in primary subclasses (*be-do-have-go* are the primary verbs).

14. Form-Meaning
Form is the most abstract meaning; meanings are individuated form. Syntax-Semantics-Pragmatics is a continuum from closed to open: semantic categories are hyponyms of syntactic categories. Pragmatics is extralinguistic.

15. Definitions
These combine semantic and pragmatic. The more primary (closed-class) a word, the more completely semantic its definition; its role is essentially intralinguistic, minimally relating to reality. The less primary (open-class) a word, the less semantic (and more pragmatic) its definition; its role is essentially extralinguistic, its definition largely a "real" definition, describing properties of a real-world referent. A vocabulary as a whole is not modularly autonomous.

16. Figurativity
The less primary a word, the more it is related directly to externalities; the more so, the more open it is to figurative extensions, based on that reality. The more primary a word, the less directly related to externalities, and thus the less possibility of figurativity.

Robert Kirsner (personal communication) observes that this book is highly programmatic: it claims much more than it substantiates. As consolation, he also says this is not a solitary failing, but rather one common to linguistics in general. I plead guilty and beg mercy on these two counts. Some failing here is (I hope) due to lack of space; in future works, I will try to give more extensive treatments of the verbs *break* and *take,* two highly primary verbs, with special attention to their semantic fields. Some failing is due to lack of prior analyses: the unsatisfactory treatment of *bear* comes from (I hope) the lack of completed analyses of the prepositions, and of the verbs (whoever they are) most closely related to *bear* (one of them has to be *have*).

One of my themes, persistent but never center stage, is that the subject matter we are considering is so overwhelmingly complex that linguistic approaches/theories/schools that appear sometimes to be irreconcilable (and thus by scholarly obligation at war) may simply be in different places of a huge forest, or at different parts of the elephant. Although this book has been fifteen wandering years in progress, the suspicion that everyone is right in some ways is one of the most recent in my thoughts, and thus this theme is one of the least developed. My biggest failing is that I have ignored too many works, misread or misappreciated others, taken of others and forgotten the debt, and even when knowing acknowledged too little. Rereading my book, I am struck by my failure to acknowledge Bolinger's (1961) emphasis on gradience. I won't correct the omission: I'll let it show. To others who are astonished to read here their own findings, without sufficient credit from me: forgive me, and let me know.

DATA REFERENCES

Abbreviations in these references are listed following this section, except for dictionary definitions, which are in "Other Abbreviations." Sentences with (BC) come from the Brown Corpus and are not listed here. (S) indicates a spoken example, (HL) a newspaper headline.

AUTHOR. SOURCE: CHAPTER.SENTENCE NUMBER,PAGE IN SOURCE

Nathan M. Adams. RD 5/76: 4.253,273

James Agee. PV: 2.70,88; *Let Us Now Praise Famous Men,* Ballantine 1939: 2.146,144; 7.109,47

Conrad Aiken. SHAPE2: 7.96,383

Joan Aiken. *The Weeping Ash,* Doubleday 1980: 6.17,379

Brian Aldis. *The Malacia Tapestry,* Harper 1976: 2.184,106; 8.107,69

Maury Allen. LHJ 5.75: 6.26,42

Neil Amdur. PB 2.78: 6.47,80

Sherwood Anderson. DOSS2: 8.186,557

V. C. Andrews. *Flowers in the Attic,* Pocket Books 1979: 7.110,8; *Petals on the Wind,* Pocket Books 1980: 8.361,127; *If There Be Thorns,* Pocket Books 1981: 8.81,298; 8.121,302; 8.349,335

Associated Press. BSUN 1.6.78: 4.121,C7; DMH 12/12/81: 1.7,2B; 12/10/77: 4.128,3B; LS 7/26/77: 2.333,A1; TP 12/28/75: 4.328,6.6; VP 6/14/77: 4.113,B7; 12/9/74: 2.276,A15; 5/10/78: 4.120,B7; 12/16/74: 4.20,B11; 5/15/77: 8.223,E3; 4/21/76: 6.7,C1; 7/11/76: 4.264,A2; VP-LS 1/13/80: 7.49,E3; 7/16/78: 4.81,A4

Tony Ardizzone. *In the Name of the Father,* Doubleday 1978: 8.155,203

Harvey Arden. NG 12/79: 2.310,826; 3.77: 8.250,345
Robert Ardrey. ESSAY: 4.279,263; *African Genesis,* Dial 1961: 2.159,326
T. W. Arnold. W3:7.23
Robert Arthur. *The Secret of Terror,* Random House: 4.187,113
Isaac Asimov. *The Early Asimov,* Doubleday 1972: 4.88,258; 4.308,281; 6.27,489
Linda C. Askey. SL 9/80: 2.344,151
Daphne Athas. *Entering Ephesus,* Viking 1971: 7.62,153; 8.56,395; 8.92,130
Louis Auchincloss. *House of the Prophet,* Houghton Mifflin 1980: 7.11,68; 7.27,81;
    7.86,55

Richard Bach. RDC: 4.230,193
David Bachman. LS 4/25/78: 2.307,C7
Anthony Bailey. NYER 9/8/75: 4.200,87
James Baldwin. FICT: 7.34,77; S29: 2.224,33; QS: 4.217,95; PV: 7.99,159; *Giovanni's
    Room,* Dell: 4.206,171
J. B. Ballard. SFCM: 8.201,371
Whitney Balliett. NYER 4/1/74: 6.3,47; 5/7/79: 2.205,161
Robert Barndoll. VP 8/31/75: 6.13,C2
Margaret Barnes. W3:7.32
Stringfellow Barr. POD: 2.261,221
John Barth. ESS: 8.169,65; SMS: 2.193,25; MT3: 2.104,660; *Giles Goat Boy,* Fawcett
    1966: 2.126, 230; 2.342,49
Joseph D. Bates, Jr. *Fishing,* Dutton 1973: 1.4,563; 4.5,302; 4.45,578; 4.192,309;
    4.199,476; 4.236,415
Gregory Bateson. *Steps to an Ecology of Mind.* Ballantine 1972: 4.134,330
Charles Baxter. MQR Sp1981: 8.298,34
Charles Beaumont. KAL: 4.235,43
Neil Bell. TIW: 8.45,313
Saul Bellow. *The Adventures of Augie March,* Viking 1953: 6.33,54;6.12,132; *Herzog,*
    Fawcett 1964: 7.37,82; *Humboldt's Gift,* Viking 1973: 4.74,434; 4.215,428;
    4.224,99; 4.229,344; 8.216,207
Dorothea Bennett. *The Maynard Hayes Affair,* Coward, McCann, & Geoghegan, 1979:
    7.114,69
Hal Bennett. LITF: 4.166,272
Meyer Berger. W3: 7.25
Carl Bernstein and Bob Woodward. *All the President's Men,* Warner 1974: 4.148,288;
    4.165,330; 4.313,266
Wendell Berry. *A Place on Earth,* Avon 1966: 2.18,289; 2.60,187; 2.122,69; 2.237,86;
    2.240,66; 2.263,158; 2.319,333; 2.328,352; 4.276,364; 4.311,216
Doris Betts. *Heading West,* Knopf 1981: 6.85,312; 8.355,215
Ann Blackman. DMH 9/30/81: 4.84,7A
Cecilia Blanchfield. MGAZ 8/15/77: 4.98,25
Corinne Demas Bliss. ESQ 4/80: 8.310,95
Fred Bodsworth. *The Sparrow's Fall,* Doubleday 1967: 4.275,7
Paul Darcy Boles. *Glory Day,* Random House 1979: 7.74,14; 7.127,51
Gail Bolger. WAVY-TV 2/28/78 (S): 4.90
Dwight Bolinger. *Aspects of Language,* 2nd ed, Harcourt Brace Jovanovich 1975:
    4.249,71

Erma Bombeck. RD 4/75: 7.31,87; VP 7/14/78: 4.54,D4
Edward Bonetti. NAR13: 8.274,230
Arna Bontemps. LITF 4.53,301
Wayne C. Booth. *Modern Dogma and the Rhetoric of Dissent,* Notre Dame 1974: 4.307,94
Hal Borland. *Country Editor's Boy,* Lippincott 1970: 8.209,196
Vance Bourjaily. *Now Playing at Canterbury.* Ballantine, 1976: 2.129,590; 4.97,393
Gamaliel Bradford. PTE: 1.31,242
Howard Breslin. *The Silver Oar,* Crowell 1954: 4.295,37
W. H. Brett. Quoted in Santillana & Dechend: 2,371,217
Jeremy Britt. *Piccadilly Circus,* BBC 7/24/77 (S): 6.43
Paul Brodeur. NYER 11/6/78: 2.7,148; 2.134,117
Wallace S. Broecker. NH 10/77, 2.164,18
Henry Bromell. BASS73: 8.16,13; 8.267,16
J. Bronowski. *Ascent of Man,* Little Brown 1973: 4.238,246; 6.15,59; 6.35,74
George Bronson Howard. DU: 7.104
Peter W. Brooks. TECH: 6.29,408
Richard G. Brown. BASS64: 8.2,21
Roger Brown. *Words and Things,* Free Press 1958: 2.204,287
William J. Buchanan. RD 8/75: 8.125,58
Pearl S. Buck. FMS: 2.311,459
Nash Buckingham. F&S 3/81: 8.161,69
Tom Buckley. BMA68: 4.260,9
E. A. Wallis Budge. Quoted in KRON 3.3: 2.177,48
Jerry Bumpus. BASS75: 8.12,28; PR 81.1: 8.136,114
Eugene Burdick. RWR3: 7.30,524
Anthony Burgess. *The Doctor is Sick,* Ballantine 1960: 2.341,124
Bill Burke. LS 9/19/78: 2.229,A1
Edmund Burke. W3: 7.29
Frederick Busch. BASS77: 8.32,12; BASS80: 8.87,42
Lord Byron. OED: 1.36

Thomas Y. Canby. NG 7/75: 4.272,9
Dorothy Canfield. CASS: 8.275,234
Truman Capote. *Other Rooms, Other Voices,* Random House 1948: 4.60,14
Otis Carney. *When the Bough Breaks,* Houghton Mifflin 1957: 8.193,26
Edmund Carpenter. MFOT: 7.77,3
A. J. Carr. NO 6/13/74,33
Gerald Carson. NH 6-7/79: 7.42,128
Willa Cather. S29: 2.235,4; Shadows in the Rock, Knopf 1931: 2.69,206
Charles E. Caton. JS: 2.271,8
Bruce Catton. AH 8/72: 1.8,98; *This Hallowed Ground,* Doubleday 1955: 4.58,213
Nancy Chaikin. BASS75: 8.139,53
R. W. Chambers. HIV: 2.144,168
Raymond Chandler. *The Lady in the Lake,* Pocket Books 1943: 4.183,107
Jerome Charyn. *Darlin' Bill,* Arbor House 1980: 8.22,30; 8.357,99
John Cheever. BASS77: 8.178,77; 8.323,34; CASS: 8.358,219; *The Collected Stories of John Cheever,* Knopf 1978: 1.28,642; 2.187,420; 2.192,251; 4.7,387

Kelly Cherry. BASS72: 8.257,43
Wayson S. Choy. BASS72: 8.39,29; 8.84,22
Creighton Churchill. AHOME 8/76: 4.204,6
Thomas Y. Canby. NG 12/77: 2.264.804
Bill Clark. SKY 8/80: 8.233,33
Mary Higgins Clark. *Where are the Children?*, Dell 1975: 4.69,166
Wilson Clark. SM 12/74: 2.387,89
Austin Clarke. NAR14: 8.328,277; WPR8: 4.208,477
Francis Clifford. *All Men Are Lonely Now,* Coward-McCann 1967: 8.206,156; *The Blind Side,* Coward-McCann 1971: 2.365,237
Jay Cocks. TIME 1/3/75: 2.318,6
Arthur A. Cohen. WPR8: 8.365,375
Richard Cohen. VP 1/15/85: 6.87,A15
Lowell Cohn. SFC 9/29/86: 6.6,57
Jackson Cole. *Mesquite Marauders,* Popular Library 1938: 2.329,27; 4.55,113; 4.179,156; 4.188,88
Joan Colebrook. *The Cross of Lassitude,* Knopf 1967: 8.112,178
Dan Collins. CHN 2/27/77: 4.261,2B
Columbo, TV show. (S): 5/9/76
Barry Commoner. O&D: 2.295,363
Neil Compton. NAR2:2.256,78–79
Cyril Connolly. In Orwell: 2.20,170
Joseph Conrad. SHAPE2: 2.41,136; SIC: 7.85,151; *Akmayer's Folly,* Doubleday 1929: 6.89,101: *Three Short Novels,* Bantam 1966: 2.119,82; 2.141,180; *Victory,* Anchor 1915: 2.44,247
Consumer Survival Kit. WHRO-TV 8/10/77 (S): 3.4
Catherine Cookson. *The Girl,* Morrow 1977: 8.204,30; 8.292,23
Ann Copeland. BASS77: 8.72,57
Edward P. J. Corbett. *Classical Rhetoric and the Modern Student,* 2nd ed., Oxford U. Press 1971: 2.84,384; 2.90,597
George W. Cornell. RWR3: 8.29,173
Donovan A. Courville. KRON 1.2: 2.211,62
Jacques-Yves Cousteau. MAINL 1/77: 2.221,40
James Gould Cozzens. *By Love Possessed,* Fawcett 1957:7.11,303
Carl and Nell Craft. VP 8/31/75: 6.25,C3
Stephen Crane. *The Red Badge of Courage and Selected Stories,* Signet 1895: 2.176,152; 2.278,22
Edward Crankshaw. *The Shadow of the Winter Palace,* Viking 1976: 2.269,213; 8.195,45
Michael Crichton. *Eaters of the Dead,* Knopf 1976: 8.119,164
Walter Cronkite. CBS News 3/5/75 (S): 4.135
Tom Crouch. SM 12/78: 6.45,43
G. E. Cruikwall. W3: 8.372
James Crumley. *The Last Good Kiss,* Random House 1978: 8.236,74; 8.279,239; 8.369,26
George Cuomo. *The Hero's Great Great Great Great Great Grandson,* Atheneum 1971: 8.15,22; 8.318,71

Clive Cussler. *Raise the Titanic,* Bantam 1976: 7.52,2; 7.58,49; 7.68,298; 7.69,33; 7.119,70–71

John Darnton. NO 5/25/80: 7/98,4–VI
Richard D. Daugherty and Ruth Kirk. SM 5/76: 4.284,70
Robyn Davidson. NG 5/78: 2.381,589
L. P. Davies. *The Alien,* Doubleday 1971: 7.35,33
Olivia Davis. *The Steps of the Sun,* Houghton Mifflin 1972: 8.150,120
Terry Davis. *Vision Quest,* Viking 1979: 8.252,140
John Dean. *Blind Ambition,* Simon & Schuster 1976: 4.146,127; 4.322,367
Mary Deasy. *The Corioli Affair,* Little Brown 1954: 4.49,221
Simone de Beauvoir, tr. Leonard M. Friedman. *The Mandarins,* Eagle Books 1956: 4.332,464–65; 8.356,23
Floyd Dell. DIMENS: 7.6,23
Vine Deloria, Jr. *God is Red,* Dell 1973: 2.52,169; 2.225,156
Benjamin DeMott. O&D: 2.359,60
Peter de Vries. MIDC: 8.325,283
Gordon R. Dickson. *Mutants,* Macmillan 1970: 7.54,196
Annie Dillard. *Pilgrim at Tinker Creek,* Harper & Row 1974: 2.118,155
Doris Miles Disney. *Shadow of a Man,* Macfadden-Bartell 1965: 8.307,153
William Diver. WORD 19.3: 4.136,419
Franklin W. Dixon. *The Tower Treasure,* Grosset & Dunlop 1959: 4.197,143; *The Shore Road Mystery,* G&D 1964: 2.135,173
Durham Morning Herald (DMH) 4/9/77: 4.138,4A; 7/27/75: 8.219,C1(HL)
John Dos Passos. *Midcentury,* Houghton Mifflin 1960: 8.142,264; *Number One,* Houghton Mifflin 1943: 8.43,19; 8.253,123; 8.364,157
Michael Douglas. PB 1/71: 4.312,244
Arthur Conan Doyle. REALM: 2.299,73
Theodore Dreiser. *An American Tragedy,* Signet 1925: 7.17,261
Elizabeth Drew. NYER 12/29/86: 4.320,93
Richard Dozer. SN 2/18/78: 4.73,54
Andre Dubus. SWR Su1975: 8.66, 394; 8.77,403; Sp1979: 8.152,215
Paul Duke. *Washington Week in Review* 9/12/75 (S): 4.39
David DuPree. WP 5/26/75: 4.11,D7
Lawrence Durrell. *Justine,* Pocket Books 1957: 2.27, 69; 2.110,45; *Mountolive,* Pocket Books 1959: 1.27,237; 2.115,117; 7.95,243

Connie Eble. (S): 4.68
Rosary Eble. (S): 4.331
David Eddings. *High Hunt,* Putnam's 1973: 8.183,117
Dorothy Eden. *Sleep in the Woods,* Fawcett 1960: 8.237,16
Albert Eisele. A 12/74: 6.28,85
Loren Eiseley. ESSAY: 2.288,411
Alexander Eliot. SM 8/76: 8.137,88
Stanley Elkin. BASS65: 8.14,86
George P. Elliott. FIFTY: 2.210, 417; BASS50: 2.370.141
William S. Ellis. NG 12/77: 2.298,855; 11/79: 7.70,723
Ralph Ellison. *Invisible Man,* Signet 1947: 7.39,226; 7.59,203

R. D. Ellman. W3: 4.240
William M. Estes. *Another Part of the House*, Lippincott 1970: 4.119,79; 4.172,65
Gareth Evans. NNNK: 2.86,200

Henry Fairlie. H 6/80: 2.89,28
James Fallows. A 12/24: 2.338, 87
William Faulkner. DOSS2: 2.145,407; REALM: 7.9,394; FIFTY: 8.263,257; FICT:
    7.16,381; *Light in August*, Modern Library 1932: 2.93,309
Ron Faust. *The Burning Sky*, Playboy 1978: 7.88,84; 8.129,71
Stephen Fay. NH 12/78: 2.316,44
Arnold Federbush. *The Man Who Lived in Inner Space*, Bantam 1973: 8.122,129
Marilyn Ferguson. *The Brain Revolution*, Taplinger 1973: 2.390,340
James W. Fernandez. LIS 8.79: 2.252,282
Carl Fincke. CHN 12/11/77: 4.106,9B
Dudley Fitts. W3: 8.375
F. Scott Fitzgerald. *The Great Gatsby*, Scribner's 1925: 2.138,182; 4.17,99
J. M. Flagler. W3: 8.374
Inglis Fletcher. *Queen's Gift*, Bobbs-Merrill 1953: 4.194,17
Walter R. Fletcher. NYT 12/29/74: 1.5,5.7
Jerry A. Fodor. *The Language of Thought*, Crowell 1975: 2.356,1
Forbes 4/15/76: 4.268,27
Jesse Hill Ford. WPR4: 8.147.150
Alan Dean Foster. *Outland*, Warner 1981: 8.11,261; 8.205,190; 8.262,179
Charles Fox. *The Noble Enemy*, Doubleday 1980: 8.162,178
Janet Frame. W3: 8.342
Harriet Frank, Jr. *Special Effects*, Houghton Mifflin 1979: 7.50,27
William L. Franklin. NG 7/81: 8.41,70; 8.63,70
George MacDonald Fraser. PB 5/73: 2.46,232; 7.51,218
Denne H. Freeman. LS 6/3/75: 2.25,A13; 4.23,A13
Mary E. Wilkins Freeman. LITF: 2.326,91; RHMM3: 4,225,345
Guy Friddell. VP 5/11/76: 6.11,B1; VP-LS 7/16/78: 4.153,F1
Betty Friedan. O&D: 7.14,244
Gertrude Friedberg. *The Revolving Boy*, Doubleday 1966: 8.168,16
Aldred Friendly. SM 8/77: 4.143,70
Robert Frost. CELEB: 8.138,376

Randy Galloway. SN 1/7/78: 4.151,45
John Galsworthy. FMS: 2.87,695
Ernest K. Gann. RDC: 4.189,360; RWAE: 4.211,32
John Gardner. *Excellence*, Harper 1961: 7.79,69
Catherine Gaskin. RDC: 1.44,60
W. H. Gass. BASS62: 8.19,135; 8.97,137; 8.277,137
Barbara Charlesworth Gelpi and Albert Gelpi. *Adrienne Rich's Poetry*, Norton 1975:
    6.36,117
Luther Gerlach. NH 1/78: 4.282,22
Jack W. Garmond and James Witcover. VP 11/25/77: 2.348,A21
T. Gertler. BASS80: 8.332,187
Margaret Gibson. SMS: 8.359,139; SWR Winter 1970: 8.42,123; 8.93:126

Anthony Gilbert. *Missing From Her Home*, Random House 1969: 2.66,56
Doug Gilbert. MGAZ 8/15/77: 4.129,15
Christopher Cook Gilmore. *Atlantic City Proof*, Simon & Schuster 1978: 2.36,175; 2.127,203; 2.197,175
Ellen Glasgow. *Barren Ground*, Farrar, Straus, Giroux 1957: 2,100, 70; 2.156,169
H. A. Gleason. (S): 7.42
Joe Goddard. SN 5/30/81: 8.230,32
Donald L. Gold. DISC4: 8.281,97
Herbert Gold. *The Magic Will*, Random House 1961: 6.10,150
William Golding. AH: 2.379
William Goldman. *Boys and Girls Together*, Bantam 1964: 4.10,20; 4.94,390
Nadine Gordimer. FICT: 2.34,438
Mark Goodman. S70: 8.146,216
Paul Goodman. *Speaking and Language: Defence of Poetry*, Vintage 1971: 4.242,51
Caroline Gordon. MSSAM1: 4.170,563
James Gorman. SCI 5–6/75: 3.8,29
John Mayo Goss. FPS: 8.329,419
Stephen Jay Gould. NH 2/84: 2.223,16; 5/77: 4.149,12; 2/78: 4.147,10
Shirley Ann Grau. *The Wind Shifting West*, Knopf 1973: 8.222,64; 8.258,180
Gerald Green. *The Last Angry Man*, Scribner's 1956: 8.191,17
Hannah Green. *I Never Promised You a Rose Garden*, Signet 1964: 2.292,106; 8.187,187
Joanne Greenberg. *In This Sign*. Holt, Rinehart & Winston 1970: 2.38,78; 8.173,61
Johnny Greene. H 4/77: 4.203,58
George Greenstein. VP-LS 7/21/85: 6.88,C2
Zane Grey. *The Lost Wagon Train*, Pocket Books 1936: 2.242,183; 4.38,111; 4.327,153; 7.177,128; 8.133,283
Francis Irby Gwaltney. *A Step in the River*, Random House 1960: 1.47,148; 8.111,230

Ben Haas. *The Last Valley*, Simon & Schuster 1966: 1.39,152; 2.378,233; 3.6,83; 8.240,281
H. R. Haldeman. *The Ends of Power*, New York Times 1978: 2.167,240, 7.46,294
Nancy Hale. *Black Summer*, Little Brown 1963: 8.49,77
Alex Haley. PE5: 4.309,303
Arthur Haley. Hotel, 1965: 7.40,405
Edward T. Hall. *Beyond Culture*, Anchor 1977: 2.24,20; 2.54,234; 2.248,262
James Norman Hall. *Lost Island*, Popular Library 1944: 1.30,95
Oakley Hall. PB 5/75: 8:159,92; 8.163,86
Martin J. Hamer. BASS65: 8.300,121
Edward Hannibal. *Chocolate Days, Popsicle Weeks*, Houghton Mifflin 1970: 4.86,109; 4.232,55; 4.324,69
Elizabeth Hardwick. OF: 6.4,204; *Seduction and Betrayal*, Vintage 1970: 2.26,29
Thomas Hardy. S29: 1.38,210
Sara Harris. *The Puritan Jungle*, Putnam's 1969: 4.239,200
Geoffrey H. Hartman. *Beyond Formalism*, Yale 1970: 2.374,369
Jim Hartz. NG 11/81: 8.211,578
Nathaniel Hawthorne. REALM: 7.112,105
Sterling Hayden. *Voyage*, Putnam's 1976: 2.30,693; 4.219,38; 4.323,18

Robert Hazel. BASS67: 8.283,129
William Hazlitt. AH: 2.183
John J. Healy. *A Game of Wits,* David McKay 1975: 2.388,284, 4.43,286
Robert A. Heinlein. *Methuselah's Children,* Signet 1958: 4.288,65; Farnham's Freehold, Berkley XXX: 4.228,75
Willi Heinrich, tr. Richard and Clara Winston. *The Cross of Iron,* Bantam 1956: 8.284,136
Joseph Heller. *Catch-22,* Dell 1955: 4.233,31; 7.36; 7.36,144
Mark Helperin. FICT: 7.67,501
Ernest Hemingway. MT3: 4.57,391; *The Old Man and the Sea,* Scribner's 1952: 2.166,76; 4.19,100; 4.237,101
William O. Hendricks. POET 11: 2.212,14
Frank Herbert. *Dune,* Berkley 1965: 4.272,134; 8.100,33; 8.149,118
James Herriot. *All Creatures Great and Small,* Bantam 1972: 1.48,334; 2.108,201; 2.124,363; 2.286,99; 2.313,270; 4.207,32; 7.28,389; 7.56,180; 7.75,406; 7.83,116
Georgette Heyer. *Frederica,* Dutton 1965: 8.145,70
Thor Heyerdahl, tr. F. H. Lyon. *Kon-Tiki,* Pocket Books 1950: 2.199,53
Archibald M. Hill, LSA Bulletin 3/80: 1.35,9
William Hjortsberg. PB 11/78: 8.124,275
Laura Z. Hobson. *The Tenth Month,* Dell 1970: 2.322,226
Matthew Hodgart. NYRB 9/11/69: 2.290,28
William Hoffman. SWR Winter1977: 8.101,45; F1975: 8.115,553
Cecelia Holland. *Until the Sun Falls,* Atheneum 1969: 8.50,264; 8.53,171; 8.85,61; 8.89,239; 8.90,216; 8.94,336; 8.130,252; 8.176,10; 8.273,115; 8.293,263; 8.335,38
E. J. Holmyard. TECH: 1.42,279
Joseph Hone. *The Private Sector,* Dutton 1972: 8.215,313
Donald Honig. *Walk Like a Man,* Sloane 1961: 8.13,42; 8.18,66; 8.67,43; 8.294,49
Paul Horgan. *Mountain Standard Time,* Farrar, Straus & Cudahy 1962: 8.24,182; 8.79,251; 8.82,209; 8.127,95; 8.134,121; 8.175;166
Barbara Howar. *Making Ends Meet,* Random House 1976: 4.122,23
Maureen Howard. BASS65: 6.41,130
Susan Howatch. *The Shrouded Walls,* Fawcett 1968: 7.80,123; 7.90,126
William Dean Howells. *The Rise of Silas Lapham,* Penguin 1983: 2.281,49
Fred Hoyle and John Elliott. *A for Andromeda,* Harper & Row 1962: 6.20,14
Carl L. Hubbs. WB66,F: 2.375,149
Langston Hughes. AE5: 4.8,48; *The Langston Hughes Reader,* Braziller 1958: 4.131,486; 6.21,354
Lois Phillips Hudson. *The Bones of Plenty,* Atlantic Monthly 1962: 2.296,37
Nancy Hunt. PEOPLE 2/12/79: 7.93,65
Hugh Allyn Hunt. BASS67: 8.324,146
Evan Hunter. *Sons,* Doubleday 1969: 4.262,20
Kristin Hunter. NF: 2.117,268; 7.63,272
Roy Hunter. BOYL 12/77: 4.169,10
Kaatje Hurlbut. BASS79: 8.80,49
Isobel Wylie Hutchinson. NG 10/54: 2.111,559

Aldous Huxley. FMS: 2.81,107; 2.239,115; SIC: 8.131,313; *The Genius and the Goddess*, Bantam 1955: 4.6,89
Noel Hynd. *The Sandler Inquiry*, Dial 1977: 8.299,138; 8.344,222

Hammond Innes. *North Star*, Knopf 1975: 2.336,127
Michael Innes. *Seven Suspects*, Dolphin 1937: 6.18,175

Blyden Jackson. S29: 2.116,389
Keith Jackson. ABC-TV Olympics 7/29/76 (S): 4.334
Janice Jacobi. (S): 4.118
John Jakes. *The Seekers*, Jove 1975: 2.74,374; 2.75,391; 2.76,358; 8.105,393; *The Titans*, Jove 1976: 2.154,207; 8.25,20; *The Warriors*, Pyramid 1977: 8.5,174; 8.38,322; 8.297,334
Julian Jaynes. *The Origin of Consciousness in the Breakdown of the Bicameral Mind*, Houghton Mifflin 1976: 2.63,389
Paul Johnstone. H 9/76: 4.318,10
James Jones. *From Here to Eternity*, Scribner's 1951: 4.250,121; 8.352,122
Madison Jones. SMS: 8.339,171; 8.363,167
Robert Paul Jordan. NG 7/79: 7.65,52
James Joyce. MT3: 2.143,185
Joseph Judge. NG 2/79: 8.54,173
Horace Freeland Judson. NYER 11/27/78: 6.86,60
Robert Jungh, tr. James Cleugh. *Brighter Than a Thousand Suns*, Grove Press 1958: 2.362,142

Roger Kahn. *The Boys of Summer*, Harper & Row 1971: 2.274,xix
Jerry Kambites. NG 7/80: 8.235,88
Stuart Kaminsky. *He Done Her Wrong*, Mysterious Press 1983: 2.306,45; 4.223,153
Steve Katz. NAR11: 8.309,147
Stanley Kauffman. O&D: 8.208,141
Hunter Kay. SMS: 2.174,196; 7.102,201; 8.17,186; 8.21,194; 8.265,187
Alfred Kazin. PB 6/73: 6.44,208
Sam Keen. *To a Dancing God*, Harper & Row 1970: 2.249,145
Carolyn Keene. *The Clue in the Old Attic*, Grosset & Dunlop 1947; 6.16,141; *The Haunted House*: 4.37,29
George F. Kennan. PV: 7.97,419
John Kerckhoff. KAL: 4.226,178
Ken Kesey. *Sometimes a Great Notion*, Bantam 1964: 8.270,115; 8.306,334; 8.334,399; *One Flew Over the Cuckoo's Nest*, Signet 1962: 2.6,198; 3.7,121; 4.185,10; 8.128,17; 8.319,83; 8.321,172
Tabitha King. *Small World*, Macmillan 1981: 3.3,37; 8.108,6; 8.171,14
Smith Kirkpatrick. SWR Sp1971: 8.271,331
Jim Kjelgaard. *Big Red*, Holiday House 1945: 4.40,118
Arthur Knight. W3: 7.20
Bill Knox. *Live Bait*, Doubleday 1978: 7.47,47; 7.91,4
Joseph Kraft. VP 4/20/78: 2.51,A13; 11/30/77: 2.58,A22; 1/29/78: 4.216,C4
Bennett Kremen. WPR8: 4.35,290; 4.109,294
A. L. Kroeber. W3: 7.21

Katharine Kuh. MFOT: 7.72,367
Sigmund Kvaløy: NORTH Su1974: 6.50,24

Howard LaFay. NG 5.67:2.282,631
Derek Lambert. *The Kites of War,* Coward-McCann 1969: 8.144,237; 8.210,207
John Lamm. SKY 11/74: 4.287,7
Michael Lamm. POPMECH 2.76: 4.263,80
W. Clyde Lammey. POPMECH 3.75: 8.224,60
Jack Lang. SN 2/8/75: 6.51,32
Ray LaRoque. TRAIL 6/76: 4.103,141
D. H. Lawrence. FON: 8.203,629; FICT: 7.66,721: REALM: 2.195,320; S29: 2.14,326;
    LXJK: 2.395,384: MT3: 2.303,293; 2.300,260; 2.312,249
John LeCarre. *The Little Drummer Girl,* Knopf 1983: 2.37,124; 4.76,102; 4.258,57;
    8.272,429
Ursula K. LeGuin. *The Lathe of Heaven,* Avon 1971: 7.44,42; *The Dispossessed,* Avon
    1974: 2.142,167; 7.12,46; *A Wizard of Earthsea,* Bantam 1968: 2.213,152; *The
    Farthest Shore,* Bantam 1972: 2.125,189; 2.114,109; 2.186,166
Max Lerner. LS 12/11/75:4.294,A6
Harry Levin. PV: 6.37,431
Sinclair Lewis: *Arrowsmith,* Harcourt, Brace & World 1924: 8.196,83
Norma Levy: PARADE 6/8/75: 2.277,11
David Lightfoot. FORMSYN: 2.279,229
Karen Lingo. SL 8/79: 1.29,69
Bob Lipper. VP 2/1/78: 4.116,B6
Robert Lipstyle. RC2: 2.287,205
Jim Liston. POPMECH 2/76: 4.190,70
Greta Little. (S): 2.334
Mike Littwin. VP-LS 5/28/78: 2.353,E3
Kimon Lolos. BASS64: 8.9,193
Jack London. SHAPE: 2.62,360; *The Call of the Wild,* Macmillan 1903: 2.16,68;
    2.102,51
Chauncey C. Loomis. WRRE: 2.262,193
Ledger Star (LS) 5/4/77: 4.150,24 (HL); 5/13/78: 4.152,TV-Guide 14 (HL)
Wilson Lucas. NORTH F1973: 8.98,11
Robert Ludlum. *Acquitaine Progression,* Random House 1984: 3.360,87; 6.91,266;
    6.92,493
Jack Ludwig. SIXT: 4/172, 141; 8.126,139
Mary Luke. *Gloriana,* Coward-McCann 1973: 2.39,125; 2.47,545; 2.50,240;
    2.243,152; 2.247,23; 2.343,142
Dudley Cammett Lunt. *The Woods and the Sea,* Knopf 1965: 2.131,276; 2.189,24;
    2.208,271; 6.9,174; 8.315,83
Alison Lurie. *Foreign Affairs,* Random House 1984: 4.125,163
Russell Lynes. SM 175: 6.8,47; SM 12/74: 6.14,42

Ian MacDonald. SN 7/30/77: 4.127,10
Ross Macdonald. *Find a Victim,* Bantam 1954: 4.181,73; 4.184,74; 7.115,136
Gary MacEoin. *Colombia and Venezuela and the Guianas,* Time Books 1971: 6.49,118
Helen MacInnes. *Above Suspicion,* Fawcett 1941: 7.116,127

Kenneth MacLeish. NG 1/75,147
Earl MacRauch. WPR4: 4.196,188
Lawrence Maddry. VP 5/9/76: 4.44,B1; 8/11/76: 4.48,B1; 7/14/78: 4.191,B1
Jeb Stuart Magruder. FAMWEEK 8/10/75: 4.271,10
J. Peter Maher. LGSCI 12/77: 2.203,7
Norman Mailer. *The Naked and the Dead*, Grosset & Dunlop 1948: 2.61,590;
    2.268,134; 7.43,115; 7.118,605; 8.7,283; 8.74,253; 8.88,171; 8.264,62; 8.305,225;
    8.317,151; *An American Dream*, Dial 1965: 8.64,98
David Zane Mairowitz. *The Radical Soap Opera*, Avon 1974: 2.301,31
Major Hoople (comic strip). W&F: 7.103,229
Bernard Malamud. SIXT: 8.177,101; 8.256,93; SSCA: 1.6,500; *Two Novels*, Modern
    Library 1957: 4.161,206
Malcolm X. TTL: 1.1,189
Joe Marcin. SN 5/12/79: 2.53,7
John P. Marquand. Wickford Point, Time 1939: 8.31,83
Gabriel Garcia Marquez, tr. Gregory Rabassa. PB 11/71: 2.289,122
Ngaio Marsh. *Enter a Murderer*, Berkley 1963: 8.20,243
John Martin. CARQUART F1972: 4.62,18
Harriet Martineau. W3: 2.85
Wesley Marx. *Acts of God, Acts of Man*, Coward-McCann 1977: 4.145,150
Jack Matthews. BASS70: 8.302,161
Peter Matthiessen. *At Play in the Fields of the Lord*, Bantam 1965: 4.220,269; 8.35,256;
    8.58,193; 8.113,134
W. Somerset Maugham. *Cakes and Ale and Twelve Short Stories*, Doubleday 1966:
    2.169,497; 7.7,391; 7.78,408
Nancy Mayer. *The Male Mid-Life Crisis*, Doubleday 1978: 3.1,14
Robert Mazzocco. NYRB 3/14/68: 7.125,31
Mary McCarthy. *Birds of America*, Harcourt Brace Jovanovich 1971: 8.167,21
George McClelland. VP 10/10/78: 2.2,B7; 12/14/75: 4.105,E2
James McCormick. NAR2: 7.41,215
Joe McGinness. PB 10/72: 8.360,98
Charles McGrath. NYER 12.29.76: 8.158,25
Matthew W. McGregor. BASS69: 2.258,156
Cathleen McGuigan. *The Sand Pebbles*, Harper & Row 1962: 2.339,277; 2.340,113;
    8.114,284; 8.148,284
Jack McKenney. POPMECH 1/75: 4.278,74
Bill McKeown. POPMECH 4/76: 4.115,85
Marshall McLuhan. *The Gutenberg Galaxy*, Toronto 1962: 2.15,40
Patrick F. McManus. F&S 6/81: 8.75,14; 8.341,14
Larry McMillen. TP 12/30/81: 8.22,3.1
John McPhee. ESSAY: 8.218,239
Melvin Merkin. BG84: 2.361,144
Richard Meyers. *Doomstar*, Warner 1978: 2.128,39
Marguerite Michaels. PARADE 4/2/78: 4.104,4
James A. Michener. *The Source*, Fawcett 1965: 2.22,106; 2.112,370; 2.231,964;
    2.304,580; 2.314,739; 2.330,322; 4.306,354; 8.95,303; *Chesapeake*, Random
    House 1978: 2.68,386; 7.57,213

Giovannia Miegge, tr. Bishop Stephen Neill. *Gospel and Myth in the Thought of Rudolph Bultmann,* John Knox 1960: 2.185,42

Alan Milberg. TIW: 2.92,341

Nancy Milford. *Zelda,* XXXX: 2.21,192

Arthur Miller. *The Crucible,* Bantam 1952: 4.5,365

Ira Miller. SFC 11/7/81: 8.243,45

Sue Miller. PSH 6.3: 8.102,34

John R. Milton. BASS69: 2.88,186

Cathy Mitchell. LHJ 8/79: 7.92,36

Donald Mitchell. *The Language of Modern Music,* St. Martin's 1970: 1.46,153; 4.296,20

N. Scott Momaday. NG 7/76: 2.45,13; BORZ4: 2.234,344

Leo Monahan. SN 10/12/77: 4.142,31

Ann Moody, KAL: 4.186,125

Brian Moore. NAR 15: 8.96,34

George Moore. REALM: 2.372,67

Rex Morgan, M.D. (comic strip). VP 4/10/76: 4.227,B2

Samuel Eliot Morison. *John Paul Jones,* Time Books 1959: 2.373,28

Herbert Morris. TMP: 2.275,305

Willie Morris. BASS70: 8.308, 205: *The Last of the Southern Girls,* Knopf 1973: 2.48,272; 8.386,184; *Fire Sermon,* Harper & Row 1971: 8.296,129

Wright Morris. BASS70: 8.308,205

Toni Morrison. *Song of Solomon,* Signet 1977: 8.44,34; *Beloved,* Knopf 1987: 8:331,136

Kathryn Morton. VP 2/15/76: 4.159,C4

Don Moser. NG 3/77: 2.255,381

Milt Moss. PARADE 5/15/77: 4.247,26

Roger Mudd. CBS News, Democratic Convention 7/12/76 (S): 8.180

William Mullen. PENSEE 9: 2.217,40

Robert Murphy. W3: 7.101; *The Stream,* Pyramid 1971: 1.2,147

William Murray. BMA67: 1.9,104

N. Richard Nash. *The Last Magic,* Atheneum 1978: 7.94,71

National Geographic (NG) 2/60: 2.113, 165; 1/78: 2.233,104; 8/71: 2.148,193; 10/65: 2.150,494

Ed Neal. SFE-SFC 3/21/76: 4.210,4C

Kent Nelson. VQR Su1975: 8.83,376; BASS 76: 2.321,177

Jay Neugeboren. BASS65: 8.78,257; 8.370,254

P. H. Newby. SM 5/79: 2.232,63

Charles Newman. BASS77: 8.95,223

J. R. Newman. W3: 7.22

New Republic (NR). W3: 8.373

News & Observer, Raleigh NC (NO) 7/11/78: 4.141,4(HL); 7/13/78: 4.316,8

Newsweek (NW). W3: 8.220

New Yorker (NYER) 2/6/78: 4.87,25; 8/14/78: 1.45,27

New York *Times* News Service: CHN 1/4/78: 4.289,2B

Margaret G. Nichols. F&S 10/75: 6.30,144

Hugh Nissenson. SHAPE2: 2.179,396

Larry Niven. SFCM: 8.120,232; 8.291,241
Larry Niven and Jerry Pournelle. *Lucifer's Hammer*, Fawcett 1972: 8.251,352
Albert Jay Nock. POD: 4.137,493
Lewis Nordan. H 1/78: 7.73,62
Christopher Norris. *The Deconstructive Turn*, Methuen 1983: 2.91,150
Frank Norris. REALM: 2.161,190

Joyce Carol Oates. BASS64: 8.65,244; BASS73: 8.179,213; NORTH 3/81: 8.347,16;
    8.354,15; *The Edge of Impossibility*, Fawcett 1972: 2.366,135; 6.93,32; 6.95,183
Jim O'Brien. SN 1/7/78: 4/168,28
Flannery O'Connor. DESFIC: 4.218,343; FICT: 8.289,960; CASS: 8.46,49; NF:
    8.61,291; DOSS2: 8.8,500; QM: 2.40,209; CFC5: 2.32,242; *Wise Blood*, Signet
    1949: 8.4,224; 8.36,157; 8.37,354; 8.48,43; 8.57,179; 8.59,396; 8.71,219;
    8.249,96
Eliabeth Ogilvie. *The Devil in Tartun*, McGraw Hill 1980: 2.198,57
Diane Oliver. MSSAM3: 2.230,157
Margery Ollingham. *The Mind Readers*, William Morrow 1965: 8.241,252
Paul Olsen. BASS70: 7.87,233; 8.261,235
Tillie Olsen. CASS: 8.326,410
William O'Rouke. *Idle Hands*, Delacorte 1981: 8.69,46
George Orwell. 1984: *Text, Sources, Criticism*, Harcourt Brace & World 1963:
    2.250,58; 8.47,8
Thomas O'Toole. VP 5/25/81: 8,166,A5
Bob Ottum. *See the Kid Run*, Simon & Schuster 1978: 8.28,248

Thomas Page. *Sigmet Active*, Times Book 1978: 7.71,43
Nell Irvin Painter. *Exodusters*, Knopf 1977: 2.254,119
Bruce Palmer. *They Shall Not Pass*, Doubleday 1971: 8.160,305; 8.345,19
Nancy Pelletier Pansing. BASS69: 4.201,219
Molly Panter-Downes. W3: 7.81
Edwards Park. SM 4/75: 2.377,52; 5/79: 4.108,36; 6/76: 6.23,46
Carolyn Bennett Patterson. NG 2/60: 8.234,264
Francis Gray Patton. *Good Morning, Miss Dove*, Pocket Books 1954: 8.330,83
Peggy Payne. CARCOUNT 8/77: 4.46,10
Charles A. Pease. *Body Building Group Method*, Ronald 1963: 8.117,63
Rachel Peden. *The Land, the People*, Knopf 1966: 2.171,246
Neal Peirce. VP-LS 5/28/78: 2.391,C11
Walker Percy. *The Moviegoer*, Popular Library 1962: 8.254,65; 8.353,20
Natalie L. M. Petesch. BASS78: 2.178,173
Jim Pettigrew, Jr. SKY 8/85: 2.228,14
Kevin P. Phillips. VP 5/16/77: 2.206,A12; 3/13/78: 4.257,A15
Ken Pickering. USAT 1/28/87: 4.89,2C
William Plomer. ODCIE: 2.12
Edgar Allen Poe. FICT: 2.175,1018
Michael Polanyi (and Harry Prosch). *Meaning*, Chicago 1975: 7.48,15
Popular Mechanics (POPMECH) 7/81: 2.42,32
Katherine Anne Porter. CASS: 8.255, 249; FJ: 2.302,72; RLF: 7.84,322; *Ship of Fools*,
    Little Brown 1962: 6.24,15
Shirley Povich. WP 6/12/77: 4.130,M3

J. H. Powell. *Bring Out Your Dead,* Time Books 1949: 2.294,56
J. L. Powers. CASS: 8.244,360
Mary Louise Pratt. *Toward a Speech Act Theory of Literary Discourse,* Indiana 1977: 2.147,192
Reynolds Price. VQR Sp1975: 8.181,292; BASS76: 2.283,214; *The Surface of Earth,* Atheneum 1975: 2.130,507; 2.136,500; 2.170,174; 2.172,137; 2.270,305; 2.284,98; 2.35,239; 6.42,318; 8.246,285
Marcel Proust, tr. C. K. Scott Moncrieff, Modern Library 1928: 2.200, 335; 2.209, 334
Anne Eisner Putnam. NG 2.60: 2.152,289
John J. Putnam. NG 1/78: 8.110,16
Thomas Pynchon. SIXT: 4.335,29; *V,* Bantam 1963: 4.70, 26; 4.195,23; 8.255,345

Norma Quarles. NBC Nightly News 4/17/79 (S): 7.120
Ellery Queen. *The Killer Touch,* Signet 1965: 8.68,92; 8.217,131; 8.242,93; 8.269,50; 8.282,125
Edgar Monsanto Queeny. NG 10/54: 2.151,507

Donald Radcliffe. BASS67: 2.227,264
Ayn Rand. *Atlas Shrugged,* Random House 1957: 2.297,487; 4.221,501; 4.222,649
Florence Engel Randall. SHAPE: 2.308,267
Anatol Rapoport. *Semantics,* Crowell 1975: 6.34,251
William Raspberry. VP 1/27/78: 4.269,A17
Marjorie Kinnan Rawlings. *Cross Creek,* Ballantine 1942: 1.3,111; 2.347,185; 7.55,113
Piers Paul Read. *Alive,* Avon 1974: 4.214,35
Jerry Reed. VP 12/13/74: 1.40,C1
Clayton Reeve. (S): 4.92
Art Reid. F&S 10/75: 4.293,111
Ruth Rendell. *Murder Being Once Done,* Bantam 1972: 4.209,115
Lisa Ress. *Flight Patterns,* U. of Virginia 1985: 4.75,12
Cynthia Marshall Rich. MIDC: 8.366,235
Barbara Rieff. *Tempt Not This Flesh,* Playboy 1979: 8.106, 46; 8.268,176
Jean Rickhoff. *The Sweetwater,* Dial 1976: 2.309,144
Bill Riley. (S): 4.126
S. Dillon Ripley. SM 12/79: 2.35,8
Harold Robbins. *The Private,* Pocket Books 1974: 2.260,113; 4.298,271; 4.300.229; 7.10,107; 7.13,319; 7.19,93
Clayton Robert. JMH 49.4: 2.389,604
Raboo Rodgers. BOYL 12/77: 4.51,42; 8.116,42
Robert Rodman. SECOL 1.1: 2.11,2
Leon Rooke. BASS80: 8.52,292
Steve Roper (comic strip). VP 2/28/78: 4.79; VP-LS 7/16/78: 4.85
Rose Rosenblatt. WPR8: 8.276,338
Sam Ross. *Windy City,* Putnam's 1979: 4.83,78
Judith Rossner. *Looking for Mr. Goodbar,* Kangaroo Book 1975: 4.99,314
Theodore Roszak. *Where the Wasteland Ends,* Doubleday 1972: 6.90,209
Henry Roth. *Call It Sleep,* Avon 1962: 2.28,280; 2.195,341; 8.30,82; 8.337,79
Philip Roth. CASS: 8.320,175; *Letting Go,* Bantam 1962: 2.9,208; *My Life as a Man,* Holt Reinhart & Winston 1970: 2.153,68; 8.202;210
Michael Rothschild. BASS76: 8.70, 236: 8.132,253; 8.338,247

Berton Roueche. W3: 8.286
Phil Roura and Tom Posta. RD 1/80: 8.34,159
Darrell Royal. VP: 12/6/76: 4.110,B10
A. J. Russell. *Pour the Hemlock*, Random House 1976: 2.72,124; 7.82,35
Bertrand Russell. *The Autobiography of Bertrand Russell*, Vol. 1: 7.113,33
Eric Frank Russell. AHL: 8.190,152
Franklin Russell. *Watchers at the Pond*, Knopf 1961: 8.117,153

William Safire. *On Language*, Times Books 1980: 8.248,185
Charlotte Saikowski. CSM 11/17/86: 1.37,37
J. D. Salinger. *The Catcher in the Rye*, Signet 1945: 4.336,11
Thomas Sanchez. WPR5: 8.51,131
Carl Sandburg. *Abraham Lincoln: The Way Years 1864–1965*, Laurel 1925: 4.338,517; *Abraham Lincoln*, one-volume edition, Harcourt Brace 1925: 4.310,36
San Francisco Chronicle (SFC) 8/11/77: 4.144,54(HL); 4/17/76: 4.282,41(HL); 6/24/81: 8.229,55
Paul Sann. *Fads, Follies and Delusions of the American People*, Bonanza 1967: 2.251,324
George Santayana. *The Last Puritan*, Scribner's 1936: 2.106,24
Georgio de Santillana and Herta von Dechend. *Hamlet's Mill*, Godine 1969: 2.216,44
Mildred Savage. *Parrish*, Simon & Schuster 1958: 8.192,291
Curtis and Kathleen Saville. SM 10/81: 8.141,204
Dorothy Sayers. W3: 7.123
John Sayles. BASS77: 8.40,307; 8.199,308
Sylvia Fromberg Schaeffer. *The Madness of a Seduced Woman*, Bantam 1983: 8.99,150
Jim Schefter. POPSCI 6/76: 4.64,85
Stephen Schmidt. KR Winter1981: 8.226,33
Mark Schorer. *The State of Mind*, Houghton Mifflin 1947: 8.322,100
Max Schott. BASS78: 8.76,247
Budd Schulberg. *Introduction to Nathanael West, The Day of the Locust*, Time Books 1939: 4.95,xxii
Terri Schultz. NORT4: 8.313,939
David M. Schwartz. SM 5/81: 8.135,120
Scientific American (SA) 9/77: 4.234,13
John Scofield. NG 9/69: 7.108.372
C. E. Scoggins. HOOS 1.41,459; 4.114,455
Bob Seagren. ABC-TV, Olympics 7/26/76 (S): 6.46
David Seltzer. *The Omen*, Signet: 4.265,194
Thalia Selz. BASS62: 8.333,373
Fred Setterberg. MQR F1980-W1981: 8.213,693
Mary Lee Settle. *Blood Tie*, Houghton Mifflin 1977: 7.45,116; *Fight Night on a Sweet Saturday*, Viking 1964: 8.336,105
Tim Severin. FLIGHT 8/78: 4.198,23
Leonard Shapiro. WP 11/5/77: 4.102,D6
Irwin Shaw. FMS: 7.15,443
Lloyd Shearer. PARADE 7/10/77: 4.67,5
David Shelf. PB 2/78: 4.91,208
Jean Shepherd. C70: 4.251,393
David Sheridan. SM 8.77: 4.297,36

David Shores. FJ: 4.205,452
Robert Silverberg. FSTA: 4.82,215
William A. Silverman. SA 6/77: 2.351,100
Clifford D. Simak. *All Flesh is Grass,* Doubleday 1965: 2.383,108
William E. Simon. PB 5/75: 4.286,62
George Gaylord Simpson. *Attending Marvels,* Time Life Books 1934: 2.31,168;
    2.259,13; 2.349,53; 4.259,191
John Skow. PB 4/73: 2.3,202
Philip Slater. *The Pursuit of Loneliness,* Beacon 1970: 2.219,108
Frank G. Slaughter. *Epidemic,* Doubleday 1961: 8.304,69
Anne Smith. VP 5/10/75: 4.314,A6
Mark Smith. *The Death of the Detective,* Avon 1973: 2.5,492; 9.245,34
Howard Smith and Leslie Harlib. VV 8/15/77: 4.158,16
Smithsonian (SM) 10/81: 8.165,82
David Snell. SM 6/76: 4/71,72
Gilbert Sorrentino. NAR15: 2.23,198
Southern Living (SL) 11/79: 2.267,264; 7/78: 2.376,177; 1/77: 8.232,25
Art Spander. SFC 8/28/75: 4.277,48
Muriel Spark, quoted by Updike in *Assorted Prose:* 2.103,240
Elizabeth Spencer. *Voice at the Back Door,* Time Books 1956: 8.33.323; 8.209,240
Sporting News (SN) 9/29/79: 1.32,22
Jean Stafford. ESQ 8/76: 4.157,16; *The Collected Stories of Jean Stafford,* Farrar Straus
    & Giroux: 2.158,20: 2.238,116
Wallace Stegner. FPS: 2.19,454; PV: 4.213,127; *Discovery,* Middle East Import Press,
    Beirut 1971: 2.10,57; 8.164,129; *A Shooting Star,* Viking 1961: 8.174:43
John Steinbeck. W3: 7.24; *The Grapes of Wrath,* Bantam 1939: 8.104,233; *East of
    Eden,* Bantam 1952: 2.94,483; 2.181,301
Stendahl, tr. Richard Coe. PPV: 2.332,45
Tony Stein. LS 1/31/78: 4.304,C1
Augusta Stevenson. *George Washington, Boy Leader,* Bobbs-Merrill 1959: 4.252,27
Charles L. Stevenson. *Ethics and Language,* Yale 1944: 2/369,35
John Stewart. POR: 7,100.199
Mary Stewart. *Crystal Cave,* Doubleday 1970: 2.234,41; 2.273,106
Geoffrey Stokes. VV 12/24/80: 8.23,35
Irving Stone. *The Origin: A Biographical Novel of Charles Darwin,* Doubleday 1980:
    8.207,390
Lawrence Stone. NYRB 8/24/67: 6.48,32
Robert Stone. BASS70: 8.287,330
The Streets of San Francisco, TV show. 6/17/76 (S): 4.330
Jesse Stuart. *Trees of Heaven,* Dutton 1940: 8.26,128; 8.109,99; 8.238,76; 8.278,317
William Styron. *Lie Down in Darkness,* Bobbs-Merrill 1951: 2.155,131; *Set This House
    on Fire,* Random House 1959: 1.120,311; 2.137,416; 2.139,29; 2.180,416;
    2.188,356; 2.190,483; 2.191,140; 2.257,114; 2.331,306; 4.182,459; 7.107,29; *The
    Confessions of Nat Turner,* Signet 1966: 2.132,245; 2.337,313
Ronald Sukenick. PR 76.1: 6.38,98
William J. Sullivan. LANGSCI 8/77: 4.117,17
Pamela Swift. PARADE 7/16/13: 4.333,13

Gay Talese. *Honor Thy Father,* Fawcett 1971: 4.246,361; 4.321,399

H. G. Tapply. F&S 5/75: 4.193,146
James Tate. NORTH Sp1976: 4.66,21
Peter Tauber. *The Last Best Hope,* Harcourt Brace Jovanovich 1977: 2.83,186; 2.95,64
Peter Taylor. CASS: 7.26,57
Dick Teresi. *Book of Bikes and Bicycling,* Popular Mechanics Books 1975: 4.62,37; 4.133,278
Carol Burton Terry. VP-LS 1/8/78: 4.154,F5
Jim Thacker. WTKR-TV (basketball game) 1/20/79 (S): 1.33
Dylan Thomas. RWR4: 4.292,117
Lewis Thomas. RFR4: 7.8,253
Lowell Thomas. *Lauterback of the China Sea.* Doubleday Doran 1930: 6.22,44; 8.140,181
William Irwin Thompson. *At the Edge of History,* Harper 1971: 4.78,63
James Thurber. *The Years with Ross,* Little Brown 1959: 2.4,136
Time (TIME) 5/22/78: 4.36,73; 11/28/77: 4.136,23; 11/28/77: 4.162,22; DA: 7.121; W3: 8.312
Anastasia Toufexis. TIME 5/27/85: 2.245,69
Glenn Tinder. NR 1/27/79: 2.293,22
Alvin Toffler. *Future Shock,* Bantam 1970: 2.160,241; 2.165,486; 2.196,150; 4.291,172
H. M. Tomlinson. *The Sea and the Jungle,* Time Books 1912: 2.29,34; 2.101,71; 2.207,299; 2.236,236; 2.325,9
Jean Toomer. DDS2: 8.301,282
Stephen Toulmin. *Human Understanding,* Princeton 1972: 7.76,175
Robert Traver. *Anatomy of a Murder,* St. Martin's 1958: 4.174,27
Lionel Trilling. FIFTY: 4.241,353; 7.60,368
Barbara W. Tuchman. *The Guns of August,* Macmillan 1962: 2.280,182
Agnes Sligh Turnbull. *The Day Must Dawn,* Macmillan 1942: 8.303,47
Andrew Turnbull. *Thomas Wolfe,* Scribner's 1967: 8.367,9
W. C. Tuttle. *Salt For the Tiger,* Avalon 1971: 4.42,151; 4.59,135
Mark Twain. POD: 2.246,519
Anne Tyler. SMS: 7.106,349; 8.259,345

Karl D. Uitti. *Linguistics and Literary Theory,* Norton 1969: 6.39,202
United Press International (UPI). VP 8/25/75: 4.202,A4
John Updike. PB 12/79: 2.8,172; 12/79: 2/173,170: WRRE: 4.301,355; *Rabbit Run,* Knopf 1960 4.164,7; 4.299,134; 6.31,344; 8.123.315; *The Centaur,* Fawcett 1962: 4.337,18; 8.154,35; *Assorted Prose,* Fawcett 1965: 4.108,162; 2.220,34; *The Coup,* Knopf 1978: 2.96,80; 2.168,182; 2.357,4; *Too Far to Go,* Fawcett 1979: 2.363,48; 2.364,54; *Rabbit is Rich,* Knopf 1981: 2.334,419

George Vecsey. VP-LS 7/26/81: 8.86,D8
Frank Vehorn. VP-LS 5/14/78: 4.139,E1
Immanuel Velikovsky. KRON 2.2: 2.149,93
Gordon Verrell. SN 1.21.78: 4.132,51
Gore Vidal. *Burr,* Bantam 1973: 2.55,346; 2.121,95; 2.214,363
Virginian-Pilot (VP) 9/3/79: 2.78,A1; 8/23/80: 2.352,A18; 5/16/76: 4.41,A1(HL); 2/15/76: 4.267,C11; 4/8/76: 4.290,A1(HL); 4/8/76: 4.302,B4(HL); 8/24/78: 4.305,A18; 2/13/76: 4.315,A1(HL); 7/2/77: 4.319,B7; 4/13/81: 8.239,A8

Virginian-Pilot—Ledger-Star (VP-LS) 178: 4.140,F7(HL)
Kurt Vonnegut, Jr. MT3: 2.80,589; BORZ4: 2.285,224

Dan Wakefield. *Going All the Way,* Dell 1970: 2.291,71; 4.50,225; 4.96,119;
    4.171,266; 4,212,82; 8.60,62
Vic Wall. W3: 8.280
Joseph Wambaugh. *The Blue Knight,* Little Brown 1972: 4.80,150; 4.93,42
Walter Wangerin, Jr. *The Book of the Dun Cow,* Pocket Books 1978: 2.157,98
G. J. Warnock. *English Philosophy Since 1900,* Galaxy 1969: 2.224,21
Robert Penn Warren. LITREF: 4.167,289; *Wilderness,* Random House 1961: 8,103,265
Richard Wasserstrom, TMP: 2.56,359
Gordon Weaver. SWR F1977: 8.295,543
Edward Weeks. *My Green Age,* Little Brown 1973: 2.194,284; 2.315,163
Theodore Weesner. BASS72: 8.346,348
H. G. Wells. REALM: 8.27,98
Eudora Welty. SMS: 2.186,402; 8.6,388; POD: 2.222,110; IL3: 8.55,41
Jessamyn West. HOOS: 4.180,261
Glenway Wescott. SIX: 2.335,289
David Westeheimer. *Von Ryan's Express,* Doubleday 1964: 8.170, 269
Edith Wharton. REALM: 8.10,172
E. B. White. BORZ4: 8.73,533; NORT4: 8.153,187
Laura White. VP 2/15/76: 4.280,C1; 11/9/75: 4.281,C1
Theodore H. White. *The Mountain Road,* William Sloan 1958: 2.241,19; *Breach of
    Faith,* Atheneum 1975: 2.215,203; 6.32,289
W. A. White. W3: 7.18
A. N. Whitehead. *Science and the Modern World,* Mentor 1925: 2.218,140
Les Whitten. *Sometimes a Hero,* Doubleday 1979: 8.188,417
Tom Wicker. *Facing the Lions,* Avon 1973: 1.43,485; 4.160,172; 4.270,352; 7.53,296;
    8.3,423; 8.182,411; 8.226,332; 8.340,95; 8.371,222
Laura Ingalls Wilder. *Little House on the Prairie,* Harper & Row 1953: 4.18,33
John P. Wiley, Jr. SM 4/80: 8.172,98
George C. Wilson. VP 8/22/75: 8.189,C5
L. Woiwode, *What I'm Going to Do, I Think,* Farrar Strauss & Giroux 1969: 8.285,288;
    8.311,168
Bob Wolf. SN 6/24/78: 4.101,50
Tom Wolfe. *The Hills Beyond,* Pyramid 1958: 2.71,236
Sally Wood. SWR Su1972: 8.314,407
Virginia Woolf. *To the Lighthouse,* Harvest 1927: 6.16,365; 8.247,252
The World of Henry Orient (movie). CBS-TV 8/6/76 (S): 4.111
Mary Worth, comic strip. 7/9/78: 4.123
Richard Wright. FIFTY: 8.260,227; MT3: 8.62,413; SHAPE: 7.61,101; S29: 2.107,61
Philip Wylie. *Generation of Vipers,* Pocket Books 1942: 8.143,8

Samuel Yellen. FMS: 7.64,555
Agatha Young. BSRDCB: 8.327,272
Dick Young. SN 2/18/78: 4.100,16

Hy Zimmerman. SN 7/23/77: 2.317,37

ABBREVIATIONS IN REFERENCES

A   *Atlantic*

AR5   *Assignments in Exposition,* 5th ed., Louise E. Rorabacher, Harper & Row 1974

AH   *American Heritage* magazine

AHL   *Above the Human Landscape,* ed. Willis E. McNelly & Leon E. Stover, Goodyear 1972

AHOME   *American Home Journal*

AP   Associated Press

BASS19##   *The Best American Short Stories of 19##* (several years), multiple editors, especially Martha Foley (hardcover, except paperback 1967), Ballantine

BG84   *Creative Computing Buyer's Guide 1984 to Personal Computers and Peripherals*

BMA67,68   *Best Magazine Articles* 1967,1968, ed. Gerald Walker, Crown 1967,1968

BORZ4   *The Borzoi College Reader,* 4th ed., ed. Charles Muscatine and Marlene Griffith, Knopf 1980

BOYL   *Boys' Life* magazine

BSRDCB   *Best Sellers from Reader's Digest Condensed Books,* 1968

BSUN   The Baltimore *Sun*

C70	*Counterpoint: Dialogue for the 70s,* ed. Conn McAuliffe, Lippincott 1970
CARCOUNT	*Carolina Country* magazine
CARQUART	*Carolina Quarterly* journal
CASS	*Contemporary American Short Stories,* ed. Douglas and Sylvia Angus, Fawcett 1967
CELEB	*Celebration: Introduction to Literature,* ed. Paul A. Parrish, Winthrop 1977
CFC2,5	*Contexts for Composition,* 2nd ed., ed. Stanley A. Clayes and David Spencer, Appleton-Century-Crofts 1969, 1979
CHN	The Chapel Hill *Newspaper,* Chapel Hill NC
CSM	*Christian Science Monitor*
DESFIC	*The Design of Fiction,* ed. Mark Josephine and Hester Harris, Crowell 1976
DIMENS	*Dimensions,* ed. Thomas H. Brown and Jeffrey T. Cross, Winthrop 1980
DISC4	*Discovery 4,* ed. Vance Bourjaily, Pocket Books 1954
DMH	Durham NC *Morning Herald*
DOSS2	*The Dimensions of the Short Story,* 2nd ed, ed James E. Miller, Jr. and Bernice Slote, Harper 1981
ESS	*The Essential Self,* ed. Paul Berry, McGraw Hill 1975
ESSAY	*The Essay,* ed. Richard L. Cherry, Robert J. Conley and Bernard A. Hirsch, Houghton Mifflin 1975
ESQ	*Esquire* magazine
F&S	*Field and Stream* magazine
FAMWEEK	*Family Week,* Sunday supplement
FICT	*Fictions,* ed. Joseph F. Trimmer and C. Wade Jennings
FIFTY	*50 Best American Short Stories,* ed. Martha Foley, Sentry 1967
FJ	*Fiction's Journey,* ed. Barbara McKenzie, Harcourt Brace Jovanovich 1978
FLIGHT	*Flightime,* magazine of Allegheny Airlines
FMS	*Fifty Modern Stories,* ed. Thomas M. H. Blair, Harper 1960
FON	*Forms of the Novella,* ed. David H. Richter, Knopf 1981
FORBES	*Forbes* magazine
FORMSYN	*Formal Syntax,* ed. Peter E. Culicover, Thomas Wasow and Adrian Akmajian, Academic Press 1977
FPS	*First-Prize Stories, 1919–1960,* Doubleday 1960
FSTA	*Final Stage,* ed. Edward L. Ferman and Barry N. Malzberg, Charterhouse
H	*Harper's*
HIV	*His Infinite Variety: Major Shakespearean Criticism Since Johnson,* ed. Paul N. Siegel, Lippincott 1964
HOOS	*Hoosier Caravan,* ed. R. E. Banta, U. Indiana 1975

I&D	*Invention and Design,* ed. Forrest D. Burt and E. Cleve Want, Random House
INSIGHT	*Insight,* ed. Emil Hurtik, 2nd ed., Lippincott 1973
JMH	*Journal of Modern History*
KAL	*Kaleidoscope,* ed. M. Jerry Weiss, Cummings 1970
KR	*Kenyon Review*
KRON	*Kronos* journal
LANGSCI	*Language Sciences* journal
LHJ	*Ladies' Home Journal* magazine
LIS	*Language in Society* journal
LITF	*Literature: Fiction,* James Burl Hogins, Science Research Associates 1974
LITREF4	*Literary Reflections,* 4th ed., ed. William R. Elkins, Jack L. Kendall, John R. Willingham, McGraw-Hill 1982
LS	The Norfolk VA *Ledger-Star*
LXJK	*Literature: An Introduction to Fiction, Poetry and Drama,* ed. X. J. Kennedy, Little Brown 1966
MAINL	*Mainliner,* magazine of United Air Lines
MFOT	*Media for Our Time,* ed. Dennis DeNitto, Holt Reinhart 1971
MFW	*Models for Writing,* James Burl Hogins and Robert Earl Yarber, Science Research Associates 1974
MGAZ	The *Gazette Montreal*
MIDC	*Midcentury,* ed. Orville Prescott, Washington Square Press 1957
MQR	*Michigan Quarterly Review*
MSSAM1,3	*Modern Short Stories,* 1st & 3rd ed., ed. Arthur Mizener, Norton 1962, 1971
MT3	*The Modern Tradition: Short Stories,* 3rd ed., ed. Daniel F. Howard
NORTH	*North American Review*
NAR#	*New American Review*
NF	*The Norton Introduction to Literature: Fiction,* ed. Jerome Beaty, Norton 1973
NG	*National Geographic* magazine
NH	*Natural History* magazine
NNNK	*Naming, Necessity and Natural Kinds,* ed. Stephen P. Schwartz, Cornell 1977
NO	Raleigh NC *News and Observer*
NORT4	*The Norton Reader,* 4th ed., ed. Arthur M. Eastman et al., Norton 1977
NR	*New Republic* magazine
NYER	*New Yorker* magazine
NYT	New York *Times*
NW	*Newsweek* magazine

O&D	*Order and Diversity,* ed. Robert B. Parker and Peter L. Sandberg, Wiley 1973
ODCIE	*Oxford Dictionary of Current Idiomatic English,* ed. A. P. Cowie and R. Mackin, Oxford 1976
OF3	*The Open Form,* 3rd ed., ed. Alfred Kazin, Harcourt Brace Jovanovich 1970

PARADE	*Parade,* Sunday supplement
PB	*Playboy* magazine
PE5	*Patterns of Exposition 5,* ed. Randall E. Decker, Little Brown 1976
PENSEE	*Pensee,* journal of Lewis and Clark College
PEOPLE	*People* magazine
POD	*Points of Departure,* ed. Arthur J. Carr and William Steinhoff, Harper 1960
POET	*Poetics* journal
POPMECH	*Popular Mechanics* magazine
POSCI	*Popular Science* magazine
POR	*Philosophers on Rhetoric,* ed. Donald G. Douglas, National Textbook Co. 1975
PR	*Partisan Review*
PROSE	*Prose: A Systematic Approach to Writing,* ed. Eva M. Burkett, Cummings
PSH	*Ploughshares* journal
PTE	*From Paragraph to Essay,* Alternative Edition, ed. Woodrow Ohlsen and Frank L. Hammond, Scribner's 1966
PV	*The Personal Voice,* ed. Albert J. Guerard, Maclin B. Guerard, Claire Rosenfield, Lippincott 1964

| QM | *Quest for Meaning,* ed. Glenn O. Carey, McKay 1975 |
| QS | *Quartet/Stories,* ed. Harold P. Simonson, Harper 1973 |

RC2	*The Reading Commitment,* Michael Adelstein and Jean G. Pival, 2nd ed., Harcourt Brace Jovanovich 1982
RD	*Reader's Digest* magazine
RDC	*Reader's Digest Condensed Books,* vol. 4, 1936
REALM	*The Realm of Fiction,* ed. James B. Hall and Elizabeth C. Hall, McGraw Hill 1977
RFR4	*Reading for Rhetoric,* 4th ed., Caroline Shrodes, Clifford Josephson and James R. Wilson, Macmillan 1979
RHMM3	*Rhetoric in a Modern Mode,* 3rd ed., ed. 1976 James K. Bell and Adrian K. Cone, Glencoe Press 1976
RLF	*The Range of Literature: Fiction,* ed. Elizabeth W. Schneider, Albert L. Walker and Herbert E. Childs, Van Nostrand 1973
RWAE	*Reading and Writing,* Alternate Edition, 1962
RWR4	*Reading Writing and Rhetoric,* 3rd ed., ed. James Burl Hogins and Robert E. Yarber, 1967

S29	*29 Short Stories,* ed. Michael Timko, Knopf 1975
S70	*The Sense of the Seventies,* ed. Paul J. Dolan and Edward Quinn, Oxford 1978
SA	*Scientific American* magazine
SFC	San Francisco *Chronicle*
SFCM	*Science Fiction: Contemporary Mythology,* ed. Patricia Warrick, Martin Harry Greenberg and Joseph Olander, Harper 1978
SCI	*Science* magazine
SFE	San Francisco *Examiner*
SHAPE2	*The Shape of Fiction,* 2nd ed., ed. Leo Hamalian and Frederick R. Karl, McGraw Hill 1978
SIC	*Structure in Composition,* ed. Eilene M. Rall and Karl E. Snyder, Scott Foresman 1970
SIX	*Six Great Modern Novels,* Dell 1954
SIXT	*12 From the Sixties,* ed. Richard Kostelanetz, Dell 1967
SJ	*Semantics: An Interdisciplinary Reader in Philosophy, Linguistics and Psychology,* ed. Danny D. Steinberg and Leon A. Jakobovits, Cambridge 1971
SKY	*Sky,* magazine of Delta Air Lines
SL	*Southern Living* magazine
SM	*Smithsonian* magazine
SMS	*Stories of the Modern South,* ed. Benjamin Forkner and Patrick Sanway, S.J., Bantam 1977
SN	*Sporting News*
SSCA	*Short Stories: A Critical Anthology,* ed. Ensaf Thune and Ruth Prigozy, Macmillan 1973
SWR	*Sewanee Review*
TECH	*A History of Technology,* Vol. 5, ed. Charles Singer, E. J. Holmyard, A. R. Hall and Trevor I. Williams, Oxford 1958
TRAIL	*Trailer Life* magazine
TIME	*Time* magazine
TIW	*Thinking in Writing,* ed. Donald McQuade and Robert Atwan, Knopf 1980
TMP	*Today's Moral Problems,* ed. Richard Wasserstrom, Macmillan 1975
TP	New Orleans *Times-Picayune*
TTL	*A Time in Their Lives,* ed. Jerry Herman, Canfield Press 1974
UPI	United Press International
USAT	*USA Today*
VP	Norfolk VA *Virginian-Pilot*
VQR	*Virginia Quarterly* Review
VV	*Village Voice*
WB66	*World Book Encyclopedia,* Field Enterprises 1966
WHRO-TV	Television station (PBS), Norfolk VA

WP   Washington *Post*
WPR4,5,8   *Works in Progress* series, nos. 4,5,8, ed. Martha Saxton, Doubleday
              1971,1972,1973
WRRE   *A Writer's Reader,* ed. Donald Hall and D. L. Emblen, Little Brown
              1976

OTHER
ABBREVIATIONS

AP	Associated Press (newspaper reports with no byline)
AH	William Morris, ed., *American Heritage Dictionary,* first edition (1969)
BC	The Brown Corpus (1961)
CC	Clark and Clark (1979)
CTG	Classical Transformational Grammar (derived from the *Aspects*-model, Chomsky (1965))
DA	Mitford M. Mathews, ed., *A Dictionary of Americanisms* (1956)
DN	Direct object nominal
DU	Eric Partridge, ed., *A Dictionary of the Underworld* (1968)
FW	Issac Funk, ed., *Funk and Wagnalls New Standard Dictionary of the English Language* (1963)
GB	Government-Binding Theory (see Chomsky (1982))
GG	Gleitman and Gleitman (1970)
GS	Generative Semantics
KF	Katz and Fodor (1963)
LS	Norfolk VA *Ledger-Star*
NO	Raleigh NC *News and Observer*
OALD	A. S. Hornsby and A. P. Cowie, ed., *The Oxford Advanced Learner's Dictionary of Current English* (1974)
ODIE	A. P. Cowie and R. Macklin, ed., *The Oxford Dictionary of Current Idiomatic English,* Volume 1 (1975)
OED	*The Oxford English Dictionary*

PN	Object of preposition nominal
RH	Jess Stein, ed., *The Random House Dictionary of the English Language*, Unabridged Edition (1966)
SFC	San Francisco *Chronicle*
SPE	*Sound Pattern of English* (Chomsky and Halle (1968))
SSP	Stockwell, Schachter, and Partee (1973)
SN	Subject nominal
TG	Transformational Grammar
UPI	United Press International (newspaper reports with no byline)
VP	Norfolk VA *Virginian-Pilot*
VP-LS	Combined VP and LS, Sunday newspaper
WNW	David B. Guralnik, ed., *Webster's New World Dictionary*, Second College Edition (1982)
W2	*Webster's Second International Dictionary* (1934)
W3	Philip B. Gove, ed., *Webster's Third New International Dictionary* (1966)

NOTES

NOTES: CHAPTER 1

1. Current views are also reinforced by the observation that many people assume naively that a word has, or should have, only one meaning. Obviously, this uncritical belief does not provide any support for claims of multiplicity.

2. Fillmore (1976: 25ff.) gives an apt example, from Coseriu (1966), of "synonyms": Greek nouns *brotos* and *anthropos*:

> They both designate man. But the first presents man as one term of a
> contrast set in which the other is god; the second presents man as one term
> in a contrast set in which the other is animal. *Brotos* designates man as
> non-god, *anthropos* designates man as non-beast. Each word simultaneously
> identifies the creature and the larger framework or context within which the
> creature is being spoken of.

This example is part of Fillmore's argument that each word has associated FRAMES: accompanying, mutually evoked contexts, linguistic and nonlinguistic, required and default. The frame considered here is the systematic semantic field.

3. Sampson (1975: 60ff), while rejecting all intuitional data, suggests that its apparent strongest justification is that it enables us to judge actual utterances as ungrammatical. I consider this so weak a justification that I haven't listed it: intuitionalists reject sentences that I find all right or at worst rhetorically inept. One of Sampson's concerns is the unavoidable factor of vested interest. But I think it is too extreme (and impossible) to reject intuitional data as completely as he does. Someone using them in the public forum by implication submits them to objective review (which sometimes is negative). The "empirical" status of actual utterances is also not as intuition-free as Sampson might like; part of that utterance is the interpretation of the other interlocuter, so what-we-think-is-the-case is always present. Granted the limitations that both Sampson and I discuss, I feel it is legitimate data nevertheless.

4. These comments have implications for Chomsky's arguments (1980: 12) for a "Galilean Style" of inquiry:

> I am interested, then, in pursuing some aspects of the study of mind, in particular, such aspects as lend themselves to inquiry through the construction of abstract explanatory theories that may involve substantial idealisation and will be justified, if at all, by success in providing insight and explanations. From this point of view, substantial coverage of data is not a particularly significant result; it can be attained in many ways, and the result is not very informative as to the correctness of the principles employed. It will be more significant if certain fairly far-reaching principles interact to provide an explanation for crucial facts—the crucial nature of these facts deriving from their relation to proposed explanatory theories. It is a mistake to argue, as many do, that by adopting this point of view one is disregarding data. Data that remain unexplained by some coherent theory will continue to be described in whatever descriptive scheme one chooses, but will simply not be considered very important for the moment.

Earlier (p. 27), Chomsky argues that "the only alternative" to this approach is "a form of natural history tabulation and arrangement of facts, hardly a serious pursuit. . . ." But these polar alternatives oversimplify. I follow, in this book, the Galilean style, but I cannot accept Chomsky's assumption that intuitional data can be clearly interpreted. The "crucial facts" are especially crucial because they can be mistakenly construed from overextended and overloaded data. The issue is whether small bases of intuitional data are sufficiently representative and whether they can be properly assessed.

Someone doing a historical survey of TG will notice how often theoretical positions have changed because new data have been "discovered". There is nothing wrong with this; it is the normal path of all scientific investigation. However, the ongoing enterprise can be aided if each investigator looks for relevant actual data before taking a theoretical position based solely on intuition.

A large part of any database must be actual use. Even extensive intuiting will not find certain kinds of data. Consciousness is limited in resourcefulness and is tacitly influenced by pretheoretical assumptions. The most damaging assumption is the one that attributes too much meaning to the language. Large collections of actual data can provide correction (though not totally) for these shortcomings.

NOTES: CHAPTER 2

1. In this chapter I am using the words *synchronic* and *diachronic* as they are currently understood; in Chapter 3, I will propose a new view.

2. I note here only a few of the relevant factors that Delancey (1984), Lakoff (1977), (1987: 54ff.) and others take as prototypic of agency. Prototypes provide two necessary factors: they allow for gradience and for perceptual salience. The latter suggests the possibility that certain types of agency may be stereotypic: those most obvious to consciousness, and thus often treated as if they were distinct, and even unique, possibilities.

Geis and Zwicky (1971) note that causation is sometimes inferred between the clauses of sentences such as *John screamed and Mary dropped the glass*. Their notion of "invited inference" was one of the inspirations for the pragmatic rules I propose in this book.

3. In the context of proposing how children conflate semantic categories into syntactic relations, Schlesinger (1981: 227) cites the following:

> (i) *The new brush was painting a still life.
>   The brush was painting the surface a bright red.
> (ii) *The pencil was scribbling a proof of the theorem.
>   The pencil was scribbling fast.
> (iii) *The knife was cutting sandalwood into a statuette.
>   The knife was cutting sandalwood.

He suggests that subject position is inherently agentive. Instruments can be assimilated into this position if they are capable of the agency required by the rest of the sentence; the first of each pair requires more human qualities. However, since the predicates, as context, imply a human(like) agent, the starred instruments fail simply because they can't measure up; it is not necessary (though possible) for the subject to be inherently agentive in any degree. Nevertheless, there must be something (at least a stereotype) behind the long tradition of linguists who believe that subjects are typically agents.

4. Fillmore (1970: 116) captures part of the reagent range with the case of COUNTER-AGENT: "the force or resistance against which the action is carried out."

An entity can be simultaneously agentive and reagentive. Saksena (1980) notes the possibility of an AFFECTED AGENT; this is morphologically explicit in some languages, and is implicit in *He bore up under the weight*. He also observes that this possibility further throws into question the positing of a few discrete "cases" (or "thematic relations") (p. 812):

> First, the notion of agent is not a single category, since agents fall into two formally distinct types: affected and non-affected. Second, the contrast between case categories is not clear-cut; the semantics of being affected by the verb activity links some agents, semantically and syntactically, to categories such as patient, dative and experiencer. Finally, since case categories can be classified as affected (patients, datives, experiencers, affected agents) vs. non-affected (not-affected agents, instrumentals, causative agents), the contrast is more fundamental and primitive than that of the case categories which it encompasses.

We can also have for *bear* a Transitivity Condition, adopted from Hopper and Thompson (1980), in which an expression is judged more transitive as it includes two participants and is active, telic, punctual, volitional, realistic, and potent, and one participant is both affected and individuated. The important point: dimensions that may be inherent, fixed and discrete for some verbs are unspecified (and thus variable and continuous) for other verbs, and for the class of verbs as a whole; similarly, the nouns accompanying verbs will be variable in complementary ways.

NOTES: CHAPTER 3

1. Bierwisch elaborates on this point (1981: 362):

> Chomsky (1980) has argued that the usual notions of learning are rather
> inappropriate to account for the process of language acquisition, which is in
> essential respects determined by highly structured internal dispositions.
> Language acquisition, he claims, consists essentially in the activation of
> these dispositions, the emerging differences between different languages
> being due to the specification of certain free parameters according to the
> actual experience coming from the child's environment. It remains to be
> seen whether these basic ideas can account not only for the development of
> grammatical rules, but also for that of lexical items. There appears to be a
> problem in this respect, as the vocabulary of a language is notoriously
> characterized by idiosyncratic peculiarities rather than by uniform and
> general structures holding for all possible languages. One might even go
> on to argue that within a single language community there are no two
> individuals with exactly the same lexical knowledge.

2. Bartsch (1984) calls it "tolerance"; he covers the topic much more thoroughly than I
do here.

3. Cantrall (1972: 22) provides, with comment, a sentence with similar variation:

> (i) John blew off the same finger that Mary blew off, his left finger.
>
> It appears that each of the two got a finger blown off rather than John
> getting his left finger blown off twice.

He notes this is similar to examples of "sloppy identity" (Ross (1967)):

> (ii) John blew off his left pinkie, and so did Mary.

His article is filled with sentences similarly problematic. I might note here (in gratitude)
that it was Cantrall, by his copious examples, who first showed me the value (and
necessity) of large databases.

Two linguists who similarly use large databases, and who also argue for
monosemy, are Bäcklund and Hines (see bibliography).

4. Both Clark (1983) and Bartsch (1984) stress the "context-dependence" of nonce
uses; however, I think this description is misleading, because all phenomena are context
dependent in some way.

NOTES: CHAPTER 4

1. Gleason (1972) and Lakoff (1982) give a number of sentences that cannot be
accounted for by CTG well-formedness. Both of these articles should be on any minimal
list of readings in syntax-semantics. Gleason notes that the sentences people speak are
often quite different from the sentences linguists study, or (by their rules) allow. Lakoff
thinks his data invalidate the whole generative enterprise, but I think they only severely
limit it.

NOTES: CHAPTER 5

1. Maher (1977a: 333) gives another example, from music, taken from C. Pratt (1969: 10):

> When the tones c and g are sounded together they produce a quality which in music is called the Fifth. That quality is neither in the c nor in the g, nor does it depend on those particular notes. Any two tones with the ratio 2/3 will be recognized immediately as a Fifth no matter in what region of the scale they may be played. Fifthness is a Gestalt which is different from either or any of its parts, and no amount of knowledge about the parts in isolation would ever give the remotest hint as to what Fifthness is like.

2. Harris (1980: 48) cites a more obvious version of this mistake, created by change:

> For Confucius, an example on non-conformity between name and thing was the use of the word *ku,* traditionally designating a type of drinking goblet with corners, but which came to be made without corners. Rather than treating this as a case where the word was no longer appropriate to the thing, or an example of a word changing its meaning, Confucius appears to have regarded it as a case of the thing no longer being appropriate to the word. It is as if, to take an English parallel, one described the situation in which the word *manuscript* is no longer applied exclusively to documents written by hand, but also to what is typewritten, by saying not that the word *manuscript* had altered or extended its meaning, but instead that manuscripts were often nowadays wrongly made (i.e., by typewriters).

NOTE: CHAPTER 6

1. Makkai (1972: 122): "Any polylexonic lexeme which is made up of more than one minimal free form or word (as defined by morphotactic criteria) each lexon of which can occur in other environments as the realization of a monolexonic lexeme is a LEXEMIC IDIOM."

NOTES: CHAPTER 7

1. In his "Poetically man dwells," Heiddiger observes:

> Man acts as though he were the shaper and master of language, while in fact, language remains the master of man. . . . For strictly, it is language that speaks. Man first speaks when, and only when, he responds to language by listening to its appeal. (Tr. Albert Hofstadter, 1971: 215–16).

I am indebted to my philosopher colleague Larry Hatab, who both told me of this observation several years ago and found the quotation for me.

REFERENCES

Anderson, J. M. (1971) *The Grammar of Case: Toward a Localist Theory*. Cambridge University Press

Anderson, Stephen R. and Paul Kiparsky, eds. (1973) *A Festschrift for Morris Halle*. Holt, Rinehart and Winston: New York

Andrews, Edna. (1976) 'Markedness theory in morphology and semantics'. *The SECOL Review* 10.3:89–103

Antilla, Raimo. (1972) *An Introduction to Historical and Comparative Linguistics*. Macmillan: New York

Bach, E. and R. T. Harms, eds. (1968) *Universals in Linguistic Theory*. Holt, Rinehart & Winston: New York

Bäcklund, Ulf. (1978) '*Quick(ly), rapid(ly)*, and *swift(ly)*—a study of a group of synonyms'. In Wölck and Garvin (1979)

_____. (1983) '*Appear* and *seem*—lexical integrity in danger?' In Morreal (1983)

_____. (1984) 'Semantic duality: *Quick(ly)* and *as*-clauses'. In Hall (1985)

Bailey, Charles-James N. and Roger W. Shuy, eds. (1973) *New Ways of Analyzing Variation in English*. Georgetown University Press

Bar Hillel, Y., ed. (1971) *Pragmatics of Natural Languages*. Reidel: Dordrecht

Bartsch, Renate. (1984) 'Norms, tolerance, lexical change, and context-dependence of meaning'. *Journal of Pragmatics* 8:367–93

Bateson, G. (1972) *Steps to an Ecology of Mind*. Ballantine Books: New York

Beach, W. A., S. E. Fox, and S. Philosoph, eds. (1977) *Papers from the Thirteenth Regional Meeting, Chicago Linguistic Society*

Berlin, Brent and Paul Kay. (1969) *Basic Color Terms: Their Universality and Evolution*. University of California Press

Bever, Thomas G., John M. Carroll and Lance A. Miller, eds. (1984) *Talking Minds: The Study of Language in Cognitive Science*. MIT Press

Bierwisch, M. (1981) 'Basic issues in the development of word meaning'. In Deutch (1981)

Binnick, Robert I., Alice Davison, Georgia M. Green, and Jerry L. Morgan, eds. (1969) *Papers from the Fifth Regional Meeting*, Chicago Linguistic Society

Bloomfield, Leonard. (1933) *Language*. Holt: New York

Bolinger, Dwight. (1961) *Generality, Gradience, and the All-or-None*. Mouton: The Hague

——. (1965) 'The atomization of meaning'. *Language* 41:555–73. Also in Jakobovits and Miron (1967)

——. (1967) 'Adjectives in English: attribution and predication'. *Lingua* 18:1–34

——. (1971a) 'Semantic overloading: a restudy of the verb *remind*'. *Language* 47:522–54

——. (1971b) *The Phrasal Verb in English*. Harvard University

——. (1972) *Degree Words*. Mouton: The Hague

——. (1975) *Aspects of Language*, 2nd edition. Harcourt, Brace Jovanovich: New York

——. (1976) 'Meaning and memory'. *Forum Linguisticum* 1.1:1–14

——. (1977a) *Meaning and Form*. Longman: London & New York

——. (1977b) 'Idioms have relations'. *Forum Linguisticum* 2:157–69

Borkin, Ann. (1972) 'Coreference and beheaded NP's'. *Papers in Linguistics* 5.1:28–45

Bjarkman, Peter C. and Victor Raskin, eds. (1986) *The Real-World Linguist*. Ablex Publishing Co.: Norwood, NJ

Brugman, Claudia. (1981) Story of *over*. M.A. Thesis, University of California, Berkeley. Available from the Indiana University Linguistics Club

Cantrall, William R. (1972) 'Relative identity'. In Peranteau et al. (1972)

Chomsky, Noam. (1955) 'Logical syntax and semantics: their linguistic relevance'. *Language* 31:36–45

——. (1965) *Aspects of the Theory of Syntax*. MIT Press

——. (1980) *Rules and Representations*. Columbia University Press

Chomsky, Noam and Morris Halle. (1968) *The Sound Pattern of English*. Harper & Row: New York

Clark, H. H. (1983) 'Making sense of nonce sense'. In Flores d'Arcais and Jarvella (1983)

Clark, E. V. and H. H. Clark. (1979) 'When nouns surface as verbs'. *Language* 55:767–811

Cobler, Mark, Susannah MacKaye and Michael T. Wescoat, eds. (1984) *Proceedings of the West Coast Conference on Formal Linguistics*, Volume 3. Stanford University Press

Cohen, L. Jonathan. (1971) 'Some remarks on Grice's views about the logical particles of natural language'. In Bar-Hillel (1971)

——. (1979). 'The semantics of metaphor'. In Ortony (1979)

Cole, Peter, ed. (1978) *Pragmatics, Syntax and Semantics*, Volume 9, Academic Press: New York

Cole, Peter and Jerry L. Morgan, eds. (1975) *Speech Acts. Syntax and Semantics,* Volume 3. Academic Press: New York

Copeland, James E. and Philip W. Davis, eds. (1981) *The Seventh LACUS Forum 1980.* Hornbeam Press: Columbia SC

Corbett, Edward P. J. (1971). *Classical Rhetoric for the Modern Student,* 2nd edition. Oxford University Press

Coseriu, Eugenio and Horst Geckler. (1974) 'Linguistics and semantics'. In Sebeok (1974)

Culler, Jonathan. (1981) *The Pursuit of Signs. Semiotics, Literature, Deconstruction.* Cornell University Press

Dahl, Östen. (1975) 'On generics'. In Keenan (1975)

Davidson, D. and G. Harman, eds. (1972) *Semantics of Natural Languages.* Reidel: Dordrecht

Delancey, Scott. (1984) 'Notes on agentivity and causation'. *Studies in Language* 8:181–213

Deutsch, Werner, ed. (1981) *The Child's Construction of Language.* Academic Press: New York

DiPietro, Robert J. and Edward L. Blansitt, Jr, eds. (1977) *The Third LACUS Forum 1976.* Hornbeam Press: Columbia SC

Dobzhansky, Theodosius. (1962) *Mankind Evolving.* Yale University Press

Eble, Connie. (1980) 'Slang, productivity, and semantic theory'. In McCormack and Izzo (1980)

————. (1981) 'Slang, productivity, and semantic theory: a closer look'. In Copeland and Davis (1981)

————. (1982) ' "What's else to say?" ' In Gutwinski and Jolly (1982)

————. (1983) 'Greetings and farewells in college slang'. In Morreall (1983)

Emonds, Joseph. (1972). 'Evidence that indirect object movement is a structure-preserving rule'. *Foundations of Language* 8:546–61

Empson, William. (1953) *Seven Types of Ambiguity,* 3rd edition. Chatto: London

Fasold, Ralph W. and Roger W. Shuy, eds. (1975) *Analyzing Variation in Language.* Georgetown University Press

Fillmore, Charles J. (1970) 'Types of lexical information'. In Kiefer (1970)

————. (1975) 'An alternate to checklist theories of meaning'. *Proceedings of the 1st Annual Meeting,* Berkeley Linguistic Society, pp. 123–31

————. (1976) 'Frame semantics and the nature of language'. In Harnad et al. (1976)

————. (1977) 'The case for case reopened'. In Heger and Petöfi (1977)

————. (1984) 'Some thought on the boundaries and components of linguistics'. In Bever, et al. (1984)

Fillmore, Charles J., Daniel Kempler and William S-Y. Wang, eds. (1979) *Individual Differences in Language Ability and Language Behavior.* Academic Press: New York

Fillmore, Charles J. and D. Terence Langendoen, eds. (1971) *Studies in Linguistic Semantics.* Holt, Rinehart & Winston: New York

Flew, A., ed. (1951) *Logic and Language,* Volume 1. Blackwell: Oxford

Flores d'Arcais, G. B. and R. J. Jarvella, eds. (1983) *The Process of Language Understanding.* Wiley: New York

Fodor, Jerry. (1981) *Representations.* MIT Press

Fodor, Jerry and Jerrold J. Katz, eds. (1964) *The Structure of Language: Readings in the Philosophy of Language*. Prentice Hall: Englewood Cliffs NJ

Fraser, Bruce. (1971). 'A note on the *spray paint* cases'. *Linguistic Inquiry* 2:604–07

Frege, G. (1892) 'On sense and reference'. In translation in Geach and Black (1952)

Garcia, Erica. (1975) *The Role of Theory in Linguistic Analysis: The Spanish Pronoun System*. North Holland: Amsterdam

Geach, P. T. and M. Black, eds. (1952) *Frege: Philosophical Writings*. Blackwell: Oxford

Geis, M. and A. Zwicky. (1971) 'On invited inferences'. *Linguistic Inquiry* 2:561–66

Givón, Talmy. (1985) 'Function, structure, and language acquisition'. In Slobin (1985)

Gleason, H. A., Jr., (1972) 'Sentences people speak and sentences linguists study'. *The Canadian Journal of Linguistics* 17:111–127

Gleitman, Lila R. and Henry Gleitman. (1970) *Phrase and Paraphrase*. W. W. Norton & Co., Inc.: New York

Gould, Stephen Jay. (1987) *Time's Arrow, Time's Cycle*. Harvard University Press

Green, Georgia. (1969) 'On the notion "related lexical entry" '. In Binnick, et al. (1969)

―――. (1974) *Semantics and Syntactic Regularity*. Indiana University Press

Greenberg, Joseph H. (1963) *Universals of Language*, 2nd edition, MIT Press

Greenberg, S. Robert. (1966) 'Families of idioms in American English'. Unpublished talk, Annual Meeting of LSA

Grice, H. Paul. (1975) 'Logic and conversation'. In Cole and Morgan (1975)

―――. (1978) 'Further notes on logic and conversation'. In Cole (1978)

Gunderson, Keith, ed. (1975) *Minnesota Studies in the Philosophy of Science*, Volume VII: Language, Mind, and Knowledge. University of Minnesota Press

Gutwinsky, Waldemar and Grace Jolly, eds. (1982) *The Eighth LACUS Forum 1981*. Hornbeam Press: Columbia SC

Hall, Robert A., Jr. (1978) 'Idiolect and linguistic super-ego', *Language, Literature and Life*, pp. 33–37. Jupiter Press: Lake Bluff IL

Hall, Robert A., Jr. ed. (1985) *The Eleventh LACUS Forum 1984*. Hornbeam Press: Columbia SC

Harnad, Steven R., Horst D. Steklis, and Jane Lancaster, eds. (1976) *Origins and Evolution of Language and Speech*. Annals of the New York Academy of Sciences, Volume 280

Harris, Roy. (1980) *The Language Makers*. Cornell University Press

Heger, K. and J. Petöfi, eds. (1977) *Kasustheorie, Klassifikation and Semantische Interpretation*. Buske: Hamburg

Heiddiger, Martin. (1971) *Poetry, Language, Thought*. Tr. Albert Hofstadter. Harper & Row: New York

Hines, Carole P. (1975) 'True statements and true friends'. In Ordoubadian and Von-Raffler Engel (1975)

―――. (1978) 'Well, . . .'. In Paradis (1978)

―――. (1979) 'Lexical integrity: *good, great* and *well*'. In Wölck and Garvin (1979)

―――. (1980) '*As well* and *as well as*'. In McCormack and Izzo (1980)

Hockett, Charles F. (1958) *A Course in Modern Linguistics*. Holt: New York

―――. (1968) *The State of the Art*. Mouton: The Hague

Hofmann, Hans. (1967) *Search for the Real and Other Essays*. Revised Edition. Ed. Sara T. Weeks and Bartlett H. Hays, Jr. MIT Press.

Hofstadter, Martin. See Heiddiger.

Homans, George C. (1967) *The Nature of Social Science*. Harbinger: New York

Hoppenbrouwers, G. A. J., P. A. M. Seuren and A. J. M. M. Weijters, eds. (1985) *Meaning and the Lexicon*. Foris: Dordrecht

Hopper, P. J. and S. A. Thompson. (1980) 'Transitivity in grammar and discourse'. *Language* 56:251–99

Householder, Fred W. (1977) 'Innateness and improvisability'. In DiPietro and Blansitt (1977)

Householder, Fred W., ed. (1972) *Syntactic Theory I: Structuralist*. Penguin Books: New York

Hymes, Dell. (1979) 'Sapir, competence, voices'. In Fillmore et al. (1979)

Itkonen, Esa. (1978) *Grammatical Theory and Metascience*. John Benjamins: Amsterdam

Jackendoff, Ray S. (1973) 'The base rules for prepositional phrases'. In Anderson and Kiparsky (1973)

———. (1977) $\overline{X}$ *Syntax: A Study of Phrase Structure*. MIT Press

———. (1983) *Semantics and Cognition*. MIT Press

Jacobs, Roderick A. and Peter S. Rosenbaum, eds. (1970) *Readings in English Transformational Grammar*. Ginn: Waltham MA

Jakobovits, Leon A. and Murray S. Miron. (1967) *Readings in the Psychology of Language*. Prentice Hall: Englewood Cliffs NJ

Jeffries, Lesley and Penny Willis. (1984). 'A return to the spray paint issue'. *Journal of Pragmatics* 8:715–29

Johnson, Mark. (1987) *The Body in the Mind: the Bodily Basis of Reason and Imagination*. University of Chicago Press

Johnson-Laird, P. N. and P. C. Wason, eds. (1977) *Thinking. Readings in Cognitive Science*. Cambridge University Press

Joos, Martin. (1972) 'Semantic axiom number one'. *Language* 48:257–65

Katz, Jerrold J. (1977) 'A proper theory of names'. *Philosophical Studies* 31.1: 1–80.

Katz, Jerrold J. and Jerry A. Fodor. (1963) 'The structure of a semantic theory'. *Language* 39:170–210. Also in Jakobovits and Miron (1967)

Kay, Paul and Chad K. McDaniel. (1978) 'The linguistic significance of the meanings of basic color terms'. *Language* 54:610–46

Keenan, E. L., ed. (1975) *Formal Semantics of Natural Language*. Cambridge University Press

Keenan, E. L. and B. Comrie. (1977) 'Noun phrase accessibility and universal grammar'. *Linguistic Inquiry* 8:63–69

Keifer, F. (1970) *Studies in Syntax and Semantics*. Reidel: Dordrecht

Kiefer, F. and J. Searle, eds. (1980) *Pragmatics and Speech Act Theory*. Reidel: Dordrecht

Kirsner, Robert S. (1972) 'About "about" and the unity of "remind" '. *Linguistic Inquiry* 3.4:489–99

Kirsner, Robert S. and Sandra A. Thompson. (1976) 'The role of pragmatic inference in semantics: a study of sensory verb complements in English'. *Glossa* 10.2: 200–240

Köhler, Wolfgang. (1969) *The task of Gestalt psychology*. Introduction by Carroll C. Pratt. Princeton University Press

Korzybski, Alfred. (1933) *Science and Sanity*. The Science Press Printing Company: Lancaster PA

Kripke, S. (1972) 'Naming and necessity'. In Davidson and Harman (1972)

———. (1977) 'Identity and necessity'. In Schwartz (1977)
Kuno, Susumu. (1987) *Functional Syntax*. University of Chicago Press
Labov, William. (1973) 'The boundaries of words and their meanings'. In Bailey and Shuy (1973)
———. (1987) 'Are black and white vernaculars diverging?' *American Speech* 62.1:5–12
Lakoff, George. (1977) 'Linguistic gestalts'. In Beach et al. (1977)
———. (1982) 'Experiential factors in linguistics'. In Simon and Scholes (1982)
———. (1987) *Women, Fire, and Dangerous Things*. University of Chicago Press.
Lakoff, Robin. (1971) 'If's, and's, and but's about conjunction'. In Fillmore and Langendoen (1971)
Lawler, John. (1972) 'Generic to a fault'. In Peranteau, et al. (1972)
Lees, R. B. (1960) *The Grammar of English Nominalizations*. Mouton: The Hague
Lindner, Susan. (1981) A Lexico-Semantic Analysis of Verb-Particle Constructions with *Up* and *Out*. Ph.D dissertation, University of California, San Diego. Available from the Indiana University Linguistics Club
Lowen, Alexander. (1958) *The Language of the Body*. Collier Books: New York
Maher, J. Peter. (1977a). 'The semantics and perception of IC structure: A Gestalt approach to color terms: Spanish and English 'green' '. In DiPietro and Blansitt (1977)
———. (1977b) ' 'Upside down' language and mind'. *Language Sciences* 48:1–10
Makkai, Adam. (1972) *Idiom Structure in English*. Mouton: The Hague
———. (1977) 'Idioms, psychology, and the lexemic principle'. In DiPietro and Blansitt (1977)
Marantz, Alec P. (1984) *On the Nature of Grammatical Relations*. MIT Press
McCawley, James. (1968) 'The role of semantics in a grammar'. In Bach and Harms (1968)
———. (1971) 'Tense and time reference in English'. In Fillmore and Langendoen (1971)
McCormack, William C. and Herbert J. Izzo. (1980) *The Sixth LACUS Forum 1979*. Hornbeam Press: Columbia SC
Morreall, John, ed. (1983) *The Ninth LACUS Forum 1982*. Hornbeam Press: Columbia SC
Morris, Charles. (1971) *Writings on the General Theory of Signs*. Mouton: The Hague
Nunberg, Geoffrey. (1984) 'Individuation in context'. In Cobler et al. (1984)
Ogden, Charles K. and Ivor A. Richards. (1923) *The Meaning of Meaning*. Harcourt, Brace & World: London & New York.
Ordoubadian, Reza and Walburga Von-Raffler Engel, eds. (1975) *Views on Language*. Inter-University Publishing: Murfreesboro TN
Ortony, Andrew, ed. (1979) *Metaphor and Thought*. Cambridge University Press
Paikeday, Thomas M. (1985) *The Native Speaker is Dead!* Paikeday Publishing Company: Toronto & New York
Paradis, Michel, ed. (1978) *The Fourth LACUS Forum 1977*. Hornbeam Press: Columbia SC
Peranteau, Paul M., Judith N. Levi and Gloria C. Phares, eds. (1972) *Papers from the Eighth Regional Meeting, Chicago Linguistic Society*
Posner, Roland. (1980) 'Semantics and pragmatics of sentence connectives in natural language'. In Rauch and Carr (1980). Reprinted from Kiefer and Searle (1980)

Postal, Paul. (1970) 'On the surface verb *remind*'. *Linguistic Inquiry* 1:37–120. Also in Fillmore and Langendoen (1971)

Pratt, Carroll C. (1969) Introduction to Köhler (1969).

Putnam, Hilary. (1975) 'The meaning of "meaning" '. In Gunderson (1975)

———. (1978) *Meaning and the Moral Sciences.* Routledge & Kegan Paul: London

Quine, Williard Van Orman. (1953) *From a Logical Point of View.* Harper & Row: New York

Rauch, Irmegard and Gerald F. Carr, eds. (1980) *The Signifying Animal.* Indiana University Press

Reddy, Michael J. (1969) 'A semantic approach to metaphor'. In Binnick et al. (1969)

Reich, Peter A. (1969) 'The finiteness of natural language'. *Language* 45:831–43. Reprinted in Householder (1972)

Reich, Peter A., ed. (1976) *Second LACUS Forum 1975.* Hornbeam Press: Columbia SC

Richards, I. A. (1936) *The Philosophy of Rhetoric.* Oxford University Press

Robinson, Richard. (1954) *Definition.* Oxford University Press

Rosch, Eleanor. (1977a) 'Classification of real-world objects; origins and representations in cognition'. In Johnson-Laird and Wason (1977)

———. (1977b) 'Human categorization'. In Warren (1977)

Ross, John Robert. (1967) Constraints on Variables in Syntax. Ph.D. Dissertation, MIT

Ruhl, Charles. (1975) 'Polysemy or monosemy: discrete meanings or continuum?' In Fasold and Shuy (1975)

Saksena, Anuradha. (1980) 'The affected agent'. *Language* 56:812–26

Sampson, Geoffrey. (1975) *The Form of Language.* Weideneled and Nicolson: London

Schlesinger, I. M. (1981) 'Semantic assimilation in the development of relational categories'. In Deutsch (1981)

Schwartz, Stephen P., ed. (1977) *Naming, Necessity, and Natural Kinds.* Cornell University Press

Schwartz, Stephen P. (1979) 'Natural kind terms'. *Cognition* 7:301–15

Sebeok, Thomas, ed. (1974) *Current Trends in Linguistics,* Volume 12. Mouton: The Hague

Simon, I. and R. Scholes, eds. (1982) *Language, Mind and Brain.* Lawrence Erlbaum: Hillsdale NJ

Slobin, Dan Isaac, ed. (1985) *The Crosslinguistic Study of Language Acquisition,* Volume 2: Theoretical Issues. Lawrence Erlbaum: Hillsdale NJ

Stockwell, R. P., P. Schachter, and B. H. Partee. (1973) *The Major Syntactic Structures of English.* Holt, Rinehart, Winston: New York

Ullman, Stephen. (1957) *The Principles of Semantics.* Blackwell: Oxford

Waisman, F. (1951) 'Verifiability'. In Flew (1951)

Warburton, I. and N. S. Prabhu. (1972) 'Anaphoric pronouns: syntax versus semantics'. *Journal of Linguistics* 8:289–92

Warren, Neil, ed. (1977) *Studies in Cross-Cultural Psychology,* Volume 1. Academic Press: New York.

Weeks, Sara T. and Bartlett H. Hayes, Jr. (1967) See Hofmann (1967)

Weinreich, Uriel. (1963) 'On the semantic structure of language'. In J. Greenberg (1963)

Whitehead, Alfred North. (1925) *Science and the Modern World.* Mentor Books: New York

Wittgenstein, Ludwig. (1953) *Philosophical Investigations.* Blackwell: Oxford

Wölck, Wolfgang and Paul L. Garvin, eds. (1979) *The Fifth LACUS Forum 1978.* Hornbeam Press: Columbia SC

Yngve, Victor H. (1960) 'A model and an hypothesis for language structure'. *Proceedings of the American Philosophical Society* 104:444–66

———. (1987) *Linguistics as a Science.* Indiana University Press

Ziff, Paul. (1960) *Semantic Analysis.* Cornell University Press

———. (1972) *Understanding Understanding.* Cornell University Press

INDEX

GENERAL

information, 31, 38, 58, 68, 80, 90, 94,
96, 100, 104, 182, 197; contextual, 6,
117; given/old and new, 31, 169
inherent lexical meaning, 13, 15, 28,
32–33, 58, 68, 83, 86, 95, 139, 146,
168, 204, 208–10, 234, 266
innate linguistic knowledge, x–xi, 8, 17,
66, 71–72, 74, 76, 101, 122, 143.
innovation, 77–85, 163
innovative denominal verb convention, 82
instrument, 12–13, 16, 23, 25–27,
29–31, 46, 83, 115, 123, 135–36, 210,
266; and agent, 32, 116, 135, 225–27;
and purpose, 116; as direct object,
210, 213, 230; as subject, 212. *See*
metonymic patterns
instrumental: meaning, ix, xi; verb, 129
instrumental-doing to (typically-
insistent)-quality-of-doing to
(typically-irresistible)-
quality-of-result-of-doing [metonymic
shifts], 83
instrument to do-(typical)-
action-with-instrument [a metonymic
shift], 83
intensional and extensional, 29, 101–2,
129, 175–76, 179–80, 196
intensity, 38, 117, 122–24
intention, 184; and accident, 137. *See*
degree; metonymic patterns
intentionality, 138, 146–49, 204; and
uptake, 148–49
interchangeability, 51
interlocuters, viii, 265
intermodularity of language and reality,
199
internal and external (to language),
15–17, 180
interpretations, 4, 6–7, 16, 31–33, 39,
51–52, 56, 62, 81, 83, 91–94, 112,
117, 126, 129, 175, 194, 205–6;
natural, 92; multiple, 31, 137
interrogative, 26, 59
intralinguistic/extralinguistic, 15, 64, 90,
129, 154, 168, 173, 197–99, 235–36
intransitive, 28–39, 42, 47, 54, 63, 84,
208, 212, 216, 230; prepositions, 24,

40, 152, 163, 165; pseudo, 230. *See*
transitive
intuition, xiv, 22–23, 49, 51, 63, 94,
122, 126–27, 150, 154–57, 164–65,
201, 203, 264–65; and use, xiv,
13–16, 234–35, 264–65. *See* data; use
invariance, 77, 79
invited inference, 266
involvement through indirection or
incompletion, 113
irony, 96, 103, 107, 222
isolation, x–xi, xiv, 7, 15, 17, 19, 21,
23, 49, 71, 88, 94, 113, 122, 126,
134–35, 139–43, 153, 194, 219

jerry-built, 18, 22, 39
jointly comprehensive hyponyms, 124

knowledge, viii, 13, 20–22, 36, 66,
69–71, 134, 144, 161, 199, 201,
205–6, 210, 267; common, 144;
conscious/unconscious, 13, 20–22;
lexical, 267; linguistic, vii–viii, 13,
20–22, 198; linguistic/extralinguistic,
70, 100, 121; scientific, 206; worldly,
6, 36, 70, 91, 100, 121, 123

label, 133, 144, 151, 199
language and reality, 79, 100–101,
129–30, 132–35, 139, 143, 146–48,
180–82, 194, 199–200, 233, 235
language capacity: modularity of, 16
language-in-the-whole, 101, 131, 154
length of string, 168–70
level of abstraction, xi, 130–31, 137,
139–45, 148, 154, 167–68, 170;
basic, 130–31
lexeme and morpheme, 153–55
lexemic and sememic idioms, 153
lexical: ability, 90; ambiguity, xii;
analysis, vii, 101; and grammatical
word classes, 129, 177, 236; content,
177; knowledge, 267
lexical meaning, 6, 33, 67–68, 234; and
inferential meaning, vii, ix, xi, 7, 33,
83, 163, 234; and syntax, 6, 33

metonymy 27, 48, 56, 65–66, 68–70,
83–85, 96–100, 106–7, 109, 111–12,
114, 122, 124, 158, 177, 193–94,
196–97, 203, 205, 212–13, 215, 217,
219, 233; pragmatic, 7–8, 13, 60–62,
97, 100, 103, 196; semantic, 97;
syntactic, 100. *See* metaphor
Middle English, 65
middle range of categorization, 131
mind, 21, 176, 178; and world, 175;
theory of, 200
minds and realities, 20–24
minimal: antonymy, 201–02; content
words, 58–59; explicit context, xi, 126
minimalists and maximalists, vii–ix
minimality bind, 202
minimizations, 15, 134, 170, 137, 191
mirror, 65, 74, 91, 133, 146, 181, 184
misleadingly obvious, 125
misplaced concreteness, 141, 144, 151
modality of power, 206
modals, 58
modifiers: and heads, 142; conditionals
as, 58; modals as, 58; negative, 58–59;
predicate, 43; prominence of, 58
modulation, xi, xiii–xiv, 20, 33, 39, 51,
69, 73, 77, 82, 85–87, 89–91, 94–96,
106, 122, 126, 139, 148, 154, 160,
168–69, 179, 194, 204, 235; and
nonmodulation, 173; implicit, xi;
pragmatic, 51, 90, 93, 160, 168, 171,
194, 204; of time, 93; of unity, 93
modular diversification, 71
modularity, 5–9, 16–17, 21, 67, 95, 169;
and mutuality, 129, 138–39, 177, 182,
184, 199–200, 235; of language
capacity, 16
modules, 16, 20, 71
monosemy, vii–ix, x–xii, 1–26, 29, 31,
47, 49–50, 64, 84, 127, 145, 151,
158, 169, 171, 173–74, 199, 204, 207,
267; and polysemy, ix, 147, 179, 212,
217; primarily variant, 180, 201
Monsemic Bias, viii, 3–5, 24–34, 90,
102, 128, 147, 152, 204, 234
morpheme and lexeme, 153–55
morphology, 189
motion, 5; and rest/stasis, 27, 44

motivation, xiv, 66, 68–69, 74, 80, 106,
124–25, 162, 165, 167, 177–78, 183,
193–94, 198, 202, 219
motive. *See* metonymic patterns
Move Alpha (GB), 7
movement, 34–37, 54, 124, 158, 171,
203, 208, 219; abstract, 48–49, 124;
and change, 186; and nonmovement,
38, 40; forward and backward
(kicking), 210; of foot and goal, 218;
pointing, 37; transformation, 171
movement verb, 34, 47, 129, 203–4,
210; and contact verb, 207, 213–215,
218, 225–27, 229–30, 232–33
multiple: cognitive models, xiv;
complications, 29; interpretations, 31,
137; means of interpreting, 4;
modulations, 73; perspectives, 4; uses,
17, 179
multiple meaning/multiplicity, vii, ix–x,
1–5, 9–10, 20, 39, 51–52, 65, 68–69,
90, 105–6, 125, 134, 152, 179, 202,
204, 264
mutability, 8–9, 16, 64, 69, 71, 76–78,
100, 141, 201
mutable and immutable, 77, 235
mutuality, 200–201; and modularity, 129,
138–39, 177, 182, 184, 199–200, 235
mythology, 49

natural, 72, 92–93, 95; and arbitrary,
178, 184, 198–99; and conventional,
78; and linguistic order, 135, 180;
consequence, 212; interpretation, 92
natural kind, 180, 191, 200; and nominal
kind, 181
necessary. *See* conditions
negation, 8, 26, 56, 58–59, 183
negative: evidence, 13; modifiers, 58–59;
status of elements in a strong system,
viii, 9
network of relationships, 203
neutral, 2, 34, 77, 81, 94, 166, 175, 179
new and old/given information, 31, 169
newsworthiness, 168, 170
nomenclature, 133–34, 177, 181–82,
200; and primary vocabulary, 199

nominal and natural kinds, 181
nominal, implicit, 23
nominal/real definitions, 129, 180
nominative, 130
nonce, 21, 69, 81, 85, 100, 267
nonexclusive, 205
norm, 86, 168; of scientific investigation,
47; motivation as a, 162.
NORMAL, 20–22, 65–66, 71–72, 150;
and IDEAL, 71
normality, 96, 122
normative rules, 96
noun to verb [a metonymic shift], 83
nouns/NP, 130, 132, 134, 181, 184–85,
188, 197–98, 207. See DN; PN; SN;
Heavy NP Shift; Extraposition; verb
number, 133, 136, 175

object: as a syntactic position, 31; as a
semantic case, 32; of preposition,
163–64. See DN; PN
objective, 122
objects: affected/effected, 216–17;
affected/manipulated, 232; created, 217
oblique syntactic position, 32
occasionally and always, 92
ODIE, OED. See dictionaries.
old/given and new information, 169
OPEN, 95, 144, 193
open, 71, 127, 200, 205, 219; class, 183,
185. See closed
open present, 66, 148
open texture, 85
openness, 64–95, 154, 191, 193, 205.
See conditions
order, 21–23, 47, 65, 72; and disorder,
23; and freedom, 72; internal (to
language) and external, 15–17, 180;
linguistic and natural, 135, 180; of
language and reality, 182
order: foundational, 19, 72, 137–38;
implicational: colors, 176–77; primary,
21, 178–79, 185
ordered classes: colors, 176
ostension, 133
overabstraction, 79, 150
overanalysis, 136

overconcretion, 79, 133
overconscious, 24, 154, 156, 201
overdistinction, 186
overemphasis on paraphrase, 171, 179
overextended explanation, xii
overgeneralization, 11, 19, 133; and
undergeneralization, 19
overhearer, 148
overhomogenization, 20, 145, 201
overidealization, 145
overloading: semantic, 7, 81, 134, 265
overparticularizing, 153
overrealistic, 160
overreferential, 133
overriding, 102, 170
oversemanticizing, 96, 149
oversimplifying, 94, 136–38, 142, 154,
203
overspecifying, 1, 2, 76, 79, 161, 179,
186, 197
oversystemizing, 71
overvaluing, 21, 66, 87

paradigm, 13, 17, 23, 25, 60, 75, 83,
87, 135, 156; and syntax, 9–10, 74,
87, 193, 203
paradigmatic-metaphoric-generalized, 193
parameters (GB), 77, 267
parallel, 4, 10, 50, 69, 91, 158, 160,
172, 200, 218, 230; contact and
movement patterns, 230; perhaps
without, 175; syntax of ground/literal
and figurative meaning, 218, 231–32;
syntax of kick and slap, 207
paraphrase, ix, 4, 13–14, 79, 86, 174,
234; overemphasis on, 171, 179
part and whole, 139–40, 219
part of speech, 142
partialization, 125, 134, 194.
partially arbitrary/partially predictable,
193–94
participants, 59
particle, 23–24, 40, 152, 163–72;
adjacency to verb, 163–67, 170, 172;
shift, 40, 164–65, 167
particle-preposition-adverb, 163, 171
particular/individual and species, 91
partitive and holistic, 233

163, 192, 199, 235; perceived and
conceived, 181; physical, 113–114;
presumption of, 183; semantic, 125;
-specific 134.
realness, 204
reanalysis, 65, 69, 193
recurrence, 141
redundancy, 83, 213; deaccenting of,
168–69
reference, vii, 29, 31–32, 35–36, 97–98,
100–101, 103, 129, 132–34, 138, 144,
151, 175, 177, 179, 182, 185, 195–96,
199–200, 205, 207, 217, 223, 235;
and inference, 68; and meaning, 129;
and nonreference, 173, 200; and sense,
129, 149; direct, 103, 181; point of,
xii; real world, 195
reference-word-concept, 133
reflexed 43–47, 50, 54, 62–63; adjunct,
54; pattern, 43–47
reflexive, 42–43, 45, 58, 159, 215–16;
and nonreflexive, 159
reflexivity, 149
register, 17, 77, 103, 107, 113, 144, 235
reinterpretation, vii, 83
rejection, 107, 222
related: conceptual units, xii; senses, x,
xii
relation: general, 201; thematic, 266
relationship: and process, figurative, 193;
form and meaning, 68–69, 199;
grammatical, 130; language and
reality, 132–33, 142, 146, 200;
network, 203, word to context, 142
relative clauses, 26, 59
relevance, 6, 15, 23, 36, 94, 126, 175
relics, 172
remote: from change, 71; from
reality/reference, 29, 177. See degree
remotivation, 69
repetition, 85
representation, mental, viii.
resemblance, family, 202–4
response. See degree
rest and motion, 27
result, 7, 12–13, 27, 216, 218, 221, 225,
230
RH. See dictionaries.

rhetoric, 58, 97, 100, 264
rhetorical heaviness, 169
ritualization, 124–25
roles, semantic, 32, 130
root of a progressively opening semantic
field, 174–76, 182, 236
rule, viii, 8, 17, 20; breaking, 22, 101;
deletion, 69–70, 100; -directed
capacity, 19; generative, 47; inference,
30; normative, 96; pragmatic, 30–31,
34, 36, 38–39, 89, 266; preference,
203, 205; PP, 164; semantic
cancellation, 146, 148, 151;
substantive and regulative, 92, 184;
system, 13

salience, 124, 132, 138, 183, 265
same thing (like), 84
sameness, 93–94
scale of abstraction, 138
scene, 49, 232
scientific, 72, 75, 133, 181–82, 195,
206; classification, 191–92;
endeavor/investigation/analysis, 17, 21,
265; knowledge, 206
secondaries in semantic field, 177
secondary/primary categories, 101
semantic, x, 13, 23, 29, 31, 63, 67, 75,
77, 83, 85–86, 91, 93, 95, 127,
131–32, 136, 146, 148–50, 155, 158,
179, 197, 200–201, 215; ambiguity, xii;
and conceptual/cognitive, viii–xiii; and
syntactic, xi, 82, 182–83, 204,
266–67; and worldly knowledge, 39;
bind, 92, 145; cancellation rule, 146,
148, 151; case, 32; category, 266;
change, 20, 64; content, 59, 200;
definition, 179; development, 27;
distinction, 28; field, 25, 185–91, 235,
264; heterogeneity, 179; overloading,
7, 81, 134, 265; reality, 125;
relationships, 129; roles, 32, 130, 155;
rules, 36; structure, xi–xii; theory, 2,
9, 132–33; unities, 186, 197–202
semantic and pragmatic, viii–xi, 9, 15,
17, 20, 31–34, 36, 38–39, 51, 55–56,
64, 67–69, 71, 80, 82–84, 92, 95,
97–98, 100, 103, 121, 123–29, 136,

PROPER NAMES
(references not included)

PREPOSITIONS

about, 43, 45, 214, 220–21
above, 44–45
across, 43–44, 163, 210–11, 214, 223, 226–28
against, 28–29, 34–41, 45, 60, 208–11, 213–14, 218, 220–22, 227–29, 232
along, 41, 46, 155, 170, 216–17
around, 37, 41, 43–44, 208, 212, 220–23
as, 4, 68
aside, 214
at, 37–38, 152–53, 208–11, 213–14, 218, 222, 227–28, 230
away, 36–37, 41, 46–47, 155–58, 167, 214–16, 221–22, 229

back, 41–42, 155–56, 210–11, 214, 220–21, 223–24, 226, 230
backward, 216
backwards, 209–11
before, 43–45
behind, 230
below, 121
beneath, 43
between, 43–44, 209, 228
by, 31, 42, 48, 50, 152, 156

down, 26–27, 30–31, 33–37, 40–43, 49, 58, 86, 88, 155, 157, 163, 168, 171–72, 209, 214, 216–17, 228–31
downwards, 30

for, 59, 120, 157, 159, 208, 224
forth, 226, 230
forward, 42, 214
from, 37, 41, 43, 50, 152, 158, 160, 166, 203, 214–16, 220–21, 225–229

in, xiii–iv, 34, 37–38, 41, 43–45, 47–48, 67, 84, 152, 156, 159, 163, 166, 172, 208–14, 216–17, 222–26, 228, 231, 233
into, xiii, 37, 41–42, 47, 84, 166, 203,

208, 210–16, 218, 220, 222–24, 227–29, 231–33

of, 22–23, 62, 81, 132, 134, 152, 182–83, 214, 216, 229, 233
off, 1, 2, 5, 23, 37, 41, 49, 67, 127, 152, 155–64, 171–72, 194, 214–16, 218, 223–25, 229, 233
on, 27, 30, 33–39, 42–46, 50, 52, 62, 81, 121–22, 152, 155–57, 159–60, 163–64, 166–67, 170, 172, 196–97, 209–11, 213–15, 218, 220, 223, 226–32
onto, 41, 225, 233
out, xiii–xiv, 22–23, 37, 41, 48–50, 62, 81, 152, 156, 163, 166–67, 172, 208–14, 216–18, 220, 222–24, 229
over, 41–44, 46–47, 155–56, 166–67, 169–70, 210–11, 224, 228–29, 231

past, 37

through, 41–42, 44, 157, 163, 166, 208, 210–11, 217, 225
to, 28–29, 34, 36–37, 40–43, 45, 49–50, 52, 62, 81, 84, 152, 156, 159, 166, 215–18, 220, 223, 228–30
toward, 33–34, 37, 41–42, 59–60, 157, 208, 214

under, 28–30, 32–33, 37, 42–44, 46–47, 55, 203, 214, 216, 221, 266
up, 26–34, 37, 40–43, 46–47, 49, 55, 81, 120, 155, 163, 166–67, 172, 207–8, 210–11, 214–18, 220, 222, 224, 229–30, 233, 266
upon, 30, 33–39, 43–44, 46, 228
upstairs, 223

with, 23, 32, 37, 43, 45–47, 50, 52, 56, 58–60, 84, 152–53, 155, 157, 170, 172, 209–10, 213–15, 219, 24–28, 230–33
within, 43, 45

VERBS

OTHER SELECTED WORDS